A Comprehensive Christian Appraisal

MODERN
PSYCHOPATHOLOGIES

MARK A. YARHOUSE

RICHARD E. BUTMAN

BARRETT W. McRAY

ivp

InterVarsity Press
Downers Grove, Illinois

InterVarsity Press
P.O. Box 1400, Downers Grove, IL 60515-1426
World Wide Web: www.ivpress.com
E-mail: email@ivpress.com

InterVarsity Press® is the book-publishing division of InterVarsity Christian Fellowship/USA®, a movement of students and faculty active on campus at hundreds of universities, colleges and schools of nursing in the United States of America, and a member movement of the International Fellowship of Evangelical Students. For information about local and regional activities, write Public Relations Dept., InterVarsity Christian Fellowship/ USA, 6400 Schroeder Rd., P.O. Box 7895, Madison, WI 53707-7895, or visit the IVCF website at <www.intervarsity.org>.

All Scripture quotations, unless otherwise indicated, are taken from the Holy Bible, New International Version®. NIV®. *Copyright ©1973, 1978, 1984 by International Bible Society. Used by permission of Zondervan Publishing House. All rights reserved.*

Tables 12.3 and 12.4 are adapted from Alan Carr, The Handbook of Child and Adolescent Clinical Psychology: A Contextual Approach *(New York: Routledge, 1999). Used by permission.*

Every effort has been made to trace and contact copyright holders for additional materials quoted in this book. The authors will be pleased to rectify any omissions in future editions if notified by copyright holders.

Design: Cindy Kiple
Images: David Oliver/Getty Images

ISBN 978-0-8308-2770-1

Printed in the United States of America ∞

Library of Congress Cataloging-in-Publication Data

Yarhouse, Mark A., 1968-
    The modern psychopathologies: a comprehensive Christian
appraisal/
    Mark A. Yarhouse, Richard E. Butman, Barrett W. McRay.
        p. cm.
    Includes bibliographical references and index.
    ISBN 0-8308-2770-6 (alk. paper)
    1. Mental illness—Religious aspects—Christianity. 2. Psychiatry
and religion. I. Butman, Richard E., 1951- II. McRay, Barrett W.,
1961- III. Title.
    RC455.4.R4Y37 2005
    616.89—dc22

                                                                    200500072

| **P** | 19 | 18 | 17 | 16 | 15 | 14 | 13 | 12 | 11 | 10 | 9 | 8 | 7 | 6 | 5 | 4 |
| **Y** | 23 | 22 | 21 | 20 | 19 | 18 | 17 | 16 | 15 | 14 | 13 | 12 | 11 | 10 | | | |

To Lori,
who has so clearly and consistently
lived out the kind of personal love for Christ,
stewardship of gifts and resources,
and sacrificial love for others discussed
throughout this book. —Mark

To Eleanor Butman,
who for more than five decades has
modeled integrity and deeply shaped my love for
the written and spoken word. —Richard

To Sydney,
who fills each day with love and laughter
for me and our children and who so clearly models
Christlike compassion and service in her
ministry and mentoring of students
. . . you are my inspiration. —Barrett

PREFACE

*T*his book has been a work in progress since the mid-1990s, when the *Diagnostic and Statistical Manual* of the American Psychiatric Association was published in its fourth edition. It was at that time that the three of us came together in initial discussions about what it means to think as Christians about psychopathology. One of our favorite discussions took place, memorably, during a kayak trip to Door County, Wisconsin. We wrote this book to sort out our convictions about integration of faith in the study of psychopathology, desiring to engage other Christians in a dialogue about ways of thinking about diagnosis and psychopathology *through the eyes of faith*. Rather than creating a radically new approach to the study of psychopathology, we draw attention to the resources already present in historic pastoral care, including an understanding of sin and its relation to contemporary categories of psychopathology.

To do this, we took several steps. The first was to consider ways in which the church has historically approached symptoms of psychological and spiritual concerns that are in some ways evident in contemporary nosologies. The next step was to clearly explain what we know about psychopathology from the best scientific studies conducted to date. We attempted to summarize existing explanatory frameworks—ways in which professionals today tend to make sense of symptoms of psychopathology. An additional step involved reflecting on these explanatory frameworks in an intentional manner—to be truly and thoroughly Christian in our analysis of contemporary psychopathology, and to do so in a way that would help other Christians in the field move forward in the task of integration.

This book is intended for a broad audience that includes students and clinicians in the mental health fields (e.g., psychology, counseling, social work, marriage and family therapy, and so on), pastors and ministers of pastoral care.

OVERVIEW OF THE BOOK

The book is divided into four parts. In part one (chapters one through four), we set the stage for the discussion of the major symptom presentations as organized by the *DSM*. Chapter one is a discussion of pastoral care and disordered desires. We begin with a review of ways in which the Christian community has historically approached various psychological and spiritual concerns. In chapter two, "Biological and Sociocultural Foundations of Mental Illness," we examine various models of psychopathology and express our commitment to a multifaceted perspective. Chapter three is concerned with classifying mental disorders. In this chapter we look at the various ways mental disorders have been classified, as well as the current debates in the classification system reflected in the *DSM*. The last chapter in part one (chapter four, "Sin and Psychopathology") is our effort to unpack the implications of sin in the study of psychopathology from a Christian perspective.

Part two of the book (chapters five through eleven) devotes one chapter to each of the major symptom presentations discussed in contemporary psychopathology (e.g., problems of mood). Each chapter contains a brief discussion of pastoral approaches to the topics covered in the book, followed by an overview of the disorders in contemporary classification, followed by research on etiology, treatment and prevention. We then discuss themes in integration, tying the discussion back to the foundational chapters from part one of the book.

Part four (chapter fourteen) reflects our desire to cast a vision for the church and for Christian mental health professionals. We want to bring together the best resources from the church and the best understandings from science and clinical practice.

ACKNOWLEDGMENTS

All three of us contributed to the content and reflections found in each chapter, but we each had primary responsibilities for specific chapters. Mark was the primary author of chapters four, seven, eleven and thirteen. Richard was the primary author of chapters two, five, six, nine and ten. Barrett was the primary author of chapters one, three, eight and twelve. Mark and Barrett were the primary coauthors of chapter fourteen.

We feel very fortunate to have worked together on this project and to have seen our friendships strengthened over the years. We have been blessed by stimulating conversations with students and colleagues for many years now. In particular we want to thank the students who took psychopathology courses over the past few years from Mark at Regent University and over many more years from Richard at Wheaton College. Your insights, narratives and questions have influenced us more than you may ever know.

We would like to thank the many people who read and critiqued various chapters of this book. Mark wishes to thank his research team members, including Erica Tan, Lisa Pawlowski, Stephen Russell, Heather Brooke, Lori Burkett, Robin Seymore, Edye Garcia, Lynette Bogey and Adam Hunter. He would also like to thank the Christian education class at Galilee Church for their thoughtful consideration of many of these issues as he taught Pursuing Emotional Wholeness in Christ.

Richard would like to acknowledge his research and teaching assistants: David Hoover, Ariel Oleari, Brian McLaughlin, Luke De-Mater, June Stroner, Amy Prescott, Justin O'Rouke and Alex Johnson. Thanks also to colleagues for their feedback, including Bob and Terri Watson, Michael Mangis, Derek McNeil, Pamela Trice, Sandy Johnston Kruse, Victor Argo, Georgina Panting, Javier Sierra, Jairo Sarmiento, Guillermo Jimenez, Stanton Jones, Ward Kriegbaum, Dorothy Chappell, Randy Sorenson, Helen DeVries, Mark McMinn, Robert Gregory, Jack and Barb Van Vessem, Chip Edgar, Don Pruessler, Tim Brown, Alexandra Tsang, Don Bosch, Brent Stenberg, Newt Malony, Walt Wright, Steve Sittig and Don Dwyer.

Barrett would like to acknowledge his research assistants Lucas Bossard and Andy Jack. He would also like to thank the colleagues and mentors whose wisdom and guidance have laid the foundation for his contribution to the views of pastoral care expressed in this book: John McRay, Mark McMinn, Rich Butman, Jim Cassens, Jerry Root, Fran White, Mark Yarhouse, Terri Watson, Stew Morton, Mike Marcey, Ed Dunkelblau and Peter Bouman.

We would all like to acknowledge our formal reviewers, Al Dueck and Randy Sanders, who provided us with constructive feedback that helped us in the fine-tuning.

Part One

Issues in Integration of Christianity and the Scientific Study of Psychopathology

1

HISTORIC PASTORAL CARE AND DISORDERED DESIRES

Why begin a book on modern psychopathologies with a chapter on historic pastoral care? Though the value of pastoral care for the life and ministry of the church may be obvious, what does it have to do with modern psychopathologies? Pastoral care, or the ministry of "the cure of souls," has been described as consisting of "helping acts, done by representative Christian persons, directed toward the healing, sustaining, guiding, and reconciling of troubled persons whole troubles arise in the context of ultimate meanings and concerns" (Clebsch and Jaekle, 1964). As such it has served as the "practical outworking of the church's concern for the everyday and ultimate needs of its members and the wider community," and it has deep roots in the Christian tradition (Hurding, 1995, p. 78). But what does historic pastoral care have to do with struggles people have with anxiety, depression or substance abuse?

We believe that the history of pastoral care provides us with insights into the human condition that predate contemporary psychology and specific theories of psychopathology. Further, we believe that Christians interested in the study of human experience, including various dysfunctions and psychopathologies, need to be informed by these insights and pastoral reflections on the experiences of "troubled persons" and the church's concern for their everyday and ultimate needs.

Historic pastoral care and reflection was quite different from what we think of as modern psychology. It was based chiefly on reflection and deduction from principles derived from Scripture and pastoral experience, whereas the modern psychologies, while also indebted to reflection and theorizing, are grounded more in behavioral science investigation characterized by inductive, empirical study. In other words, the pastoral language, categories and methodologies for understanding human experiences are significantly different from those used by contemporary mental health professionals. These differences led to the neglect of historic pastoral care, in part out of disdain for premodern wisdom and its tendency to privilege reductionism, naturalism and empiricism (Oden, 1980). Although much has been gained through advances in the behavioral sciences, we wish to make connections that have been all but lost as Christians attempt to think *as Christians* about contemporary mental and spiritual health concerns. Toward that end we consider historic pastoral care and the insights of pastoral writers on the human condition.

Hurding (1995) traces some of the earliest expressions of pastoral care to the Old and New Testaments, in which pastoral care was experienced as

- *prophetic care,* evidenced in warnings concerning judgment as well as promises of renewal
- *shepherdly care,* images of God shepherding his people and the expectation of a Messiah-shepherd
- *priestly care,* especially in the Levites and their roles as representatives of God's people, a role ultimately fulfilled by Christ
- *physicianly care,* seen in language suggesting God is a compassionate healer who brings wholeness, and this desire for wholeness is demonstrated through the healing ministry of Christ and his followers

These earliest themes and expressions of pastoral care can be seen in the early church and throughout the history of pastoral care.

From the church's birth at Pentecost, its writings bear witness to the significance given the task of care for one another and especially for those in need. Recognition is given not only to the importance of this work but also to the knowledge and skill needed to provide care to those who are suffering. Christ and his apostles laid the foundation for a church committed to the care of each member and instructed believers to make this a central aspect of life within the body of Christ. The early church fathers taught about the need for "physicians of the soul" skilled in the care of those whose woundedness hindered their faithful obedience to Christ or deprived them of fullness of life in the community of faith (Clebsch and Jaekle, 1964). For example, Origen writes in the second century that Christians should look carefully for a "physician" of souls to whom they could confess their sin and "lay bare the cause of [their] ailment, who knows how to be infirm with the infirm" (quoted in Kemp, 1947, p. 27). Throughout the history of the church, this ministry of soul care has been central to its life and mission.

The history of the mental health field from its origins in Greek philosophy to the development of contemporary theories of psychotherapy reveals an intensifying focus on systematic understandings and categorizations of the problems people experience in their psychological health (see Jones and Butman, 1991). This field of study—identified as the study of psychopathology or abnormal psychology—provides the basis for the diagnostic categories and terminology used by contemporary health and mental health providers in their care for persons in mental, emotional, behavioral and relational distress. These diagnostic categories have evolved through numerous iterations and revisions and continue to do so as theories mutate, societal values change, and continuing research offers a greater breadth of understanding.

Pastors, elders, ministry leaders and Christian mental health professionals, in their desire to better understand how and why people hurt and ways to be helpful in response to their pain, have sought to understand the diagnostic categories of psychopathology and to appraise them in light of the truths of the Scriptures and the teachings of the Christian church. It is our hope that this book will serve as a resource to those who wish to better grasp this integrative endeavor and as a guide to those who might wish to join in the ongoing task of understanding the nature of human suffering and responding to those in distress.

Western society's growing fascination with popular psychological understandings of the person has catapulted concern about psychopathology and wounds of the soul to the mainstream. Many people, when faced with emotional problems, will turn to mental health professionals to sort out the complexities of their concerns. Symptoms are almost without exception organized and conceptualized with reference to contemporary diagnostic nosology (e.g., the *Diagnostic and Statistical Manual of Mental Disorders,* APA, 1994), and this may inform case conceptualization and treatment planning, though it may also foreclose prematurely on other resources, including those found within the historic pastoral care literature. As Oden observes, "It is time to listen intently to the scriptural text and early Christian writers. It is time to ask how classical Christianity itself might teach us to understand the providence of God in the midst of our broken and confused modern situation" (1991, p. 36).

It is toward this end of "listening intently" to the Scriptures and the voices of Christians who have gone before us and paved the way for our understanding of human experience that we consider the "roots" of Christian caregiving in the historic ministry of pastoral care and some of the more contemporary "shoots" in theology and psychotherapy. Unfortunately, these contemporary trends, coupled with numerous other forces such as the advancement of the empirical study of human behavior, have led to the segregation of psychological and spiritual aspects of care and understandings of mental and emotional suffering.

THE ROOTS OF CHRISTIAN CAREGIVING

Scriptural foundations. The Scriptures, of course, do not use the language of contemporary psychopathology. Furthermore, it is not the intent of any of the biblical writers to offer a systematic categorization of psychological dysfunctions. Therefore we must be careful not to look to the Scriptures to find evidence of "God's view" of psychopathology. It apparently was not God's intent in inspiring the scriptural writers to teach us the exact nature and breadth of our psychological functioning. However, in many places the Scriptures do offer instruction about the nature of our human condition before God and before one another. These truths have tremendous bearing on our understanding of issues related to psychopathology, and these teachings laid a foundation for the development of the church's understanding and approach to human suffering and eventual categorizations of these experiences.

A number of theological truths emerging from the pages of the Scriptures have bearing on our understanding of these issues. These include the nature of humans as created beings and image bearers of God and the impact of sin on that nature. These truths also include

God's design for the church's response to the suffering that results from the evil that is now part of this world. So here, after a brief discussion of humans as created beings and image bearers of God, we turn our attention to the impact of sin and the church's response.

The nature of humans. It is beyond the scope of this book to offer a comprehensive theological anthropology. However, we affirm the Christian view that human beings are created by God, that they are "created persons," to use Hoekema's phrase (1986, p. 6). That is, human beings are created and dependent on God (created) while relatively independent and capable of making decisions and setting and meeting various goals (persons).

Also, to be human is to be created in the *image* of God *(imago Dei)*. Numerous scholars have proposed various ways we image God—through reason, will, the soul, relationality and so on—but suffice it to say that there are many aspects of human nature and being that set us apart from other creatures and seem to reflect something of who God is. There may be many facets to human beings' imaging of God, and we affirm that God intended from creation to set humanity apart for his purposes.

As created persons, as image bearers of God and in a number of other ways, human beings, whether or not they acknowledge it, are always in relation to God and to transcendent reality. We assume, then, that God created human beings to function in certain ways and that those functions include both "internal" thoughts, feelings and experience of one's conscience and "external" behaviors and ways of relating to others. When we are not functioning properly, we place ourselves at risk of spiritual, emotional and physical health concerns, and these domains are not discrete but interrelated and complex.

The impact of sin. Although we were created as image bearers of God and were made in relation to him, we exist in a fallen state. This fallen condition is referenced by Paul in Romans: "Sin entered the world through one man, and death through sin, and in this way death came to all men, because all sinned. . . . Through the disobedience of the one man the many were made sinners" (Rom 5:12, 19). Sin refers to both a state (of fallenness) and specific acts. We have all "sinned and fall short of the glory of God," and we face the consequences of that sin, which is death (Rom 3:23; 6:23).

Specific acts of sin not only remind us of our fallen condition but demonstrate specific, concrete ways in which we fail to act according to God's will for our lives and relationships. Sin undoubtedly interacts with a number of other dimensions of human experience, and we will discuss these issues further in chapter three.

The impact of sin (as a state) is everywhere and experienced by everyone. But the message of the gospel is that God has not left us in this state of hopeless despair. He had compassion on us (Ps 145:9; Is 30:18; 49:13; Rom 5:8). "All have sinned and fall short of the glory of God, *and are justified freely by his grace through the redemption that came by Christ Jesus. . . .* For the wages of sin is death, *but the gift of God is eternal life in Christ Jesus our Lord"* (Rom 3:23-24; 6:23).

The Scriptures acknowledge that sin has left us in a state of brokenness and helplessness (not worthlessness, as some would assert). We are unable to change our condition. God alone can redeem us; he alone can bring hope and healing. Our intended nature was changed as a result of Adam and Eve's sin, and we each at some point willfully participate in that legacy of sinfulness. Our condition is not as it was intended to be, and God responds to this condition in two seemingly opposing ways—wrath and judgment for the evil at work within us (Rom 1:18) and compassion and comfort for the suffering that we bear (2 Cor 1:4).

Eric Johnson (1987) proposes that these two aspects of our fallen nature (that for which God holds us responsible and that for which he does not) have significant implications for a Christian understanding of psychopathology. He suggested that the Scriptures teach a distinction between "sin" and "weakness": "sin" *(hamartia)* refers to the changes in our nature and behavior for which we are responsible, while "weakness" *(astheneia)* refers to those changes in our nature for which we are not responsible. God responds to our sin with judgment tempered by grace, while his response to weakness is tenderness and compassion (Rom 8:26; 1 Cor 15:43; 2 Cor 12:9-10; 13:4; Heb 4:15; 11:34). This latter category and the overlap between the two, Johnson concludes, may have relevance for the many manifestations of human brokenness that are the focus of contemporary psychopathology. In other words, we have weaknesses that place us at risk of sinning, and we live in a world that is tainted by sin (as a state of affairs), and these dynamics, taken together with a variety of other factors, may account for a person's susceptibility to psychopathology.

THE CHURCH'S RESPONSE

As Jesus looked on the crowds of people, he was moved to compassion for them because of the many ways they suffered and because of their need for a shepherd (Mt 9:35; 14:14; 15:32; 20:34). His response to people in pain is the model for the church.

> In the ministry of Jesus is found the source, the inspiration, the ideal.... No other influence in the history of humanity has done so much to relieve human suffering, to create a spirit of compassion, and to inspire others to give themselves in an attempt to understand and to serve their fellow-men.... The stories and incidents revealed in the four gospels present one who had a unique insight into the needs and problems of people, one who understood with a clarity that has never been equaled or surpassed the meaning of life and human nature.... Jesus felt that ... his mission was to relieve human suffering ... to alleviate suffering in any manner in which he met it, whether it might be physical, mental, moral, or spiritual. (Kemp, 1947, pp. 6-7)

The Scriptures assume the reality of suffering and the need for care and make it clear that this is not only central to the mission of the church but part of the law of Christ—"bear one another's burdens and so fulfill the law of Christ" (Gal 6:2). The prevailing scriptural metaphor for the care and comfort of the wounded, weak and oppressed is a shepherd's care for the flock: "When [Jesus] saw the crowds, he had compassion on them, because they were harassed and helpless, like sheep without a shepherd" (Mt 9:36). Peter extols elders to be "shepherds of God's flock that is under your care" (1 Pet 5:2). Jesus refers to himself as the "Good Shepherd" in John 10, and Peter refers to God as the "Shepherd and Overseer of [our] souls" (1 Pet 2:25). In Psalm 23, David gives perhaps the most vivid picture of this metaphor of tender care as he describes God's love in response to his weakness and woundedness: "he restores my soul" (Ps 23:3).

The English word *pastor* is derived from the Latin *pastor,* which means shepherd. Those who would lead God's church and care for his people must see themselves as shepherds. Without understanding the role of the shepherd of Old and New Testament Israel, one cannot grasp the profound nature of this teaching. Shepherds were social outcasts, considered unclean because they lived among animals. Yet it was a shepherd whom God chose as king over Israel, and it was to shepherds that the angel Gabriel first announced Jesus' birth. Benner explores some of the richness of this metaphor of Christian ministry:

"Shepherds lead their sheep to places of nourishment and safety, protect them from danger, and are regularly called upon for great personal sacrifice. They are characterized by compassion, courage, and a mixture of tenderness and toughness" (1998, p. 25). Through this metaphor of a humble shepherd we see the breadth of God's compassion and his call for us to be people of compassion, and this metaphor provides the foundation for the church's response throughout history to people in pain.

We are to be people of compassion who seek to comfort one another with the comfort we have received from God—a comfort that produces "patient endurance" to persevere amid trials and sufferings (2 Cor 1:3-7). We are to serve one another with the humility Christ displayed in his sacrifice (Phil 2:5-11). And those entrusted with the specific responsibilities of "shepherding" are to "keep watch over themselves and over all the flock of which the Holy Spirit has made you overseers" (Acts 20:28). In the New Testament church, shepherding was not about status or position but about a vital responsibility of service. That service included leading by demonstrating a life of trustworthiness and Christlike service (1 Tim 3:1-7; Tit 1:6-9; 1 Pet 5:1-3) and preserving unity in the church so the spiritual gifts of all the believers could be brought together to meet the needs of the community and glorify God (1 Cor 12; Eph 4:1-16). This mutuality of caring in community, facilitated and overseen by the pastoral leadership of shepherds, formed the foundation for the ministry that has been referred to throughout the history of the church as "the care of souls" or "pastoral care."

THE LITERATURE OF THE CHURCH

Throughout the history of the church, understandings of the nature of human suffering and the human condition have varied, as have the responses of the church to those who are suffering. Both the need for a "remedy" for sin and the need for assistance in spiritual growth have been central to the church's response to the human condition. The focus of this response, though varied in its precise theology and practice, has most often been on the need for redemption in the life of believers who suffer as a result of sin (Kemp, 1947; McNeill, 1951; Clebsch and Jaekle, 1964; Benner, 1998). We will highlight a few examples of these variations in perspective and care.

The impact of sin. The theologians of the early church believed that the soul is stained with sin and that in the believer this arouses inner turmoil between the desires that God created for humans to experience and the perversion of those through sin. All suffering, disability and trials can in the end be traced back to sin, and therefore an understanding of these struggles in life begins with an awareness of the sinfulness of the human condition. Origen, an Alexandrian theologian writing in the early third century, attempted to tease out the complexity of human dispositions that may impede one's ability to live out life as God intended:

> I do not think it is possible to explain easily or briefly how a soul may know herself; but as far as we are able, we will try to elucidate a few points out of many. It seems to me, then, that the soul ought to acquire self-knowledge of a twofold kind: she should know both what she is in herself, and how she is actuated; that is to say, she ought to know what she is like essentially, and what she is like according to her dispositions. She should know, for instance, whether she is of good disposition or not, and whether or not she is upright in intention; and, if she is in fact of an upright intention, whether, in thought as in action, she has the same zeal for all virtues, or only for necessary things and those that are easy; furthermore, whether she is making progress, and gaining in understanding of things, and growing in the virtues; or whether perhaps she is standing still and resting on what she has been able to achieve thus far; and whether what she does serves only for her own improvement; or whether she can benefit others, and give them anything of profit, either by the word of teaching or by the example of her actions. . . . And the soul needs to know herself in another way—whether she does these evil deeds of hers intentionally and because she likes them; or whether it is through some weakness that, as the Apostle says, she works what she would not and does the things she hates, while on the contrary she seems to do good deeds with willingness and with direct intention. Does she, for example, control her anger with some people and let fly with others, or does she always control it, never give way to it with anyone at all? So too with gloominess: does she conquer it in some cases, but give way to it in others, or does she never admit it at all? (*The Song of Songs* 2, quoted in Oden, 1987, 3:35)

Origen's accounts reflect an appreciation not only for the complexities of human disposition but also of the importance of self-examination so that a person understands his or her propensity to act in ways that promote (or fail to promote) spiritual and emotional well-being.

Classifications of sin became a specific focus of the early church, and "in the experience of life and the practice of soul guidance, attention was inevitably drawn to a variety of grave offenses of thought or action for which repentance was required" (McNeill and Gamer, 1938, p. 18). Lists of these sins began to be circulated in the church and would form the foundation for the church's response to sin and the formulation of appropriate guidelines for pastoral counsel. In the second century, Hermas identified twelve sins that required repentance: unbelief, incontinence, disobedience, deceit, sorrow, wickedness, wantonness, anger, falsehood, folly, backbiting and hatred. A list by Cyprian, the third-century bishop of Carthage, included eight sins: avarice, lust, ambition, anger, pride, drunkenness, envy and cursing (ibid.).

Augustine, bishop of Hippo in North Africa at the beginning of the fifth century, considered sin to be a *disordering* of that which God had originally created to be good. Thus the disorders of the soul could be described as the distortion of a virtue that God had ordained. In particular, Augustine wrote of what he called "disordered loves":

> The person who lives a just and holy life is one who . . . has ordered his love, so that he does not love what it is wrong to love, or fail to love what should be loved, or love too much what should be loved less (or love too little what should be loved more), or love two things equally if one of them should be loved either less or more than the other, or love things either more or less if they should be loved equally. No sinner, *qua* sinner, should be loved; every human being, *qua* human being, should be loved on God's account; and God should be loved for himself. And if God is to be loved more than any human being, each person should love God more than he loves himself. Likewise, another human being should be loved more than our own bodies, because all these things are to be loved on account of God whereas another person can enjoy God together with us in a way in which the body cannot, since the body lives only through the soul, and it is the soul by which we enjoy God. All people should be loved equally. (*On Christian Teaching* 1.59-60, p. 21)

This emphasis on disordered loves or disordered desires would characterize much of historical pastoral care, as theological insights aided pastors in their "understanding and interpretations of human experience" (Tidball, 1988, p. 493).

John Cassian, a fifth-century monk who introduced Eastern monastic life to the Western church, categorized the disordered desires under what became known as the "eight principal vices" of gluttony, fornication, avarice, anger, dejection, languor, vainglory and pride. He offered not only a description of these sins but guidance for their "treatment" (McNeill and Gamer, 1938). At the close of the sixth century, Pope Gregory revised Cassian's ordering of sins and their remedy, giving emphasis to pride (a revolt of the spirit against God) and lust (a revolt of the flesh against the spirit). His list in order included pride, vainglory, envy, anger, dejection, avarice, gluttony and lust.

Pope Gregory extended his classification of human nature further, acknowledging that people possess different qualities of character and therefore "one and the same exhortation is not suited to all" (Gregory, 1978). This was an important pastoral insight. He suggested that the approach of the pastor in soul care should be "adapted to the character of the hearers, so as to be suited to the individual in his respective needs, and yet never deviate from the art of general edification" (ibid., p. 89). He proceeded to offer a classification system for understanding various polarities of character or state that ought to be taken into consideration by the pastor giving counsel or admonition. In addition to the categories of gender, age and social position, these included such categories as joyful and sad, wise and dull, impudent and timid, insolent and fainthearted, impatient and patient, kindly and envious, sincere and insincere, hale and sick, fearful and impervious, taciturn and loquacious, slothful and hasty, meek and choleric, humble and haughty, obstinate and fickle, gluttonous and abstemious, generous and thieving, discordant and peacemakers. These categories evidence both conditions of the souls due to sinful vices and conditions due to what might be called temperament.

By the end of the sixth century, Celtic writers in Ireland were producing a flow of penitential books that would govern the experience of penance and the practice of guidance. Most of these books were written by followers of Cassian or Gregory, and their influence would shape the focus of pastoral guidance throughout the medieval period of the church.

The Middle Ages brought with it greater emphasis on sacramentalism, though this was hardly the only development in pastoral care. Other emphases included Bernard of Clairvaux's (1090-1153) and

Hildegard of Bingen's work in practical spirituality (Hurding, 1995). Additional developments were in the area of concern for the destitute, and perhaps Francis of Assisi is most well known for his outreach to the poor.

In the sixteenth century, Ignatius Loyola described the nature of the soul as being subject to "desolation" and said it was only through the process of "consolation" that the soul could be restored:

> I call it consolation when the soul is aroused by an interior movement which causes it to be inflamed with love of its Creator and Lord, and consequently can love no created thing on the face of the earth for its own sake, but only in the creator of all things. . . . I call consolation any increase of faith, hope, and charity and any interior joy that calls and attracts to heavenly things, and to the salvation of one's soul, inspiring it with peace and quiet in Christ our Lord. I call desolation all that is contrary to the third rule, as darkness of the soul, turmoil of the mind, inclination to low and earthly things, restlessness resulting from many disturbances and temptations which lead to loss of faith, loss of hope, and loss of love. It is also desolation when a soul finds itself completely apathetic, tepid, sad, and separated, as it were, from its Creator and Lord. For just as consolation is contrary to desolation, so the thoughts that spring from consolation are the opposite of those that spring from desolation. (*Spiritual Exercises,* quoted in Oden, 1987, 4:73)

Advances in pastoral theology during the Reformation were seen in the work of Martin Bucer, Martin Luther and John Calvin. Protestant pastors began to offer teaching on the nature of sin and the role of the pastor in guiding souls. Perhaps the most systematic writing on pastoral care is seen among the Puritans. Interestingly, the writings of the Puritans evidenced an awareness of the distinction between spiritual and natural causes of any number of concerns. For example, natural depression, called "melancholy" in Puritan times, was understood as a condition quite apart from depression due to spiritual causes. Natural depression had no known cause, though it was presumed to be due to what we might think of as psychological causes. Puritan writers focused most of their attention on spiritual causes and cures, viewing bouts with spiritual depression as best remedied through resources available to the Christian, such as the reading of Scripture, pastoral counsel, corporate worship, prayer and the work of the Holy Spirit.

Through all of these periods of church history, it is evident that although there was a growing awareness of differences between spiritual and "natural" causes of various concerns, the impact of sin on the human soul has been the primary concern of the shepherds of the church, whose responsibility it was to offer instruction, guidance and care.

THE CHURCH'S RESPONSE

At the close of New Testament times, the church faced severe persecution as it grew and began to spread throughout the world. New offices and increasing structure emerged within the church in response to its growth and the persecution it was enduring. Pastoral ministry was often centered on sustaining people within the community in the face of tremendous trial. Anticipation of the imminent return of Christ gave the community strength and hope to persevere, and this anticipation contributed to the gradual rise of the practice of confession as central to the life of the church. By the second century, standard methods for private guidance and public confession had developed within the church (Holifield, 1983). The church's response to and remedy for the condition of sin was confession to one another (Jas 5:16; 1 Jn 1:9) and repentance (Lk 5:32; Acts 5:31; 2 Cor 7:10; 2 Pet 3:9), and these would form the foundation of the church's response until the modern era (Benner, 1998).

All indications are that confession was public and was a central element in the regular meetings of the church. The *Didache*, written about one generation after the close of the New Testament, instructed the church to gather on the Lord's day to "confess your sins, and not approach prayer with a bad conscience" and to "break bread and give thanks, first confessing your sins so that your sacrifice may be pure" (quoted in Richardson, 1970, pp. 173, 178). Gradually, however, confession became a more private practice. In the fourth century, Basil, bishop of Caesarea, suggested that confession of sins should follow the same principles followed with physical illnesses. Just as persons do not disclose their bodily infirmities to everyone but only to those skilled in their cure, so confession of sins should be made to one who is able to offer a spiritual remedy. In the fifth century, Pope Leo the Great declared it sufficient that confessions be made in secret to a priest. He felt that continuance of public confession was dangerous, that many would avoid penance if public confession was required (Kemp, 1947).

This change from public to private confession not only demonstrated movement toward the idea that value resides in individual confession of sin to a qualified caregiver but also acknowledged a growing desire for a confidential framework for confession. The second synod of Davin in Armenia ensured confidentiality by decreeing that any priest who divulged the content of a confessional should be anathema. This later became known as the Seal of the Confessional (Kemp, 1947).

With the rise of the confessional as a central focus in soul care came an emphasis on penance as part of the process of confession. This emphasis eventually was codified in the form of the "penitential" in about the sixth century. Perhaps inspired by St. Gregory's *Pastoral Care* (originally published in 591), numerous volumes appeared, which functioned as handbooks for priests in their role as confessors. Whereas Pope Gregory's work focused primarily on the qualities of pastoral leadership and the most effective ways for responding to people with various styles and temperaments, the penitentials that followed were largely composed of lists of commonly recognized sins and the penance necessary to receive forgiveness for each. In addition, they outlined methods for priests to use in receiving and dealing with penitents (McNeill and Gamer, 1938).

The penitentials were an important factor in the shift from public to private confession. Many used the metaphors, ideas and language of then current models of medicine. The *Penitential of Columban* from the seventh century stated:

> For even the physicians of bodies prepare their medicines in various sorts. For they treat wounds in one way, fevers in another, swellings in another, bruises in another, festering sores in another, defective sight in another, fractures in another, burns in another. So therefore the spiritual physicians ought also to heal with various sorts of treatment the wounds, fevers, transgressions, sorrows, sicknesses, and infirmities of souls. (McNeill and Gamer, 1938, p. 251)

Similarly, in the eighth century a penitential attributed to the Venerable Bede suggested that a "physician of the soul" should allow for different spiritual and circumstantial conditions, in the same way that a physician of the body prescribes varying remedies depending on the disease.

Though at times harsh in their instruction, the penitential authors demonstrated a "sympathetic knowledge of human nature and a desire to deliver men and women from the mental obsessions and social maladjustments caused by their misdeeds" (McNeill and Gamer, 1938, pp. 45-46). They sought to understand the conditions of sinners and the factors that might affect these conditions and the church's response to them. The *Bigotian Penitential* from the eighth century suggested that the process of confession and penance should take into consideration "the age and sex of the penitent, his training, his courage, with what force he was driven to sin, with what kind of passion he was assailed, how long he continued in sin and with what sorrow and labor he was afflicted" (Kemp, 1947, p. 29).

> The penitentials offered to the sinner the means of rehabilitation. He was given guidance to the way of recovering harmonious relations with the church, society and God. Freed in the process of penance from social censure, he recovers the lost personal values of which his offenses have deprived him. He can once more function as a normal person. Beyond the theological considerations, we see in the detailed prescriptions the objective of an inward moral change, the setting up of a process of character reconstruction which involves the correction of special personal defects, and the reintegration of personality. (McNeill and Gamer, 1938, p. 46)

As a group, the penitentials sought to cure souls by what they termed the "principle of contraries": each vice must be replaced by a corresponding virtue. The theology behind them was clearly legalistic, and the penalties were often so severe as to be inhumane. Their goal, however, was to care for the spiritual health of sinners lost in their sin. The place of confession and penance in the life of the church also solidified the role of the priest as the physician of the soul.

In 1215 the Fourth Lateran Council dictated that everyone must confess their sins to their local priest at least once each year, and by the twelfth century a full sacramental theory of priestly absolution was developed. The systematized response of the church to sin and confession seemed to reach some completion in the sixteenth century with the elaboration of a complex body of casuistry—the application of general principles to particular cases—which undertook to remedy every spiritual dilemma imaginable (Holifield, 1983).

With the Reformation came a renewed emphasis on the role of the pastor as a "shepherd" in the community and a focus on mutual responsibility and care—the priesthood of all believers. The Protestant Reformers wrote of the primary role of the pastor as offering the same tender care to the flock as that described by Paul in his first letter to the church in Thessalonica: "As apostles of Christ we could have been a burden to you, but we were gentle among you, like a mother caring for her little children. We loved you so much that we were delighted to share with you not only the gospel of God but our lives as well, because you had become so dear to us" (1 Thess 2:7-8).

In the seventeenth century Richard Baxter wrote, "We must feel toward our people as a father toward his children; yea the tenderest love of a mother must not surpass ours" (Baxter, 1931, pp. 178-79). Baxter felt his success as a pastor was due to his efforts in pastoral care. He had a custom of family visitation and said, "I find more outward signs of success [from this ministry], than from all my public preaching to them" (Baxter, 1829, p. 80). Utilizing family visits, pastoral counsel and preaching, Baxter spoke to the spiritual condition of those under his care. Although the Puritans were known for their emphasis on theological truths, their concern was really that God work in the hearts of his people so that true faith "claims the affections as well as the intellect" (Packer, 1990, p. 132).

Baxter's *Christian Directory* (1673) is perhaps the most comprehensive and far-reaching Puritan work on pastoral care. It was written for pastors who were younger and less experienced in "practical divinity." The Puritans viewed people as spiritually sick, and their remedy was to bring about healing:

> Truth obeyed, said the Puritans, will heal. The word fits, because we are all spiritually sick—sick through sin, which is a wasting and killing disease of the heart. The unconverted are sick unto death; those who have come to know Christ and been born again continue sick, but they are gradually getting better as the work of grace goes on in their lives. The church, however, is a hospital in which nobody is completely well, and anyone can relapse at any time. (Packer 1990, p. 65)

Emphasis was placed on self-examination so that pastors could accurately diagnose spiritual disease and offer biblical remedies. Biblical remedies were expositions of Scripture directed to the conscience through the conviction of the Holy Spirit.

Thomas Oden highlights five recurring themes in the literature of pastoral care that he contended describe the historic view of the church on the nature of an effective relationship of soul care, and these are strikingly similar to what is being reported in the literature on "empirically supported relationships": "(1) accurate empathic listening; (2) congruent, open awareness of one's own experiencing process, trusting one's own soul, one's own most inward experiencing, enabling full self-disclosure; (3) unconditional accepting love; (4) rigorous self-examination; and (5) narrative comic insight" (Oden, 1987, 3:7). There are reasons to see the relationship between the helper and recipient of care as the heart of the matter—no doubt reflective of our intrinsically relational identities.

Catherine of Sienna, a fourteenth-century Italian mystic who devoted her life to care for the poor and sick, evidenced a passion for empathy:

> They made themselves infirm with those who were infirm, so that they might not be overcome with despair, and to give them more courage in exposing their infirmity, they would ofttimes lend countenance to their infirmity and say, "I, too, am infirm with thee"! They wept with those who wept, and rejoiced with those who rejoiced; and thus sweetly they knew to give every one his nourishment, preserving the good and rejoicing in their virtues, not being gnawed by envy, but expanded with the broadness of love for their neighbours, and those under them. They drew the imperfect ones out of imperfection, themselves becoming imperfect and infirm with them, as I told thee, with true and holy compassion, and correcting them and giving them penance for the sins they committed—they through love endured their penance together with them. For through love, they who gave the penance, bore more pain than they who received it. (*A Treatise of Prayer*, quoted in Oden, 1987, 3.8-9)

Ambrose, bishop of Milan in the fourth century, wrote in his work *Duties of the Clergy* about the need for those who care for souls to know themselves: "Blessed, plainly is that life which is not valued at the estimation of outsiders, but is known, as judge of itself, by its own inner feelings" (quoted in Oden, 1987, 3.19). The apostle Peter reveals that if we love one another deeply, such love has the power to "cover over a multitude of sins" we may commit against each other (1 Pet 4:8). Thomas Aquinas, in the thirteenth century, offered similar words to those who care for souls: "When the people see that you unfeignedly love them, they will hear any thing and bear any thing from you. . . . We ourselves will take all things well from one that we know entirely loves us" (*Commentary on Sentences* 1, Distinction 27, q.1.a.1-4, quoted in Oden, 1987, 3.8-9).

In the eleventh century, the Benedictine abbot William of St. Thierry wrote about the importance of examining oneself rigorously to know the motives of the heart and the actions that follow:

> To try to escape ill-health of the soul by moving from place to place is like flying from one's own shadow. Such a man as flies from himself carries himself with him. He changes his place, but not his soul. He finds himself the same everywhere he is, except that the constant moving itself makes him worse, just as a sick man is harmed by jolting when he is carried about. (*The Golden Epistle* 95; quoted in Oden, 1987, 3.42)

George Herbert, a sixteenth-century Anglican pastor, addressed the need for some humor and "pleasantness of disposition" in the ministry of caring for the souls of others. He contended that "instructions seasoned with pleasantness both enter sooner and root deeper" (*The Country Parson*, pp. 94-95; quoted in Oden, 1987, 3.47).

Throughout all of these, we see evidence of a compassionate response of soul care physicians to the specific needs of people, with keen awareness of the nature of their sin and their suffering.

THE SEGREGATION OF THE PSYCHOLOGICAL AND SPIRITUAL

Throughout Christian history the church has been dedicated to the care of souls; these efforts have been undergirded by the basic understanding that sin is the cause of human suffering and dysfunction and that the remedy can be found only in a compassionate pastoral response to the realities of both sin and pain. Thus pastoral care within the church has always utilized and benefited from contemporary understandings of the nature of humanity and the soul (psychologies) and existing models of caring (psychotherapies).

> In every historic epoch, pastoring has utilized—and by utilizing has helped to advance and transform—the psychology or psychologies current in that epoch. . . . Nowhere in history has Christianity adumbrated solely from its own lore a distinct psychology, either theoretically or popularly understood. To ap-

preciate traditional pastoring is to stand ready to adopt and adapt current psychological insights and applications without abdicating the distinctly pastoral role. (Clebsch and Jaekle, 1964, pp. 68-69)

This is evident in the literature of the pastoral writers right up to the twentieth century. In his 1918 book *The Disease and Remedy of Sin,* W. M. MacKay described three categories of diseases of the soul— diseases of the flesh, diseases of the heart and diseases of the spirit— and their remedies in metaphoric language drawn from then current concepts of medicine and psychology. In the preface, he explains his purpose this way:

> It is the aim of these pages to show that true religion, so far from being apart from real life, is the very essence of it; that its truths are the laws of Spiritual Health, and that, far from being a dispensable luxury, they are more necessary than the bread we eat or the air we breathe. With this end, the various experiences of the soul in health and disease have been examined from a medical point of view. This volume therefore may be described as an Essay in the Psychology of Sin and Salvation from a medicinal standpoint. Christianity is everywhere regarded as the care and cure of spiritual disease. The prevalent category of thought is "spiritual health": the commanding goal is "eternal life." (MacKay, 1918, vii)

Nevertheless, the distinctly Christian nature of such understandings of the human condition and corresponding remedies for sin and suffering have been challenged in the twentieth and twenty-first centuries by the rise of contemporary psychopathology and psychotherapy. Materialistic ideologies, attempting to break from religious or supernatural worldviews, also gave rise to efforts to understand the human condition and offer remedy. They rapidly gained acceptance and prominence as they offered a more "scientific" approach to understanding human suffering and its remedy. Distinctly Christian pastoral models began to fall into the background as the church slowly became fascinated with this "new" field of study. Clebsch and Jaekle contend that the presence and prominence of modern psychology in our culture have silenced the church and produced a fundamental rift in the once vital ministry of the cure of souls (1964). Thomas Oden adds:

What happened after 1920? It was as if a slow pendulum gradually reversed its direction and began to swing headlong toward
modern psychological accommodation. . . . Pastoral care soon
acquired a consuming interest in psychoanalysis, psychopathology, clinical methods of treatment, and in the whole string of
therapeutic approaches that were to follow Freud. . . . Classical
pastoral wisdom fell into a deep sleep. (1988, pp. 22-23)

David Benner argues that the rise of modern psychotherapies led
to an artificial separation of the spiritual and psychological aspects of
persons. Such compartmentalizing the soul into psychological and
spiritual, he contends, "resulted in the church being judged to be relevant only to the spiritual part of persons." Therefore "the church
largely abandoned efforts to chart or offer guidance regarding matters of the inner life in its totality. This ultimately led to the displacement of clergy by psychotherapists as curates of the soul" (pp. 13-14).

We are now left with a perspective on the nature of persons that
segregates psychological and spiritual into separate domains. Diseases and remedies for each have become the purview of almost totally separate disciplines with separate ideologies, separate pathways
of training and separate professional identities. Specialists in the "psychological" nature of persons can be trained without regard for the
"spiritual" nature of persons, and experts in the "spiritual" nature of
persons can be trained with little or no regard for the "psychological"
nature of persons. We have accepted the idea of a fragmented soul,
and so our attempts to understand the psychological nature of human
pain and struggle (psychopathology) are often undertaken without regard for spiritual realities, historic Christian perspectives or an understanding of the spiritual implications of these views.

Contemporary works in psychopathology occasionally describe the
historical conceptions of abnormal behavior. For example, Barlow
and Durand (2002) distinguish between supernatural, biological and
psychological traditions. We discuss the biological and psychological
traditions in greater detail in chapter four. In their discussion of the
supernatural tradition, Barlow and Durand note that deviant or abnormal behavior was often seen as a battle between "good" and
"evil." Though this is a simplistic account, there is a kernel of truth to
it. What is interesting, however, is the distinction between the supernatural, the biological and the psychological. These distinctions point
to the state of affairs and the challenges faced by Christian mental

health professionals who want to acknowledge spiritual influences and transcendent reality while demonstrating regard for advances in biological and psychological bases for behavior.

We must desegregate the soul in our thinking, and we must rejoin spiritual and psychological methodologies for responding to the sin and suffering of persons. In so doing, Christian pastoral care traditions must reemerge within the ministries of the church, once again leading the church in its response to sin and suffering and intentionally integrating the advances of current psychologies. "A major effort is needed today to rediscover and remind the classical models of Christian pastoral care and to make available once again the key texts of that classical tradition following about fifty years of neglect, the depths of which are arguably unprecedented in any previous Christian century" (Oden, 1988, p. 17).

DESEGREGATION OF THE SOUL

The shepherding ministry of the church has historically drawn on both spiritual and psychological resources for the care of souls. Within the past century, these have become compartmentalized, and psychological resources have been largely separated out from the church's ministry. Psychological care is considered the domain of professional mental health practitioners and spiritual care the domain of professional clergy. Though there can be wisdom in specialization, we believe that the segregation that is evident today is both unbiblical and neglectful of the history of soul care within the church. Christian providers of psychological care and Christian providers of spiritual care must rejoin their efforts and recognize their joint responsibility for a more holistic care of the soul (as a "psychospiritual whole," see Benner 1998). Of course, our awareness of the great traditions of pastoral care does not in and of itself qualify us to be practitioners, but this awareness is a starting point for integration.

Such an integrative approach to soul care would be rooted in a biblical understanding of the nature of the soul. Benner argues convincingly for a view of the soul rooted in the theology, anthropology and psychology of Scripture, encompassing "all of our personhood":

> The soul is the meeting point of the psychological and the spiritual. This means that soul care that draws on both the best insights of modern therapeutic psychology as well as the historic Christian approaches to the care and cure of persons will never

again be able to accept the artificial distinction of the psychological and spiritual. A proper understanding of the soul reunites the psychological and the spiritual and directs the activities of those who care for the souls of others in such a way that their care touches the deepest levels of people's inner lives. (1998, p. 62)

Some have attempted to bridge this divide; however, those efforts most often take the form of attempts to inform the one of the expertise of the other. For example, Johnson and Johnson (2000) produced a helpful resource for pastors that summarizes the major diagnostic categories of psychological disorders and their most common treatments—an attempt to inform pastors of the expertise of psychology. Roberts (1993) has provided a thought-provoking analysis of the views of persons championed by prominent contemporary psychotherapeutic models, concluding that they are insufficient and offering his Christian interpretation of selfhood—an attempt to inform those in psychology of the expertise of theology. It is time for a desegregation of the soul in our thinking about what causes psychological and spiritual disorders and a unification of our efforts of care for the soul.

Soul care that attends to both the spiritual and psychological wounds of people is the kind of soul care that has been done throughout the history of the church. We must return to these roots while drawing on advances in the behavioral sciences. In many places today, pastors are attempting to counsel the spiritual without considering the psychological, and counselors are attempting to counsel the psychological without considering the spiritual. This must be changed. There is great need for counselors to be better trained theologically and for pastors to be better trained in psychology.

Our hope is that this work may contribute to increasing efforts to reconceptualize the work of Christian soul care, drawing on the rich history of distinctly Christian understandings and practices and the best that contemporary psychopathology and psychotherapy have to offer. In the twelfth century, Aelred of Rievaulx offered a prayer for the work of soul care that captures the vision for what is needed.

Teach me your servant, therefore, Lord, teach me, I pray you, by your Holy Spirit, how to devote myself to them and how to spend myself on their behalf. Give me, by your unutterable grace, the power to bear with their shortcomings patiently, to share their griefs in loving sympathy, and to afford them help according to their needs. Taught by your Spirit may I learn to comfort the sorrowful, confirm the weak and raise the fallen; to be myself one with them in their weakness, one with them when they burn at causes of offence, one in all things with them, all things to all of them, that I may gain them all. Give me the power to speak the truth straightforwardly, and yet acceptably; so that they all may be built up in faith and hope and love, in chastity and lowliness, in patience and obedience, in spiritual fervor and submissiveness of mind. And, since you have appointed this blind guide to lead them, this untaught man to teach, this ignorant one to rule them, for their sakes, Lord, if not for mine, teach him whom you have made to be their teacher; lead him whom you have bidden to lead them, rule him who is their ruler. Teach me, therefore, sweet Lord, how to restrain the restless, comfort the discouraged, and support the weak. Teach me to suit myself to everyone according to his nature, character and disposition, according to his power of understanding or his lack of it, as time and place require, in each case, as you would have me do. (*Treatises, The Pastoral Prayer*, quoted in Oden, 1987, 3.11)

Bringing together Christianity and the science of psychology is a challenging and exciting prospect. The joining of a Christian perspective on historic pastoral care and contemporary advances in the behavioral sciences may provide new insights for Christian mental health professionals. One of the many areas for discourse is a distinctly Christian perspective on abnormal behavior. That is the purpose of this book: to consider what it means to see psychopathology through the eyes of faith.

RECOMMENDED RESOURCES

Benner, D. G. (1998). *Care of souls: Revisioning Christian nuture and counsel.* Grand Rapids, MI: Baker. This book offers a prophetic vision for a view of the soul and soul care that unites the psychological with the spiritual dimensions of persons.

Clebsch, W. A., and Jaekle, C. R. (1964). *Pastoral care in historical perspective: An essay with exhibits.* Englewood Cliffs, NJ: Prentice-Hall. This offers the reader a brief journey through the history of pastoral care combined with powerful excerpts from the writings of the church.

Nouwen, H. J. M. (1972). *The wounded healer.* New York: Doubleday. A heartfelt call to pastoral care despite our common woundedness.

Gregory the Great. (1950). *Pastoral care* (Henry Davis, Ed. and Trans.). New York: Newman Press. A classic in pastoral care literature, this book reveals the heart of a shepherd of souls who holds high the responsibility and ministry of pastoral care.

McMinn, M. R. (2004). *Why sin matters.* Wheaton, IL: Tyndale. This is a thoughtful and challenging consideration of the connection between sin and grace.

Oden, T. C. (1987). *Classical pastoral care.* Grand Rapids, MI: Baker. This is a helpful four-volume anthology of writings from the history of the church related to key areas of pastoral care.

REFERENCES

American Psychiatric Association. (1994). *Diagnostic and statistical manual of mental disorders* (4th ed.). Washington, DC: Author.

Augustine. (1997). *On Christian teaching.* (Orig. A.D. 427. R. P. H. Green, Trans.). Oxford: Oxford University Press.

Barlow, D. H., and Durand, V. M. (2002). *Abnormal psychology: An integrative approach* (3rd ed.). Belmont, CA: Wadsworth.

Baxter, R. (1829). *The reformed pastor: Or, the duty of personal labors for the souls of men* (Rev. and abridged by W. Brown). New York: American Tract Society.

Baxter, R. (1931). *The autobiography of Richard Baxter* (J. M. Lloyd Thomas, Ed.). New York: E. P. Dutton.

Benner, D. G. (1998). *Care of souls: Revisioning Christian nurture and counsel.* Grand Rapids, MI: Baker.

Clebsch, W. A., and Jaekle, C. R. (1964). *Pastoral care in historical perspective: An essay with Exhibits.* Englewood Cliffs, NJ: Prentice-Hall.

Gregory the Great. (1978). *Pastoral care* (Orig. A.D. 591. H. Davis, Trans.). In J. Quasten and J. Plumpe (Eds.), *Ancient Christian writers* (Vol. 11). New York: Newman.

Hoekema, A. A. (1986). *Created in God's image.* Grand Rapids, MI: Eerdmans.

Holifield, E. B. (1983). *A history of pastoral care in America: From salvation to self-realization.* Nashville: Abingdon.

Hurding, R. F. (1995). Pastoral care, counseling and psychotherapy. In D. J. Atkinson, D. F. Field, A. Holmes and O. O'Donovan (Eds.), *New dictionary of Christian ethics and pastoral theology* (pp. 78-87). Downers Grove, IL: InterVarsity Press.

Johnson, E. L. (1987). Sin, weakness and psychopathology. *Journal of Psychology and Theology, 15*(3), 218-26.

Johnson, W. B., and Johnson, W. L. (2000). *The pastor's guide to psychological disorders and treatments.* New York: Haworth Pastoral Press.

Jones, S. L., and Butman, R. E. (1991). *Modern psychotherapies: A comprehensive Christian appraisal.* Downers Grove, IL: InterVarsity Press.

Kemp, C. F. (1947). *Physicians of the soul: A history of pastoral counseling.* New York: Macmillan.

MacKay, W. M. (1918). *The disease and remedy of sin.* London: Hodder & Stoughton.

McMinn, M. R. (2004). *Why sin matters.* Wheaton, IL: Tyndale House.

McNeill, J. T. (1951). *A history of the cure of souls.* New York: Harper & Brothers.

McNeill, J. T., and Gamer, H. M. (1938). *Medieval handbooks of penance: A translation of the "Libri poenitentiales" and "Selections from related documents."* New York: Columbia University Press.

Oden, T. C. (1980). Recovering lost identity. *Journal of Pastoral Care, 34*(1), 4-18.

Oden, T. C. (1983). *Pastoral theology: Essentials of ministry.* San Francisco: Harper & Row.

Oden, T. C. (1984). *Care of souls in the classic tradition.* New York: Fortress.

Oden, T. C. (1987). *Classical pastoral care: Vol. 4. Crisis ministries.* Grand Rapids, MI: Baker.

Oden, T. C. (1987). *Classical pastoral care: Vol. 3. Pastoral counsel.* Grand Rapids, MI: Baker.

Oden, T. C. (1988). Recovering pastoral care's lost identity. In L. Aden and J. H. Ellens (Eds.), *The church and pastoral care* (pp. 17-32). Grand Rapids, MI: Baker.

Oden, T. C. (1991). *After modernity . . . what?* Grand Rapids, MI: Zondervan.

Packer, J. I. (1990). *A quest for godliness: The Puritan vision for the Christian life.* Wheaton, IL: Crossway.

Richardson, C. C. (1970). *Early Christian fathers.* New York: Macmillan.

Roberts, R. C. (1993). *Taking the Word to heart: Self and other in an age of therapies.* Grand Rapids, MI: Eerdmans.

Tidball, D. J. (1998). Pastoral theology. In S. B. Ferguson, D. F. Wright and J. I. Packer (Eds.), *New dictionary of theology* (pp. 493-94). Downers Grove, IL: InterVarsity Press.

2

BIOLOGICAL
AND SOCIOCULTURAL
FOUNDATIONS OF
MENTAL ILLNESS

*T*here are four broad models of abnormality in the field: biological, psychosocial, sociocultural and spiritual. Perhaps best known to our readers are the psychosocial and spiritual models. Especially in Christian circles, mental illness is often seen as a direct expression of choices made by an individual, be it their cognitive interpretive framework or a pattern of deception and evil (see our discussion on sin and psychopathology in chapter three). Our focus in this chapter will be on two other important models that seem to be less appreciated by even well-informed Christians—the biological and sociocultural traditions. We will try to make a case for "responsible eclecticism" (Jones and Butman, 1991, chap. 15), a perspective that adopts a "biopsychosocial" and integrative mindset. A careful reading of the available evidence makes it impossible, we believe, to adopt a single model mindset that would adequately explain all aspects of abnormality. Thus we intend to promote a more holistic approach, avoiding the extremes of psychological or spiritual reductionism—what we will call the sin of "nothing-but-ism."

It is exceedingly rare to see a case of mental illness that does not reflect an almost bewildering combination of biological, psychosocial, sociocultural and spiritual factors. Our explicit or implicit notions of causation, however, usually fail to reflect a carefully nuanced understanding of human pain and suffering. Not only is this possibly superficial and potentially harmful, but it can also suggest a strong desire to deny the existence of the distasteful in everyday life (McLemore, 1978).

THE PSYCHOSOCIAL MODEL REVISITED

This is the model most favored by the majority of practicing clinicians. It is an extremely broad paradigm or set of assumptions and concepts that help us explain or interpret mental illness. Within this tradition there are psychodynamic, behavioral, cognitive, humanistic and existential emphases, with scores of variations on often similar themes. In a related InterVarsity Press text (*Modern Psychotherapies: A Comprehensive Christian Appraisal*), efforts were made to compare and contrast emerging notions of personality, psychopathology and psychotherapy from a Christian perspective (Jones and Butman, 1991). The psychosocial model is often rather deterministic and reductionistic, interpreting mental illness as an expression of underlying personality dynamics, environmental factors, internal thinking processes or learned patterns (habits) of self-determination—concepts that seek to help us make sense of disorders that were previously incomprehensible.

More than a century of careful study has given us a wealth of theory and research to explore, with much potential relevance for the church and society. Part two of this volume will draw heavily on this material as we explore the major clusters of clinical disorders. Perhaps no other model has offered as many keen insights with helpful implications for treatment and prevention. The major challenge in the twenty-first century will be to find creative ways to integrate the different perspectives and specify the factors that are especially pertinent to particular problems and populations (Nathan and Gorman, 1998). Perhaps the most significant breakthroughs in the treatment of serious mental illness during the twentieth century occurred when pharmacological (biological model) and psychotherapeutic (psychosocial model) interventions were combined in actual clinical practice

(Barlow, 1993). It is now possible to offer much clearer direction and specificity in treatment planning (Jongsma and Peterson, 1995). Mental health services no longer need to be hit or miss, limited by the theoretical assumptions or biases of the clinician.

As practicing clinicians as well as academicians, we appreciate the psychosocial tradition for helping us to see more clearly how an individual's "raw material" might influence their mental health and well-being. For those of us who take both Scripture (special revelation) and reason/science (general revelation) seriously, it is extremely important how we define psychological health—and that such concepts include considerations of faith (McLemore, 1978). As Butman (2001) has noted, religion has the potential for being an important resource for coping with the demands of everyday living. Still, it is possible for a person to "be the paragon of mental health as this is traditionally defined, and yet be living without faith in God through Christ" (McLemore, 1978, p. 182). Or a person could be "holy" from a faith perspective yet be living a life that is "toxic" in terms of interpersonal relationships (McLemore, 2003). Suffice it to say that the psychosocial model has greatly sensitized us to our propensity toward impression management and almost infinite capacity to be deceitful in the ways we relate to others, ourselves and our Creator God.

We have become increasingly convinced that the presence of psychological problems in someone's life does not in any way invalidate—or even cast doubt on—their personal faith commitment. The psychosocial model has helped us come to see ourselves and our clients as works in progress, as cracked vessels with clay feet (Manning, 1988; Nouwen, 1992). We are all fallen persons, and we live in a world that is deeply flawed. This model has shown us the utter futility of pretending that things are not this way, and how cautious we should be in making judgments about anyone's character or convictions, except our own (Malony, 1995).

RELIGION, HEALTH AND WELL-BEING

The spiritual model encompasses more than an emphasis on sin and psychopathology (Plantinga, 1995). It also includes our notions of identity (Cooper, 2003), how we deal with pride and self-acceptance (Myers, 2000) and how we cope with the demands of everyday living (Pargament, 1997). Further, it has much to do with how we structure our congregations and communities (Bilezikian, 1997), the social psychology of religious organizations (Kauffmann, 2000), and what ultimately gives us hope, meaning and purpose (Smedes, 1998). Perhaps most telling, decisions about our worldview and lifestyle speak directly to how we might deal with the situational or developmental crises that arise in the course of our life (Sittser, 1996).

As Paloutzian has observed, "religious persons, as far as personality and psychological adequacy are concerned, appear to be neither better off nor worse off than other persons. They are only different—slightly better off and worse off, each in specialized ways" (1996, p. 260). Interestingly enough, rates of psychopathology (as defined by the *DSM-IV-TR*) are not significantly different for churched and unchurched populations (Hood, Spilka, Hunsburger and Gorsuch, 1996), with only modest exceptions that will be discussed in part two. Obviously, "keeping the law" does not necessarily guarantee physical, emotional or fiscal well-being. Rates of mental illness around the world show that nobody is immune from the stressors or vulnerabilities that can lead to mental illness. It is hard for us to understand how anyone who possesses this information and is a biblical realist could possibly believe in a "prosperity gospel." There are simply too many people who, despite their best efforts (or those of family and friends), are ravished by serious symptoms of mental and emotional distress.

Again, this should not surprise us. Scripture does not teach that Christians should somehow be immune from mental illness. Granted, some expressions of mental disorder are a direct result of sin— whether sin of omission or of commission—or due to structural or systemic deception and evil (Bixler, 1999). As Philip Yancey has observed, "Jesus did not come into the world to explain suffering—or to take it away—but to fill it with His presence in His time" (1984). As Sittser (1996) notes, suffering does bring potential for the enlargement of our soul, but certainly no guarantee.

Within the tradition of this model, then, it is more important to decide what gives us meaning and purpose in our lives (values), how we draw upon the resources of families and friends (social support) and whether we believe that what we do can actually make a difference in any particular situation (sense of efficacy and hope). The available data do not support the belief that a particular creed or set of convictions in and of itself makes us any better at coping (Pargament, 1997). How we apply those attitudes and beliefs concretely and specifically seems more telling—a theme that we will revisit throughout part two of this book.

BIOLOGICAL FOUNDATIONS OF MENTAL ILLNESS

The biological model is the major alternative to the psychosocial model in mental health circles. Often called the "medical perspective," the core assertion is that mental disorders reflect malfunctions within the individual, usually centered in the brain or nervous system. Interestingly enough, this tradition developed in direct opposition to the role and influence of the church—especially in medieval times, when demon possession was the major paradigm of mental illness (Comer, 2004). As noted in chapter one, there have been periods of collaboration and periods of competition between the church and health care professionals throughout the centuries (Clebsch and Jaekle, 1975; Tidball, 1986).

In the past two decades of mental health research, there has been a virtual explosion of biologically oriented research. The impressive advances made in the development of psychotropic medications for the most serious expressions of mental illness (e.g., schizophrenia, bipolar disorder, depression) have brought nothing short of a revolution in clinical practice and care. Miller and Jackson (1995) call the availability of so many more treatment options a "Godsend." Treatment with medications is not without certain risks, including side effects and a tendency toward biological reductionism among practitioners and recipients of services alike. The current milieu of "managed care" has no doubt contributed to the tendency to see persons in less than holistic and integrated ways.

A major focus of study in this tradition has been brain anatomy and functioning. As we will see repeatedly in part two of this text, nearly every major cluster of disorders has been linked with deficits or vulnerabilities in neuroanatomy, brain chemistry, genes or viral infections. The model has gained considerable respect in the field and has been enormously fruitful in generating new and often effective treatment strategies. Still, the model is far from being as complete or conclusive as proponents would have us believe. And many Christians are profoundly ambivalent about the widespread availability of psychotropic medications, wondering whether their use will interfere with "character development" or contribute to the avoidance of "legitimate suffering" (Stapert, 1994).

Academicians, clinicians and researchers tend to talk about the development (etiology) of mental disorders in terms of a *stress-diathesis* understanding. Specifically, they argue that "problems in living" tend to develop when acquired or inherited weaknesses or vulnerabilities become strained by internal and/or external factors (stress). Given sufficient stress over time, many of us might develop mental disorders (e.g., posttraumatic stress disorder as the result of exposure to abusive combat or violence). The challenges that we face include finding out what those diatheses might be or how the stressors might be experienced through the individual's interpretive framework. This should make us cautious about making sweeping generalizations about causation or responsibility. The more time we spend in the field, the more we are willing to acknowledge the incompleteness of our understanding of significant causal factors of any person's experience of serious mental illness. We need to cultivate a stance of humility and a deep respect for persons and their pain. Generic assumptions and broad generalizations seldom contribute to a deepened understanding of the inner world of mental illness. We cringe when we hear easy answers being offered in churches or communities. It is natural, of course, to want to keep things from being difficult or confusing. The urge to intervene or offer a quick fix can be overwhelming in difficult and painful situations (Nouwen, 1997).

It is our growing conviction that life events can have direct effects on neuroanatomy and neurochemistry. We would argue for a "holistic dualism" (see chapter eight) that stresses the essential unity of mind and body. The evidence is simply compelling that significant crises, losses or traumas can irreversibly affect mental, emotional and physical well-being and perhaps even spiritual health. Study after study (for a review, see Comer, 2003) has consistently shown that not only do we *feel* our pain but that pain becomes an important part of us and can affect the ways we think and behave. Perhaps this is most clearly evident in the way our "lifestyle choices" (such things as diet, exercise and rest) influence our physical as well as mental health.

Apart from a growing sophistication in making sense of life events from a more holistic and integrative perspective, the biological model offers some tangible treatment strategies that tend to polarize lay and professional circles alike. There are now at least three generations of antianxiety, antidepressant and antipsychotic medications (significant modifications and improvements have been made since the 1950s). The evidence available suggests that these medications are most useful adjuncts to treatment for serious expressions of anxiety and mood disorders and essential for stabilizing persons struggling with psychosis (Nathan and Gorman, 1998). The problems usually arise when they are seen as "cures" for mental illness or inappropriately prescribed without careful assessment or any offer of potentially less obtrusive therapeutic alternatives. For decades claims have been made about the "perfect drug," providing benefits without any side effects or need to take responsibility for self-care. This desire speaks more of the human condition than it does of the current state of research in psychopharmacology.

Consider, for example, the highly publicized and widespread availability of Viagra, the anti-impotence drug. None of us would disparage the legitimate use of this medication as a part of a larger treatment plan for improving a couple's sexual relationship. Yet it is often offered without any conversation about improving communication patterns (see Balswick, 1998 and Van Leeuwen, 2002 for discussions of aberrations of "responsible dominion" and of "male inexpressiveness").

Expectations about what psychotropic medication can and cannot do are huge for practitioners and clients alike (Comer, 2003). We have grave reservations, however, about the medicalization of nearly all mental and emotional disorders and the sense of diminished responsibility that often comes with a "nothing-but" mindset about psychopharmacology (Meyer and Deitsch, 1996). Medication should be used as an aid or adjunct to treatment rather than a complete treatment in and of itself. It pains us to learn that socioeconomic class is often a more important determinant of what kind of care a person receives that what the available evidence would suggest is most helpful (Antony and Barlow, 2002).

A biological understanding of mental illness need not limit our awareness of the complexity of human pain and suffering. We are convinced, in fact, that a responsible eclecticism should take seriously the biological foundations of nearly all expressions of psychopathology. This is true whether biology is a primary cause (as in the case of senile dementia), a precipitating cause (as in the cause of bipolar disorder) or a contributing cause (as often is the case in posttraumatic stress disorder). As Brand and Yancey have carefully noted (1980; 1984), we are "fearfully and wonderfully made," and our neuroanatomy and neurochemistry are part of the creational image, so that insult and injury to the brain and nervous system—or viral infections— can greatly diminish our ability to deal with the tasks of everyday living. No doubt lifestyle choices can affect the "hardware" or "software" of these brain-behavior connections, but to assume all these matters are functions only of our own choice is terribly naive and potentially harmful, especially in our understanding of the pain and suffering of another human being.

The inconsistencies in the compassion and understanding we show toward victims of terrorist bombings versus persons struggling with dementia or depression are striking and often telling about our deeper assumptions about "legitimate suffering" and realistic, biblical hope (Corey-Seibolt, 1984). When a friend gets cancer, we often reach out boldly and confidently. In contrast, if a friend becomes clinically anxious or depressed, a more probable response is mutual disengagement, perhaps because the problem is too confusing. The friend may be wracked with guilt, shame and fear of ridicule, and avoidance or denial can sometimes be a far easier response. It's easier to know what to do about a broken limb: instead of launching into an inner moral debate about choice and responsibility, we call 911. Even in a suicidal crisis, however, we can pretend it is not happening or assume the friend can just "snap out of it."

We have found it helpful to assume that there are almost always biological underpinnings in any particular expression of suffering. Mental and emotional distress is experienced in multiple dimensions of personhood, including the biological domain. There may be disturbances in appetite, movement or rest. More subtle and perhaps even more damaging are changes in levels of neurotransmitters, injury to the brain and nervous system, or bacterial or viral infections. The biological model teaches us to look for such dimensions and take them seriously.

SOCIOCULTURAL FOUNDATIONS OF MENTAL ILLNESS

The sociocultural model of abnormality focuses first and foremost on social and cultural forces that influence individuals, families, communities and even entire countries. Not only are demographic variables (age, gender, race/ethnicity, socioeconomic class) deemed to be essential to our understanding of mental illness, but so too are social norms (values) and roles chosen in private or public settings (Van Leeuwen, 2002). More than any other model of abnormality, this tradition has sensitized us to the broad *context* in which psychopathology is expressed or observed. It is not surprising, then, that growing numbers of academicians, clinicians and researchers are adopting a community or systemic mindset, seeking to understand how external forces can influence the ways in which we think, feel and act.

Historically, this model focused on poor societal conditions as a major determinant of mental illness. Poverty, for example, has been studied for decades and has been especially implicated in stress and

.adjustment disorders, problems of mind and body, and some of the most serious expressions of mental illness (psychosis, bipolar disorder, personality disorders, substance-related disorders). The incidence of mental illness has always been higher in lower socioeconomic classes. (This demographic is huge in understanding the etiology and maintenance of mental illness.) As Comer (2003) has noted, these individuals are often "doubly disadvantaged": not only is there a greater risk of mental illness, but they are far less likely to get adequate or effective mental health services. Perhaps one of the most powerful predictors of reported abuse or domestic violence is a downward trend in the economy; unemployment is a huge risk factor for "acting out," especially among men.

The sociocultural model has also sparked tremendous interest in the possible prevention of mental illness. Obviously, no one is immune from all risk factors associated with psychopathology. Most of us know at least one family member or friend who struggles with anxiety, depression or drug abuse. Billions of dollars are spent on mental health care yearly in the United States, and billions disappear due to lost productivity (Kass, Oldham and Pardes, 1992). Seeking assistance early is not part of the cultural mindset, especially in regard to mental health concerns. As any internist or general medical practitioner will tell you, it often takes chronic pain or a major health crisis before many individuals will even seek help. Given the shame, guilt or embarrassment often associated with mental disorders, avoidance often seems to be the rule (Clinebell, 1972). Despite decades of community education and consciousness raising, stereotypes abound and countless falsehoods persist. The net result far too often is a "conspiracy of silence and superficiality" (McLemore, 2003). Problems persist—that is, become chronic—and wreak havoc on individuals, families and friends. Our allopathic mindset ("don't fix it till it's broke") reflects our rather limited notions of health and well-being, poor stewardship of human resources, and propensity toward impression management rather than truthfulness and integrity.

George Albee, a longtime professor of psychology at the University of Vermont, is widely considered to be the father of preventative psychology. He once remarked that "the greatest untapped mental health resource in this country are the churches and synagogues that are empty six and a half days a week" (quoted in Kauffmann, 2000). Certainly many religious organizations are trying to find more effective ways to reach out to hurting persons in the community and congregation (Benner and Hill, 1999, cf. articles on prevention and community mental health). There is debate regarding to what extent this should be central to the mission and task of the church (Crabb, 1999). But if one-third of all Americans will suffer a serious mental problem at some point, committed Christians would be wise to consider the implications for worship, service and fellowship (Kauffmann, 2000). This in no way diminishes the crucial importance of evangelism, discipleship and training in the local church, but to ignore the reality that a significant portion of the congregation is suffering in any given week runs the risk of further isolating or marginalizing already demoralized persons (Clinebell, 1972).

Primary prevention is whatever can be done to improve the mental health of all persons, including early detection and screening, meaningful employment, adequate housing, strong social support systems. *Secondary* prevention involves efforts to identify high-risk groups and intervene as soon as possible (e.g., victims of violence and abuse, persons experiencing catastrophic losses, families struggling to provide necessary care for seriously ill parents or children). *Tertiary* prevention is the attempt to facilitate access to competent caregivers in good therapeutic settings and restore greater health and wholeness.

Countless programs have been developed and implemented in recent decades, and many of them have been remarkably helpful. Unfortunately, it has often been hard to sustain the vision as well as support the work long term, especially when it comes to some of the more chronic forms of mental illness. Careful study of the treatment of impaired individuals throughout the centuries, and across cultures, shows that these efforts, however noble, have been enormously difficult to maintain (Comer, 2003). Perhaps our remedial mindset—or avoidance of so much human suffering and pain—belies our professed belief in the inherent dignity and worth of all persons (Nouwen, 1992), or reveals our inability to see life as a school for character development and not just our personal fulfillment (Packer, 1990).

Less than 2 percent of the billions of dollars spent on mental health treatment in the United States is spent on prevention efforts or research; that is, 98 percent is being spent on treatment of problems in living "after the fact" (Kass, Oldham and Pardes, 1992). Rosalynn Carter, a deeply committed Christian and a longtime community advocate for the mentally ill, has offered us a great service in her book *Helping Someone with Mental Illness* (1998, with S. M. Golant). The former First Lady does a remarkable job of dispelling myths and stereotypes about mental illness, discussing treatment options from a lay perspective, and offering a vision for prevention and more community-based services. No doubt deeply influenced by her own work with afflicted persons in her extended family and immediate circle of friends, she is an exemplar of that priestly and prophetic witness that is desperately needed in the church and the culture at this moment in history (Wolterstorff, 1980).

All three of us have had the opportunity to work in mental health settings with "low resourced" individuals—persons who face overwhelming stressors in managing the tasks of everyday living. We have learned much about the importance of being their advocates, the painful realities of dealing with structures and systems that are not always receptive or open, and the ongoing challenge of empowering them for transformation (Nouwen, 1997). Whether the task is to gain access to a competent healthcare provider, to find affordable housing or to gain meaningful employment, we have come to see how everyday stressors can strain individuals and families to their breaking point (the stress-diathesis perspective). Perhaps where we most need to stretch as well-resourced persons in a land of plenty is to open our hearts and hands to the suffering in our midst. Responding to their needs may be one of the most important antidotes to our own spiritual hunger or poverty (Myers, 2000). We suspect that sustained immersion in altruistic service will teach us much about our shared humanity and brokenness (Manning, 1988).

The sociocultural model also teaches us the importance of healthy communication and conflict management. These are foundational competencies for spiritual and emotional well-being (McLemore, 2003). It takes people to make people sick, and it takes people to make people well. Good interpersonal relationships and strong social support systems are perhaps the cornerstone of mental health. A report from the American Psychological Association's Division of Psychotherapy Task Force suggests that 40 percent of change in therapy can be attributed to extratherapeutic change—influences from outside of the professional relationship, such as family relationships, friendships, clergy support and outside readings (Lamber and Barley, 2002). In any case, the sociocultural tradition has greatly increased our understanding of family structures and systems and how even social organizations (e.g., work or church settings) can parallel healthy (or unhealthy) family dynamics (Smedes, 1989).

Especially valuable work in this tradition has been done on social roles and expectations. Diagnostic labels, for example, can become self-fulfilling prophecies (Comer, 2003). Patients and providers as well as extended families and social networks can easily confuse the person with the diagnostic label and treat them accordingly. Clients themselves can learn to play the "sick role" to save face or for real or imagined gain. *People who seek out professional services are more than the sum of their symptoms.* They are more than a diagnostic label and should not be referred to with labels—"the borderline I saw in therapy yesterday" versus "the person who suffers from symptoms of borderline personality disorder." One approach undercuts the image of God in the person; the other reminds us of what we share.

In our culture we have a tendency to be harsh and judgmental toward others—especially those who behave in maladaptive, abnormal ways or don't conform to societal expectations. We are prone to fundamental attributional errors, minimizing the impact of internal or external stressors and perhaps exaggerating the extent to which an individual can exercise free will. Yet when we are suffering or experiencing significant distress, we are acutely conscious of factors that seem beyond our control (Plantinga, 1995). Such dynamics are messier than many Christians would like, but understanding them can deepen our appreciation for the complex relationships between sin and psychopathology.

Treatments based on the sociocultural model involve an attitude or mindset more than a specific set of psychotherapeutic interventions. A *systemic* or *community* approach is first and foremost appreciative and respectful of cultural differences. The classic symptoms of mental illness may also be signs or symbols of what has gone awry in a specific context. Interventions that are not age-, culture- or gender-sensitive may be less than helpful, even toxic or oppressive, especially if they reflect ethnocentric biases or stereotypes (Fenton, 1973). Christian mental health professionals simply must become more cognizant of the impact of the broader social network (couples, families, groups) on how we make sense of living in the world. There is growing evidence that treatment that includes significant others is more effective and promotes longer-lasting change in more diverse settings (Jones and Butman, 1991).

The sociocultural model has helped us to understand psychopathology both within and across cultures but is perhaps less helpful in predicting abnormality for any given individual. Still, it has greatly sensitized us to the importance of demographic variables (age, gender, race/ethnicity, socioeconomic status) and social networks or the lack thereof. Finally, it has raised awareness about the importance of community, including the work of churches and parachurch organizations. As one colleague has asked—at least rhetorically—"if the church was truly the church, who would need counseling?" (Warren, 1972).

BACK TO BASICS

Certain themes have been central to part one of this text, and they will be foundational to our subsequent presentation of the various clinical syndromes. We have chosen to emphasize four major models of psychopathology: biological, psychosocial, sociocultural and spiritual. Each paradigm might be best viewed as a perspective on causation. The psychosocial and spiritual models have aroused especially intense debate within Christian circles for decades, perhaps even centuries. In more secular settings the debate tends to be "either-or" rather than "both/and" regarding the biological and psychosocial perspectives. There has been a lively discussion in academic and professional settings about the importance of "spirituality" as a relevant variable, but more in terms of private, subjective experience than of organized or collective worship, service and fellowship (Kauffmann, 2000).

It is our strong conviction that the available evidence supports a holistic, integrative understanding of mental illness, a stance of epistemic humility that has been called "responsible eclecticism." Throughout the remainder of the book, then, we will use "biopsychosocial model" to communicate an interactional understanding of psychopathology. Problems in living ought to be viewed as multiply determined. This mindset reduces the risk of naive realism or needless reductionism (e.g., "depression is just a neurochemical anomaly").

We also think it best to see psychopathology as *multiply maintained*. What keeps an individual in the vicious cycle of pain and suffering? No doubt personal choice plays a significant role in certain expressions of mental illness. Perhaps more common, however, are roles and social expectations, disengagement and escape, mutual withdrawal or unhelpful reinforcement, or an intense desire to avoid further pain and suffering. As Kauffmann (2000) has noted, the nature of social support a person experiences before, during and after a significant crisis, loss or trauma is probably the single most powerful predictor of recovery and eventual healing (cf. Worden, 2002). Our personal and collective response to pain and suffering, then, significantly affects both the etiology and maintenance of psychopathology.

We have much to learn from the history of pastoral care throughout the centuries. Church-based services have at times been a blessing, and at times they have been a burden. Contemporary debates about the reality of evil and the demonic need to be informed by reason, Scripture and tradition rather than anecdotal accounts limited to subjective experience. A balanced view that appreciates the power of sin and evil yet respects human freedom and agency is not easily achieved. Such an approach would emphasize the worth and dignity of every human being as well as offer a deeper understanding of the influence of the spiritual world on day-to-day functioning. At its best, the church can provide a strong social support network (community), offer a vision of life that gives meaning to suffering (Sittser, 2000) and teach essential life skills that can help us cope and adjust with the challenges of everyday living (Pargament, 1997).

Attempts to classify mental health concerns have a long history as well. Not until recently has the field moved toward a holistic and integrative understanding of etiology and maintenance (biopsychosocial model), nor have proponents of differing models always demonstrated "convicted civility" (Mouw, 1992). The recent biological revolution and increasing respect for sociocultural factors have unevenly influenced academicians, clinicians and researchers.

Clearly, the relationship between the culture and church on such matters has not always been collaborative or helpful. The church has too often demonized and marginalized those who have suffered from psychopathologies. Our constructs reflect differing emphases on thinking, feeling and behaving, or greater emphases on either within-the-person or external-to-the-person influences on human action. "Education for responsible action" (Wolterstorff, 1980) demands that we take seriously the findings of reason (science) as well as the claims of Scripture on our lives and communities. Compassion toward broken and wounded persons is a biblical mandate and a clear expression of what truly lies in the depth of our soul (Crabb, 1999).

Finally, we make an effort to speak directly to ways we see both Scripture and reason (science) speak clearly on issues of etiology (causation), treatment and prevention. We will take seriously what we believe has been the priestly and prophetic witness of the church throughout the ages. And we will adopt a respectful stance toward hurting persons and the cumulative experiences of practicing clinicians, who daily have to deal with the painful and challenging realities of struggling persons who often feel "hopeless, helpless and powerless" and without a skillful shepherd (Haas, 1966). It is our hope and prayer that this information will help all of us, layperson and professional alike, to become more competent, compassionate and committed to the care of the mentally ill.

RECOMMENDED RESOURCES

Halgin, R. (2000). *Taking sides: Clashing views on controversial issues in abnormal psychology.* Guilford, Conn.: Dushkin/McGraw-Hill. An excellent reader on issues that have often polarized laypersons and professionals alike.

Shwartzberg, S. (2000). *A casebook of psychological disorders.* Boston: Allyn and Bacon. A text that does a remarkable job of sensitizing the reader to the complexity of psychopathology as well as the human face of emotional distress.

Sittser, G. (1996). *A grace disguised: How the soul grows through loss.* Grand Rapids, MI: Zondervan. This is perhaps the best book in print on "the problem of pain" and human suffering from a faith perspective.

Worden, W. (2002). *Grief counseling and grief therapy* (3rd ed.). New York: Springer. This, the most widely used text in the field of loss and bereavement, was written by a deeply committed Christian psychologist who teaches at Harvard.

REFERENCES

Antony, M., and Barlow, D. (Eds.). (2002). *Handbook of assessment and treatment planning for psychological disorders.* New York: Guilford.

Balswick, J. (1992). *Men at the crossroads.* Downers Grove, IL: InterVarsity Press.

Barlow, D. (Ed.). (1993). *Clinical handbook of psychological disorders.* New York: Guilford.

Benner, D., and Hill, P. (Eds.). (1999). *Baker encyclopedia of psychology and counseling* (2nd ed.). Grand Rapids, MI: Baker.

Bilezikian, G. (1997). *Community 101: reclaiming the church as community of oneness.* Grand Rapids, MI: Zondervan.

Bixler, W. (1999). Sin, psychological consequences of. In D. Benner and P. Hill (Eds.), *Baker encyclopedia of psychology and counseling* (2nd ed.) (pp. 1124-25). Grand Rapids, MI: Baker.

Brand, P., and Yancey, P. (1980). *Fearfully and wonderfully made.* Grand Rapids, MI: Zondervan.

Brand, P., and Yancey, P. (1984). *In his image.* Grand Rapids, MI: Zondervan.

Butman, R. (2001). Psychology of religion. In W. Elwell (Ed.), *Evangelical dictionary of theology* (2nd ed.) (pp. 968-71). Grand Rapids, MI: Baker.

Carter, R., and Golant, S. M. (1998). *Helping someone with mental illness.* New York: Random House.

Clebsch, W., and Jaekle, C. (1975). *Pastoral care in historical perspective.* New York: Jason Aronson.

Clinebell, H. (1972). *The mental health ministry of the local church.* Nashville: Abingdon.

Comer, R. (2003). *Abnormal psychology* (4th ed.). New York: Worth.

Cooper, T. (2003). *Sin, pride and self-acceptance.* Downers Grove, IL: InterVarsity Press.

Corey-Seibolt, M. (1984). Arrogant optimism or realistic hope? Address presented at chapel service, Wheaton College, IL.

Crabb, L. (1999). *The safest place on earth.* Nashville: Word.

Fenton, H. (1973). *The trouble with barnacles.* Grand Rapids, MI: Zondervan.

Garber, S. (1996). *The fabric of faithfulness.* Downers Grove, IL: InterVarsity Press.

Hood, R., Spilka, B., Hunsberger, B., and Gorsuch, R. (1996). *The psychology of religion* (2nd ed.). New York: Guilford.

Jongsma, A., and Peterson, M. (1995). *The complete psychotherapy treatment planner.* New York: Wiley-Interscience.

Jones, S., and Butman, R. (1991). *Modern psychotherapies: A comprehensive Christian appraisal.* Downers Grove, IL: InterVarsity Press.

Haas, H. (1966). *The Christian encounters mental illness.* St. Louis: Concordia.

Kass, F., Oldham, J., and Pardes, H. (1992). *The Columbia University College of Physicians and Surgeons complete home guide to mental health.* New York: Henry Holt.

Kauffmann, D. (2000). *My faith's OK: Reflections in psychology and religion.* Goshen, IN: Goshen College Bookstore.

Lamber, M. J., and Barley, D. E. (2002). Research summary on the therapeutic relationship and psychotherapy outcome. In J. C. Norcross (Ed.), *Psychotherapy relationships that work* (pp. 17-32). New York: Oxford University Press.

Malony, N. (1995). *The psychology of religion for ministry.* New York: Paulist.

Manning, B. (1988). *Reflections for ragamuffins.* New York: Harper & Row.

McLemore, C. (1978). *Clergyman's psychological handbook.* Grand Rapids, MI: Zondervan.

McLemore, C. (1982). *The scandal of psychotherapy.* Wheaton, IL: Tyndale House.

McLemore, C. (1984). *Honest Christianity.* Philadelphia: Westminster Press.

McLemore, C. (2003). *Toxic relationships and how to change them.* New York: Wiley-Interscience.

Meyer, R., and Deitsch, S. (1996). *The clinician's handbook.* Boston: Allyn and Bacon.

Miller, W., and Jackson, K. (1995). *Practical psychology for pastors* (2nd ed.). Englewood Cliffs, NJ: Prentice-Hall.

Mouw, R. (1992). *Uncommon decency: Christian civility in an uncivil world.* Downers Grove, IL: InterVarsity Press.

Moyers, W. (1989). *A world of ideas.* New York: Doubleday.

Myers, D. (2000). *The American paradox: Spiritual hunger in an age of plenty.* New Haven, CT: Yale University Press.

Nathan, P., and Gorman, J. (2002). *A guide to treatment that works* (2nd ed.). New York: Oxford University Press.

Nouwen, H. (1992). *The return of the prodigal son.* New York: Doubleday.

Nouwen, H. (1997). *Mornings with Henri Nouwen.* Ann Arbor, MI: Servant.

Packer, J. (1990). *A quest for godliness: The Puritan view of the Christian life.* Wheaton, IL: Crossway.

Paloutzian, R. (1996). *Invitation to the psychology of religion* (2nd ed.). Boston: Allyn and Bacon.

Pargament, K. (1997). *The psychology of religion and coping.* New York: Guilford.

Plantinga, C. (1995). *Not the way it's supposed to be: A breviary of sin.* Grand Rapids, MI: Eerdmans.

Sittser, G. (1996). *A grace disguised: How the soul grows through loss.* Grand Rapids, MI: Zondervan.

Sittser, G. (2000). *The will of God as a way of life.* Grand Rapids, MI: Zondervan.

Smedes, L. (1989). *Caring and commitment: Learning to live the love we promise.* San Francisco: Harper & Row.

Smedes, L. (1998). *Standing on the promises: Keeping hope alive for a tomorrow we cannot control.* Nashville: Thomas Nelson.

Stapert, J. (1994). Will pharmacological Calvinism protect me? *Perspectives.* Grand Rapids, MI: Pine Rest Christian Hospital. June/July 9-10.

Tidball, D. (1986). *Skillful shepherds: An introduction to pastoral theology.* Grand Rapids, MI: Zondervan.

Van Leeuwen, M. (2002). *My brother's keeper.* Downers Grove, IL: InterVarsity Press.

Warren, N. (1972). If the church was truly the church, who would need counseling? Typescript, Fuller Theological Seminary, Pasadena, CA.

Wolterstorff, N. (1980). *Until justice and peace embrace.* Grand Rapids, MI: Eerdmans.

Worden, W. (2002). *Grief counseling and grief therapy.* New York: Springer.

Yancey, P. (1984). Talk given at Faith Covenant Church, Wheaton, IL.

3

CLASSIFYING
MENTAL DISORDERS

*T*he apostle Paul wrote in his letter to the church in Rome that as a result of sinfulness, God gave humanity over to a "depraved mind, to do what ought not to be done" (Rom 1:28). Because of their sin, people's "thinking became futile," and their "foolish hearts were darkened" (1:21). Human beings became disordered—all of us. As a result, we do not function as we were intended to function. Our thoughts, emotions, behaviors and relationships are not what they should be—not what they were created to be. We live in a world deformed by sin, and we treat each other in sinful ways. All of us struggle to live and to function in this reality.

Some adapt to this reality and find ways to function and even thrive. For others, the struggle seems to be overwhelming. For reasons not yet fully revealed to us by God, some are allowed to experience a life relatively free from pain and trial, surrounded by supportive relationships, while others suffer oppression, abuse and deprivation.

Christians acknowledge this disordered reality. We are all disordered, and we live in a disordered world. This is a spiritual truth, and as we discussed in the previous chapter, the church throughout history has striven to address the human condition and classify disordered behavior. Two related questions have been at the core of these efforts: What is righteousness? What is the distinction between sinful and righteous behavior?

The field of psychopathology considers the same disordered reality and looks not to its deviance from God's design but to behavior that is deviant from societal norms. Two similar related questions have been at the core of efforts within the field of psychopathology to understand human experience and behavior: What is normal? What is the distinction between abnormal and normal human functioning? The focus here is not whether the behaviors are right or wrong but whether they are maladaptive, dysfunctional, incongruent or perhaps antisocial. The term "mental disorder" is commonly applied to these categories of abnormal human functioning, but it is in reality inadequate. It does not do justice to the complexity of cognitive, emotional, spiritual, behavioral and relational factors that are at work in the development and maintenance of a "mental" disorder.

Though no universally accepted definition exists for the term or concept, most of the definitions share common emphases, sometimes referred to as " 'the four D's': deviance, distress, dysfunction, and danger" (Comer, 1996, p. 2). The American Psychiatric Association has defined and explained a "mental disorder" as

> a clinically significant behavioral or psychological syndrome or pattern that occurs in an individual and that is associated with present distress (e.g., a painful symptom) or disability (i.e., impairment in one or more important areas of functioning) or with a significantly increased risk of suffering death, pain, disability, or an important loss of freedom. In addition, this syndrome or pattern must not be merely an expectable and culturally sanctioned response to a particular event, for example, the death of a loved one. Whatever its original cause, it must currently be considered a manifestation of a behavioral, psychological, or biological dysfunction in the individual. Neither deviant behavior (e.g., political, religious, or sexual) nor conflicts that are primarily between the individual and society are mental disorders unless the deviance or conflict is a symptom of a dysfunction in the individual, as described above. (APA, 1994, pp. xxi-xxii)

Throughout history, attempts have been made to understand and categorize abnormal human functioning. From Egyptian descriptions of abnormal behavior as early as 2600 B.C. to early classification schemes of the Greek philosophers and physicians beginning around the fifth century B.C. to the complex and comprehensive national and international classification systems of today, we have sought to understand why we behave as we do. Our ability to understand that has depended largely on our efforts to adequately classify and study these "disorders."

NOSOLOGY: THE SCIENCE OF CLASSIFICATION

Nosology refers to the scientific task of categorizing and classifying phenomena. Not all are in agreement on the value of nosology for the work of mental health care. Some stress that it is the most vital element necessary to maintain the scientific integrity and viability of the discipline. For example, Adams and Cassidy contend that "a science can develop only so far as it is able to classify the information in its field," and, quoting Norman Sartorius, they assert that "no other intellectual act is of equal importance" (Adams and Cassidy, 1993, p. 3). Others disagree and stress the limiting biases that emerge from attempts to force individualized experience into preconceived categories.

Two conceptual approaches to nosology have dominated historical approaches to classifying psychopathology, and a third is emerging in the field. The first, referred to as the *monothetic approach,* the *classical categorization model* or the *neo-Kraepelin model,* is based on the idea that categories of psychopathology form around distinct naturally occurring phenomena that are readily evident to all observers. Disorders in this model are considered to be homogeneous, "qualitatively distinct entities . . . [with] sharply distinct, non-overlapping boundaries. . . . Membership in a category is considered on a 'yes-or-no ('all or nothing') basis" (Reeb, 2000, pp. 11-12). Nathan and Langenbucher summarize assumptions about the process of classification made by this model:

(a) the presence of universally accepted criteria for class membership (e.g., all squares have four sides, and all schizophrenic individuals are autistic)

(b) high agreement about class membership among classifiers (e.g., everyone agrees on what is a square, just as everyone agrees on who is schizophrenic)

(c) within-class homogeneity of members (e.g., all squares look alike, and all schizophrenic persons behave the same way) (2003, p. 4)

Cantor, Smith, French and Mezzick (1980) describe a second model of categorization, *prototypic categorization* (also referred to as the *polythetic approach*), which they contend is much more consistent with the nature of psychopathology and the process of classifying syndrome patterns most commonly used in mental health. Disorders in this model are considered to exist on a continuum from very clear to very unclear cases and to be "heterogeneous. . . [with] overlapping ('fuzzy') boundaries" (Reeb, 2000, p. 12). Very clear cases are seen as "prototypes," and membership in a category of disorder requires only a certain number of symptoms from a specified list associated with that disorder. Nathan and Langenbucher describe assumptions of this model that make it more suitable, in their opinion, for psychopathology classification:

(a) correlated—not necessarily pathognomonic—criteria for class membership

(b) high agreement among classifiers only when classifying cases that demonstrate most of the correlated criteria for class membership

(c) heterogeneity of class membership because criteria are only correlated, not pathognomonic (2003, pp. 4-5)

A third approach, the *dimensional approach,* does not seek to determine the presence or absence of a disorder (as with the above approaches) but rather attempts to rate a person on a defined scale according to certain attributes of functioning—for example, personality traits, cognitions, emotions, behaviors or levels of functioning) (Reeb, 2000). Dimensional models do not focus on qualitative distinctions between normal and abnormal functioning but rather view psychopathology on a continuum of health, as "representing extreme versions of normal traits" (Reeb, 2000, p. 15). According to Reeb, recent editions of the *DSM* have used a hybrid model, drawing on all three approaches to classification.

The assumptions one brings and the approach one uses in the task of categorization have tremendous bearing on the ability of any classification model to identify and differentiate specific observable reoccurring phenomena. Some have debated whether classification in psychopathology can ever approach the standards of "scientific" categorization. For example, Birley (1975) believed that psychiatric diagnosis should be seen as more an art than a science. He believed that the best the process of diagnosis can offer is a "condensed, symbolic representation [which would] communicate a truth about [a] slice of

nature," similar to a work of art (quoted in Nathan and Langenbucher, 2003, p. 5).

The general trend, however, has been to view the diagnostic process as a scientific endeavor. Nathan and Langenbucher (2003) summarize the work of Blashfield and Draguns (1976) who outlined the
scientific purposes of diagnostic classification thus:

(a) communication, because without a consensual language, practitioners could not communicate

(b) a means for organizing and retrieving information, because an
item's name is a key to its literature and knowledge accrues to the
type

(c) a template for describing similarities and differences between individuals

(d) a means of making predictions about course and outcome

(e) a source of concepts to be used in theory and experimentation (p. 5)

Contemporary systems for classifying psychopathology have developed over a long and often conflictual history. They continue to elicit
extensive deliberation and revision. In this chapter we will survey the
historical development of the classification of psychopathology, contemporary systems of classification used by health care and mental
health care providers and researchers, and a few key issues related to
these. We will consider challenges to contemporary systems and
points of specific interest for Christian psychologists and mental
health care providers who must work within the limitations of these
systems.

HISTORICAL DEVELOPMENT OF CLASSIFICATION

As noted, endeavors to classify abnormal human functioning have a
long and varied history (see appendix A). The first recorded efforts
date back to the third millennium B.C., with Egyptian and Sumerian
documents that make reference to senile dementia, melancholia and
hysteria. Common among the Greeks and Romans of the late centuries B.C. and early centuries A.D. were descriptions of five categories of
psychopathology (Pincus and McQueen, 2002). Most notable of these
was Hippocrates, who in the fifth century B.C. delineated these five
categories as "*phrenitis*, an acute disturbance with fever; *mania*, an
acute disturbance without fever; *melancholia*, all chronic disorders;
hysteria, a female disorder noted by agitation, pain and convulsions;

and *epilepsy,* the only disorder of the group possessing the same name and meaning today" (Millon, 1969, p. 11). With little revision, this system was accepted and utilized until the fall of Rome in the fifth century A.D.

Rome's fall marked the beginning of a period of rejection of naturalistic explanations of disease in favor of spiritualized ones. In the thousand-year Dark Ages, an increasing religious fanaticism in Europe sought to blame demonic forces for widespread famine and pestilence. Societal responses to mental illness ranged from initial fear and compassion for people understood to be seized by demonic forces against their will to eventual hatred and torturous revenge against those believed to be in collaboration with the devil. Witch hunts, inquisitions, torture and execution became characteristic of the treatment of the mentally ill, unwitting objects of the rage and anguish of societies plagued by hunger, disease and superstition.

Not until the sixteenth century did voices began to emerge challenging the barbaric treatment of the mentally ill, which was rooted in superstitious and ill-informed spiritualized understandings of psychopathology. Some began to return to premedieval explanations of psychopathology, and the Hippocratic system of classification began to find a renewed following (Nathan and Langenbucher, 2003). The work of physicians such as Paracelsus (Swiss) and Johann Weyer (Dutch), who vigorously opposed superstitious explanations of psychopathology and inhumane treatments, contributed to a climate of intense debate and volatile reactions. Paracelsus, though he continued to embrace some superstitious explanations, was the first to espouse chemical origins of mental disorders. He added three categories to the classification system of Hippocrates: *"vesania,* disorders caused by poisons, *lunacy,* a periodic condition influenced by phases of the moon, and *insanity,* diseases caused by heredity" (Millon, 1969, p. 11).

Felix Plater, a Swiss physician who followed after Paracelsus, developed a system based on observable symptoms. He proposed the following categories of psychopathology: *"consternatio mentis,* disturbances of consciousness, *mentis alienato,* disorders of violence, sadness, delirium or confusion, *mentis defatigatio,* mental exhaustion and *imbecillitas mentis,* mental deficiency and dementia" (ibid.).

By the eighteenth century, physicians like Philippe Pinel began to reform treatment of the mentally ill in some hospitals and to train others in a more naturalistic understanding of the origins of psychopathology. Pinel's student Jean Esquirol published the first modern work on psychopathology in 1838, *Des maladies mentales* (the maladies of the mind). Expanding research and a growing body of knowledge in anatomy and physiology fortified an emerging emphasis on disease-oriented classification. In 1845 Wilhelm Griesinger, a German psychiatrist, published *Mental Pathology and Therapeutics*, in which he made the bold claim that "mental diseases are brain diseases" (ibid., p. 12). An alternate naturalistic system emerged at the same time, given its most substantive form by German psychiatrist Karl Ludwig Kahlbaum. His system categorized disorders not by disease but by their course and outcome. These two approaches remained oppositional until Emil Kraepelin (1856-1926) successfully bridged them with his classification system, which attempted to consider both symptom patterns and patterns of onset, course and outcome. Kraepelin's system, published in his *Textbook of Psychiatry* (first edition, 1883), became the standard for the field. He was working on the ninth edition at the time of his death.

Contributions to Kraepelin's nosology were made in the United States by Adolf Meyer and in Switzerland by Eugen Bleuler. The combination of their efforts with Kraepelin's system formed the basis of our contemporary system of classification. "In this 'traditional' classification," according to Millon, "Kraepelin's clinical categories are retained as the basic framework, and Meyer's and Bleuler's psychological notions provide guidelines to the patient's inner processes and social reactions" (ibid., p. 13).

Theodore Millon summarizes the varied history of classification in psychopathology thus:

> What patterns, trends and directions can we extract from this history? For one, it is likely that the reactions of any group of naïve individuals faced with mental disorder in their midst would follow a parallel course to what had in fact taken place. At first, such a group would react with perplexity and fear, followed shortly by efforts to avoid or eliminate the disturbing behavior. Because of their lack of knowledge, their crude efforts would fail, leading to frustration and, in turn, to anger, punitive action and hostility. In due course, the obvious helplessness and innocence of the ill would evoke protests against harshness and cruelty. A new compassion and sympathy would arise and awaken a search for methods of humane treatment. But goodwill alone would not be sufficient to deal with the illness. Proper

treatment requires knowledge, and knowledge can be derived best from systematic study and research. And so, in its course of progress, this imaginary group would move step by step from perplexity, fear and cruelty, to scientific analysis and humane treatment. It is at this point that we stand in our study of psychopathology today. Despite periodic regressions and fads, progress toward humanism, naturalism and scientific empiricism has continued. (ibid., p. 34)

CONTEMPORARY CLASSIFICATION

Contemporary efforts to classify abnormal psychological functioning offer little more consistency and uniformity than has been true throughout history. Kendler (1990) identified three general approaches that have been characteristic of psychopathology classification over the past two centuries. Kendler referred to these as (1) reliance on great professors, (2) reliance on the consensus of experts and (3) reliance on empirical data.

Reliance on great professors. This approach, which dominated the nineteenth and twentieth centuries, relied on the work of esteemed psychopathologists to identify and categorize mental disorders into systems consistent with their theoretical approaches. As noted above in discussion of the history of psychopathology classification, the work of a key theorist dominated the perspectives of the scientific and mental health communities, at times for decades, until another theorist's work supplanted it. Examples were theorists such as Pinel, Greisinger and Kraepelin. Kraepelin's understanding of psychoses, in particular, had wide acceptance during the early twentieth century (Reeb, 2002).

Reliance on the consensus of experts. During the twentieth century the influence of key individual theorists gave way to committees and organizations interested in developing systems of classification that could be embraced by the broader mental health community, both nationally and internationally. Attempts were made to reach consensus on categories of classification. Irreconcilable disagreements were settled by majority vote, leaving much room for conflict between opposing perspectives.

In 1948 the World Health Organization published the sixth edition of the *International Classification of Diseases (ICD),* which was the first major organizational classification system to include a section on mental disorders (World Health Organization, 1948). The American

Psychiatric Association soon followed with the 1952 publication of the *DSM-I*. The *DSM-II* (1968) also relied on a consensus approach to classification and majority vote on issues of conflict.

Reliance on empirical data. By the latter part of the twentieth century, the search for universally reliable and valid criteria for psychopathology classification and diagnosis led to significant revisions in the process by which these organizations developed, evaluated and modified diagnostic categories. According to Reeb, in the *DSM-III* (1980), *DSM-III-R* (1987) and *DSM-IV* (1994), the American Psychiatric Association innovated the process of classification of psychopathology in the following ways:

1. Preeminence was given to available empirical data for the determination of diagnostic categories. With the *DSM-IV*, a three-stage empirical process was employed, which utilized literature reviews, reanalysis of data sets and issue-focused field trials.

2. Specific criteria used to make judgments about the presence or absence of a disorder were operationally defined.

3. A biopsychosocial approach to psychopathology was chosen in an attempt to be neutral regarding the many competing etiological theories of psychopathology that dominated the "great professors" approach to classification (we will address these theoretical perspectives in more detail later in the chapter).

4. A multiaxial system of diagnosis was developed enabling mental health clinicians to evaluate persons on five dimensions of functioning.

    a. Axis I   all disorders and syndromes, except . . .
    b. Axis II   personality disorders and mental retardation
    c. Axis III   medical conditions relevant to psychological functioning
    d. Axis IV   psychosocial or environmental problems
    e. Axis V   rating of global psychosocial functioning

5. An explicit definition of a mental disorder was given differentiating abnormal and normal functioning.

6. An emphasis was placed on vocabulary reflecting the diagnosis of the disorder as opposed to a diagnosis of the person; labeling terms like *schizophrenic* and *alcoholic* were avoided.

7. Disorders were categorized according to essential (required) features, associated (frequently present but not required) features, age

at onset, course, impairment, complications, predisposing factors, prevalence, gender ratio, familial pattern and differential diagnosis (a description of features that differentiate the disorder from closely related ones).

8. Correspondence to the ICD system of classification was improved. (Reeb, 2002, pp. 7-8)

No one classification system is embraced by all health care and mental health care providers. In fact, Lamberts et al (1998) identify no fewer than seven options stemming from three major systems of classification for mental disorders available to primary care physicians—who still are responsible for most of the care given patients who suffer with psychological disorders. These systems and variant options include the following:

• *International Classification of Diseases (ICD-10),* which includes all physical as well as mental disorders. Chapter F of *ICD-10* focuses on mental disorders and appears in three versions:

1. *ICD-10 Clinical Descriptions and Diagnostic Guidelines:* intended for general clinical, educational and service use

2. *ICD-10 Diagnostic Criteria for Research:* intended for clinical research and contains criteria for diagnosis that are more restrictive and exclusive

3. *ICD-10-PC,* for primary care: intended for use in primary care settings, describes only a selection of common mental problems

• *Diagnostic and Statistical Manual of Mental Disorders (DSM-IV),* produced by the American Psychiatric Association, has three versions:

1. *DSM-IV Text Revision (DSM-IV-TR):* intended for use by psychiatric and psychological service providers

2. *DSM-IV International Version:* intended for use by the international mental health community, contains the text of the *DSM-IV* but uses *ICD-10* diagnostic codes

3. *DSM-IV Primary Care Version (DSM-IV-PC):* intended to facilitate the education of primary care physicians about mental disorders and to be compatible with other diagnostic systems used in primary care settings

• *International Classification of Primary Care (ICPC),* which includes all physical and mental disorders that might be encountered by primary care physicians and the reason a patient might seek care for these.

Lamberts and colleagues conclude that primary care physicians' task of choosing the most helpful system for their work in understanding the psychopathology of their patients and communicating with other care providers is still complex and cumbersome and in need of simplification and uniformity.

Among mental health providers in the United States the *DSM-IV* is the most commonly used system of categorization, whereas the *ICD-10* is commonly used in other parts of the world (Sadler, 2002, cf. articles on classifying mental disorders). These two systems were developed independently, and therefore there was potential for inconsistency in diagnostic criteria between them. In the development of the fourth edition of the *DSM* and the tenth edition of the *ICD*, efforts were made to coordinate the two systems. It was feared that if the systems were not coordinated, "the resulting multiple and inconsistent criteria for the same psychiatric diagnosis would impair communication among clinicians and the generalizability of research, especially internationally" (Frances, Widiger and Pincus, 1989, p. 373). Throughout this book we will use the *DSM* categories of classification for the sake of cohesiveness and clarity.

A concluding comment. DSM categories of psychopathology are utilized not only by health and mental health providers but also increasingly by pastors and other ministry leaders. It is used, for example, in Johnson and Johnson's book *The Pastor's Guide to Psychological Disorders and Treatments* (2002), whose authors state their purpose thus:

> This book is designed to be a quick and easy reference source for pastors interested in the essential concerns posed by common psychological (psychiatric) disorders. . . . We have written this guide in hope of offering pastors a useful and fruitful resource as they attempt to help children, adults, and families in their churches. We hope it comes to be a tattered and much referenced guidebook for those who counsel as part of their ministries. Most of all, we hope this guide will serve God's kingdom as pastors find the right services for parishioners in need. (pp. 4-5)

Implicit is the assumption that the contemporary nosology in psychopathology is "useful and fruitful" for pastors who want to help people and "find the right services for parishioners in need."

As contemporary society, and increasingly the church, continues to embrace understandings of human suffering rooted in the nosology of psychopathology, clarity about the nature of that nosology and its applicability is essential. Three issues related to the nature of the contemporary *DSM* nosology will be examined here, with a summary of some limitations of that system identified in the literature of psychopathology: theoretical perspectives on psychopathology, the question of etiology and the values inherent in the *DSM* system of classification.

THEORETICAL PERSPECTIVES IN CONTEMPORARY CLASSIFICATION

Historically, theoretical perspectives on the classification of psychopathology have differed as dramatically as have the perspectives on their treatment (see Jones and Butman, 1991). Theodore Millon, in his classic work *Modern Psychopathology* (1969), grouped these perspectives into four major categories:

- *biophysical* theories, which assume that physiological processes are the primary determining factors of psychopathology

- *intrapsychic* theories, which assume that psychological factors determine abnormal psychological functioning

- *phenomenological* theories, which stress the unique experience and perception of each individual and how that perception is lived out

- *behavioral* theories, which assume that the process of learning through reinforcement shapes pathology in the individual (see appendix B)

We will look briefly at these theoretical perspectives, as they provide a historical picture of some of the foundational theoretical chasms evident in attempts to understand psychopathology.

Biophysical theories. Biophysical theories in general contend that abnormal psychological symptoms indicate the presence of a biological defect of some sort. These theories generally group around two perspectives: (1) most psychopathology is rooted in hereditary conditions or naturally occurring differences in individual biology, and (2) most psychopathology results from external invasive factors (e.g., toxins, infectious diseases, traumas, malnutrition, hereditary defects) that disrupt normal healthy functioning. Biophysical theorists typically center their research efforts on questions related to heredity, constitution (normal variation in human physiology and its relation to psychopathology) and/or neurophysiology.

Intrapsychic theories. Intrapsychic theories in general contend that abnormal psychological symptoms reflect attempts by a person to compensate for, adapt to or defend against some form of psychological trauma or inner conflict, most often experienced during formative periods of childhood. Three specific categories of experience are most often targeted as the root of pathological development: (1) frustration of basic needs and instinctual drives, (2) exposure to conflictual experiences, and (3) the nature of the settings in which the developmental process occurs and the attitudes of primary caregivers. Psychopathology is generally understood to represent unresolved conflict or repressed anxiety.

Phenomenological theories. Phenomenologists view each person as having the capacity for self-actualization and consider pathology to result from the impairment of a person's ability to be self-authenticating. They stress that a person reacts to the world only through her own unique experience and perception of it. This individualized perception and the ability to embrace it fully and courageously are foundational to healthy functioning. Psychopathology exists when a person is unable to embrace his or full inner potential and becomes "depleted by self-frustration and broken by despair" (Millon, 1969, p. 70).

Behavioral theories. Behaviorists reacted to what they perceived as subjective introspection in the intrapsychic and phenomenological theories, rejecting notions of authentic choice and internal processes in favor of a belief that reinforced adaptive behavior as the sign of healthy functioning. Psychopathology merely represents behavior that has been reinforced in a maladaptive or socially unacceptable direction. As Millon states, "By reducing the reality of experience to abstract stimuli and responses, psychopathology becomes a barren pattern of mechanical reactions" (ibid., p. 69).

As is evident from this cursory overview, the theoretical presuppositions and biases of those who attempt to understand the nature and causes of psychopathology have a tremendous bearing on the factors they will consider relevant to the task. Theoretical perspectives pose the risk of blinding clinicians and researchers to other valid and valuable ways of understanding psychopathology; however, without them no framework would exist for understanding and categorizing human functioning. As Kendler points out, "Validation of a psychiatric disorder cannot . . . occur in a vacuum" (1990, p. 970). Widiger adds,

> What is often necessary for the interpretation of data is a theoretical model that guides the understanding of the relevance of alternative validators (More, 1991). The validation of a mental disorder is inherently the validation of a particular theoretical

formulation of the diagnosis, and it cannot occur in the absence of this formulation (Follette and Houts, 1996; Widiger and Trull, 1993). The choice among competing formulations that place a different emphasis on alternative validators is a choice between competing theoretical formulations of the disorder. (Widiger, 2002, p. 38)

Which actually precedes the other is a question debated among researchers. Is the theoretical perspective foundational to the classification system as Widiger suggests, or vice versa, as Adams and Cassidy propose?

Most mental health professionals, including humanists, behaviorists, psychodynamic theorists, and those with a biological orientation, would agree that the study of human beings begins with the observation of their behavior. It is the implications and explanations of that observed behavior that constitute the various theoretical orientations. It is imperative that an adequate classification system precede the development of these theories. Although the temporal order is often confused in actual practice, the sequence of the development of a science involves classification, then measurement, and then theories as a basic prerequisite for knowledge. (Adams and Cassidy, 1993, pp. 8-9)

No gold standard exists for establishing which theoretical perspective is the right one or holds the most validity (Widiger, 2002). Proponents of each perspective have levied strong criticisms on the other perspectives and on the role theoretical perspectives have historically played in the field of psychopathology. For example, in his critique of psychopathology theories, Millon states,

The formal structure of most theories of psychopathology is haphazard and unsystematic; concepts often are vague and procedures by which empirical consequences may be derived are confused. Many theories are written in a hortatory and persuasive fashion. Facts are mixed with speculations, and literary allusions and colorful descriptions are offered as substitutes for testable hypotheses. In short, instead of presenting an orderly arrangement of concepts and propositions by which hypotheses may be clearly derived, these theories present a loosely formulated pastiche of opinions, analogies and speculations. Brilliant as many of these speculations may be, they often leave the reader dazzled rather than illuminated. (Millon, 1969, p. 69)

In this climate of fundamental disagreement and debate, the most current revisions of the *DSM* classification system have striven for an atheoretical approach. The *DSM-IV* states that its approach attempts to be "neutral with respect to theories of etiology" (APA, 1994, p. xviii). The result is a lack of ownership for the theoretical perspectives implicit within the classification system. It is imperative that clinicians and researchers be forthright about their theoretical perspectives and the impact of those on their research and practice.

Christians engaged in the work of mental health care and research bear no less of a responsibility to know the theoretical biases and presumptions behind the diagnostic systems we use, to disclose our own theoretical perspectives in our work and (perhaps most important) to understand the relationship our faith has to the theoretical perspectives we embrace. Those who profess to believe in God and the veracity of the Scriptures embrace common elements of a distinct view of persons—that human beings are created in the image of God, are disordered by sin and await transformation into the likeness of Christ in eternal life (see Jones and Butman's chapter "A Christian View of Persons," 1991, pp. 39-62). These beliefs must have impact on our theoretical understandings of psychopathology and the ways we use a nosology devoid of similar understandings.

ETIOLOGY IN CONTEMPORARY CLASSIFICATION

Historically, the task of diagnosing psychopathology has not been a quest for etiology (Schaffner, 2002). Identifiable, distinct and isolatable causes for particular diagnoses have not been the norm, as the etiological factors at work in the formation of psychopathological symptoms are multifaceted. This has been a source of significant tension between two major perspectives on the work of psychopathology, which Comer (1996) identifies as the *somatogenic* perspective, which holds that abnormal psychological functioning results from physical causes (a view with a 2300-year history, dating back to the work of Hippocrates), and the *psychogenic* perspective, which contends that psychological causes are responsible for the development of psychopathology (originated in the nineteenth century in the work of Anton Mesmer, Jean Charcot, Josef Breuer, and ultimately Sigmund Freud and his students).

Some hold so closely to a somatogenic perspective that they argue that no truly scientific nosology can be developed for psychopathology until its etiologies can be irrefutably reduced to neurochemical and biological mechanisms (e.g., Lilienfeld and Marino, 1995; Kendler, 1990; Kendell, 1989). Others argue that etiology should not be the focus of classification and diagnosis of psychopathology and that it should be seen as distinct from the work of classification and diagnosis of physical illness. For example, Schaffner (2002) quotes the following disclaimer in the preface of Goodwin and Guze's (1974/1996) book *Psychiatric Diagnosis:*

> There are few explanations in this book. This is because for most psychiatric conditions there *are* no explanations. "Etiology unknown" is the hallmark of psychiatry as well as its bane. Historically, once etiology is known, a disease stops being "psychiatric." Vitamins were discovered, whereupon vitamin-deficiency psychiatric disorders no longer were treated by psychiatrists. The spirochete was found, then penicillin, and neurosyphilis, once a major psychiatric disorder, became one more infection treated by non-psychiatrists. (quoted in Schaffner, 2002, p. 271)

Prior to the time of Paracelsus, diagnoses were rooted in assumptions of the causes of pathology. For example, Hippocrates believed the etiology of illnesses he diagnosed was in various fluid imbalances in the body. Paracelsus changed the focus from etiology to groups of signs and symptoms (syndromes) that were believed to occur in patterns and characterize pathology. This emphasis on description of symptom patterns rather than causes continues in our contemporary system. According to Nathan and Langenbucher, "In Paracelsus' system, as well as in each succeeding step toward the modern approach epitomized by the . . . DSM-IV, the etiology of the illness was presumed to be unknown and hence unnecessary for the diagnostic task" (Nathan and Langenbucher, 2003, p. 5).

As we mentioned in chapter one, the idea of cause is central to the nosologies of the church in its understanding of the disordered human condition. Sin as a state and sinful behavior as a choice are basic to historical Christian approaches to understanding human functioning. Contemporary nosology in psychopathology lacks a coherent foundation in etiology, and some see no need for it. This is an important aspect of our contemporary system of classification and warrants careful consideration by clinicians and researchers, Christian and non-Christian alike.

DSM "VALUES" IN CONTEMPORARY CLASSIFICATION

The values of the DSMs are answers to the "should" questions that are the most fundamental for a diagnostic manual; such questions include: Should we have a diagnostic manual? What should it include? How should we put it together? Whom should we include in making such a manual? To whom should we direct this manual? How should we decide which methods and scientific data are meritorious and which are not? (Sadler, 2002, pp. 7-8, cf. articles on classifying mental disorders)[1]

"The DSM-IV is not a value-free, apolitical scientific classification of mental disorders" (Widiger, 2002). The very concept of a mental disorder assumes a societally shared value in the idea of "normal," "healthy," psychological functioning, because the diagnosis of a mental disorder suggests a value judgment about "abnormal" or "unhealthy" functioning. In addition, as Thomas Widiger points out, the exact "point of demarcation" between functioning that is normal and abnormal is debatable and subject to personal and societal values (cf. Clark, Watson and Reynolds, 1995). He argues one step further that there is also "no clear or qualitative point of demarcation between . . . mental and physical disorders, or between mental and relationship disorder . . . ; persons disagree on where to place the point of demarcation. If the demarcation is along a continuum of functioning, some amount of uncertainty, ambiguity, and disagreement is to be expected and should be tolerated" (Widiger, 2002, p. 28).

Consider the diagnosis of mental retardation. Current standards suggest that the point of demarcation is an assessed intelligence quotient (IQ) of 70. According to Widiger, this point of demarcation does not represent a "nonarbitrary, qualitatively distinct point along the continuum of intelligence" that exists in nature and is unquestionable to all who observe the phenomena. It merely represents a consensus reference point established by clinicians, researchers and scientists at which they believe it is meaningful to characterize significantly limited intelligence functioning. He concludes, "The presence of a continuum and debatable points of demarcation do not diminish the va-

---

[1]We are indebted to John Sadler (2002) and his colleagues for our discussion of values in psychopathology classification. We draw liberally from their comprehensive work, *Descriptions and Prescriptions: Values, Mental Disorders, and the DSMs*, for our discussion of these issues and recommend their work to our readers who wish to research the issue of values in classification in more depth.

lidity of the construct of mental retardation; they question only the validity of a qualitative dichotomy between normal and abnormal intelligence" (ibid., pp. 28-29).

The *DSM-IV* classification system strives toward an evidence-based approach to classification. Kendler (1990) identifies key challenges to this approach. With an evidence-based system, specific empirical testing is necessary to validate each hypothesis in the nosological system; therefore little credibility is given to historical traditions, clinical judgment or common sense. Consensus regarding the construct of particular diagnoses may be difficult to reach (e.g., depression can be understood as a mood disorder or cognitive disorder). In addition to the construct of the disorder, clinicians may disagree over the significance of various contributing factors such as family history or clinical course, making scientific testing difficult (see also Sadler, 2002, cf. articles on classifying mental disorders).

Though the developers of the *DSM*s have striven to produce a classification system that is at its core scientific, they have in the process produced a document that has tremendous social implications (Widiger and Trull, 1993). Diagnostic categories can have significant positive or negative ramifications for specific groups and individuals within our society (Frances et al., 1990). The potential influence of the *DSM*s on the development of public policy for these groups can lead to challenges to the scientific integrity of the classification process, as pressures may be placed on researchers to produce specific results.

In the wake of the revolution in science of the 1960s and 1970s, which challenged the fabric of empiricism, rationality and logical positivism and convincingly showed that all science is laden with the values of the scientist (e.g., Feyerabend, 1978; Kuhn, 1970), the *DSM-II* was under revision. Robert Spitzer, the head of the revision committee, acknowledged a personal agenda to depathologize homosexuality, contending that its identification as a disorder was based on value judgments rather than good science (Spitzer, 1981). According to Sadler, "The whole controversial mess around this change brought to popular awareness the notion that psychopathology involved value judgments" (2002, p. 4; cf. articles on classifying mental disorders).

Some have unabashedly advocated the use of political pressure and agendas in the formulation of diagnostic criteria. For example, Walker states that the "political advocacy of the battered woman's movement, along with the feminist mental health network, managed to force the psychiatrists . . . to place in the appendix several . . . newly proposed diagnoses" (1989, p. 699). In response to the dangers of such socially and politically motivated research agendas, some have accused the American Psychiatric Association of using the *DSMs* as an instrument to gain "economic wealth, social influence and political power" (Widiger, 2002, pp. 32-33; cf. Caplan, 1995; Follette and Houts, 1996; Kirk and Kutchins, 1992; Rogler, 1997; Schacht, 1985; and Zimmerman, 1988).

Individual as well as organizational political influence is an important challenge to the scientific integrity of the classification process. Though values in the form of research biases and political ideologies are an inescapable reality in the scientific process, scientific integrity demands that researchers, scientists and clinicians strive to minimize their role in the formulation of diagnostic categories and criteria. As Frances, Widiger and Pincus state, "The ideal is to reach the conclusions a person with no fixed preconceptions (a consensus scholar) would discover from a comprehensive overview of the entire research literature, not confined to any particular research program or theoretical orientation" (1989, p. 374; quoted in Widiger, 2002, p. 35).

Some have suggested that resolving problematic values in the process of diagnosis and treatment can be done only through the diagnostician's willingness to boldly embrace and disclose those values (Simola, 1992; Kirmayer, 1994; Kleinman, 1988). "Neutrality is both a myth and a fallacy," says Simola, who contends that it is better to be openly biased than to fail in an attempt to be neutral or value-free (1992, p. 399). Others challenge this notion, asserting that the "optimal method for overcoming problematic cultural biases is the continued application of a critical scientific perspective" (Widiger, 2002, p. 30).

> To the extent that the final decisions reflect simply the a priori viewpoints of the persons in closest proximity to the decision-making power, the process can become (or at least appear to become) more political than scientific. The decisions become based not on the scientific literature but on the amount of control, power, or influence one has over the decision-making process. An individual researcher's impact on the DSM would be a matter not of the quality of the research but of the proximity to the position of influence. (Widiger, 2002, p. 35)

A different perspective on "values" is taken by Sadler (2002; cf. articles on classifying mental disorders), who contends that values and evaluation are and should be seen as the complementary other half of the "universe" of psychopathology. Without values, Sadler asserts, with only the descriptive and factual elements of the work of psychopathology, mental health care would be an "impoverished field."

> Values shape what is clinically relevant (what the clinician sees or doesn't see); what clinical evidence is salient, useful, or otherwise important; the criteria of pathology; the credibility of the diagnostic process, even the priorities in designing a classification. . . . For every delusion there is a complementary jealousy, fear, or family member's tears; for every addiction there is a tragedy; for every depression there is at least one lament. (2002, pp. 5-6; cf. articles on classifying mental disorders)

Differences among cultures can affect the degree to which general psychological functioning or a given behavior is considered pathological. Healthy or adaptive functioning and behavior are to some degree determined within a given society, and these values may or may not be shared by other cultures (Kirmayer, 1994; Kleinman, 1996; Rogler, 1996). Such differences can complicate the process of diagnosis and attempts to develop universally accepted classification systems (Mezzich et al., 1996).

LIMITATIONS OF CONTEMPORARY CLASSIFICATION

Clearly, all are not in agreement regarding the value and utility of the systems of classification. Some who challenge their use suggest that the limitations of categorization outweigh the benefits. Some of the suggested limitations include the following:

1. *DSM* categories are descriptive rather than explanatory. The categories are based on visible symptom patterns and clusters rather than etiological (causal) considerations.

2. *DSM* categories focus on individual pathology. It is not within the classification system to consider family dysfunction, societal injustice or disorder, or other systemic problems. Therefore, pathology is (whether intended or not) attributed to the life of the individual at the risk of perpetuating societal injustice.

3. *DSM* categories propagate diagnostic labels which can be destructive in the life of individuals.

4. *DSM* categories promote a medical model of psychological practice that can limit social or psychological approaches from being reimbursable.

5. *DSM* categories strive to be atheoretical.

6. *DSM* categories were developed as a product of committee and intended to serve multiple functions. Sadler states, "The manual seeks to serve the needs of clinical practice, research, administrative record keeping and coding, and third-party reimbursement (see the introduction in the DSM-IV, APA, 1994). . . . Many criticisms of the DSMs have been leveled precisely at this all-things-to-all-people aspect" (2002, p. 315, cf. articles on classifying mental disorders)

DSM categories are not scientific enough. As Sadler says, "The thrust of science-based criticisms is that the DSM is too compromised a piece of science to warrant a meaningful claim for scientific status. The other practical (nonscientific) interests (user-friendliness, compatibility with the ICD, relevance to treatment selection, etc.) are too prominent to make the DSM a credible document" (2002, p. 315, cf. articles on classifying mental disorders).[2]

A significant challenge to the classification and diagnosis of psychopathology has been the lack of any uniformly accepted standard for validation of the diagnostic criteria. "The absence of the kind of definitive, documented etiological mechanisms, with associated laboratory findings, by which the diagnoses of many physical disorders are confirmed—a gold standard for comparative purposes—has made establishing the validity of many DSM . . . diagnoses a good deal more difficult" (Faraone and Tsuang, 1994, quoted in Nathan and Langenbucher, 2003, p. 9). Various validation criteria have been considered over the past several decades, including symptom consistency, family studies, the course of the illness, genetic studies and more recently neurophysiology (Andreasen, 1995).

ADDITIONAL CONSIDERATIONS

The classification process of the *DSM*s is a multidimensional process, with allegiances that can at times be counterproductive. Sadler identifies three such processes: "(1) scientific processes, (2) professional-interest or guild processes, (3) organizational-practical processes"

---

[2]These limitations are drawn from the following sources: Nathan and Langenbucher, 2003; Sadler, 2002 (cf. articles on classifying mental disorders); Caplan, 1995; Kirk and Kutchins, 1992; Eysenck, 1986; Faust and Miner, 1986; Schacht, 1985; Spitzer, 1985; Kendell, 1991; Garfield, 1986; Chodoff, 1986; Denton, 1989; Rothblum, Solomon and Albee, 1986; Strong, 1993.

(2002, p. 301, cf. articles on classifying mental disorders). He suggests that those guiding the *DSM* classification processes have been faced with the challenge of balancing a desire for empirically valid and reliable research in psychopathology with the need for a system that is of practical value in clinical practice. "Processes of classification cannot overlook the central ethic of their entire activity, which is to aid individuals and families who suffer from mental disorders" (2002, p. 302, cf. articles on classifying mental disorders).

> The idea that scientific knowledge is perspectival, incomplete, and infected with values and interests generates legitimate anxiety in all of us—for if we cannot anchor ourselves with scientific knowledge, on what basis can we rationally choose to act on the important problems that face us? But it is exactly this question—On what basis can we rationally choose to act?—that we must confront, scientist and layperson, patient and clinician. Scientists must choose as we all do: What are the important questions for research? Which methods will give us the most credible results? On what criteria shall we decide between conflicting theories and data? Whom should we admit as colleagues, and what should their qualifications be? It is in the particular answers to these questions that the politics of science emerges, and the DSM's science is no exception. (Sadler, 2002, p. 306, cf. articles on classifying mental disorders)

> Classification systems are neither inherently self-evident nor given. On the contrary, they emerge from the crucible of human experience; change and variability, not immutability, are characteristic. Indeed, the ways in which data are organized at various times reflect specific historical circumstances. (Grob, 1991, p. 421)

For the Christian, the discussion must be extended even further. If we agree with some of the leading thinkers in the field that the knowledge base from science is incomplete and classification systems are variable, then the Christian is left to constantly critique existing systems of classification and, further, to consider whether there is a distinctively Christian understanding of classification that is not part of the broader contemporary discussion.

Consider what classification systems would look like were they developed out of differing cultural contexts. As noted above, the *DSM-IV* and the *ICD-10* sought to bridge major differences that had been present prior to that time. But what if there were multiple classification systems? What if they were to emerge out of different cultural contexts? Would this not speak volumes to sociocultural dimensions of many contemporary psychopathologies?

We would argue that while all psychopathologies have a sociocultural dimension, this dimension is weighted differently in different expressions of psychopathology. For example, schizophrenia may be one of the more biologically based expressions of mental illness (and in some respects carries less sociocultural weight), while anorexia nervosa and bulimia nervosa are two of the most recent illnesses and two expressions of psychopathology that carry greater sociocultural weight. Biology may very well factor into these expressions of psychopathology, but the weight is distributed differently among them.

A Christian view of society would have implications for how we view psychopathologies. If, for example, anorexia and bulimia are more directly constructed by an American (or Western) social reality, then integration would take seriously what a *Christian* social reality might look like. And this has implications for that society's categorization of psychopathologies, because the social reality contributes in important and often subtle ways to what is deemed pathological. Do we dare consider what a Christian social reality looks like? Does this social reality help us construct what is pathological? Can a Christian social reality ever be completely separated out from the broader culture, or will different Christian "cultures" create different social realities and thus different psychopathologies? Or will there be some least common denominators related to social justice, for example, so that pathologies that are related to institutional sexism and racism are found across all Christian communities?

These are important questions for our consideration. We hope that by raising these questions we will begin to help Christians in the field wrestle with the proper relationship between their Christian faith and the study and classification of psychopathology.

RECOMMENDED RESOURCES

Adams, H. E., and Sutker, P. B. (2001). *Comprehensive handbook of psychopathology* (3rd ed.). New York: Plenum. This is a definitive and current consideration of the theory and research in the field of psychopathology.

Johnson, W. B., and Johnson, W. L. (2000). *The pastor's guide to psychological disorders and treatments*. New York: Haworth Pastoral Press.

This is an attempt by two psychologists to translate the *DSM* nosology of psychopathology to a pastoral audience.

Koocher, G. P., Norcross, J. C., Hill, S. S., III. (1998). *Psychologists' desk reference*. New York: Oxford University Press. This is a helpful reference work that offers short articles on many issues related the psychopathology (e.g., epidemiology, current research, treatment modalities, etc.)

Spitzer, R. L., Gibbon, M., Skodol, A. E., Williams, J. B. W., and First, M. B. (2001). *DSM-IV-TR casebook: A learning companion to the diagnostic and statistical manual of mental disorders, fourth edition text revision*. Washington, DC: American Psychiatric Association. This book offers vignettes that bring the *DSM* categories of psychopathology to life.

REFERENCES

Adams, H. E., and Cassidy, J. F. (1993). The classification of abnormal behavior: An overview. In P. B. Sutker and H. E. Adams (Eds.), *Comprehensive handbook of psychopathology* (2nd ed.) (pp. 3-25). New York: Plenum.

American Psychiatric Association. (1994). *Diagnostic and statistical manual of mental disorders* (4th ed.). Washington, DC: American Psychiatric Association.

Andreasen, N. C. (1995). The validation of psychiatric diagnosis: New models and approaches. *American Journal of Psychiatry, 152*, 161-62.

Birley, J. L. T. (1975). The history of psychiatry as the history of an art. *British Journal of Psychiatry, 127*, 383-400.

Blashfield, R. K., and Draguns, J. G. (1976). Toward a taxonomy of psychopathology. *British Journal of Psychiatry, 42*, 574-83.

Cantor, N., Smith, E. E., French, R. deS., and Mezzich, J. (1980). Psychiatric diagnosis as a prototype categorization. *Journal of Abnormal Psychology, 89*, 181-93.

Caplan, P. J. (1995). *They say you're crazy: How the world's most powerful psychiatrists decide who's normal*. Reading, MA: Addison-Wesley.

Chodoff, P. (1986). *DSM-III* and psychotherapy. (Editorial). *American Journal of Psychiatry, 143*(2), 201-3.

Clark, L. A., Watson, D., and Reynolds, S. (1995). Diagnosis and classification of psychopathology: Challenges to the current system and future directions. *Annual Review of Psychology, 46*, 121-53.

Comer, R. J. (1996). *Fundamentals of abnormal psychology*. New York: W. H. Freeman.

Denton, W. H. (1989). *DSM-III-R* and the family therapist: Ethical considerations. *Journal of Marital and Family Therapy,* 15(4), 367-77.

Eysenck, H. J. (1986). A critique of contemporary classification and diagnosis. In T. Millon and G. L. Klerman (Eds.), *Contemporary directions in psychopathology: Toward the DSM-IV* (pp. 78-98). New York: Guilford.

Faraone, S. V., and Tsuang, M. T. (1994). Measuring diagnostic accuracy in the absence of a "gold standard." *American Journal of Psychiatry, 151,* 650-57.

Faust, D., and Miner, R. A. (1986). The empiricist and his new clothes: *DSM-III* in perspective. *American Journal of Psychiatry, 143*(8), 962-67.

Feyerabend, P. (1978). *Against method.* London: Verso.

Follette, W. C., and Houts, A. C. (1996). Models of scientific progress and the role of theory in taxonomy development: A case study of the *DSM. Journal of Consulting and Clinical Psychology, 64,* 1120-32.

Frances, A. J., Pincus, H. A., Widiger, T. A., Davis, W. W., and First, M. B. (1990). *DSM-IV:* Work in progress. *American Journal of Psychiatry, 147,* 1439-48.

Frances, A. J., Widiger, T. A., and Pincus, H. A. (1989). The development of *DSM-IV. Archives of General Psychiatry, 46*(4), 373-75.

Garfield, S. L. (1986). Problems in diagnostic classification. In T. Millon and G. L. Klerman (Eds.), *Contemporary directions in psychopathology: Toward the DSM-IV* (pp. 99-113). New York: Guildford.

Grob, G. N. (1991). Origins of *DSM-1:* A study in appearance and reality. *American Journal of Psychiatry, 148*(4), 421-31.

Jones, S., and Butman, R. (1991). *Modern psychotherapies: A comprehensive Christian appraisal.* Downers Grove, IL: InterVarsity Press.

Kendell, R. E. (1989). Clinical validity. *Psychological Medicine, 19,* 45-55.

Kendell, R. E. (1991). Relationship between the *DSM-IV* and the *ICD-10. Journal of Abnormal Psychology, 100*(3), 297-301.

Kendler, K. S. (1990). Toward a scientific psychiatric nosology: Strengths and limitations. *Archives of General Psychiatry, 47,* 969-73.

Kirk, S. A., and Kutchins, H. (1992). *The selling of DSM: The rhetoric of science in psychiatry.* New York: Aldine DeGruyter.

Kirmayer, L. J. (1994). Is the concept of mental disorder culturally relative? In S. A. Kirk and S. D. Einbinder (Eds.), *Controversial issues in mental health* (pp. 2-9). Boston: Allyn and Bacon.

Kleinman, A. (1996). How is culture important for *DSM-IV?* In J. E. Mezzich, A. Kleinman, H. Fabrega, and D. L. Parron (Eds.), *Culture and psychiatric diagnosis: A DSM-IV perspective* (pp. 15-25). Washington, DC: American Psychiatric Press.

Kuhn, T. S. (1970). *The structure of scientific revolutions* (2nd ed.). Chicago: University of Chicago Press.

Lamberts, H., Magruder, K., Kathol, R. G., Pincus, H. A., and Okkes, I. (1998). The classification of mental disorders in primary care. *International Journal of Psychiatry in Medicine, 28*(2), 159-76.

Lilienfeld, S. O., and Marino, L. (1995). Mental disorder as a Roschian concept: A critique of Wakefield's "harmful dysfunction" analysis. *Journal of Abnormal Psychology, 104,* 411-20.

Millon, T. (1969). *Modern psychopathology: A biosocial approach to maladaptive learning and functioning.* Philadelphia: W. B. Saunders.

Millon, T., and Klerman, G. L. (1986). *Contemporary directions in psychopathology: Toward the DSM-IV.* New York: Guilford.

Nathan, P. E., and Langenbucher, J. (2003). Diagnosis and classification. In G. Stricker and T. A. Widiger (Eds.), *Handbook of clinical psychology: Clinical psychology* (Vol. 8:3-26). New York: John Wiley & Sons.

Pincus, H. A., and McQueen, L. (2002). The limits of an evidence-based classification of mental disorders. In J. Z. Sadler (Ed.), *Descriptions and prescriptions: Values, mental disorders and the DSMs* (pp. 9-24). Baltimore, MD: Johns Hopkins University Press.

Reeb, R. N. (2000). Classification and diagnosis of psychopathology: Conceptual foundations. *Journal of Psychological Practice, 6*(1), 3-18.

Rogler, L. H. (1996). Framing research on culture in psychiatric diagnosis: The case of the *DSM-IV. Psychiatry 59,* 145-55.

Rogler, L. H. (1997). Making sense of historical changes in the *Diagnostic and statistical manual of mental disorders:* Five propositions. *Journal of Health and Social Behavior, 38,* 9-20.

Ross, P. A. (2002). Values and objectivity in psychiatric nosology. In J. Z. Sadler (Ed.), *Descriptions and prescriptions: Values, mental disorders and the DSMs* (pp. 45-55). Baltimore, MD: Johns Hopkins University Press, 2002.

Rothblum, E. D., Solomon, L. J., and Albee, G. W. (1986). A sociopolitical perspective of *DSM-III.* In T. Millon and G. L. Klerman (Eds.), *Contemporary directions for psychopathology: Toward the DSM-IV* (pp. 167-89). New York: Guilford.

Sadler, J. Z. (Ed.). (2002). *Descriptions and prescriptions: Values, mental disorders and the DSMs.* Baltimore, MD: Johns Hopkins University Press.

Schacht, T. E. (1985). *DSM-III* and the politics of truth. *American Psychologist 40*, 513-21.

Schaffner, K. F. (2002). Clinical and etiological psychiatric diagnosis: Do causes count? In J. Z. Sadler (Ed.), *Descriptions and prescriptions: Values, mental disorders, and the DSMs* (pp. 271-90). Baltimore, MD: Johns Hopkins University Press.

Simola, S. K. (1992). Differences among sexist, nonsexist and feminist family therapies. *Professional Psychology: Research and Practice, 23*, 397-403.

Spitzer, R. L. (1981). The diagnostic status of homosexuality in *DSM-III:* A reformulation of the issues. *American Journal of Psychiatry, 138*(2), 210-15.

Spitzer, R. L. (1985). *DSM-III* and the politics-science dichotomy syndrome: A response to Thomas E. Schacht's "*DSM-III* and the politics of truth." *American Psychologist, 40*, 522-26.

Strong, T. (1993). *DSM-IV* and describing problems in family therapy. *Family Therapy, 32*, 249-53.

Walker, L. E. A. (1989). Psychology and the violence against women. *American Psychologist, 44*, 695-702.

Widiger, T. A. (2002). Values, politics and science in the construction of the *DSMs*. In J. Z. Sadler (Ed.), *Descriptions and prescriptions: Values, mental disorders and the DSMs* (pp. 25-41). Baltimore, MD: Johns Hopkins University Press.

Widiger, T. A., and Trull, T. J. (1993). The scholarly development of *DSM-IV*. In J. A. Costa e Silva and C. C. Nadelson (Eds.), *International Review of Psychiatry* (1:59-78). Washington, DC: American Psychiatric Press.

World Health Organization. (1948). *Manual of the international statistical classification of diseases, injuries, and causes of death: Sixth revision of the international lists of diseases and causes of death.* Geneva: W.H.O.

Zimmerman, M. (1988). Why are we rushing to publish *DSM-IV?* *Archives of General Psychiatry 45*, 1135-38.

APPENDIX A
Historical Development of the Naturalistic View of Psychopathology

6th century B.C.	Alcmaeon	Greek physician considered by some to be the founder of empirical psychology. He concluded that the brain is the source of sensation and reasoning, and therefore problems in reasoning are the result of brain pathology.
5th century B.C.	Hippocrates	Greek physician who challenged the prevailing magical and mythological explanations of disease by suggesting that biological imbalances (specifically of four bodily fluids) are the cause of disease and treatments should directly address these causes. He sorted mental disorders into five categories.
4th century B.C.	Plato	Greek philosopher who addressed sociocultural factors in the cause of some mental illness and argued for humane treatments. He did hold to some spiritual explanations of mental illness.
2nd century B.C.	Asclepiades	Roman physician who strongly supported the idea that mental illness stems from naturalistic causes and adhered to humane treatments, though rejecting Hippocrates's humoral theory. He emphasized understanding environmental influences in the etiology of mental illness. Considered the first to have differentiated between hallucinations and delusions, and was the first to categorize disorders as either acute or chronic.
1st century B.C.	Aretaeus	Roman physician who believed that mental illness is primarily an exaggeration of normal mental processes. Developed a differentiation of disorders according to symptom patterns.
	Celsus	Roman academic who reorganized Hippocrates's classification system into distinct groups of disease entities.
2nd century A.D.	Soranus	Roman physician who built upon Celsus's reorganization of the Hippocratic nosology, revising and extending this basic system of classification.
	Galen	Roman physician who also built upon this same system with minor revisions. This basic nosology would remain intact through disregard during the Dark Ages and reemerge with the Renaissance.
5th century A.D.	Dark Ages	Period in which mystical and magical explanations of psychopathology were embraced and naturalistic explanations rejected.

15th century A.D.	Summis Desiderentes Affectibus	Document in which Pope Innocent VIII called on Christians to identify and rid Christendom of all those who practice witchcraft. Most accused of witchcraft were mentally ill.
	Maleus Maleficarum	Published after the above document, this manual described procedures for identifying, interrogating and sentencing witches. It fueled a barbaric period of torture and oppression of the mentally ill, whose abnormal behavior was thought to arise from occult involvement.
16th century A.D.	Juan Luis Vives	Spanish philosopher who stood against the tide of inquisitional fervor, suggesting that abnormal mental functioning is not of magical or spiritual origin. He called for compassion for the mentally ill.
	Paracelsus	Swiss physician who advocated natural causes of mental illness—a return to premedieval thinking—and was persecuted for his work.
	Jean Fernel	Physician who revived and extended the classification system of Hippocrates and first used the term *physiology*.
	Johann Weyer	Dutch physician, considered by some the father of modern psychiatry, who vigorously challenged the inhumane treatment of the mentally ill, publishing an attack on the *Maleus Maleficarum*. He advocated naturalistic explanations of mental illness, called for humane treatment and was the first physician to specialize in treatment of the mentally ill.
18th century A.D.	Philippe Pinel	Physician who instituted reforms for the treatment of the mentally ill. His work led to the practice of keeping systematic records and case histories of patients.
	Jean Esquirol	Physician and successor to Pinel who continued his reforms in humane treatment and published the first modern work on mental disorders: *Des maladies mentales*.
19th century A.D.	Dorothea Lynde Dix	Schoolteacher who fought for reform of U.S. hospitals and asylums and brought about significant legislative reforms, resulting in the modern principle of public responsibility for the mentally ill.
20th century A.D.	Clifford W. Beers	Former patient in U.S. asylums for three years who published a penetrating account of his experiences, *A Mind That Found Itself*, which led to improved hospital conditions and education of the public and the establishment of the Society for Mental Hygiene.

APPENDIX B

Major Theoretical Approaches to Psychopathology (adapted from Theodore Millon's discussion of psychopathology theories [1969, p. 71])

1. **Biophysical Theories** (disease model of psychopathology)

   Founding theorists: Kraepelin, Bleuler, Sheldon, Meehl, Hoskins, Kallman

   Definition of pathology: biological dysfunctions and dispositions

   Assumed etiology of pathology: heredity, constitution, defects

   Significant concepts: genes, temperament, constitution, defects

   Categories of pathology: traditional psychiatric disorders

   Data considered: heredity, anatomy, physiology, biochemistry

2. **Intrapsychic Theories** (adaptation model of psychopathology)

   Founding theorists: Freud, Hartmann, Erikson, Jung, Fairbairn, Adler, Sullivan, Horney

   Definition of pathology: unresolved conflicts, repressed anxieties

   Assumed etiology of pathology: instinct deprivation, childhood anxieties

   Significant concepts: instincts, ego, unconscious, defense mechanisms

   Categories of pathology: symptom disorders, character patterns

   Data considered: free association, memories, dreams, projective tests

3. **Phenomenological Theories** (dissonance model of psychopathology)

   Founding theorist: Rogers, Maslow, May, Boss, Binswanger

   Definition of pathology: self-discomfort

   Assumed etiology of pathology: denied self-actualization

   Significant concepts: self, self-regard, *eigenwelt*

   Categories of pathology: impoverishment, disorganization

   Data considered: self-reports of conscious attitudes and feelings

4. **Behavioral Theories** (learning model of psychopathology)

   Founding theorists: Dollard, Miller, Wolpe, Eysenck, Bandura, Rotter, Skinner

   Definition of pathology: maladaptive behavior

   Assumed etiology of pathology: deficient learning, maladaptive learning

   Significant concepts: conditioning, reinforcement, generalization

   Categories of pathology: numerable specific behavior symptoms

   Data considered: overt behavior observed and recorded objectively

4

SIN AND
PSYCHOPATHOLOGY

*T*he field of psychology has slowly grown in appreciation of some of
the benefits of religion. Several works on religion and psychotherapy,
religious coping, and religion and meaning making have been published by the American Psychological Association and other prominent
publishers (e.g., Emmons, 1999; Pargament, 1997; Shafranske, 1996).
These doors may have opened in part thanks to increased awareness of
ways in which religious affiliation and practice promotes physical health
and psychological well-being. For example, religious affiliation is associated with lower blood pressure (Levin and Vanderpool, 1989), lower risk
of cardiovascular disease (Hummer, Rogers, Nam and Ellison, 1999) and
lower risk of cancer (Jarvis and Northcott, 1987). To some these correla-
tions have suggested that religious affiliation may lead to longer life, as
suggested by a recent meta-analysis (McCullough et al., 2000), while to
others the associations are suggestive but inconclusive.

Christians are well aware that the field of psychology has not always shown much interest in religion. And within psychology, psychopathology has been one of a few focused areas of study that have
been slow to recognize religion as an important primary variable in
promoting well-being. Religion is often portrayed as a phenomenon

that has shaped human understanding of mental illness in negative ways. In mainstream psychopathology textbooks, mention of religion is limited to historical footnotes regarding ways religion has shaped various cultures' views of normal and abnormal behavior, often in "restrictive" or "judgmental" ways. For example, in one undergraduate abnormal psychology text (Barlow and Durand, 2002), religion is subsumed under the "supernatural tradition" as a historical footnote on abnormal behavior. The reader is left with a truncated view of Christianity, which is placed alongside practices of turning to the moon and stars for insights into abnormal behavior. Discussing the belief that unusual behavior reflects "the battle between good and evil," Barlow and Durand note: "One strong current of opinion puts the causes and treatment of psychological disorders squarely in the realm of the supernatural. During the last quarter of the 14th century, religious and lay authorities supported these popular superstitions, and society as a whole began to believe in the reality and power of demons and witches" (2002, p. 8). The authors note that this tradition is "alive and well" though "relegated . . . to small religious sects in this country and to nontechnological cultures elsewhere" (2002, p. 10).

We can see evidence of this tradition in the history of pastoral care. Some pastoral writers believed in spiritual and demonic forces in the etiology of many of what we refer to today as mental health concerns. For example, Origen speaks of the challenges facing those who would cure people suffering from "lunacy":

> First let us inquire how he who has been cast into darkness and repressed by an impure and deaf and dumb spirit is said to be a "lunatic," and for what reason the expression to be a "lunatic" derives its name from the great light in heaven which is next to the sun, which God appointed "to rule over the night." Let physicians then, discuss the physiology of the matter; inasmuch as they think that there is no impure spirit in the case, but a bodily disorder, and inquiring into the nature of things let them say, that the moist humours which are in the head are moved by a certain sympathy which they have with the light of the moon, which has a moist nature. . . . It is evident that this disorder is very difficult to cure, so that those who have the power to cure demoniacs sometimes fail in respect of this, and sometimes with fastings and supplications and more toils, succeed. (Origen *Commentary on Matthew*, quoted in Oden, 1987, p. 263)

Christians must acknowledge that the church has contributed to what we witness today as the bifurcation between sin and mental illness. Still, it may be difficult for Christians to know how to think through these issues if they do not see a full engagement of their faith in the study of psychopathology. They may conclude that a religious perspective has no place in the study of abnormal behavior.

Of course there are kernels of truth in the historical analyses exemplified by Barlow and Durand. At times psychopathology has been demonized, ignored, hidden and shamed by the church. But when religion is referenced only briefly and negatively in texts, there appears to be an implicit bias against religion in the scientific study of psychopathology.

In discussions of substance use disorders, most psychopathology texts refer to several models of alcoholism, including the "moral model," the view that moral weakness leads to the misuse of alcohol. That is, alcohol represents a temptation, and those who succumb to it lack the character to do otherwise. The moral model has its adherents both within the church and in the broader mental health community, and some would argue that there are benefits to it, at least with low-severity alcohol abusers (see Babor, 1994). But such text references hardly constitute a full and sympathetic engagement of religion as a primary variable.

But mention of the moral model does raise the question of the proper relation between sin and psychopathology. In the case of alcoholism and other substance use disorders, Christians may be tempted to fall back on simplistic understandings in an attempt to honor God by framing the issue in moral terms. However, by making a simplistic conceptualization we do a disservice to the reality of the experience and to the God of that reality.

We have yet to see a full and sympathetic engagement of religion as a primary variable in the meaning structures and behaviors of persons who contend with symptoms of psychopathology. In the study of psychopathology, a full and sympathetic engagement with Christianity would entail a discussion of the relationship between sin and psychopathology.

SIN, SICKNESS OR CRIME?

In *Whatever Became of Sin?* Karl Menninger observes that the language of sin had been replaced by language of either crime or sickness. We talk of criminal behavior and mental illness far more than we talk of sinful behavior or sin as a state or condition. Menninger observes a "transfer of authority" from churches and homes to the state that has resulted in the legislation of rules for behavior (1973, p. 25). The fallout was more than mere legislation; it also included new explanatory frameworks ("criminal activity" or "mental illness") that made "the designation of sin increasingly pointless from a practical standpoint" (ibid.). Sin departed from the public arena, and ultimately "sin as sin became a strictly personal matter" (ibid.).

As this shift was happening, the emerging field of "mental health" provided an alternative explanatory framework for understanding certain behaviors. As Menninger puts it, the construct of sin was soon displaced by "a new social philosophy and a new code of morality" (ibid., p. 38). This new social philosophy was reflected by hypnosis, psychoanalysis, behaviorism, psychopharmacology and scientific methodology. For the first time the question was asked whether a particular behavior was a "sin or a symptom" (ibid., p. 47). Implicit in the question is a move away from confession, repentance and forgiveness toward interventions that would bring about "improved functioning."

Although "crime" and "sickness" displaced "sin," Menninger observes a shift in which crimes were even being thought of as illnesses: "Some of the 'sins' . . . were increasingly seen as really not sinful, nor immoral, nor wrong. The general conclusion seemed to be that if behavior is really wrong, it is a crime—unless it is a disease" (ibid., p. 45). In fact, the language and explanatory framework of mental illness has largely replaced both the language of sin and the language of criminal conduct. We have become a culture of ubiquitous pathology. We see mental illness everywhere.

There is no one person who is responsible for this shift. However, O. Hobart Mowrer identifies Sigmund Freud as a key figure in the shift away from "sin" toward a language of "sickness." Neurotic expressions of mental illness, according to Freud, can be traced back to one's overinvolved superego, "which is the product of too strenuous socialization of the individual at the hands of harsh, unloving parents and an intolerant society" (1960, p. 301). In this explanatory framework, "repression" rather than "sin" lies at the heart of "neurotic" behavior.

Stirring as Mowrer's analysis of sin and sickness is, it still falls far short of a Christian critique, because Mowrer reduces sin to behaviors that lead to mental illness. For Mowrer, sin is not an expression of a fallen humanity; it has nothing to do with transgressions against a moral law, nor is sin in any way tied to transcendent reality: "Hell is still very much with us in those states of mind and body which we call neurosis and psychosis; and I have come increasingly, at least in my own mind, to identify anything that carries us toward these forms of perdition as *sin*" (ibid.). What Mowrer wants is a discussion of sin that allows for moral responsibility, even if he has to fundamentally change the concept and definition of sin.

McMinn has articulated several valuable ideas in his book *Why Sin Matters: The Surprising Relationship Between Our Sin and God's Grace* (2004). He would join Menninger (and to a lesser extent Mowrer), we believe, in lamenting the sweeping denial in our society of the reality of sin and of a language to communicate that reality. He would want us to pay more attention to a language of sin. As McMinn observes, "Some people are sick, and some are criminals, but we all are sinners" (2004, p. 90). Rather than seeing mental illness as a common denominator or common construct for language and communication, we would do well to return to a shared understanding of our fallen condition and the behaviors and consequences of acting out of that fallen state. In other words, we may pay a price for using "permissive" and "widely inclusive" notions of grace and acceptance that may be seen in "love without limits" or "affirmation without accountability" approaches.

Taking a different approach from Menninger, Mowrer and McMinn, Dueck (2002) prefers to conceptualize the differences in language between sin and psychopathology as having to do with the shift away from a modern society to a postmodern society. The language of sin and the language of psychopathology have become increasingly constricted over time, he says, so that neither speaks to the other in any meaningful way. The problem, according to Dueck, is that we are assuming that language is essentially referential:

> There are those who think that if a problem is perceived as physical, it must naturally be a medical issue; if emotional, it must be a psychological concern; or, if spiritual, a religious matter. It is assumed that each language describes a different objective reality and each domain demands experts in the language that describes it. . . . It may well be that the syntax of our inherited Western language allows us to carve up the human being in such a way in the first place. . . . The language of religion remains private and the language of medicine and psychology determines the public definitions of illness. (2002, p. 22)

Dueck is not the only contemporary Christian scholar to consider the role language plays in shaping human experience and constructs of mental health and pathology. Roberts (1993), for example, describes human beings as verbivores. He believes we are word eaters, that we eat and digest words and these words come to characterize us as persons over time. Roberts sees the modern psychotherapies as essentially offering people words to live by, words found in the theories of health and abnormality within each school of psychotherapy. These words, while they vary from theory to theory, hold in common an ability to shape our experience of ourselves and of who we become in terms of our character.

Roberts (1993) sees each of the modern psychotherapies as having something to say about mental illness, because each prescribes a healthy life and a way to get there. When we fall short of that life, we can look to the particular psychotherapy to tell us why we are off base and how to get back on track.

Whether the transfer of authority is due to language and legislation, a shift from modernity to postmodernity, the role words play in shaping our character or all of the above, what keeps Christians in the mental health field from drawing on the language and explanatory framework of sin? One reason Christians may be reluctant to discuss sin is that we want to distance ourselves from "moralistic bullyboys," though they, as Menninger states, are more concerned with "legality and vengeance" than with sin (1973, p. 47). Christians do seem to fear that if they reference sin they will be associated with those who essentially use the explanatory framework to bully others. They may want to avoid seeming more concerned with morality than with facilitating people's mental health and well-being. Of course we must consider the reasoning behind this assumption: it may well be that an accurate understanding and working through of sin may facilitate greater well-being in the long run than a denial of the reality of sin.

Another concern of Christian practitioners may be that their secular peers will view them as unscientific. They may believe that if they reference sin in their explanatory framework, they will be dismissed by the broader scientific community of which they hope to be a part and which they hope to influence. As Mowrer (1960) observed, the concept of sin has fallen out of favor in *both* science *and* theology. If the language of sin is avoided in theology, how much more so in the field of psychology? In any case, if the concept of sin is passé, then the person who references it will not be welcomed to the table of those who are making decisions that affect the mental health field.

There is a double-edged sword here. One may feel pressure to be sufficiently respected to have a place at the table of scientific discourse—and that only those at the table will influence the field. So with the best of intentions, one may avoid discussing sin for the very purpose of eventually influencing the field. But what is brought to the table once essential dimensions of a Christian explanatory framework, such as sin, have been jettisoned?

The other edge to the sword is that those who engage in in-depth discussion of sin and other aspects of a Christian explanatory framework risk removing themselves from broader discussions in the field and, consequently, any hope of transforming the broader culture. We can lose our sphere of influence if we end up speaking only to other Christians within an evangelical ghetto. We may very well edify other believers, but we will not transform the structures of society within the mental health establishment.

Before considering how to bring the concepts of sin and psychopathology into a meaningful relationship, let's unpack the meaning of "explanatory framework" and consider how explanatory frameworks help us make sense of symptom clusters in psychopathology.

EXPLANATORY FRAMEWORKS

There are several competing and potentially complementary explanatory models in the study of what we refer to as psychopathology. Freud, for example, offered an explanatory framework for understanding "neurotic" behavior: such behavior is the result of an overactive superego, which can lead to the repression of impulses.

Freud's theory is an example of a broader, global explanatory framework. But there are also more specific explanatory models. Barash (2003) uses the example of Asperger's syndrome to help us understand how various frameworks come into existence and provide us with a sense of understanding. According to Barash, Asperger's syndrome was simply "unavailable to mental health professionals until 1944, and has only been widely recognized since the 1990s" (2003, p. B11). Today many professionals diagnose Asperger's, and many services have been developed for clients and their families. Asperger's may very well be a real thing—a real syndrome—but according to Barash, it can be seen only because we now have an explanatory model, a kind of " 'seeing' that is facilitated by the existence of an explanatory model." He discusses the relationships among disease, normality and anomaly: "A disease syndrome is by definition an anomaly (with normality being the default condition), and once again, anomalies tend to be ignored unless and until they can be retro-recognized within a grander interpretive framework" (ibid.).

As Barash observes, diagnoses of psychopathology is more subjective than say, a broken arm or leg, and "they are notoriously difficult to verify." This is "a matter of recognizing and taking seriously what genuinely exists but had not previously been acknowledged" (ibid.).

To apply this reasoning to the present discussion of sin and psychopathology: Before we labeled mental illness, people experienced and suffered from (in many cases) comparable clusters of symptoms, and other attributions were made to explain those symptoms. The question is, how ought we make sense of a cluster of symptoms so that we can see the syndrome for what it is? A Christian psychology and psychopathology that accounts for sin would have to be a "new," alternative, comprehensive explanatory model. Anything short of that will look as if it is merely explaining anomalies, which will be largely ignored by the broader mental health community.

This critique allows for the possibility that a Christian perspective might provide a more accurate explanatory framework. But it also raises the question whether any of what we refer to as "mental illnesses" exist at all or whether they are just social constructions (Barash, 2003). What Christians do not have is an adequate alternative explanatory framework. We will see mental illness because of our training; we are acculturated into a way of seeing symptoms as indicators of pathology, and many Christian mental health professionals may not feel equipped to see sin because it has typically not been part of their training.

So bringing a Christian perspective to bear on the study of psychopathology is a challenge. What it would mean to bring the concepts of sin and psychopathology into a meaningful relationship?

WHAT A CHRISTIAN EXPLANATORY FRAMEWORK BRINGS TO PSYCHOLOGY

The Christian perspective is that God created this world, and all of what he created he declared "good." This theme of the good of creation is witnessed in the Old Testament, and we see a corresponding affirmation of creation in the New Testament.

Christians also understand that we are all fallen creatures. Although we bear the image of God, we are tainted by the Fall, and all aspects of who we are and of this world reflect this fallen condition. So it should come as no surprise that behavioral, emotional and cognitive dimensions of human experience are in some way affected by the Fall. These various dimensions of human experience fail to perform as originally intended. They both reflect our fallen condition and are expressions of that condition through the decisions we make as incomplete and fallen persons.

Each of us struggles with unique expressions of our fallenness, and mental health is the stage on which many of us express that drama. The best question to ask, then, is not, Does sin affect mental health and psychopathology? but, In what ways does sin affect mental health and well-being? Our mental health functions as a kind of barometer of our experience in a fallen and incomplete environment (which includes our own fallen behavioral, emotional and cognitive faculties). There are challenges that all of us face in parent-child relationships and disordered family life, sometimes exacerbated by divorce, loss of life, financial struggles and other major stressful experiences. There is also a tendency to think in ways that undermine our mental health. There is a tendency to seek short-term gratification and to fragment others so that we can relate to them as mere objects for our own interests instead of people created in the image of God to be respected and valued.

But God does not leave humanity in its fallen condition. A proper understanding of redemption and glorification is essential to a Christian approach to sin and psychopathology. God steps into our fallen world through the incarnation, through the person of Jesus, and he fully intends to redeem believers, to sanctify or make them holy, to set them apart for his purposes.

So we want to view human mental health and well-being in the context of God's redemptive plan. Some struggle with anger. Others struggle with lust to the point of sexual addiction. Still others struggle to delight in their relationship with their spouse, their children, or their neighbors and coworkers. These exemplify how our mental health is not what God intends for us. They are expressions of our fallenness. Yet Christians hold out hope that God is at work redeeming these experiences and that we glimpse something of our future glory with him when we see gains made in our mental health and well-being.

From this brief sketch of a Christian understanding of the biblical drama, we see that it involves an affirmation of the *inherent goodness of creation.* A Christian perspective also affirms that creation is *tainted and incomplete.* So each of us is created in the image and likeness of God, and therefore of infinite worth. But we are marred by the Fall—we are broken, incomplete, deceitful persons. However, redemption and the hope of resurrection tell us never to give up; God's grace is sufficient to cover all our wrongs if we are in a right relationship with God.

In addition, a Christian understanding of sin and psychopathology should be based on a holistic view of the person in relation to self, other, God and one's physical surroundings. The Hebrew word for this is *shalom,* which connotes justice and peace in relationships to the point of delight in them (Wolterstorff, 1983).

An explanatory framework that takes account of sin brings an increased awareness of personal responsibility. As we have seen, a Christian understanding of sin is far more than an awareness of personal responsibility, but it is certainly not less. Menninger, who wanted to avoid being perceived as a "moralistic bullyboy," nevertheless "pursued the possible usefulness of reviving the use of the word 'sin'—not for the word's sake, but for the reintroduction of the concepts of guilt and moral responsibility" (1973, p. 48). Menninger later makes the following observation:

> We would condemn clergymen for offering only pastoral counsel as therapy to a man suffering from syphilis or "schizophrenia." Would we withhold all censure from a psychiatrist who is giving psychotherapy for "neurotic" symptoms of sleeplessness or sexual inhibition to a man involved in rascality and wickedness of notable degree? (ibid., p. 49)

Throughout Scripture and Christian theology, people are considered responsible for what they do with what they have been given. These are concepts that have been all but lost in contemporary discussions of psychopathology, as symptom reduction rather than personal responsibility has become the primary focus of intervention.

In addition to increased awareness of personal responsibility, an explanatory framework that takes sin seriously will increase our awareness of *corporate responsibility.* Not only does sin affect individual choices and their consequences (McMinn, 2004), but sin pervades the very structures of society (Wolterstorff, 1983).

WAYS TO INCORPORATE A CHRISTIAN EXPLANATORY FRAMEWORK

The field of psychopathology, it seems, could benefit from gaining an understanding of sin within a broader Christian explanatory frame-

work. The question of how to incorporate this understanding into actual work being done in the field of psychopathology presents a challenge. Mowrer (1960) rejects the Freudian notion that the person
suffering from neurosis is best helped by relaxing the grip of the superego. Instead, Mowrer argues that the path to health is through acknowledging one's sin (recall that Mowrer defines sin as acts that
bring one closer to mental illness), coming to terms with it:

> But the moment he (with or without "assistance") begins to ac-
> cept his guilt and his sinfulness, the possibility of radical refor-
> mation opens up; and with this, the individual may legitimately,
> though not without pain and effort, pass from deep pervasive
> self-rejection and self-torture to a new freedom, of self-respect
> and peace. (ibid., p. 304)

Even these strong claims fall far short of a Christian perspective on
sin and psychopathology. For Mowrer, sin has nothing to do with a
living and transcendent God.

So what would it mean to incorporate a Christian explanatory
framework in psychopathology, including an understanding of human incompleteness, the effects of others' sin on a person, the effects
of one's own sin on one's struggles with psychopathology, the ways
sin affects the structures of society, and the role of grace? We are not
talking about looking at different things, but about *looking at things differently, through the eyes of faith.*

Human nature. A Christian explanatory framework includes an understanding of human nature. According to Roberts, the question is
this: "What are we made for, what would our most fundamental
yearnings and interests be if they were fully wise and self-conscious,
fully in accord with our essential nature as persons?" (1997, p. 76). As
noted already, human beings were made for delight in relationship
with God, themselves, each other and the rest of creation. In other
words, for a human being to flourish, he or she must address these
most fundamental yearnings, and these associations are tied in to essential aspects of what it means to function properly as human beings.

How, then, do human beings move to reach their full potential?
Roberts (ibid.) suggests several ways human beings are structured to
actualize our potential. Two of these basic structures most closely associated with a Christian understanding of sin: *human agency* and *in-
wardness.* Concerning human agency, Roberts notes that we have a

limited freedom which allows us to express and shape our character over time. God gives us increasing access to the possibility to choose even greater freedom:

> The word of God enables us to see possibilities, without the seeing of which we would lack the real options needed for our freedom. We are liberated from our bondage to sin by a word of grace that declares we have been made righteous in Christ. And thereby actions become open to us that would otherwise have remained in the dark night of pure potentiality. (ibid., p. 82)

As Roberts observes, we are more than the sum of our behaviors. Our heart and mind are shaped by what we come to care about, what we think about and plan for:

> Proper personhood as actualized in the Christian virtues, by consequence, is not merely a set of dispositions to behave properly, but above all a rightly qualified inwardness—patterns of thought, wish, concern, emotion, and intention shaped by the Christian story and the truths about God, ourselves, and the world, that follow from that story. (ibid., p. 84)

Human beings have wishes, desires and longings, and a Christian understanding notes that our thoughts and motivations reveal who we really are and what we really care about.

Human incompleteness. As noted in chapter one, sin can be thought of as specific acts and as a state or condition. When we refer to sin as an act, we are saying that a thought or behavior (or lack of behavior) misses the mark of God's standard of morality. As a state or condition, sin is ubiquitous: the human condition is affected by the Fall and tainted by sin. McMinn's image of white noise is apt for the background experience of sin we live with daily. We assume that sin is like a light switch: either it is on or off—we sin or we do not sin. But the reality is that "the white noise is always on" (McMinn, 2004, p. 29).

The *DSM* is not a catalog of sin but a kind of catalog of the state and consequences of sin. The mass-media news, says McMinn, is in effect a "daily damage report" of the state and consequences of sin (2004, p. 47). Further, we see descriptions of the Fall in a casual perusal of an introductory psychology textbook (let alone a text on psychopathology): "you are likely to encounter descriptions of how serotonin deficits contribute to clinical depression, and how dopamine excesses are implicated in schizophrenia" (ibid., p. 13). In a prefallen state, these neurotransmitters would be properly balanced, along with the other structures and functions of the body, "but in a fallen world we live in imperfect bodies, which we take care of imperfectly and end up with all manner of maladies and ailments" (ibid.).

Kenny was a promising college athlete. However, in his junior year he began to display unusual behavior and increased paranoia. He was eventually diagnosed as suffering from paranoid schizophrenia. Although he occasionally responded well to different medications, his experience of schizophrenia, like most, ran a chronic course, and he never fully recovered from this mental illness.

Does seeing Kenny's deficits as more than just decreased levels of serotonin mean anything in psychopathology? We think it does. Seeing decreased levels of serotonin as reflections of our fallen existence normalizes them to some degree. An increased awareness of the reality of the Fall thus helps us put in perspective the challenges and constraints that we and others face in this life. This helps us rebut the notion that actualizing our potential in humanistic terms is the pinnacle of existence, that self-actualization is what we are owed, what we must all strive toward.

The effects of others' sin. The idea of identifying the effects of the sins of others on our clients is perhaps a little more accessible. For the most part therapy is an individualistic exercise, and as we work with an individual, we tend to privilege their account of the harm done to them by others.

Janice entered the college counseling center in tears. She told the on-call counselor that she had met a young man the previous week and began dating, but things went further than she wanted last night. Despite her protests, she was raped, and she is now having a difficult time sleeping and concentrating on her studies. Clearly Janice's acute post-traumatic stress is the direct result of sin done to her—a sexual assault.

Fay came for help with parenting skills. She was having difficulty setting limits for her ten-year-old daughter, in part because in her own growing-up years Fay had been a victim of verbal abuse. Now, every time she tried to set firm limits, the extreme and vicious words of her own father rang in her ears. As a result, she allowed her daughter to negotiate every decision and to essentially set the rules and expectations in the home.

Not only did the experience of verbal abuse have a devastating impact on Fay, but it traced down through another generation, affecting the upbringing of Fay's daughter, who would benefit from boundaries and limits, if they could be set clearly and consistently.

The effects of a client's own sin. What may be more challenging is to identify the effects of the sins of our clients on their difficulties. Most Christian mental health professionals are not trained to make such a connection, and few Christians would want to discuss a client's sin because of the fear of being viewed as judgmental.

We know of countless men who have been diagnosed with antisocial personality disorder and have committed serious crimes, including taking lives and destroying families. But many sin issues are much more subtle. *People of the Lie,* by M. Scott Peck, is about the reality of evil. It is one of only a handful of books on the topic of sin and human evil, and it is worth reading. When we identify evil in a person, we can run the risk of keeping sin at arm's length. *Sin is located in another person who acts in certain ways,* we might say to ourselves, and thus keep ourselves from acknowledging the painful reality of sin in our own life.

McMinn observes the *noetic* effects of sin; that is, "sin blunts our intellect and even our ability to discern sin," and thus "the fact that we discern sin so rarely is itself a symptom of sin" (2004, p. 14). We need to press beyond our natural inclination to compartmentalize sin as particularly evil deeds committed by a very small percentage of people.

Let's return to Fay, who was a victim of verbal abuse as a child and is now struggling with setting limits for her own child. It will not be so important to point out her acts of sin as to note that as she progresses in understanding how she came to struggle with setting limits, she will face decisions about whether to continue down a path toward forgiveness of her father and coming to terms with her own history, so that she can properly parent her daughter, who needs limit-setting.

One factor that helps distinguish among sin, crime and sickness, according to Menninger, is the degree of voluntariness associated with the behavior. "A crime, as with a sin, even when serving the same dynamic psychological function as a symptom, is assumed to be largely a voluntary act. As the symptom of an illness, on the other hand, the act must be largely *'involuntary'*" (1973, p. 75). Unfortunately, degree of voluntariness is very difficult to determine with precision, and such a standard presumes that these are either-or categories rather than behaviors that might be influenced by multiple factors.

Johnson distinguishes between the biblical concepts of sin and weakness. He noted that sin is "considered to be a power not created by God but by the sinner," and so "sin is something for which the sinner is held responsible" (1987, p. 218). In contrast, weakness "is a *given* limitation upon a normal or natural human ability or condition" (ibid.). A Christian understanding of moral fault encompasses both sin and weakness and notes that they combine in ways that are idiosyncratic and person specific. In its application to contemporary psychopathology, Johnson provides several examples, including alcohol dependence: some people may have a genetic predisposition to alcohol dependence (weakness), but for them active alcohol misuse clearly falls short of God's will (sin; see 1 Cor 6:10).

There will be points of conflict between Christian and secular societal views of psychopathology: "While recognizing that personal discomfort and societal norms both contribute to a consideration of what is normal, the Christian would see both these dimensions as flowing out of God's law as manifested in human consciousness (a revelation sometimes flawed by sin)" (Johnson, 1987, pp. 223-24). At the same time, Christians should expect to experience disagreement regarding what is sin and what is normal (Johnson's examples include homosexuality, pride and materialism), just as society can pathologize behaviors that reflect spiritual insight and maturity, such as sacrificial living.

Sin's effects on the structures of society. Sin is not reflected only in emotional or psychological disturbance, of course. There is a praxis-oriented dimension to a Christian explanatory framework that seeks to transform the structures of society. As noted in chapter two, psychopathology and its categories can be related to the structures of society. A Christian vision for society would then have implications for how we view various pathologies, as well as whether we "see" certain pathologies. A Christian explanatory framework reflects on the current social situation and seeks to be instrumental in its transformation. Applying this to the modern psychopathologies, the Christian will want to reflect on the care being provided to those who suffer from symptoms of psychopathology, as well as the ways society and the mental health community conceptualize mental illnesses and provide care for those in need. For example, might institutional sexism be related to some expressions of depression? Are some expressions of depression socially shaped, since twice as many women as men are depressed in our society? Is there a relationship between power and some expressions of depression?

Similarly, we mentioned in chapter two that anorexia nervosa and bulimia nervosa are two of the more recent "socioculturally weighted" psychopathologies. That is, they appear to have been constructed in part by American (Western) social values regarding what is beautiful at the expense of what is healthy. In the cases of depression and the eating disorders, as well as all the other contemporary psychopathologies to one extent or another, Christian integration must consider seriously what a Christian social reality might look like and how distortions of that ideal begin to construct what a society categorizes as psychopathology.

This critique can be extended beyond specific symptom clusters. Following Wolterstorff (1984), Christians need to ask whether a given system is functioning properly. Take the mental health care system. As Wolterstorff puts it, "We owe it to God and to our fellow human being to see to it that our society's array of institutions adequately serves the life of its members—that they serve the cause of justice and shalom" (ibid., p. 62).

Does the mental health care system work well? Would the functions assigned to the mental health care system be better addressed by other systems? What role ought the church play in serving those suffering from psychopathology? What is the place of prevention? How much of what is done in the mental health community is to turn a profit rather than meet needs? Is the familiar treatment model of the fifty-minute hour a just and effective model? What would it mean to think creatively about alternative approaches, including preventive efforts?

A proper understanding of the effects of sin on the structures of society has profound implications for the Christian interested in the integration of faith and the scientific study of psychopathology. But Christian integration extends beyond sin and incorporates an understanding of grace.

Appreciation of grace. If we commit ourselves to properly understanding sin and psychopathology, we have to be willing to look at new approaches to healing that incorporate grace and redemption. As McMinn observes, "Good therapy works because it is a place that emulates grace" (2004, p. 37). If this is true, than Christians in the field need to unpack the implications and applications of such a claim. In his closing thoughts on sin, Mowrer seeks some "new source of strength" (1960, p. 304) to endure the discussion of moral responsibility, but he does not have a language for that source of strength. The Christian community does have such a language: grace.

Though underdeveloped at this time, a Christian understanding of grace and its thoughtful application to the field should have far-reaching implications that help guide practitioners toward what is being referred to as positive psychology, a move away from focusing exclusively on pathology and toward an emphasis on strengths and resilience. In health psychology and neuropsychology, experts are discussing salutogenic mechanisms of the brain, that is, functional contributions to health that are tied to brain function and neuropathways (Smith, 2002).[1] Even in neuropsychology, then, we are witnessing an increased appreciation for ways our bodies can contribute to health-promoting functions that reflect and facilitate greater resilience and well-being.

Perhaps a place to begin is to return to Roberts's discussion of what it means to be a human being. He says that we are word eaters—"verbivores." We eat and digest words, assimilating them into "the construction of the self":

> In being verbivorous, humans are unique among the earth's creatures. We have a different kind of life than nonverbal animals, a kind of life that we can call generically "spiritual." Since we become what we are by virtue of the stories, the categories, the metaphors and explanations in terms of which we construe ourselves, we can become spiritual Marxians by thinking of ourselves in Marxian terms, spiritual Jungians if we construe ourselves in Jungian terms, and so forth. It is because we are verbivores that the psychologies have this "edifying" effect on us . . . : They provide diagnostic schemata, metaphors, ideals for use to feed upon in our hearts, in terms of which our personalities may be shaped into one kind of maturity or another. (Roberts, 1997, p. 81)

CONCLUSION

Are there costs associated with using the language of sin in psychology? There certainly may be, both large and small. For example, psychologists may not receive reimbursement if their incorporation of an understanding of sin in their case conceptualization and treatment planning is viewed as nonscientific and thus does not meet the standards of mental health services based on scientific foundations. So Christians have to do their homework. They may have to research the

[1]We would like to thank our colleague Scott Sautter for introducing us to the concept of salutogenic mechanisms of the brain.

construct of sin and its various dimensions. They may have to make a case for the incorporation of the language and construct of sin. Does this make Christians beholden to empiricism? No, but if Christians want to transform the field, they must be conversant in the primary language of behavioral sciences being spoken today.

The costs might also be more sweeping. What if a Christian view of society leads Christians in psychopathology to establish their own classification system? What if, over time, a growing number of Christians find that the evolving American social reality—which shapes expressions of psychopathology and limits our understanding of what constitutes psychopathology—has an incomplete construction of what is pathological? There may be a time when Christians feel that they must provide a more religiously congruent, complementary nosology, one that takes seriously a Christian understanding of sin in its varied meanings.

RECOMMENDED READING

McMinn, M. R. (2004). *Why sin matters: The surprising relationship between our sin and God's grace.* Wheaton, IL: Tyndale House. This is a helpful resource. It is very accessible to the layperson and a wonderful source for personal reflection.

Peck, M. S. (1983). *People of the lie: The hope for healing human evil.* New York: Simon & Schuster. This is one of very few resources that explicitly discusses evil. It is a good starting point for the Christian psychologist.

Plantinga, C., Jr. (1995). *Not the way it's supposed to be: A breviary of sin.* Grand Rapids, MI: Eerdmans. A challenging book by one of the most thoughtful Christian scholars writing today.

Roberts, R. C., and Talbot, M. R. (1993). *Limning the psyche: Explorations in Christian psychology.* Grand Rapids, MI: Eerdmans. This is a terrific edited volume from scholars in psychology, philosophy and theology.

REFERENCES

Babor, T. F. (1994). Avoiding the horrid and beastly sin of drunkenness: Does dissuasion make a difference? *Journal of Consulting and Clinical Psychology, 62*(6), 1127-40.

Barash, D. P. (2003). Believing is seeing. *Chronicle of Higher Education,* June 27, pp. B10-B11.

Barlow, D. H., and Durand, V. M. (2002). *Abnormal psychology: An inte-*

grative approach (3rd ed.). Belmont, CA: Wadsworth.

Dueck, A. (2002). Speaking the languages of sin and pathology. *Christian Counseling Today, 10*(1), 21-24.

Emmons, R. A. (1999). The psychology of ultimate concerns. New York: Guilford Press.

Hummer, R. A., Rogers, R. G., Nam, C. B., and Ellison, C. G. (1999). Religious involvement and U.S. adult mortality. *Demography, 36,* 273-85.

Jarvis, G. K., and Northcott, H. C. (1987). Religion and differences in morbidity and mortality. *Social Science and Medicare,* 25, 813-24.

Johnson, E. L. (1987). Sin, weakness, and psychopathology. *Journal of Psychology and Theology, 15,* 218-26.

Levin, J. S., and Vanderpool, H. Y. (1989). Is religion therapeutically significant for hypertension? *Social Science and Medicine, 29,* 69-78.

McCullough, M. E., Hoyt, W. T., Carson, D. B., Koenig, H., and Thoresen, C. E. (2000). Religious involvement and mortality: A meta-analytic review. *Health Psychology, 19,* 211-22.

McMinn, M. R. (2004). *Why sin matters: The surprising relationship between our sin and God's grace.* Wheaton, IL: Tyndale House.

Menninger, K. (1973). *Whatever became of sin?* New York: Hawthorn.

Mowrer, O. H. (1960). Sin, the lesser of two evils. *American Psychologist, 15*(5), 301-4.

Oden, T. C. (1987). *Classic pastoral care: Vol. 3. Pastoral Counsel.* Grand Rapids, MI: Baker.

Pargament, K. I. (1997). *The psychology of religion and coping.* New York: Guilford Press.

Roberts, R. C. (1997). Parameters of a Christian psychology. In R. C. Roberts and M. R. Talbot (Eds.), *Limning the psyche: Explorations in Christian psychology* (pp. 74-101). Grand Rapids, MI: Eerdmans.

Smith, D. F. (2002). Functional salutogenic mechanisms of the brain. *Perspectives in Biology and Medicine, 45*(3), 319-28.

Shafranske, E. (Ed.). (1996). *Religion and the clinical practice of psychology.* Washington, DC: American Psychological Association.

Wolterstorff, N. (1983). *Until justice and peace embrace.* Grand Rapids, MI: Eerdmans.

Part Two

CLINICAL PRESENTATIONS

5

PROBLEMS OF ANXIETY

*A*ll anxiety is normal, not neurotic. It is ontological, a constituent of our being. To be alive is to be anxious. One's neurosis lies in one's response to anxiety. Persons try to subdue it by perpetuating an inauthentic philosophy of life. In the face of anxiety, they engage in all types of evasive maneuvers and manipulations to quell its stridency except by surrendering their inauthenticity. They refuse to give up their self-protective perspectives on themselves. Anxiety persists, as the wrenching experience of spirit's urging to search their depths for a more meaningful orientation toward life. Even overwhelming anxiety is an ally. It powerfully confronts one with the fact that something is inwardly awry. Anxiety lessens as one begins the process of reorientation, as one embarks on the slow and painful process of confronting inauthentic strategies and starts to reduce the pattern of relating to oneself and to others and to God. (Weyerhaeuser, 1980, pp. 9-10)

Life is difficult. . . . Life is a series of problems. Do we want to moan about them or solve them? Do we want to teach our children to solve them? . . . [A] tendency to avoid problems and the emotional suffering inherent in them is the primary basis of all human mental illness. Since most of us have this tendency to a greater or lesser degree, most of us are mentally ill to a greater or lesser degree, lacking complete mental health. Some of us will go to quite extraordinary lengths to avoid our problems and the suffering they cause, proceeding far afield from all that is clearly good and sensible in order to try to find an easy way out, building the most elaborate fantasies in which to live, sometimes to the total exclusion of reality. (Peck, 1978, pp. 15-17)

*N*either of these passages makes for easy reading. Both were written by Christian mental health professionals—one a psychologist, the other a psychiatrist. The discerning reader will quickly recognize the existential and psychodynamic emphases on the significance of symptoms in the broader context, rather than simply the distress and inner turmoil they represent for afflicted individuals. In trying to make sense of stress and anxiety disorders from a faith perspective, we will have to face this tension. That is, do we focus on "roots" or "shoots"? And perhaps more telling, how will our notions of etiology and maintenance influence our attempts to intervene or even prevent some of these troublesome disorders?

Most of us know at least one family member or friend who is crippled by an intense fear of flying, especially since the events of September 11, 2001. We have observed how little their fears respond to "logic" or even well-meaning advice. The *DSM-IV-TR* classification system calls this a "specific phobia—situational type." Perhaps somewhat less familiar are the struggles of persons who have been repeatedly exposed to abusive combat or domestic violence, trauma that comes to dominate the way they organize their way in the world (van der Kolk, 2002). That same classification system describes this as either an "acute" or "posttraumatic" stress disorder, a phenomenon often graphically portrayed in the media in these days of frequent terrorist bombings, natural disasters and horrific sexual exploitation.

Stress and anxiety disorders are complex and multifaceted expressions of pain and human suffering. Viewing them from a biopsychosocial perspective seems especially important. As with any problem in living, we are somewhat limited in our comprehension since we only have the self-report of the afflicted person and our direct observation of his or her struggles. Once again, it is important to always be humble in our judgments and deeply respectful of our shared humanity. Everyone has times of feeling anxious and vulnerable or overwhelmed by a stressful situation. The thin line between normality and abnormality seems especially permeable with this group of disorders *(there but for the grace of God go I . . .).*

THEMES IN PASTORAL CARE

It has been conjectured that after the Fall, Adam and Eve experienced anxiety in their awareness of their nakedness and in their immediate response of hiding from God. Indeed they were likely nervous in anticipation of their next divine encounter. "For the first time in the history of humanity there was a sense of vulnerability and an apprehension that something bad was about to occur" (Rainwater, 1999, p. 88). These words describe *anxiety*, an emotional experience that is not what God intends for us.

Jesus calls us not to be anxious but to put our faith in God's sovereignty (Mt 6:25-32). As Rainwater (1999) observes, Jesus contrasts material and spiritual matters, suggesting that undue focus on the material leads to worry and anxiety, while focus on the spiritual and on God leads to peace. This is the view that "Christian belief is totally relevant to one's sense of perspective" (Chave-Jones, 1995, p. 164), a perspective grounded in our eternal destiny and God's provision for us between where we are today and heaven (2 Cor 4:18).

Martin Luther in "Consoling an Anxious Man" provides a good example of this approach:

Christian have . . . the very greatest future blessings certainly awaiting them; yet only through death and suffering. Although they, too, rejoice in that common and uncertain hope that the evil of the present will come to an end, and that its opposite, the blessing will increase; still, that is not their chief concern, but rather this, that their own particular blessing should increase, which is the truth as it is in Christ, in which they grow from day to day, and for which they both live and hope. But beside this they have, as I have said, the two greatest future blessings in their death. The first, in that through death the whole tragedy of this world's ills is brought to a close; as it is written, "Precious in the sight of the Lord is the death of His saints"; and again, "I will lay me down in peace and sleep." . . .

The other blessing of death is this, that it not only concludes the pains and evils of this life, but (which is more excellent) makes an end of sins and vices. (quoted in Clebsch and Jaekle, 1964, pp. 221-22)

Unfortunately, problems of anxiety can become quite complicated, and most difficulties in this area are not resolved through meditation on Scripture, as important as that is. When we interact with pastors or Christian workers, we usually find they are vitally interested in the problems of anxiety. They usually report that they regularly interact with individuals who feel overwhelmed by anxiety, fear or stress. When the church or organization in which they minister is functioning well, they can often bear witness to the healing potential of good worship, fellowship and service (Kauffmann, 2000). Those who preach often reflect on passages in Scripture that deal with anxiety, fear or worry (e.g., Matthew 6). Many Christians keep lists of key verses on this topic in a personal study Bible. But it becomes readily apparent to most pastors or Christian workers that meditation on key Scriptures rarely "fixes" serious anxiety struggles, any more than the regular singing of "Amazing Grace" helps a struggling person feel like she or he is God's beloved (Manning, 1994). God's grace, and the truths of Scripture, must be incarnated (fleshed out) in the context of everyday living.

Pastors and Christian workers often tell us that they see striking individual differences in how persons respond to crises and life events. This implies that there are certain life skills or coping strategies that are essential for dealing effectively with the demands of life. Some individuals seem to have a good repertoire of these skills; others struggle with even the thought of being in a social setting where they might feel vulnerable. Some persons seem resilient, while others can barely cope with the most basic tasks. Those who had good support, adequate supervision and appropriate structures in their formative years have a greater potential to thrive and not merely survive. Without adequate "scaffolding" in those critical periods, there is a much higher probability of eventual breakdown, especially if social support remains lacking (Malony, 1995).

One of the most discussed books in Christian higher education today is Steven Garber's *The Fabric of Faithfulness: Weaving Together Beliefs and Behaviors During the University Years* (1996). Garber is convinced that those who stay committed for the long haul made some important choices in the critical years of late adolescence and young adulthood. First, they interacted regularly with healthy role models and exemplars of truth (mentors). Second, they were committed to a group of people who effectively combined affirmation with accountability (community). Third, they exerted the necessary effort to develop a Christian worldview complex enough to withstand the challenges of pluralism (conviction). Although Garber's primary focus was on the predictors of long-term faithfulness, they are strikingly similar to what is known about coping and adjustment in general (Pargament, 1997). Certainly this bears relevance to pastoral care.

Having social support is absolutely essential. Pastors and Christian workers often tell us that when people are not connected with others they do not cope as well (Bilezikian, 1997). Finding a sense of meaning and purpose in life is also very important, as well as a belief that one can do certain things well (a sense of efficacy). A barrier or obstacle might be interactional styles that are "toxic" or self-defeating (i.e., how we relate to others and how we want them to relate to us). As McLemore (2003) has observed, unhealthy interpersonal relationships have the potential to intensify and magnify nearly every type of emotional distress and suffering.

We suspect that yet another factor that affects coping and adjustment is pride, which is certainly one of the most important themes in Scripture (cf. chapter three). As McLemore notes:

> Prideful creatures that we are, it is hard for us to acknowledge what we do not like or respect, or what we sense others will disparage. It is so much easier, so more convenient, at least in the moment, to deny the existence of the distasteful. God, however, is truthful, and to truthfulness he calls us. He wants us to know ourselves, so that in the process, we can grasp just how much he loves us. We need not fear what is inside us, however heinous, however awful, however base. God already knows all about it, and he loves us anyway—which is, in fact, the good news of Jesus Christ. . . . Our life with God will thrive only to the extent that we purpose in our hearts, sincerely and relentlessly, to reckon with truth—about him, about others, about ourselves. (1984, p. 12)

How we view the symptoms of stress and anxiety disorders may have something important to do with the biblical mandate to be truth tellers and truth seekers. Our ability to be candid and congruent with our own struggles, and our willingness to listen carefully and sacrificially to the distress of others, may directly affect our interpretation of the symptoms.

These days there is a renewed emphasis on spiritual discipline for "ordinary people" (Ortberg, 1997). Making sense of those things that make us feel anxious, vulnerable or afraid, and finding more effective ways to cope, is good stewardship of talents (Kauffmann, 2000). This perspective seems to resonate deeply with almost everyone we know who works full time in Christian ministry.

Effective pastoral care with the problems of anxiety seems to be a function of good worship, fellowship and service. Authenticity in word and deed is essential, as well as a deep commitment to developing a thoughtful Christian worldview. Finally, it involves the modeling, prompting, shaping and reinforcing of healthy and holy lifestyles that will develop the essential life skills. Since we differ so widely in terms of our "raw material" (biopsychosocial model) and know little about others' acquired or inherited vulnerability (stress-diathesis perspective), we should be exceedingly cautious about making moral judgments about character, choice and responsibility (again, *there but for the grace of God go I*).

THEMES IN PSYCHOPATHOLOGY

It can be a challenge to differentiate between popular concepts of anxiety and more professional understandings. When mental health professionals talk about anxiety, they usually describe it as a state of alarm in response to a vague sense of threat or danger. Fear is seen as immediate alarm in response to a serious, known threat (Comer, 2003). Physiologically these states are indistinguishable (changes in respiration, muscle tension, perspiration—the classic fight-or-flight response).

When we talk about being anxious, it can mean we are eager or excited to face some new opportunity or challenge, or it can suggest some very unpleasant internal feelings, even angst or agony (Miller and Jackson, 1995). We all know what it feels like to be anxious, afraid or vulnerable, but we experience that sense at vastly different levels of intensity, frequency and duration. When the feeling significantly impairs our ability to deal with the demands of everyday living or causes significant distress, the symptoms tend to be described as *clinical,* potentially demanding a pastoral or professional response.

It would be best to understand anxiety as excessive worry about life circumstances that has no factual or logical basis and persists on a daily basis for a significant period (cf. Jongsma and Peterson, 1995). Symptoms can include motor tension (e.g., restlessness, tiredness, shakiness), hypervigilance (always feeling on edge, difficulties in sleeping or concentrating) or autonomic nervous system overarousal (e.g., heart palpitations, shortness of breath, nausea). Obviously many of these symptoms are experienced as "physical," so it is not surprising that they often come to the attention of physicians rather than pastors or mental health professionals, at least initially.

Our ability to tolerate these symptoms varies widely across cultures and among individuals. A rather lively debate within the field has to do with the extent to which these responses are adaptive or useful and at what point they become too severe, or so long-lasting that they become disabling or inappropriate (as in the case of posttraumatic stress disorder).

When someone says they are feeling anxious, the Christian mental health professional should not simply assume they know what the person means. A too-quick assumption often leads to simplistic "solutions." Dealing effectively with the problems of anxiety requires great clarity in determining exactly what the problem is, what might be causing it and what if anything needs to be done about it (Miller and Jackson, 1995, p. 251).

Despite differences in interpreting the symptoms, researchers agree that stress and anxiety disorders are the most common form of mental disorders in Western industrialized societies. Significant anxiety is experienced by 10-15 percent of general medical outpatients and an equal number of inpatients. In healthy populations, perhaps 25 percent of all individuals will become "clinically anxious" (as defined by *DSM-IV-TR* criteria) at least once in their lifetime (Scully et al., 1990). A large majority of these same individuals will experience two or more of the major stress and anxiety disorders in that same time period; that is, they tend to cluster. Obviously, millions suffer with the problems of anxiety, and countless more—family and friends—are affected as well.

There is a growing recognition that stress and anxiety disorders are more than a response to internal or external stressors. They appear to reflect biological factors as well (i.e., acquired or inherited vulnerabilities). Six major categories are discussed in the classification system of *DSM-IV-TR:* generalized anxiety disorder (GAD), phobias, panic disorder, obsessive-compulsive disorder (OCD), acute stress disorder and posttraumatic stress disorder (PTSD). Across the disorders, the long-term objectives for treatment include reducing the intensity, duration or frequency of anxiety-related symptoms, increasing the ca-

pacity to deal with tasks of everyday living, and resolving the core con-
flict(s) at the root of the anxiety (Jongsma and Peterson, 1995, p. 19).

Generalized anxiety disorder (GAD). GAD is a troublesome disorder
of chronic autonomic (sympathetic) nervous system overarousal. The
autonomic nervous system is the part of our physical self that is most
directly related to our experiences of joy and anger, fear and sadness
(Miller and Jackson, 1995). Consistent strain and stress on the autonomic nervous system can seriously damage the immune system and
lead to any of a number of serious, even life-threatening diseases.
Suffering with GAD is like being flushed with regular injections of
adrenaline. Sooner or later the person is wasted—all available resources are spent. As medical doctors (and grandmothers) have been
wisely telling us for decades, "Rest or you will get sick." Persons with
GAD have no real sense of what it means to take a sabbatical or to
fully enjoy sabbath rest.

Persons who struggle with GAD tend to engage in apprehensive rumination and suffer from chronic muscular tension. They are always
worrying about what they perceive to be insurmountable threats in
their environment. Perhaps as much as 4 percent of the adult population of the United States experiences this disorder on a regular basis
(Comer, 2003). Women are twice as likely as men to be diagnosed,
perhaps reflective of sociocultural factors. Symptoms usually appear
first in childhood and adolescence, which suggests a developmental
pattern as well.

Phobias. Phobias are defined as persistent and unreasonable fears
of particular objects, activities or situations. When asked to confront
the feared stimulus, the phobic individual will experience intense
feelings of dread and worry as well as bodily symptoms of arousal of
the sympathetic nervous system (increased rates of respiration, perspiration, heart palpitations). *Phobia* comes from the Greek word for
fear, and scores of phobias have been identified throughout the centuries, including fear of spiders, flying, public speaking, heights, and
dating and intimate involvement. Persons who struggle with phobias
make every effort to avoid the objects, activities or situations that
make them feel uncomfortable. A phobia becomes a matter of clinical
or pastoral concern when it is especially intense, leads to an almost ir-
resistible desire to avoid the feared object or situation, or causes significant distress in daily functioning.

The available data would suggest that phobias are remarkably
common as well. Approximately 10 percent of the adult population

experiences phobias at least once annually, and 14 percent experience a phobia at some point in their lifetime (Comer, 2003). As with GAD, women are twice as likely as men to be diagnosed; it is unclear whether this reflects differing stressors or differing vulnerabilities. Symptoms usually first appear in childhood and tend to persist throughout the lifespan. The vast majority (90-plus percent) of persons who struggle with these symptoms do not seek help. Besides fears of specific objects or situations (e.g., animals, insects, heights, enclosed places or thunderstorms), "social phobias" are defined as severe, persistent or unreasonable fears of social or performance situations in which embarrassment might occur. Our conversations with Christian colleagues lead us to suspect that these are especially common in competitive environments that encourage a performance-based identity (Smedes, 1993). In short, phobias are disproportionate, disturbing and disabling (Meyer and Deitsch, 1996, p. 109).

Panic disorder. This disorder is evident in a person who (usually without warning) has a massive discharge of autonomic nervous system overarousal. Such "panic attacks" are periodic short bouts of striking affective and bodily discharge. For the sufferer, they are extremely distressing ("I thought I was going to die, go crazy or lose control"). It is possible for anyone to experience intense anxiety at a difficult and stressful time, but panic attacks tend to occur repeatedly, unexpectedly and without apparent reason. Persons who have experienced these bouts persistently worry afterward about a recurrence and what will happen if an attack comes when they are away from home and help is unavailable. For some this fear becomes so severe that they are unable or unwilling to leave home without a supportive friend or carefully formulated plan of action. When certain *DSM-IV-TR* diagnostic criteria are met, this is usually diagnosed as *agoraphobia*. Panic disorder is most often accompanied by agoraphobia.

Panic attacks usually develop in late adolescence or early adulthood. Approximately 2 percent of the adult population will experience a panic disorder in any given year. The gender differences (once again) are striking: women are twice as likely to be diagnosed as men. Panic disorder should not be confused with the hyperventilation syndrome that is quite common before a major competition or performance event. Panic attacks are intense but short lived, yet the sufferer does not always know (or believe) this to be the case. Hence there is a high probability that the person will increasingly restrict his or her activities. However, the prognosis for overcoming this problem is excellent when prompt and proper treatment is offered (Miller and Jackson, 1995, p. 254).

Obsessive-compulsive disorder (OCD). This disorder is widely recognized in the culture and frequently portrayed in the media in less than charitable or humane ways, as in some of the classic films of Woody Allen or the work of former San Francisco detective Monk in the weekly television drama. At least in our circles, it is quite common to hear persons who are perceived as rather uptight or rigid described as "anal," a pejorative term for the symptoms of OCD.

The actual disorder has two important components: obsessions and compulsions. Obsessions are persistent thoughts, ideas or impulses that seem to intrude into the person's consciousness on an almost continual basis. Compulsions are actions that the individual feels compelled to carry out in order to prevent or reduce anxiety. As with most stress and anxiety disorders, a diagnosis of OCD cannot be made unless the symptoms feel excessive or unreasonable, consume huge blocks of time, cause significant distress or interfere with the tasks of everyday life. Anxiety arises when the obsessions or compulsions are avoided or when the person is prevented from acting on his or her seemingly overwhelming urges.

About 2 percent of the adult population struggles with OCD in any given year. Interestingly enough, unlike most other anxiety and mood disorders, there are no gender differences in the occurrence of OCD. Technically it is possible to have OCD without both obsessions and compulsions, but this is rare. Compulsions seem most often to be attempts to help control obsessions, which can be deeply troubling, confusing or frightening.

Symptoms of OCD are often first noted in childhood or adolescence and usually reach full expression in early adulthood. The disorder is much more likely to occur in middle- or upper-class individuals, especially among those who are intelligent and greatly value achievement and efficiency (Meyer and Deitsch, 1996). How it might also be related to a religious worldview and lifestyle has been the topic of intense discussion for decades (Malony, 1995). It is not uncommon for a Christian clinician to learn that a client who struggles with OCD is deeply convinced that he or she has committed an unpardonable sin—often related to intense feelings about anger or sexuality (Yancey, 1997).

Acute stress disorder. How we respond to major events or trying circumstances can be highly idiosyncratic. Some things seem inherently stressful for almost all persons—for example, accidents, natural disaster, domestic or sexual violence, intense physical pain, exposure to abusive combat. Certainly, loss can be one of the pivotal experiences of life (Sittser, 1996). Other situations may be uncomfortable for many persons but in very different, even unique ways (cognitively, affectively, behaviorally or physically). "Much of what distresses, frightens, angers or worries people lies in their own interpretation of the situation," according to Miller and Jackson (1995, p. 251). In a very real sense, stress and anxiety are in the eye of the beholder: they reflect an interpretive grid or conceptual framework. Stress can play an important role in both psychological and physical disorders (see chapter eight, "Problems of Body and Mind"). The key issue appears to be how we cope and respond as well as how others react to disturbing or distressing events.

In the most widely used classification system available *(DSM-IV-TR)*, a distinction is made between *acute* and *posttraumatic* stress disorders. In both cases, the person has been exposed to a traumatic event (or events) and responded strongly. Significantly, these intense experiences of arousal and fear are set in motion by the hypothalamus, which activates both the autonomic nervous system and the endocrine system. Stress is not just "in your head." Both our "hardware" and "software" are programmed for a fight-or-flight response. We all differ widely in our general level of anxiety *(trait anxiety)* and our perceived sense of threat *(state anxiety)*. When we face difficult or painful situations, our responses may differ widely, ranging from potentially adaptive to clearly self-defeating. Stress can best be understood as a process that affects every aspect of personhood—mind, body and spirit.

With acute stress disorders the symptoms begin within four weeks of the event and last for less than a month; they are temporary. With PTSD, symptoms can begin at any time following the event and last for longer than one month. As was clearly evident in the United States after the events of 9/11, PTSD can develop from an acute stress disorder and lead to a host of medical and psychological complications.

In both acute and posttraumatic stress disorders, the precipitating event(s) most often involve(s) actual or threatened serious injury to self or others (e.g., terrorist actions). During and immediately after trauma, many people become highly anxious and depressed (Worden, 2002). Classic symptoms include reexperiencing the traumatic event(s) through flashbacks and nightmares, along with increased physiological arousal, reduced capacity to respond to external cues, obvious signs of distress and a pattern of avoidance.

These disorders have been observed throughout people's lifespan and across many cultures. In any given year, as many as 4 percent of the U.S. adult population may be affected, and about 8 percent of the same group at some point over the lifespan. It is assumed that women are more vulnerable and exposed to more traumatic events, since the ratio of women to men is twice as high for both disorders (cf. Van Leeuwen, 2002). Far less is known about how trauma affects children and adolescents (Worden, 1996).

Posttraumatic stress disorder (PTSD). PTSD is a delayed distress response to an atypical and significantly traumatic event, something negative and disturbing that would probably have overwhelmed most of us if we had been exposed to it (Meyer and Deitsch, 1996, p. 1117). Most of what we have learned about PTSD has come from work with soldiers or veterans who have been exposed to abusive combat or associated horrors of war. The imprint of that trauma comes to dominate how the individual organizes his or her way in the world (van der Kolk, 2002). Not only do sensory reminders of the trauma need to be tolerated in order for healing to occur, but the afflicted person must "physically experience efficacy and purpose in response to stimuli that once triggered feelings of helplessness and dependence" (van der Kolk, 2002, p. 381).

Data reported in Meyer and Deitsch (1996, p. 1117) suggest that the incidence of PTSD ranges from 34 to 78 percent in rape victims, from 3 to 37 percent in assault victims and from 15 to 31 percent in Vietnam vets. Ongoing research in the Middle East would suggest comparable rates for civilians in that troubled region of the world (1-9 percent depending on the location, race/ethnicity, gender or faith tradition). Overall, it has been estimated that as many as 20 percent of women and 8 percent of men will develop PTSD after direct exposure to significant trauma. The stress-diathesis understanding of mental illness seems especially relevant for shedding light on this form of suffering and pain.

For all the stress and anxiety disorders, it is essential to study closely the situational factors, cognitive frameworks, physical underpinnings, coping strategies and social consequences that can combine to lead to subjective distress.

ANTECEDENTS TO PROBLEMS OF ANXIETY

Frances and First observe:

Natural selection has favored those creatures that were blessed with the capacity to experience fear. Responding to danger well is probably the most basic of all survival skills. We humans have evolved as a fairly fearful species for the very simple reason that this has kept us alive in a pretty dangerous world. Any completely fearless individual does not make it for long in the hazardous environments our species must negotiate, whether jungle or corporate boardroom. The anxiety disorders represent the price we pay for the gift of fear. People with anxiety disorders have fears that occur for no reason at all or the fears occur out of proportion to any realistic danger, as if the fear mechanism is poorly calibrated or has too quick a trigger. (1998, p. 79)

These authors, both psychiatrists and key players in the development of the *DSM-IV-TR* classification system, make an important point. As we consider the factors that seem implicated in the etiology and maintenance of the six major stress and anxiety disorders, it may be helpful to see them as "the price we pay for the gift of fear." The great mystery is, why is "the fear mechanism [sometimes] poorly calibrated or has too quick a trigger"? As Carter and Golant note in *Helping Someone with Mental Illness* (1998), there is little debate that with stress and anxiety disorders, a normal, natural protective response in the body, our fight-or-flight response, is triggered by psychological or environmental factors that make a person feel extremely vulnerable. What is much harder to understand is why many different factors seem to be involved, how those factors interact and why there is much variability between individuals with the same diagnosis. A very similar combination of biological, psychosocial and/or sociocultural factors in different people do not necessarily lead to the same type of disorder. No responsible mental health professional would talk about PTSD or GAD as if they were unitary phenomena. As physicians are prone to say, it can be as important to know what type of person has the disease as what disease the person has. To that maxim we would add, and their sociocultural and interpersonal context as well.

Generalized anxiety disorder (GAD). The biological evidence is suggestive but not conclusive. With reference to GAD, contemporary research efforts focus primarily on family pedigree studies (genetics), the role of a specific neurotransmitter (NT) in regulating the normal fear reaction (gamma-aminobutyric acid or GABA), and potential problems in the feedback system of the brain and nervous system. When a blood relative has GAD, you have a greater risk of it. The benzodiazepine drugs (e.g., Valium, Xanax) appear to reduce anxiety, perhaps because GABA is released and inhibits neuron firing. Insult and injury to the brain or nervous system can significantly affect arousal and responsiveness to perceived threats to safety and security, leading to "poor calibration or too quick a trigger." From a biological perspective, it is probably safe to assume that there is at least one type of acquired or inherited vulnerability (stress-diathesis) that predisposes an individual for GAD.

Within the psychosocial model, theories about GAD abound. Perhaps the oldest theory, the psychodynamic one, sees GAD as a severe breakdown of the defense mechanisms, especially repression. More recently, humanistic thinkers have asserted that the symptoms of GAD reflect harsh self-standards or a lack of "unconditional positive regard" in the formative years. Research efforts, however, strongly suggest that maladaptive or dysfunctional thinking is at least a trigger if not a primary cause of GAD. Specifically, it is argued that people with GAD are prone to pay unusually close attention to social or situational cues that they perceive to be threatening. Further, these same persons are likely to hold many unrealistic ("irrational") beliefs about the world and have exaggerated expectations of danger. Changing these maladaptive assumptions by improving self-instruction or "self-talk" is assumed to be essential for dealing with the troublesome symptoms of GAD (Comer, 2003). We find the cognitive perspective compelling. There is also growing evidence to suggest that biological vulnerabilities, when coupled with cognitive aberrations, have a synergistic interactive effect (Meyer and Deitsch, 1996). In other words, our cognitive framework can significantly affect our bodily functioning, and vice versa.

With reference to the sociocultural model, GAD can develop as a direct result of exposure to aversive life circumstances. Repeated exposure to traumatic events has been demonstrated to be at least a trigger for GAD. Perhaps the strongest evidence for a risk factor for GAD is the incredible societal stress of poverty: rates of GAD are higher in lower socioeconomic-status groups. When poverty is coupled with chronic unemployment or impoverished educational resources, the strain can be overwhelming (Kozol, 1996). What seems less clear is why more "low-resourced" individuals do not have an exaggerated fight-or-flight response to threatening stimuli.

Phobias. Phobias have been the focus of intense study and research for decades. The accumulated evidence strongly suggests that phobias can best be understood from a biological-behavioral perspective (Meyer and Deitsch, 1996). It appears that there is a species-specific biological predisposition to develop certain fears. Specifically, certain objects or situations (e.g., snakes, heights) are potentially more dangerous than others. A heightened consciousness throughout the centuries left an imprint on human beings; that is, we are biologically predisposed to be afraid of certain objects or situations. The support for this theory would be the uneven incidence rates of the various phobias. It is far easier to avoid what we fear than to face it. Phobias, then, are the residuals of a fight-or-flight response gone awry.

More compelling to us is the behavioral explanation (psychosocial model), and this is supported by robust research (Comer, 2003). Behaviorists assume that phobias develop through avoidance conditioning. The fears are modeled by others, observed, imitated and strongly reinforced through avoidance of the feared object or situation. As any careful observer can confirm, fears also tend to generalize to other objects and situations (Miller and Jackson, 1995). Phobias "work" because they push painful things out of consciousness and are highly reinforcing due to avoidance conditioning (or the "support" of well-meaning family and friends). More than for any other type of stress and anxiety disorder, treatment protocols are widely available (Jongsma and Peterson, 1995) and are usually remarkably effective, further suggesting the biological-behavioral basis for this group of disorders.

Panic disorder. The etiology and maintenance of panic disorder appear to be a synergistic combination of biological and cognitive factors (Francis and First, 1998). In the biological model, the culprit appears to be a neurotransmitter called norepinephrine that is irregular in persons who have frequent panic attacks. Certain antidepressant medications can help the vast majority of persons who have regular panic attacks; 40 to 60 percent recover markedly or fully. These medications appear to act on a specific location in the brain, the locus cereleus, where norepinephrine is especially active. How exactly the neurotransmitter affects the "hardware" (neuroanatomy) or "software" (neurochemistry) is not understood. There is also some suggestive evidence from family pedigree studies that there may be a modest genetic predisposition for developing a panic disorder (Comer, 2003).

As with GAD, some rather impressive data would suggest that the psychosocial model is helpful as well. Cognitive theorists argue that persons who are prone to panic attacks have an all too predictable tendency to misinterpret bodily events or situational cues (Miller and Jackson, 1995). In other words, those who struggle with agoraphobia or panic attacks tend to be overly sensitive to certain bodily sensations (e.g., the symptoms of autonomic nervous system arousal) and misinterpret them as signs of an impending medical catastrophe. As Carter and Golant sensitively note, "It [is] almost like sensory overload. . . . You can have one panic attack in your life and the rest of your life be haunted by it" (1998, p. 161). Statistically speaking, panic attacks are much more likely to occur at times of significant change, loss or transition, further suggesting a sense of heightened awareness and consciousness.

Perhaps this is where the sociocultural model can be helpful. Lack of social support, poor coping skills, an unpredictable childhood and overly protective parents have all been associated with a greater risk of developing agoraphobia or panic attacks. Broadly speaking, an environment that is not safe, predictable or supportive can be toxic (McLemore, 2003).

Obsessive-compulsive disorder (OCD). OCD has been the focus of extensive research in recent decades. Once viewed primarily from a psychoanalytic perspective (fear of id impulses), it is largely viewed today as a synergistic combination of biological, cognitive and behavioral factors (Miller and Jackson, 1995). Perhaps the most exciting breakthrough discoveries have been in the biological realm.

There are two major biological theories. One stresses the role of the neurotransmitter serotonin. As with GAD and panic disorder, it appears that certain antidepressants reduce the symptoms of OCD for many sufferers, possibly suggesting some kind of causal relationship. The other theory focuses on two important regions of the brain: the orbital region of the frontal cortex and the caudate nucleus. At the risk of gross oversimplification, portions of the brain and nervous system are directly involved in conveying sensory information to our thoughts and actions. When these acquired or inherited vulnerabilities are coupled with stressors, OCD symptoms become a distinct possibility. Recent research suggests that serotonin plays a very active role in the operation of the orbital region and caudate nucleus and that low serotonin activity may trigger distressing obsessions or troublesome compulsions (Comer, 2003). Biology alone, however, cannot account for striking differences pastors or practitioners see in the specific content (obsessions) and behaviors (compulsions).

Both cognitive and behavioral perspectives (psychosocial model) offer keen insights into the etiology and maintenance of OCD. Through trial and error, certain actions become associated with a temporary reduction of fear and anxiety. Through avoidance conditioning, these associations become strong, compelling and highly reinforcing. The compulsions of OCD first occur randomly (accidentally) and in time become deeply ingrained through repetition and reinforcement.

The cognitive perspective has been even more helpful in identifying possible triggers of OCD symptoms (Scully et al., 1990). In brief, it is assumed that persons with OCD have a rather predictable tendency to blame themselves for normal (although repetitive and intrusive) thoughts and assume that dire consequences are inevitable. Interestingly, this theme was posited by Christian psychologists decades ago in regard to intense feelings of guilt and shame (e.g., Grounds, 1976; Haas, 1966). Since such feelings are extremely uncomfortable (ego dystonic), every effort is made to neutralize them through certain thoughts or actions. If a particular obsession or compulsion works, at least temporarily, it is readily incorporated into the coping repertoire. We find this explanation to be very compelling.

What is less clear is why only certain persons seem to develop the symptoms of OCD. Obviously, we all have certain thoughts we find obtrusive. And if you ask close family members or friends, they will probably tell you that you engage in certain rather predictable rituals. In contrast, persons who struggle with OCD are *far* more likely to be depressed. The research mentioned in chapter two illustrates that the biology of mood and anxiety disturbance can be strikingly similar. The truth of the matter is that it can be hard to determine if it is a predisposing or precipitating cause—or a perpetuating and reinforcing cause (see discussion of causal factors in chapter two). As both Haas (1966) and Grounds (1976) note, they tend to have extremely high standards of morality and conduct. They strongly believe that they should always have perfect control over *all* their thoughts and actions; they are often pejoratively called "control freaks." Further, they are deeply convinced that there is a direct link between all their troublesome thoughts and their chosen rituals, and that real harm will come to them (or others) if they are prevented from doing "what needs to be done." Obviously, this is a vicious, self-defeating script by which to live one's life.

Acute stress disorder. Any extraordinary trauma can cause a stress disorder. But the event alone cannot explain why some people develop an acute stress disorder and others do not. The best work we have available (e.g., Worden, 1996; 2002) suggests once again that the roots lie in a synergistic combination of biological, psychosocial and sociocultural factors.

Clearly, trauma can be a serious insult and injury to the brain and nervous system. It is now possible to state scientifically that life events can *directly* affect brain-behavior relationships. Specifically, levels of norepinephrine (a neurotransmitter) and cortisol (a hormone) can change dramatically when there is significant insult and injury to one's sense of self. When there is a preexisting biological or genetic predisposition (acquired or inherited), exposure to abusive combat or domestic violence can lower the threshold of resistance and lead to the development of an acute stress disorder or PTSD (cf. Van Leeuwen, 2002). Nobody is infinitely resilient when it comes to serious changes, losses and transitions (McLemore, 1984).

Psychosocially, our premorbid history (what we were like before exposure to the trauma) seems especially important. Without a good repertoire of coping skills, a strong support system and sense of meaning and purpose in life, we are at far greater risk for developing problems in living (Pargament, 1997). If there has been significant wear and tear on our sense of self in our formative years (e.g., domestic abuse and violence, chronic mental illness in the home, ongoing marital or familial discord), we just do not cope as well, either on a daily basis or after exposure to trauma. Generally speaking, how our worldview and lifestyle are actually fleshed out in everyday living will be a powerful predictor of our hardiness and resiliency when horrific things happen to us or to our loved ones (Malony, 1995).

Posttraumatic stress disorder (PTSD). Much of what has been said about the etiology of acute stress disorders from both a biological and psychosocial perspective is equally valid with PTSD. Again, the key difference between the disorders is the intensity, duration and frequency of the symptoms. With PTSD, the internal and external stressors tend to be even more intense and overwhelming. Clearly, acquired or inherited vulnerabilities are involved. As Worden (1996; 2002) has clearly demonstrated, however, how we respond to the hurting person—and how they respond to us—is predictive of potential recovery from trauma (or maintenance of the symptoms).

Without a doubt, it seems helpful to be able to talk through the traumatic event in the presence of supportive and understanding persons, especially if they have gone through similar experiences (Miller and Jackson, 1995). In addition, sufferers need desensitizing and tension-reducing strategies so they can learn to tolerate sensory reminders of the event and find ways to *physically* experience a sense of efficacy, meaning, and social support (van der Kolk, 2002). Perhaps most important, however, is the need to have someone who will seriously listen to them and offer acceptance and understanding (McLemore, 1984). Unfortunately, such persons are hard to find, so it is not surprising that those struggling with PTSD often are convinced that telling the truth would prove more costly than pretending. Such disengagement is a significant risk factor in the maintenance of the symptoms of PTSD.

TREATMENT OF PROBLEMS OF ANXIETY

As academicians and clinicians, we are greatly encouraged by the development of evidence-based treatment strategies for stress and anxiety disorders. Although the field still tends to be driven more by theory than by outcome research (cf. Nathan and Gorman, 1998), things are changing—and we think for the better. This assumes, of course, that sufficient time is taken to carefully define the problem(s), determine what might be causing it and what if anything needs to be done about it (Miller and Jackson, 1995, p. 251).

Before we turn to the specific disorders, a number of caveats are required. First, we think it is essential that a pastor or nonmedical practitioner maintain a strong, collaborative relationship with a physician. Except possibly in the case of phobias or acute stress disorder, a referral to a physician for a medication consultation seems imperative for anyone who is suffering intense anxiety. This does not imply a reductionistic assumption that all problems of anxiety are biologically based. Rather, it expresses respect for what it means to be "fearfully and wonderfully made." The right medication at the right dosage level can be a godsend (Carter and Golant, 1998).

Rightly viewed, medication should be seen as an adjunct or aid to treatment, but it is rarely a complete treatment in and of itself (recall chapter four's discussion of Viagra as the "solution" to problems of intimacy in our culture). Responsible physicians, pastors and mental health professionals know that there is seldom a quick fix for problems in living, especially when it comes to stress and anxiety disorders. As we will see shortly, the "best practice guidelines" almost always combine medication and psychotherapeutic intervention. To insist rigidly on an extreme "nature" (medication only) or "nurture" (therapy only) position seems naive, and even potentially life threatening, in light of what is known about effective treatment strategies.

Likewise, it is imperative to stay current with the literature. The field is changing rapidly. The proliferation of medications for the treatment of mental health concerns is nothing short of incredible. Without regular consultation and continuing education, there is potential to do much harm. Monitoring side effects and communicating clearly with one's health care provider is essential. With reference to the psychotherapeutic literature, this is equally important. A "one size fits all" mentality when it comes to treatment is simply irresponsible. The proper stance for the Christian pastor or practitioner, we believe, is *responsible eclecticism,* that is, a willingness to carefully examine all available evidence in light of a thoughtful Christian worldview.

Finally, there must be a commitment to lifelong personal and professional development. Change agents not only are competent and compassionate people, but they are men and women of substance and depth of character. They are able to forge a therapeutic relationship, can instill a sense of hope, have adequate knowledge of technique, and are deeply respectful of contextual and situational variables (cf. Jones and Butman, 1991, chaps. 15, 26). Human beings are infinitely complex, and a cookie-cutter approach to treatment could produce cruel and unusual punishment, or at least would be terribly naive and misguided.

Generalized anxiety disorder. The emerging consensus on the treatment of GAD is that the best strategy is to combine cognitive-behavioral therapy with medication and relaxation training (Nathan and Gorman, 1998). Benzodiazepine (Valium, Xanax) or azaspirones (Buspar) are usually recommended, because they seem to target the inactivity of GABA and other key neurotransmitters that mediate the fear reaction (see previous section on etiology). Barbiturates (sedative-hypnotic drugs) are not usually recommended, although they were used widely before the 1950s.

Since the symptoms are extremely uncomfortable, it is quite possible for a sufferer to develop a substance-related disorder (see chapter seven) or engage in some form of self-medication or other addictive behavior.

If addictions are likely among GAD sufferers, what treatment is recommended to prevent them? In the realm of cognitive-behavioral strategies, efforts are made to explore assumptions and beliefs that underlie the interpretation of anxiety- or stress-producing events or situations and replace those with healthy, reality-based messages that will build confidence and a sense of efficacy (Jongsma and Peterson, 1995). In addition, considerable efforts are exerted in teaching relaxation techniques (e.g., imagery techniques, biofeedback and progressive muscle relaxation), healthy self-talk and effective communication skills. Such techniques are described for a professional audience in texts like Antony and Barlow, 2002; Barlow, 1993; and Meyer and Deitsch, 1996, and for a more general audience in Comer, 2003, and Miller and Jackson, 1995. Some of these strategies do not require professional direction and can readily be applied in lay or pastoral counseling settings or even used as self-help strategies (cf. Miller and Jackson, 1995). What makes treatment of GAD more complicated than treatment of some other problems of anxiety is that there is no specific object of fear to address either in vivo or through one's imagination. Free-floating anxiety may simply reflect the human condition, and this can be addressed in treatment.

Whenever possible, persons struggling with GAD should be carefully assessed by both a physician, to explore any need for medication, and a competent mental health professional knowledgeable about cognitive-behavioral strategies. Left untreated, these symptoms can become severely disabling and lead to other serious mental health concerns or medical complications from the effects of chronic autonomic overarousal (Comer 2003). Early detection and prompt treatment are absolutely essential.

Phobias. There is little debate about what needs to be done to effectively treat a phobia. The evidence is simply overwhelming that *exposure-based* procedures are the treatment of choice (Nathan and Gorman, 1998). These are behavioral techniques (e.g., systematic desensitization, flooding and modeling) that teach a person to eventually face his or her feared object or situation directly. Relaxation training is combined with one or more imagery techniques in a safe and supportive setting, followed by exposure to the actual (in vivo) environment or object to which the phobia is connected (cf. Corey and Corey, 2002). College students often learn about such procedures in their introductory course in psychology. Many of us use them informally to self-treat some of our troublesome habits or patterns of avoidance.

There are no widely prescribed medications used to treat phobias. As noted earlier, persons struggling with phobias rarely seek professional help. This is tragic, since exposure-based techniques are almost always effective if they are properly implemented. Like any life skill, they require lots of practice and a strong commitment to change. The pattern of avoidance conditioning can be so strong that change can seem impossible to sufferers, so they suffer in silence or laugh about it with their friends and confidants. This serves only to further reinforce the pattern of avoidance (called "secondary gain" by clinicians).

Less is known about the treatment of social phobia, a phenomenon that is increasingly on the rise in our competitive and fast-paced culture. In addition to using the exposure-based treatment strategies described above, it seems essential to teach important social and interactional skills (Antony and Barlow, 2002). An overwhelming social fear may reflect a significant lack of social skills. College professors who work closely with students are well acquainted with this phenomenon. They usually find that any lasting change requires coaching and a lot of modeling and reinforcement (Corey and Corey, 2002). In more severe cases, antianxiety drugs may be necessary to raise the threshold of fear tolerance (Carter and Golant, 1998). For those struggling with identity or intimacy issues, psychotherapy may be indicated until a strong enough sense of self emerges (Miller and Jackson, 1995).

Panic disorder. With panic disorder (with or without agoraphobia), the available research strongly suggests that both medication and psychotherapeutic interventions are necessary to bring about any lasting change (Nathan and Gorman, 1998). Antidepressant medications (especially selective serotonin reuptake inhibitors) or benzodiazepines (Xanax) are usually recommended (Meyer and Deitsch, 1996). The assumption is that they break the cycle of attack, anticipation and fear. They most likely act on the norepinephrine receptors in the locus cereleus region of the brain (see previous section). Comer (2003) reports that these medications bring at least some immediate relief for up to 80 percent of the clients studied, and that 40 to 60 percent recover markedly or fully—impressive data indeed!

Unfortunately, the symptoms tend to return for most persons when they stop taking the medications. Consequently, much work is being done to teach cognitive-behavioral skills to panic-disorder sufferers. Efforts are geared toward reducing a person's responsiveness to internal and external stressors (diathesis-stress perspective). Clients are taught to more accurately interpret their bodily sensations, to which they tend to be overly sensitive. "Anxiety sensitivity" can reflect a limited repertoire of coping skills, a lack of social support or toxic relationships (McLemore, 2003). If they can get access to quality mental health services and the appropriate medication(s), there is a high probability of significant improvement. This most likely will involve finding more effective ways to self-calming, including cognitive, affective or behavioral strategies. Without a more comprehensive and holistic approach, relief of symptoms is highly unlikely (Barlow, 1993). The work of Pargament (1997) on the predictors of coping and adjustment—the importance of social support, sense of efficacy, sense of meaning and purpose—seems especially apropos.

The available evidence would suggest that cognitive-behavioral therapies are at least as helpful as antidepressant or antianxiety medications (Antony and Barlow, 2002, cf. articles on anxiety disorders). A combination can be synergistic for some persons (Meyer and Deitsch, 1996). Whatever strategies are eventually chosen (if any), the real challenge is to find ways to deal with a "fear mechanism that is poorly calibrated or has too quick a trigger" (Frances and First, 1998, p. 79).

Obsessive-compulsive disorder (OCD). Not surprisingly, the treatment of choice for the symptoms of OCD is cognitive-behavioral therapy involving exposure and ritual prevention methods combined with antidepressant medications, especially selective serotonin reuptake inhibitors, or SSRIs (Nathan and Gorman 1998). At an intuitive level at least, this makes a lot of sense. The link between thoughts (obsessions) and actions (compulsions) must be broken for any lasting change to occur.

In terms of the biology of OCD, serotonin, and the role it plays in the orbital region and the caudate nuclei, is the focus of intense research. Serotonin-based antidepressants like Anafranil, Prozac and Luvox appear to help 50 to 80 percent of those who struggle with the symptoms of OCD. It is wonderful that these medications are available to alleviate some of the suffering (Stapert, 1994). Along with our colleague Michael Boivin (2003), we believe it is fully possible to preserve a Christian view of persons amid the biopsychosocial revolution of contemporary mental health care (cf. the final section of this chapter).

In terms of psychotherapeutic interventions, several components seem to be involved in effective therapy (Miller and Jackson, 1995). Clients must be repeatedly exposed to anxiety-producing stimuli and be prevented from responding with compulsions. They need opportunities to observe credible role models who can teach them alternative coping strategies. Finally, they need to find effective ways to neutralize distressing thoughts and actions through healthy self-talk, relaxation techniques or rewarding behavioral options (Antony and Barlow, 2002, cf. chapters on various anxiety disorders). These strategies usually require extensive training and adequate supervision. Attempts to alleviate OCD symptoms on one's own (self-help) or in informal settings (e.g., lay counseling) are rarely effective (Meyer and Deitsch, 1996). Based on the available evidence, the first step in effective treatment is to get a medication consultation with a competent physician and then explore options for effective mental health care.

Acute stress disorder. There has been an explosion of theory-driven literature on trauma and recovery in recent years. Interest in that information seems especially keen since the events of September 11, 2001, besides the ongoing reports of terrorism, natural disasters, domestic violence, sexual exploitation and endless warfare. Our awareness of painful losses, difficult life transitions and unexpected changes is heightened when it affects persons we know and love.

Obviously, effective treatment depends on the nature of the trauma and the resources that are available to the affected individual(s). If the person has access to a competent physician, he or she might prescribe an antianxiety or antidepressant medication (Nathan and Gorman, 1998), at least as an interim solution. Perhaps even more important is access to a respected, knowledgeable and compassionate caregiver (Miller and Jackson, 1995), someone who is able to absorb some of the pain and is willing to be a supportive companion throughout the difficult and often perplexing sojourn of suffering (McLemore, 1984). Ideally, this person can eventually model, prompt, shape and reinforce good coping skills (Corey and Corey, 2002). In time, peer support, especially from peers who are struggling with similar changes, losses or transitions, is essential for healing and recovery (Comer, 2003).

Acute stress disorders test the depth and quality of the available communities (Bilezikian, 1997). We all differ in the degree to which we want to allow our pain to be public or kept private; however, there is little debate that some important human connections need to be made, if only to help in gaining perspective (Crabb, 1999). Loss is one of the pivotal experiences of life (Worden, 2002), and thus all us need to learn more about what it means to deal effectively with grief (Sittser, 1996).

Posttraumatic stress disorder (PTSD). PTSD goes beyond "normal" bereavement in terms of the intensity, duration and frequency of the symptoms. Decisive action usually needs to be taken (Nathan and Gorman, 1998); initially that may include antianxiety or antidepressant medication. The nature of trauma in PTSD is such that the brain and the nervous system and immune system can simply be overwhelmed by chronic overarousal (van der Kolk, 2002). It is now possible to say that severe trauma leaves a *subcortical imprint* (Worden, 2002). Not only does it seem essential to talk through the trauma, but the individual needs to *physically* experience efficacy, meaning and purpose, and social support. Medication may help with this.

Along with Worden (1996; 2002), we think it is helpful to differentiate between normal bereavement and pathological bereavement. The former involves fewer associated physical and mental disorders; generally this type of grief reaction or PTSD responds well to lay and professional intervention. In contrast, pathological bereavement tends to be much more treatment resistant and almost always requires work with practitioners who are highly skilled and well trained in grief counseling and grief therapy. We agree with Miller and Jackson (1995) that it is very difficult to find these types of practitioners. Examples of pathological bereavement include cases of men who have been exposed to abusive combat and women (or children) who have been repeatedly traumatized by abuse or violence (cf. Van Leeuwen, 2002).

Critical incident stress debriefing (Comer, 2003) is a community-based intervention that attempts to meet the physical and emotional needs of survivors ASAP. This form of crisis intervention is considered essential in order to normalize the distressing thoughts and feelings and actions that are often associated with stressful life events or crises. Many members of the New York City police and fire departments were trained in such intervention and knew well what it meant to be present in word and deed to the persons who were directly affected by the events of 9/11. As Worden (2002) has noted, relief workers who intervene in significant tragedies are often deeply affected by their work with hurting persons and may require supportive care themselves.

The available evidence on the effective treatment of PTSD strongly suggests that a variety of clinical interventions might be necessary, including individual, group or family therapy. Trauma affects entire families and communities, both directly and indirectly, and those effects are experienced cognitively, affectively and physically. There is a growing sense in this literature that beyond essential social support we all need to strengthen our self-help and coping skills. Clinicians call such preventive action *stress inoculation* (Miller and Jackson, 1995). The assumption behind stress inoculation is that we all need to be prepared for life's inevitable changes, losses and transitions. Our hardiness or resilience in the face of internal and external stressors is reflected in how we cope when tested by difficult circumstances (Sittser, 1996).

PREVENTION

Reading about stress and anxiety disorders can be pretty overwhelming in and of itself. GAD and OCD seem to be very deeply ingrained styles or patterns of coping. Acute and posttraumatic stress disorders raise both fears and concerns, especially about our own vulnerabilities or those of the ones we love the most (McLemore, 1984). Phobias and panic disorder sound all too familiar and can easily be understood as exaggerations of our fears and anxieties about dealing with the tasks of everyday living. We ask ourselves, What can be done to build more resourceful communities? How can we do a better job of teaching essential life skills? And how can we find competent and compassionate care providers whom we can trust and respect?

Mental health professionals increasingly recognize that most of the work they are doing is *remedial*, that is, treatment of problems after the fact. As noted in chapter four, the great bulk (98 percent) of the dollars spent on mental health care in the United States go to such remedial efforts, and only 2 percent is spent on prevention or education for responsible action (Kruse and Canning, 2002). This is poor stewardship and a waste of human potential, for example when persons become simply incapacitated by anxieties, fears or overwhelming stress. What might actually reduce the incidence and severity of stress and anxiety disorders?

Primary prevention. Primary prevention is something that can be done to improve anyone's physical or emotional well-being (Comer, 2003). Developing the kinds of communities that would do a better job of providing adequate housing, meaningful and gainful employment, access to competent providers of health care and human services, adequate nutrition, and sufficient opportunities for recreation and socialization would be a basic starting point (Kruse and Canning, 2002). Much more could be done to reduce obvious injustices in certain sectors of Western societies (cf. Wolterstorff, 1980). Oppressive life circumstances, especially poverty, are a significant factor in the etiology of maintenance of many stress and adjustment disorders.

The need for primary prevention is related to more effective educational programs. With reference to stress and anxiety disorders, myths and stereotypes abound throughout both religious and secular communities. These contribute to further marginalization and isolation for those who suffer, along with needless shame, guilt and embarrassment. The net result is what one colleague has called a "conspiracy of silence and superficiality" (McLemore, 1984) and mutual disengagement. We applaud the efforts of Carter and Golant (1998) and Francis and First (1998) to more widely distribute accurate and helpful information about the reality of mental illness. Each of us has had multiple opportunities to present similar information in church and community settings over the years. On nearly every occasion, people respond, "I never knew this."

Primary prevention also requires strengthening our social support systems (cf. Crabb, 1999) and the resources of the local church (Mouw, 2002). As Pargament (1997) has clearly demonstrated, social support is probably the single most important predictor of coping and adjustment. All of us need to have a clear sense that we are not alone (Miller and Jackson, 1995). Kauffmann (2000) has done of remarkable job of describing what this might mean for healthier communities and how that might help all of us to have a more proactive (preventative) mindset about seeking and receiving help. A work by McLemore, *Toxic Relationships and How to Change Them* (2003), can help construct such a primary prevention mindset, and it deserves a broad hearing.

We would all be wise to learn specific techniques of stress management. Especially relevant are the cognitive-behavioral strategies detailed in many books on personal adjustment (e.g., Corey and Corey, 2002). We all need to find more healthy, effective ways to deactivate overwhelming stimuli and neutralize distressing thoughts and feelings. It makes a huge difference whether we see ourselves as hopeless, helpless and powerless or able to act creatively, boldly and confidently, with a sense of efficacy.

Finally, consistent with the opening remarks of this chapter, it can be helpful to reflect on the meaning and significance of our symptoms. How we interpret or make sense of them is very important. There is a danger of being so focused on our overt symptoms (the "shoots") that we fail to pay sufficient attention to biological, psychosocial or sociocultural factors that might undergird them (the "roots"). Although we do not go as far as Peck (1978) or Weyerhauser (1980) on this matter, we do agree that we need to take time to reflect on the significance of the things that cause us much distress. This makes sense, because it reflects our appreciation for the other major predictor of coping and adjustment and sense of meaning and purpose (Pargament, 1997). We believe that a clearly articulated Christian worldview and a congruent and credible Christian lifestyle constitute a form of primary prevention. Reflection on our struggles can help us see what truly matters from the perspective of kingdom values.

Secondary prevention. Secondary prevention is generally understood in the field as identifying individuals or groups that are at risk for developing problems in living (Kruse and Canning, 2002). Obvious candidates would include virtually any person or group that is "low resourced" in terms of their living environment or their repertoire of coping skills—for example, the poor, the very young or elderly, the victims of social injustice, or those facing chronic health concerns. Less obvious are individuals facing major life changes, losses or transitions (Worden, 1996; 2002). Many of these persons could use concrete and specific help—not only more open and receptive communities but also essential coping skills and strategies.

We have seen wonderful examples of programs targeted to specific issues or concerns in a wide variety of community and church settings. For example:

- We are especially impressed with the work of Stephen Ministries (Miller and Jackson, 1995), a church-based program that pairs hurting persons with a well-trained and carefully supervised peer.

- Outreach Community Center in Carol Stream, Illinois, has become the largest private provider of human services in DuPage County, home to more than a million Chicagoland residents. This community-based agency specializes in early detection and intervention and is sponsored by a consortium of churches and businesses. It is intentionally located in the center of the largest concentration of poverty and ethnic diversity in the county.

- At Wheaton College in Illinois, the Center for Psychology and Church Collaboration has partnered mental health providers with churches and parachurch organizations around the globe (cf. links at <www.wheaton.edu>).

Finally, we are thrilled to see the growing number of self-help and advocacy groups throughout the United States and abroad (cf. Francis and First, 1998; Carter and Golant, 1998). Most of them have done important work in raising public awareness and providing supportive networks for those seeking help. Further, a bit of surfing the World

Wide Web (e.g., www.mentalhealth.com) reveals the Internet's potential for promoting greater public awareness and increased access to resources.

Tertiary prevention. Tertiary prevention is largely understood as efforts to assist individuals in getting the right kind of care as soon as possible or to reduce relapse or recidivism in those who have already sought treatment (Comer, 2003). Two crucial issues seemed to be involved. First of all, we need to be educated about treatment options so we can make informed recommendations and referrals (cf. Meyer and Deitsch, 1996). It is our hope and prayer that this book might be a modest contribution toward tertiary prevention. Second, it is essential to provide aftercare (follow-up) when somebody is no longer in treatment, whether in a formal or informal context. Unless sufficient attention is paid to ways in which desired changes can be generalized to posttreatment settings for a sustained period, health and wholeness may remain elusive.

In our society considerable attention is paid to adequate follow-up for former prisoners and persons who have suffered addictions. Perhaps because the potential social consequences are not as obvious, this is rarely the case for persons who have struggled with stress and anxiety disorders. The quick-fix mindset of our culture has huge consequences socially, financially and morally: we have a collective pattern of "avoidant conditioning" and lack willingness to provide structures, support and supervision needed to bring about more lasting change.

People struggling with stress and anxiety symptoms would profit from regular checkups with a trusted provider (like an annual physical checkup or regular meeting with a priest or pastor), especially if the provider has skill in assessing progress toward stated goals. It's important to keep them connected with a strong support system, helping them to find greater meaning and purpose in their suffering and develop a greater sense of efficacy.

Finally, as believers, we need to embrace the ongoing challenge of "helping the church to become the church" (Malony, 1995). Responding to the "incarnational challenge" (Kauffmann, 2000) of fleshing out truth in word and deed in our communities and churches is clearly a biblical mandate. As we seek to imitate Christ in our work and relationships, we must always seek to see good in others, recognize the painful realities of their brokenness and offer realistic, biblical hope, even when everything seems to be falling apart in their world (Smedes, 1998).

INTEGRATIVE THEMES

There are a number of related integrative themes in our discussion of problems of anxiety: classification as a mental illness, the issue of disordered desires, and how problems of anxiety relate to sin and our fallen human condition.

Issues in classification. Symptoms of problems of anxiety can function as signs and symbols. We are all too quick to make judgments and intervene. Careful assessment requires a deep appreciation of the incredible complexity of expressions of fear gone awry. The amazing variability of symptoms within any given disorder (stress-diathesis perspective), as well as the striking differences in expression across cultures and contexts, ought to remind us that we ought not to try to make anyone fit into a neat diagnostic category. One of the ongoing challenges in pastoral and clinical work is to preserve the dignity and worth of every person we encounter, especially those who are seriously incapacitated by an overwhelming sense of fear and distress. We do those we are trying to help a tremendous disservice when we confuse the essence of the person with a diagnostic label. It is incredibly difficult to avoid the sin of "nothing-but-ism" (Malony, 1995), treating persons as objects or in a condescending and patronizing manner.

We appreciate the efforts of Peck (1978) and Weyerhauser (1980) to get us to look beyond the *DSM-IV-TR* criteria to the broader developmental, social or situational context in which a person's symptoms first become apparent. It is essential to think about what certain symptoms do to us—and for us—in our attempts to be both holy and whole (McLemore, 2003). If we are honest with ourselves, few of us can tolerate more than a little fear and anxiety in daily life. How we respond to a sense of stress and distress probably tells us something about the nature of our character and convictions and the qualities of the communities of which we are a part (Garber, 1996).

But we can go much too far with this kind of thinking. After years of working with persons whose fight-or-flight response has gone awry, we think it is naive and potentially harmful to try to imbue their struggles with *too much* meaning or significance (Stapert, 1994). We do not think that our Creator God wants us to suffer any more than is necessary. Granted, Scripture offers no promise of relief or explanation of suffering in this life, but we think it would be a gross injustice to withhold care that has proved effective until a sufferer can develop a greater measure of "holy indifference to suffering." The symptoms of stress and anxiety disorders should not be seen simply as "gifts" to build character or convictions.

Sin and psychopathology. Our biological vulnerability to psychopathologies reflects our fallen condition. So it is important for Christians to take the brain and nervous system seriously. With the possible exception of the phobias, all of the stress and anxiety disorders have been shown to be connected to biological vulnerabilities. These vulnerabilities rarely cause stress and anxiety disorders, but they can be huge risk factors. The hard work done in the recent decades on neurotransmitters and brain-behavior relationships suggests that there is a reasonable basis for a biological revolution in mental health care. We find the evidence of numerous acquired or inherited factors to be powerful and convincing.

Unfortunately, among Christians the immaterial dimensions of human personhood (e.g., spirit, self) have received a disproportionate amount of attention compared to neuroanatomy and neurochemistry, which have been largely neglected or ignored. Jones and Butman (1991) speak of the risks of offering a *disembodied* understanding of persons in working with troubled persons (i.e., a mind without a body). A disembodied view is especially unhelpful when thinking about persons struggling with stress and anxiety disorders. It is far more important to understand why the fear response is out of proportion to any realistic danger than to understand how an individual "feels." Responsible eclecticism would demand that we seek to understand why the fear mechanism is poorly calibrated or too quick to trigger in the first place (Francis and First, 1998, p. 79). Problems of anxiety are undoubtedly a biopsychosocial phenomenon.

We are most impressed with the power of psychotropic medications when they are properly administered and carefully monitored. There are certainly risks of inappropriate applications or premature intervention if careful assessment is not done. There are potential side effects and medical complications; there is no "perfect drug" for all persons and all needs. But when there is a good collaborative relationship between a patient and a doctor, and between the physician and provider of mental health services, the risks are reduced. Along with Boivin (2003), we do not believe God will be found in Prozac, or Prozac in God. But when medication is used judiciously and responsibly, it can make all the difference in the world for those who suffer needlessly and those who try to help them. Medication is often a necessary (but not always sufficient) prerequisite for healing and change with the problems of anxiety.

In addition to medications, it is increasingly clear that healthy relationships are imperative. Clinicians often remark that it "takes people to make people sick, and it takes people to make people well." Healthy relationships are foundational for mental health and spiritual well-being (Bilezikian, 1997). Sadly, it is quite rare for the persons we work with to tell us that they really feel connected in their church and community. Ideally, as Crabb (1999) has noted, the church should be the safest place on earth. But as readily becomes obvious to anyone who is deeply involved in the hard work of building and maintaining community, conflict and tension are inevitable (Kauffmann, 2000). How we respond to that painful reality can be very telling; it is easy to revert to a pattern of escape and disengagement. When covenants are broken on a regular basis—and few persons honor the promises they have made—far too many people begin to slip through the cracks. Yet Christians do not have a choice about being in community (Malony, 1995). Scripture calls us to love our brothers and sisters, including our enemies.

The theme of social networks runs throughout the literature on stress and anxiety disorders. Without social support, we just do not cope well. With it, we have the potential to be more resilient. Learning how to respond to "toxic" relationships (ones that are potentially harmful and damaging) is a most basic and essential life skill (McLemore, 2003). Learning how to face our fears and anxieties *together*—not just alone—can make all the difference in the world.

The sociocultural model has helped to prompt our thinking on this most important theme. That tradition encourages us to closely examine roles, communication patterns and our core values (Van Leeuwen, 2002). Our roles tend to define us and shape our worldview and lifestyle. Clearly, this relates to how we find meaning and purpose in life, one of three most powerful predictors of coping and adjustment in the literature (Pargament, 1997).

We admit that we are inclined to follow our theoretical preferences and personal assumptions when making judgments about the treatment of the stress and anxiety disorders. As was stated in chapter four, practicing clinicians tend to have a strong bias toward either biological or psychosocial explanations of psychopathology. Rarely do they (or we) pay sufficient attention to possible sociocultural or spiritual factors.

With reference to treatment of stress and anxiety disorders, what is indefensible is a reductionistic mindset (the sin of "nothing-but-ism"). Treatments that work reflect a deep appreciation for the interface between cognition, affect and behavior, as well as the biological and sociocultural foundations of behavior.

Even a cursory reading of the emerging literature on neuroanatomy and neurochemistry (brain behavior relationships) can give us a renewed understanding of the nature of persons. Neurotransmitters like GABA, norepinephrine and serotonin are fascinating entities and have deeply enriched our understanding of the biological bases of certain behaviors that were once even more confusing and bewildering. Further, knowing more about effects of abject poverty on coping has opened our hearts and our hands as we have traveled and served in low-resourced communities both here and abroad.

We are learning to read Scripture and science with a strong desire to develop more effective social support systems, expand and refine the repertoire of useful coping skills, and find a renewed sense of meaning and purpose in everyday work and relationships. It is our hope and prayer that Christian academicians, clinicians and researchers will be even more directly involved in not just reading and interpreting the available literature but contributing to it as well.

Our vision for shalom has been expanded by our study of stress and anxiety disorders ("until justice and mercy embrace"). Certainly we are vitally concerned about facing such important challenges as gender (Van Leeuwen, 2002) and racial reconciliation (Wolterstorff, 1980). Community-based interventions can be a most worthwhile investment of time, energy and resources. Work on prevention is good stewardship. Since stress and anxiety disorders are so costly (and so common), it makes sense to be more collaborative and proactive.

Our vision for the church would include the teaching of essential life skills (Malony, 1995). We agree with Kauffmann (2000) that the church is a greatly underutilized resource for healing and growth. The available evidence is that Christians are no better (or worse) at coping with the demands of everyday living (Grounds, 1976). Much has been written about the sense of meaning and purpose that faith can imbue (Garber, 1996), and about how strong community has the power to heal (Bilezikian, 1997), and so little is written for discerning and thoughtful Christians committed to strengthening their existing social support systems. Unless beliefs are more directly linked with actions, the impact of any desired changes will be greatly limited (Miller and Jackson, 1995).

Within the context of good churches and communities, it is absolutely imperative for all of us to get more serious about managing the stressors of everyday living through better diet, exercise and rest. We need to see life as a marathon—not a series of hundred-yard dashes—and train and pace ourselves accordingly. It is not just our Christian worldview that needs to be developed if we are to face the challenges of everyday living, but our lifestyle choices as well.

An additional consideration. Realistic, biblical hope is critical for the Christian mental health professional working with clients struggling with problems of anxiety. For the writers of this book, perhaps one of our most important roles as professors is to help others find competent and compassionate caregivers. In a very real sense, we are gatekeepers to the often-confusing world of contemporary mental health care. Competence means knowing when people need to seek professional help and being aware of the resources and treatment options that are actually available.

Reviewing treatment outcome data, we are greatly encouraged by reported rates of improvement and even full recovery. Whether the issue is OCD or GAD, there is a reason to be hopeful. Obviously, no guarantee of healing and change can be offered; that depends on a host of interpersonal and situational variables.

But the thought of counseling and psychotherapy continues to remain troublesome for a significant number of committed Christians. Some of those concerns are very understandable, and others may reflect unrealistic fears. What encourages us, however, is that growing numbers of clinicians are learning research-based strategies and finding effective ways to use them in their actual work. Helping others find these practitioners can indeed be a gift.

God's good creation has been distorted and corrupted to the point that it is hard to even see clearly anymore. But central to our faith is the belief that things will not always be the way they are. We share with Smedes the hope for "global remolding":

> This is the hope of those of us who love this world, grief for its sins and sorrows, and have a stubborn faith that God can fix it. Rebuild it. Make it new—all of it. But especially the human part: our lives together, our lives with Him. We do not want the world to end. We hope for what the Bible calls Shalom, a grand word packed with every good thing that any human heart could want or need: Peace, Prosperity, Love. And joy, abounding joy. All

fairly distributed; a world remolded . . . made new, a world that will make God and His children happy again, yet the very same world He created. . . . What I hope for is a remaking of God's immensely lovely world. And in this hope, I, too, find a "great peace and a great joy." (1998, pp. 166-67)

The resurrection of Jesus is our guarantee that right will someday triumph over wrong and evil—and the painful effects of a fear response gone awry.

A CONCLUDING THOUGHT

Vernon Grounds, a Christian psychologist and longtime seminary president, once remarked: "People have problems. No statement is more trite than that, yet no statement is more tragically true" (1976, p. 17). Stress and anxiety disorders are especially painful reminders of those problems. Anxiety is indispensable to ensure survival, but it can be destructively malignant as well. Consider the parable of the talents (especially Matthew 25:24-25), where Jesus clearly states that anxiety and fear can squelch responsibility and choice and greatly inhibit useful activity.

Perhaps the greatest tragedy (at least from a faith perspective) of destructive anxiety is that it greatly reduces initiative and risk-taking and drains off much-needed courage. As Grounds notes, such a person "plays it safe and so fails to exploit [his] opportunities and develop [his] potential" (p. 22). We would add, that person is greatly limited in the capacity to enjoy God's creation forever, including the grace that is desperately needed.

RECOMMENDED READING

Carter, R., and Golant, S. M. (1998). *Helping someone with mental illness.* New York: Random House. The senior author of this book is former First Lady of the United States and a long-term advocate for mentally ill.

Francis, A., and First, M. (1998). *Your mental health.* New York: Scribner. This text offers helpful criteria for differentiating between normality and abnormality.

McMinn, M. (1996). *Making the best of stress: How life's hassles can form the fruit of the Spirit.* Downers Grove, IL: InterVarsity Press. A wonderfully helpful resource for spiritual growth, written by a very competent and compassionate psychologist who teaches at Wheaton College.

Miller, W., and Jackson, K. (1996). *Practical psychology for pastors* (2nd ed.). Englewood Cliffs, NJ: Prentice-Hall. The best single volume for cognitive behavioral strategies for applied ministry settings.

Pargament, K. (1997). *The psychology of religion for coping: Theory, research, practice.* New York: Guilford. The definitive work on the psychology of religion for coping and adjustment across a wide variety of health care and mental health concerns.

Smedes, L. (1998). *Standing on the promises: Keeping hope alive for a tomorrow we cannot control.* Nashville: Thomas Nelson. We know of no more helpful book on realistic, biblical hope.

REFERENCES

Antony, M., and Barlow, D. (Eds.). (2002). *Handbook of assessment and treatment planning for psychological disorders.* New York: Guilford.

Barlow, D. (Ed.). (1993). *Clinical handbook of psychological disorders* (2nd ed.). New York: Guilford.

Bilezikian, G. (1997). *Community 101: Reclaiming the church as a community of oneness.* Grand Rapids, MI: Zondervan.

Boivin, M. (2003). Finding God in Prozac or finding Prozac in God. *Christian Scholar's Review, 33*(1), 159-76.

Carter, R., and Golant, S. M. (1998). *Helping someone with mental illness.* New York: Random House.

Chave-Jones, M. (1995). Anxiety. In D. J. Atkinson, D. F. Field, A. Holmes and O. O'Donovan (Eds.), *New dictionary of Christian ethics and pastoral theology* (pp. 163-64). Downers Grove, IL: InterVarsity Press.

Clebsch, W. A., and Jaekle, C. R. (1964). *Pastoral care in historical perspective.* New York: Harper & Row.

Comer, R. (2003). *Abnormal psychology* (5th ed.). New York: Worth.

Corey, G., and Corey, M. (2002). *I never knew I had a choice* (7th ed.). Pacific Grove, CA: Brooks/Cole.

Crabb, L. (1999). *The safest place on earth.* Nashville: Word.

Frances, A., and First, M. (1998). *Your mental health: A layman's guide to the psychiatrist's Bible.* New York: Scribner.

Garber, S. (1996). *The fabric of faithfulness: Weaving together beliefs and behaviors during the university years.* Downers Grove, IL: InterVarsity Press.

Grounds, V. (1976). *Emotional problems and the gospel.* Grand Rapids, MI: Zondervan.

Haas, H. (1966). *The Christian encounters mental illness.* St. Louis: Concordia.

Jones, S., and Butman, R. (1991). *Modern psychotherapies: A comprehensive Christian appraisal.* Downers Grove, IL: InterVarsity Press.

Jongsma, A., and Peterson, M. (1995). *The complete psychotherapy treatment planner.* New York: Wiley-Interscience.

Kauffmann, D. (2000). *My faith's OK: Reflections in psychology and religion.* Goshen, IN: Goshen College Bookstore.

Kozol, J. (1995). *Amazing grace: The lives of children and the conscience of a nation.* New York: HarperCollins.

Kruse, S., and Canning, S. (2002). Practitioner's perceptions of the vocational rewards in work with underserved groups: Implications for "rightsizing" the psychology workforce. *Professional Psychology: Research and Practice, 22*(1), 1-7.

Malony, N. (1995). *The psychology of religion for ministry.* New York: Paulist.

Manning, B. (1994). *Abba's child: The cry for intimate belonging.* Colorado Springs: NavPress.

McLemore, C. (1984). *Honest Christianity.* Philadelphia: Westminster Press.

McLemore, C. (2003). *Toxic relationships and how to change them.* New York: Wiley-Interscience.

McMinn, M. (1996). *Making the best of stress: How life's hassles can form the fruit of the Spirit.* Downers Grove, IL: InterVarsity Press.

Meyer, R., and Deitsch, S. (1996). *The clinician's handbook* (4th ed.). Boston: Allyn and Bacon.

Miller, W., and Jackson, K. (1995). *Practical psychology for pastors* (2nd ed.). Englewood Cliffs, NJ: Prentice-Hall.

Mouw, R. (2002). *The smell of the sawdust: What evangelicals can learn from their fundamentalist heritage.* Grand Rapids, MI: Eerdmans.

Nathan, P., and Gorman, J. (1998). *A guide to treatments that work.* New York: Oxford University Press.

Ortberg, J. (1997). *The life you've always wanted: Spiritual disciplines for ordinary people.* Grand Rapids, MI: Zondervan.

Pargament, K. (1997). *The psychology of religion and coping.* New York: Guilford.

Peck, M. S. (1978). *The road less traveled.* New York: Touchstone.

Rainwater, A. J. (1999). Anxiety. In D. G. Benner and P. C. Hill (Eds.), *Baker encyclopedia of psychology and counseling* (2nd ed.) (pp. 88-91). Grand Rapids, MI: Baker.

Scully, J., Bechtold, D., Bell, J., Dubovsky, S., Neligh, G., and Peterson, J. (1990). *Psychiatry* (2nd ed.). Malvern, PA: Harwal.

Smedes, L. (1993). *Shame and grace: Healing the shame we don't deserve.* New York: HarperCollins.

Smedes, L. (1998). *Standing on the promises: Keeping hope alive for a tomorrow we cannot control.* Nashville: Thomas Nelson.

Sittser, G. (1996). *A grace disguised: How the soul grows through loss.* Grand Rapids, MI: Zondervan.

Stapert, K. (1994). Will pharmacological Calvinism protect me? *Perspectives,* June/July, 9-10.

van der Kolk, B. (2002). Posttraumatic therapy in the age of neuroscience. *Psychoanalytic Dialogues, 12*(3), 381-92.

Van Leeuwen, M. (2002). *My brother's keeper.* Downers Grove, IL: InterVarsity Press.

Weyerhauser, W. (1980). Introductory essay. In N. Maloney (Ed.), *A Christian existential psychology* (pp. 1-12). Washington, DC: University Press of America.

Wolterstorff, N. (1980). *Until justice and mercy embrace.* Grand Rapids, MI: Eerdmans.

Worden, W. (1996). *Children and grief.* New York: Guilford.

Worden, W. (2002). *Grief counseling and grief therapy* (3rd ed.). New York: Springer.

Yancey, P. (1997). *What's so amazing about grace?* Grand Rapids, MI: Zondervan.

6

PROBLEMS OF MOOD

A college student in the midst of overwhelming depression wrote:

It is hard to describe the feeling of depression. Maybe the best explanation is to picture yourself as the captain of a ship, because that's what it was like for me. It was as though I was sinking, sinking, sinking, only there was no hole in my ship. I looked around and examined the hull, thinking, "Hmm, this is very interesting, because my boat looks fine. I'm taking pretty good care of it, keeping it clean and polished, and we've been cruising along fine until now. I must have hit something, an iceberg or something."

There's no ice though, and no hole in your hull. So quickly you examine whether or not water is coming over the side, something you hadn't noticed. But you're still only sinking very slowly, so you're not overly concerned. So slow is the sinking that it's barely perceptible. It's a little bit troublesome though, because you're accustomed to having everything just right on your ship. Not only does everything operate smoothly, but also you have a good-looking ship. People are always very impressed with how well you, as captain, are able to maintain your ship. "How do you find the time?" they ask. But there is trouble. Pretty soon it's like the *Titanic,* and you're sinking really fast. And it is terrifying.

It's terrifying because there is no explanation, and you're bailing the water over the edge as fast as you possibly can, but you can't keep up. You send the women and children into the lifeboats. Some of the most valued crew members are trying to help, but there really isn't much they can do. The anxiety and stress is so overwhelming. In your confusion, you can't even tell them what they can do to help. Then they try to help by telling you, "Come on, just patch up the hole and everything will be fine. You've just got to put your mind to it." Now you are crying, "I just don't know why the boat is sinking. If I knew I would do something about it. I just don't know why this is happening."

Finally, you tell them, "Save yourselves and leave me alone. It is my ship and there is nothing you can do to help, so just get into the lifeboats and row away from me." So, confused, they lower the last lifeboat into the crashing seas and row away. And as they leave you think maybe you would have liked to go with them, but it is too late now, and you're left alone, with your sinking ship, and only the sound of the waves as they break over the bow of the boat.

A year later, this same student wrote:

Zoloft was, for me, like putting a patch on the invisible hole in my boat. It was as though some greater boat expert, who knew more than I could ever hope to understand, came in a little Coast Guard boat and just fixed what was making my boat sink. I still don't know what was making my boat go down, but the repair is made. No, my ship will never look quite the same again, but it is still the same ship. It is not quite as pretty as it used to be, and we don't make such risky journeys as we once did, but my boat is much stronger now. And with the help of the Coast Guard, we've stayed afloat. I never really understand what that guy does when he comes buzzing by—I just know he's doing something important that keeps me above water.

I've decided that taking antidepression medication (Zoloft) without the help of therapy would be as productive as patching up the hole in my ship without doing the cleanup. It might not sink, but it wouldn't be worth anything. What good is a nondepressed person who has no capability to function in everyday life? But I function quite well now, and with the help of an anonymous crew, I think I'm doing just fine.

Depression has been recognized as a common problem for at least two thousand years (Collins, 1980). It has been called the "common cold of psychopathology," perhaps because it is so prevalent and we are all susceptible. Often called *melancholia* since the time of the Greeks and Romans, it is one of the two prominent symptoms of the mood disorders, the other being *mania,* a state of breathless euphoria and frenzied energy. Its effects can be no less devastating and debilitating. As Miller and Jackson (1995) have noted, we all struggle with painful feelings of sadness, grief or shifting moods, but persons who struggle with mood disorders (so diagnosed in light of the intensity, duration or frequency of their symptoms) can be truly impaired or even totally incapacitated. More than with any other group of disorders, the risk of suicide is greatly increased, so these can be life-threatening conditions that require immediate and intensive professional treatment.

Millions of persons struggle with serious mood disorders in the United States at any given time. Apart from the pain and suffering caused to these individuals and their loved ones, the impact on the nation's economy is enormous, perhaps in excess of $40 billion (Comer, 2003). As we will see in this chapter, mood disorders are not only common but often complicated conditions than can be difficult to assess and challenging to treat. In light of the available theory and research, compelling arguments can be made for a biopsychosocial or diathesis-stress perspective.

THEMES IN PASTORAL CARE

Grief, loss and suffering are prominent themes in Scripture. Powerful psalms such as 69, 88 and 102 express the pervasive nature of despair. Realistic, biblical hope is often contrasted with the overwhelming sense of abandonment and intense suffering. Some of the great figures in Scripture, such as Job, Moses, Jonah, Peter, Jeremiah and Elijah, candidly and poignantly reveal their inner agonies and struggles. It might even be said that the whole nation of Israel was well acquainted with depression throughout the wilderness wanderings or in the periods of prolonged captivity. As Yancey (1988) has noted, depression prompts difficult questions: Is God unfair? Is God silent? Is God hidden?

Sensitive observers throughout the centuries have noticed the incredible realism that characterizes the Bible. Consider the words of Jesus in Gethsemane, "My soul is overwhelmed with sorrow to the point of death" (Mt 26:38), or the Lamentations of Jeremiah the prophet. Belief in God does not always bring relief of suffering (or an explanation), but only the promise of his presence in his time (Yancey, 1988). In the interim, our ongoing challenge is to continue to worship, fellowship and serve (Grounds, 1976).

In medieval times depression was sometimes viewed as a sin (Lastoria, 1999). In other contexts, depression and isolating behaviors were seen as reason to stir pastoral care providers to seek out the sufferers:

> Seek for that which is lost. Do not permit one who is despondent of salvation, on account of the enormity of guilt, utterly to perish. Search out those who have grown sleepy, drowsy, and sluggish, those who have lost touch with the value of their own lives. Look for those in a stupor, who dwell at greatest distance from others in the flock. These are most in danger of falling among the wolves, and being devoured by them. Bring these souls back by admonition. Exhort them to be watchful. Engender hope. (*Constitutions of the Holy Apostles,* quoted in Oden, 1987, p. 264)

Depression has often been associated with a "generalized sense of isolation" in which the sufferer feels that "God has forgotten or deserted" her or him; in fact, "the sufferer's own Christian faith comes into question" (Chave-Jones, 1995, p. 300). A downward spiral begins: "A sense of guilt also compounds the misery. Thus prayer becomes impossible and Bible reading meaningless by the very nature of the illness, not necessarily because of any spiritual failure" (ibid.).

Pargament (1997) has clearly demonstrated the importance of attending to the need for social support and finding a sense of meaning and purpose in the midst of distress and suffering. Unfortunately, persons struggling with serious mood disorders are not likely to initiate interpersonal connections or strive to develop a more coherent worldview. The more likely tendency is for the afflicted person to withdraw and disengage from the tasks of everyday living. Further, they often feel overwhelmed by a sense of helplessness and hopelessness rather than a sense of efficacy or control. As McLemore (2003) notes, they tend to move away from rather than toward people. And if the symptoms themselves make the unafflicted uncomfortable, there is the very real risk that they will disengage (Bilezikian, 1997).

There seems to be a growing recognition in pastoral circles that the ongoing challenge for being present to individuals struggling with serious mood disorders is to find the right context for treatment, be it lay or professional, and to make it available as soon as possible and for as long as necessary (Jones and Butman, 1991). Rarely do these problems respond to even well-meaning advice and counsel. Apart from the obvious distress and suffering, perhaps the greatest tragedy is that the symptoms of mood disorders can become major obstacles in the development of the gifts of members of the community of faith, thereby impeding the mission of the church (Kauffmann, 2000). Rates of depression and mania are no less common in church-based communities (Malony, 1995). The biblical mandate for good stewardship suggests that denial of the existence of the distasteful can prove very costly, but proactive and preventive responses are a good investment (Crabb, 1999).

THEMES FROM PSYCHOPATHOLOGY

Mood disorders are characterized by abnormal feelings of depression or euphoria (mania), with associated symptoms that can significantly affect physical, mental, emotional or even spiritual well-being. According to recent studies, about 5-10 percent of the U.S. population will experience severe depression in any given year (Comer, 2003). In the absence of significant mania, clinical levels of depression are usually called *unipolar* (depression alone). When there are significant cycles of euphoria as well, the condition is usually called a *cyclothymic* or *bipolar* disorder (i.e., the afflicted individual experiences the lows of depression and the highs of mania). Perhaps 1.5 percent of adults in the world suffer from some type of bipolar condition at any given time. Milder forms of depression (dysthymia) are also quite common (3-5 percent), suggesting that some 18 percent of the world's people will experience unipolar depression in their lifetime. Obviously, this means that few extended Christian families do not have at least one member who battles with some expression of an affective (mood) disorder on a regular basis.

Unipolar depression. In almost all cultures studied, the ratio of women to men with unipolar depression is two to one. Explanations for this striking difference range from biological vulnerabilities (nature) to socialization and stress (nurture). Van Leeuwen (2002) suggests that it also has to do with how our capacity for relatedness can go awry or become fundamentally misguided. From a Christian perspective, the biblical mandate for responsible dominion can be corrupted or distorted through the direct and indirect effects of the Fall. In contrast, the bipolar condition is equally common in men and women.

Depression tends to be transient (50 percent of those who experience it seem to recover within six weeks even without treatment). Although it is possible to have a single episode of unipolar depression, it is far more likely to recur.

There is simple mnemonic device, M SIG E CAPS, for recalling the major criteria for depression (Gregory, 1997). According to the *DSM-IV-TR*, for major depressive disorder, one of the key symptoms is either depressed mood or loss of interest. Then at least five of the symptoms below must be evident in the last two weeks:

M   mood depressed
S   sleep disturbance (insomnia or hypersomnia)
I   interest loss (nothing brings pleasure)
G   guilt (feelings of worthlessness)
E   energy depleted (fatigue)
C   concentration problems (indecisive)
A   appetite disturbance (weight gain or loss)
P   psychomotor change (retardation or agitation)
S   suicide preoccupation (thoughts of death)

There are emotional, motivational, behavioral, cognitive and physical symptoms of depression; it is a holistic phenomenon. Symptoms can vary considerably from person to person. As with most disorders, symptoms can also "wax and wane" for afflicted individuals, often depending on levels of perceived or situational stress. In contrast to the major depressive disorder (MDD), the *dysthymic disorder* is mild but chronic; that is, symptoms are longer lasting but less disabling. A dysthymic disorder can develop into MDD, as well as the not uncommon phenomenon of double depression, in which a person struggles with both MDD and dysthymia. Perhaps most important, it should be noted that there is a 6-15 percent risk of suicide for an individual who has severe depression.

Depression can rob individuals of their effectiveness and pleasure in life. The symptoms (M SIG E CAPS) tend to interact and reinforce each other. Emotional symptoms (feeling intensely sad and dejected) can feed into motivational symptoms (lack of drive and initiative). Behavioral symptoms (psychomotor slowing and lack of energy) can interface with cognitive (negative view of self) or somatic (physical ailments) symptoms. These reciprocal interactions can become vicious and extremely self-defeating patterns of coping. It is not surprising that family members can quickly become discouraged and frustrated.

Bipolar disorders. The bipolar condition tends to be more chronic and insidious than unipolar depression, ebbing and flowing with levels of personal and situational stress. The key signs of mania are racing and disorganized thoughts, extreme self-esteem, decreased need for sleep, distractibility and poor judgment. These are carefully delineated in the *DSM-IV-TR.* The milder form of the bipolar condition is called *cyclothymia,* which is characterized by multiple episodes of less disabling depression and euphoria (hypomania). *Cyclothymic disorder* also causes social or occupational distress as well as interpersonal turmoil (McLemore, 2003).

With the bipolar condition, women tend to experience more pronounced depressive than manic cycles. Age of onset varies between fifteen and forty-four, often triggered by traumatic or painful life events (diathesis-stress). Just as dysthymia can develop into full-blown unipolar depression, cyclothymia can develop into the more serious and potentially life-threatening bipolar disorder.

The contrast between depressive and manic symptoms in the bipolar disorder can be striking, with the shift often occurring within a relatively short period, even hours. Maniclike symptoms are perhaps less obvious to the layperson, since they may be of "adaptive" benefit in the building stages (such as a great burst of productivity during a student's finals week). But when sufferers become controlling, manipulative or exploitive, they are clearly destructive and self-defeating. A person who is perceived as "passionate and intense" or "quite the comedian" under normal circumstances may find their behavior socially sanctioned or reinforced. But true manic symptoms are rarely adaptive or effective coping strategies and seem to cause only suffering for afflicted persons and their family and friends.

A person in a state of true mania seems to be governed by dramatic, inappropriate and disproportionate elevations of euphoria, enthusiasm, hyperactivity, optimism and energy. Few of us can tolerate this state for very long without eventual collapse and exhaustion. How the manic individual can sustain it for such long periods is often a mystery to the uninitiated and unaware family member or friend.

ANTECEDENTS OF THE PROBLEMS OF MOOD

Unipolar depression. It should be said at the onset that depression is not a unitary phenomenon. Symptoms of unipolar depression can vary considerably from person to person, and a person can experience depression differently at different times in their life. Depressive symptoms tend to be transient: they can ebb and flow considerably or remit within weeks or months. At any given time, emotional or motivational symptoms may be prominent, while behavioral, cognitive or physical symptoms may be more obvious at other times. Few persons consistently fit a neat textbook profile. Expect variations and changes in presentation as the norm.

As with the anxiety and stress disorders, the biopsychosocial model of etiology and maintenance makes the most sense for problems of mood. Stress can be a significant trigger for depression (Hart, 1978). Historically, clinicians made a distinction between depression that seemed reactive (due to situational factors) and endogenous (due to internal factors). The available evidence today supports a more holistic understanding of mind and body, so that distinctions between these factors are potentially dualistic or reductionistic.

There does seem to be overwhelming evidence for an acquired or inherited diathesis for unipolar depression (McGrath, 1998). This seems especially true for those with an artistic temperament (Jamison, 1993). Family pedigree, twin and adoption studies are certainly suggestive (Antony and Barlow, 2002, cf. articles on mood disorders). For identical twins, the concordance rate for unipolar depression is 46 percent (20 percent for fraternal twins). More compelling is recent work on neurotransmitters and hormones—specifically the levels of serotonin and norepinephrine at the synapse sites—or abnormal levels of cortisol in the endocrine system (Comer, 2003). Nearly three decades of careful work with psychotropic medications like the selective serotonin reuptake inhibitors, or SSRIs, have transformed our understanding of the biological bases for unipolar depression (Meyer and Deitsch, 1996). Few responsible clinicians today would deny that there are usually biological foundations for problems of mood (Jongsma and Peterson, 1995). When these are coupled with the often self-destructive lifestyle choices we make, it is not surprising that the mood disorders are epidemic in Western industrialized societies (Peck, 1978).

Other organic variables that are often ignored or minimized include abuse of prescription drugs, over-the-counter medications or even illegal substances. Serious depressive symptoms can be direct results of poor choices about chemically controlling our mood states. In our drug-taking culture, far too often we look for the "perfect drug" (no risks and a lot of benefits). When substance abuse is coupled with an unhealthy diet or irregular eating patterns, mood states can be significantly altered. An irregular or nonexistent pattern of exercise, disturbance of normal sleep rhythms, reduced exposure to sunlight in winter or a sheer depletion of physical resources are all risk factors for mood disturbance.

There are many psychological theories about the etiology and maintenance of unipolar depression. Significant changes, losses or transitions can be factors. Grief, for example, often coexists with unipolar depression (Sittser, 1996). Without meaningful rituals, supportive family members or friends, or a sense of meaning and purpose in life, profound losses can incapacitate the griever (Worden, 2002). Those going through turmoil and transition are also vulnerable to mood disturbance. The college student, for example, must make lots of decisions in a challenging and not always supportive environment; the middle-aged adult must try to balance many competing demands with limited time and resources but may have few coping skills. Assuming full adult responsibilities and dealing effectively with life's major losses and transitions is an ongoing challenge for all of us, and especially for low-resourced individuals.

Cognitive factors have received a great deal of attention in the literature as well (Grayson and Meilman, 1992). Negative self-talk is almost always present in unipolar depression, as are irrational attitudes and beliefs (Barlow, 1993, cf. articles on mood disorders). Further, it is argued that depressed people are especially prone to errors in their thinking or automatic thoughts, and this contributes to their struggles with the demands of everyday living. When depressed, these persons are highly selective in their attention and memory and tend to develop an all-pervasive pessimistic mindset that can dramatically influence how they interpret specific life events (Miller and Jackson, 1995). The resulting rather predictable *attributional errors* reflect a tendency to see oneself, the world and the future in the least favorable light (McGrath, 1998).

As anyone knows who has tried to "reason" with a clinically depressed person, cognitive patterns can become increasingly rigid and impervious to logic. Lay and professionals alike thus readily assume that depression is *nothing but* these errors in thinking and self-assertion. Whether these are primary causes of unipolar depression or results of a synergistic combination of stressors and vulnerabilities is a matter of intense debate in the field (Nathan and Gorman, 1998).

Behavioral theorists add that depressed people tend to experience fewer rewards in everyday life: they exist on a "thin reinforcement schedule." *Learned helplessness* often occurs when depressed people no longer believe that they have any control over the reinforcements in their life, yet they are responsible for this sense of powerlessness they feel—so they just give up. Not surprisingly, when depressed persons have feelings of helplessness, they are likely to make other incorrect attributions about events *(it's always my fault)*. To use more religious language, they experience a *theology of extinction:* all attempts to assert or express themselves are experienced as abysmal, catastrophic failures (Smedes, 1993). Social support is often nonexistent, and a pattern of isolation and withdrawal only intensifies the dysmorphic mood state. Mutually satisfying interpersonal relationships are a dream rather than a reality for many depressed persons, especially those who fear intimacy and conflict (McLemore, 2003).

Sociocultural factors have been implicated in depression as well. Mood disturbance is assumed to be a universal phenomenon, but its expression may differ from culture to culture. In rural Honduras, for example, depression is likely to be reported as a physical rather than psychological condition. As the culture becomes more affluent and Western, the pattern tends to be reversed. Much has been written about how the complexities of roles for women in contemporary society may help explain some of the striking gender differences in incidence of depression (Van Leeuwen, 2002). Ageism, racism, sexism and socioeconomic injustices may also be triggers or *maintaining variables* in the vicious cycle that characterizes serious depression.

In short, unipolar depression seems to be an expression of many intertwined causes. Few clinicians or researchers would doubt the important role that biological factors play in the most severe forms of depression; an acquired or inherited vulnerability appears to be a major factor. Still, "biology is not destiny!" (Boivin, 2003). Without effective management of personal and situational stressors, the risk for expression is much greater. For individuals who are presumed to have diatheses, the healthy management of life events is critical. Effective treatment, be it self-help or professional, must be holistic, integrative and custom-tailored to the person's particular experience of depression.

The precise relationship between the many causal factors is not always clear, so single-causal attributions remain dangerous and unwise. Yet it appears that certain risk factors precede and predict depression (e.g., negative cognitions, life stress or self-dissatisfaction), whereas others seem to result from depression (e.g., impoverished social relationships, fewer reinforcements). Neurotransmitter levels may respond to cognitive, behavioral or emotional patterns, or vice versa. No doubt the absence of a vital faith and the lack of a supportive and challenging community can be risk factors as well.

Bipolar disorders. Many of that factors that cause unipolar depression are also relevant for our understanding of bipolar disorders. The major breakthroughs made in recent decades have been more biological than psychosocial or sociocultural (Jamison, 1993). It is assumed that significantly higher levels of norepinephrine at the synapse sites are related to mania. Indeed, drugs that reduce these levels (e.g., reserpine or lithium carbonate) appear to result in fewer manic symptoms. It was also assumed that high levels of serotonin contribute to mania. Recent research (Comer, 2003) suggests, however, that low levels of serotonin and norepinephrine may cause depressive symptoms, but a low level of serotonin and high level of norepinephrine lead to manic symptoms. When synapses fire too easily, mania may occur. If they resist firing, depression may result. In either case, neurotransmitters, the ions that carry messages between the synapses, have gone awry. The fact that lithium carbonate (a mineral salt) is quite effective in treating some of these symptoms suggests that there is probably some kind of "hardware" or "software" problem in brain-behavior connections, the exact nature of which is still largely a mystery.

In addition to findings regarding neurotransmitters and ions, there is some suggestive genetic data. If an identical twin develops bipolar disorder, there is a 40 percent chance his or her twin will develop it as well, compared to a 5 to 10 percent chance for fraternal twins. How specifically this reflects neuroanatomy (hardware) or neurochemistry (software) is still a matter of intense debate and study.

Apart from these important biological vulnerabilities, cognitive, emotional and behavioral factors are no doubt involved. In manic states, thinking responses are distorted in often dramatic ways; the affected person may evidence a marked sense of entitlement, grandiosity and an inflated sense of self. Affect is intense and exaggerated and often inappropriate and labile. Behavioral or situational cues are misinterpreted or ignored, which makes responsible and informed choices exceedingly difficult, if not impossible. Family members and friends are often confused, frightened and frustrated, not knowing how best to react or respond. Chaos often ensues since the person's beliefs and behaviors can appear to be widely inconsistent. Delusions,

false and persistent beliefs that are impervious to logic, can be prominent, reaching even psychotic proportions (the individual seems to
lose all contact with reality).

In the midst of all this craziness, the dignity and worth of the person remains. Kay Redfield Jamison, a professor of psychiatry at Johns
Hopkins University School of Medicine, has written a truly remarkable memoir, *An Unquiet Mind*, in which she describes her own recovery from manic-depressive illness. As has been noted for decades,
many artists struggle with serious mood disorders. Beyond the biological diatheses, be they inherited or otherwise acquired, they may
struggle with certain stressors peculiar to their chosen pursuits. The
so-called artistic temperament demands a cognitive-perceptual and
expressive style that is not widely known, appreciated or respected; research on this is not well developed at this time (see Yarhouse and
Turcic, 2003). This places an additional burden on vulnerable persons who may have a prophetic (nonconforming) vision and voice.
Think of religious leaders like John Calvin and Martin Luther who
were exemplars of risk-taking and critical insight in worlds that
stressed compliance and conformity. Perhaps in the extremes of the
mania or depression, such persons are actually unusually aware and
discerning, and their insights may have redeeming value.

TREATMENT OF THE PROBLEMS OF MOOD

When we interact with people in the midst of profound depression or
mania, it often becomes difficult to believe that their mood will ever
return to normal. Yet more than 60 percent of these persons can be
helped through a wide variety of lay and professional strategies.
Whether they recover spontaneously or through deliberate treatment, there is reason to be hopeful and encouraged. Both psychosocial and biological interventions abound for unipolar depression
(Antony and Barlow, 2002, cf. articles on mood disorders). Fewer
treatments, however, are available for bipolar disorders apart from
pharmacological management (e.g., lithium carbonate).

Unipolar depression. Seeking professional help for depression is becoming increasingly acceptable in our Western culture and in American churches. Health care and human service professionals are quite
aware of this "normalizing" trend and are far more knowledgeable
about the biopsychosocial bases for serious mood disorders than they
were even a decade ago. There is a growing consensus that depression needs to be treated holistically and in an interdisciplinary man-

ner. For well-resourced individuals (persons with good insurance policies), this usually includes a thorough medical evaluation and possible consideration of psychotropic medication(s).

The many antidepression medications available today have brought significant relief to countless persons struggling with unipolar depression. The earliest such medications included monoamine oxidase inhibitors or tricyclic antidepressants. Since the 1980s, practitioners have preferred the selective serotonin reuptake inhibitors (SSRIs), also called the second generation of antidepression medications (after the tricyclics). Prozac and Zoloft are some of the better-known SSRIs. They appear to act on the neurotransmitter (NT) serotonin. Newer medications target norepinephrine alone and serotonin and norepinephrine simultaneously (unipolar depression may be related to both NTs).

Electroconvulsive therapy (ECT) has been used for the most serious forms of clinical depression, especially those that are nonresponsive to psychotropic medications. This was and is still controversial, but it does seem to be effective with the majority of patients for whom it is indicated. It usually requires six to twelve sessions in a hospital setting, where it is carefully monitored for maximum safety and effectiveness. ECT is not without risks, but it has significantly improved the lives of many persons who were not responsive to less obtrusive procedures.

Virtually every type of verbal psychotherapy has been attempted with unipolar depression, including psychodynamic, cognitive-behavioral and humanistic-existential approaches (Jones and Butman, 1991). The available evidence (Carter and Golant, 1998; Jongsma and Peterson, 1995) strongly suggests that behavioral strategies are helpful for mild to moderate levels of depression and that cognitive and interpersonal approaches are valuable for persons with the full range of depressive symptoms (see also Antony and Barlow, 2002; cf. articles on mood disorders). More "dynamic" approaches seem relatively ineffective, perhaps because depressed clients are too passive or fatigued to fully engage the counseling relationship.

Cognitive approaches that directly target negative self-talk, irrational attitudes and beliefs, selective attention and memory, a pessimistic mindset, guilt over real or imagined wrongs, and shame about poor performance can match the rates of improvement seen with medication alone (50-60 percent). Interpersonal approaches that target deficits in communication skills and conflict management have also proved to been quite helpful for afflicted individuals (McLemore,

2003), especially those facing significant life changes and losses. In both cases, the focus is on teaching much-needed life skills or problem-solving strategies (Francis and First, 1998). Perhaps an expanded repertoire of coping skills gives the depressed individual a new sense of efficacy and hope, the belief that *what I do can make a difference in my life* (Corey and Corey, 2002).

Behavioral strategies focus on supporting depressed persons for healthy and adaptive (risk-taking) actions. The assumption is that it is more worthwhile to catch people doing something right than to focus on what they do wrong. As any wise and compassionate observer knows, it can be a real challenge to avoid exclusive support for depressed behavior (Nathan and Gorman, 1998). Behavioral strategies strive to help the afflicted person develop essential social skills and strengthen support systems. It is assumed that this will make it more reinforcing to engage others and stay active than to maintain avoidance and disengagement. Modeling effective ways to reinforce oneself for doing things right (responsible self-assertion and self-care) can help a struggling person escape the vicious cycle of depressive symptoms (Miller and Jackson, 1996).

Learning effective stress management or stress reduction techniques can also be important. Good psychoeducation may be seen as a type of stress-inoculation for the "common cold of psychopathology."

Recent research findings on *outcome-based treatments* (investigating what types of treatments work with what types of persons) suggest that multiple strategies work well for individuals struggling with unipolar depression. This is encouraging but not surprising, considering the complexity of the depressive experience. Cognitive, interpersonal and biological therapies, then, are all effective treatment approaches, and combinations of strategies may be especially effective for the full range of depressive symptoms (Scully et al., 1990).

Ancillary support for family members and friends may also be indicated, since depressive symptoms can have a dramatic impact on the sufferer's key relationships. Instruction in how best to react and respond not only helps the afflicted individual but the coping of loved ones as well (Lazarus and Lazarus, 1997). Sensitive and informed family members and friends can do a great deal to help preserve the dignity and worth of the distressed person (Schwartzberg, 2000).

Bipolar disorders. The roller coaster of emotions experienced by persons afflicted with a bipolar disorder can be difficult to observe and incredibly painful to endure. A colleague who recovered from that nightmare of an existence reports thus on the experience:

> The doctors always talked about me, not to me. They forgot that I was a real person and frequently ignored my complaints about side effects. I developed a mild case of Tardive Dyskinesia while taking Thorazine. I felt like a walking zombie as a result of taking so many strong medications for highs and lows. I was rarely taken seriously and constantly reminded of how seriously ill I was. Family and friends gave up on me—and I gave up on myself. I felt like I was trapped inside someone else's body and lost hope that anyone would ever hear my cries for help.
>
> After my ninth hospitalization, my doctor sent me to a clinic that specialized in the treatment of mood disorders. I was instructed to keep a daily mood chart so I could better understand the triggers and consequences of my emotional lability. My medications were greatly reduced, and I was stabilized with Lithium and Tegretol. The staff began to treat me like a vital, worthwhile human being. Eventually, I was discharged from the hospital—and to this day, I haven't had a serious relapse.
>
> But it took me years to rebuild my self-esteem—and it is something that I still have to work on daily. I still feel like I lost important years of my life when perhaps all I really needed was a medication change—and to be treated like a human being. My wish for you is that you do not place struggling persons in nice and neat little boxes so you can forget about who might be inside. Always try to see the worth and dignity of the affected person—and don't just try to fit them in a set of diagnostic criteria like the DSM. Most important, please remember that when a person has either a manic or depressive episode, they are probably far more aware than you might suspect. Actually, some might remember nearly every detail—and have to work through all the guilt and shame that they might feel.

Historically, it was assumed that precious little could be done to help persons struggling with bipolar disorders. If the resources were available, an extended hospitalization was often recommended, if only to stabilize the individual and to protect them from further injury or harm, including suicide. ECT was generally ineffective, and antidepressant medications often increased the risk of further manic symptoms (Maxmen and Ward, 1995).

Lithium therapy, the "gold standard" of treatment for bipolar disorders, has proven effective in the majority of cases for nearly half a century (Carson, Butcher and Mineka, 2002). The challenge with using lithium carbonate is to find the right dosage for the individual. If it is too low, there is no effect; if it is too high, it can be toxic (Jamison, 1995). When the drug is properly titrated for the affected individual, improvement can be striking for at least 60 percent of patients. Its effects on manic symptoms are most dramatic, but it appears to be effective for many of the depressive symptoms as well. The assumption is that lithium affects synaptic activity (not unlike the SSRIs), but that exact mechanism is still a mystery (Jamison, 2001). If lithium is ineffective, there are other treatment options, but none of them appear to be as generally efficacious as this amazing mineral salt (Sutker and Adams, 1993, cf. articles on mood disorders).

Still, much more needs to be done once the person is stabilized and the "peaks and valleys" are lessened. Ongoing compliance with the medication regimen can be a challenge; most afflicted persons tend to self-medicate depending on their mood state. Psychotherapy is needed to help them monitor their highs and lows and learn to identify the triggers and consequences. This is usually supplemented with cognitive-behavioral and interpersonal strategies to model, prompt, shape and reinforce more effective coping strategies (Jongsma and Peterson, 1995). As for any person who is easily overwhelmed by internal or situational stressors, developing a sense of efficacy *(I know what I need to do)* is absolutely imperative (Pargament, 1997). Since these skills can help strengthen their support system, they reduce the risk of further hospitalization. And as with unipolar depression, ancillary services to educate concerned family members and friends can do a great deal to normalize the mood swings and decrease the likelihood of further decompensation (Hood et al., 1996).

SUICIDE AND SUICIDE PREVENTION

Suicidal behavior has been a problem in our culture and throughout the world for centuries. In the United States, at least thirty thousand persons take their own life every year. Countless more make attempts that fortunately are not successful (this is usually called a "parasuicide"). Comer (2003) estimates that there are approximately twenty parasuicides for each death due to suicide. Obviously, suicide is a major health care crisis.

Suicidal behavior has been carefully studied for decades (Frederick, 1983). As one reads this literature, it becomes readily apparent that there are many common myths and stereotypes about suicide—for example, that only [fill in the blank] people commit suicide. Miller and Jackson note:

> In general, the risk of suicide is elevated for people who are in difficult situations, particularly if there seems to be no escape (such as chronic illness, financial ruin, or divorce), for those who have other problems that result in poor judgment (alcoholism or delusions), and for people who are depressed and severely self-critical. Elderly people are at highest risk of suicide, although there has been an upswing in suicides among those under the age of thirty. One of the highest risk indicators, however, is a previous attempt, particularly if it is a serious one. (1995, p. 237)

Meyer and Deitsch (1996) and Frederick (1983) offer especially helpful and detailed summaries of the available theory and research on the many risk factors that can trigger a suicide. We don't really understand, however, what moves a person from suicidal ideation to the actual attempt, and we have no foolproof criteria for determining whether someone is "really going to do it." Consequently, we should take any talk about life-threatening beliefs or behaviors very seriously.

Many of us fear that if we ask someone directly whether she wants to kill herself, we might increase the likelihood that she will try it. Actually, it appears that most who contemplate suicide are relieved to be asked; they usually are ambivalent and may have some strong thoughts and feelings on the matter that they would be willing to explore (Faiver, Eisengart and Colona, 2003). Depending on how they respond, it may be important to inquire whether they have a concrete plan or the means to carry it out. Immediate professional intervention (a suicide prevention center or a local hospital emergency room) may then be called for.

We recommend that all persons of faith have a contingency plan for preventing a suicide attempt. At a minimal level, this would probably mean not leaving the person alone until the right type of help can be found—better safe than sorry.

Frederick (1983, pp. 167-68) offers some wonderfully helpful steps for responding to someone in suicidal crisis. These are basic, essential and potentially life-saving actions.

1. Listen and hear.
2. Be sensitive to the relative seriousness of the thoughts and feelings.
3. Determine the intensity and severity of the emotional disturbance.
4. Take any suicidal complaint seriously.
5. Inquire directly about thoughts of suicide.
6. Do not be misled by comments that the emotional crisis is past.
7. Be affirmative and supportive.
8. Evaluate the resources available.
9. Act definitively.
10. Do not avoid asking for assistance and consultation.
11. Never demean or respond pejoratively to suicidal expressions.
12. Make a contract when appropriate.

It is beyond the scope of this book to offer more specific guidelines, but clearly some awareness of "psychological first aid" is imperative. We can all work harder on empathic listening, educate ourselves about risk factors, gather relevant information when we sense someone is contemplating suicide, and develop a contingency plan for responding to an emergency. We need to be aware of the resources that are available in our community, especially in local churches.

Many of us have already been grieved by suicides, and countless more will be affected in their lifetime. One bereaved colleague remarked,

> So many others have gone through the grief of a lost family member or friend. I call "civilians" those who don't understand this unique kind of death and loss, and "soldiers" those who have been through such a tragic kind of loss. To the soldiers, it feels like we have been through a war that is never "over"—so we can only try to carry on like faithful and loyal brothers and sisters.

There is a growing recognition that surviving family members and friends need help as well (Worden, 2002). Working through such a tragic loss requires special skills and sensitivities (Sittser, 1996) and unusual measures of grace, compassion and hope (Smedes, 1998). The value of social support and a sense of life's meaning and purpose at such a painful and difficult time cannot be underestimated (Hood et al., 1996).

PREVENTION OF PROBLEMS OF MOOD

What can be done to reduce the intensity, duration and frequency of affective symptoms in the culture at large and in the church in particular? Problems of mood reflect our vulnerabilities—acquired or inherited—and a synergistic combination of personal and situational stressors. Some of these factors can be controlled, others cannot. Not all of us have the same resources to draw on, and far too many persons live under limitations caused by social injustices and inequities (Wolterstorff, 1980). Mood disorders are one more painful reminder that we are living "after Eden" and this is not the way life is supposed to be (Grounds, 1976).

But much could be done. The patterns of mood disorders have been clearly delineated for decades. Unfortunately, our remedial or allopathic mindset ("don't fix it until it's broke") still hangs on. Mood disorders are treatable, but we need a vision for looking at the deeper "roots" and not just the "shoots" (symptoms). Apart from the things we can all do to improve our own mental health, are we willing to look at structures and systems that may be contributing to the problem? In other words, we want to envision the benefits of promoting shalom so that "justice and mercy can fully embrace" (Wolterstorff, 1980; Kruse and Canning, 2002). We want to find ways to build more resourceful communities, improve access to competent and compassionate providers of mental health services, and more effectively teach essential life skills (Corey and Corey, 2002).

Primary prevention. Primary prevention includes any efforts to improve the physical and emotional well-being of all persons. This might start with efforts to build communities that do a good job of providing adequate housing, offer meaningful and gainful employment, provide healthy nutrition, support lots of educational opportunities, and provide outlets for recreation and socialization across the lifespan. No perfect society exists in a world marred by the effects of the Fall, but we still need to dream about "what could yet be" (Smedes, 1998). Opportunities for healthy interactions in such contexts can be cost effective and contribute significantly to more effective coping (Manning, 1994; McLemore, 1984). No doubt, oppressive life circumstances are important risk factors (stressors) for those who are already vulnerable because of acquired or inherited diatheses.

But we also need to create communities that are more accepting of the painful reminders of our brokenness and humanity. Ben Patterson comments on this very factor in his recovery from depression:

Two things stand out in my mind as I battled with the depression and began to recover from it. Both were important in my recovery from that traumatic time. My counselor at the time was a very supportive, nurturing kind of man. Although I had taken enough counseling classes to know what he was doing—I just gave myself over to the counseling. What he did for me more than anything else was to give me permission to not have to be strong. He kept saying that it was okay to quit what I was doing, it was okay to fail, it was okay to fall down and cry. I didn't need to be the athlete, the leader, and the spiritual whatever I felt I had to be. It was okay to be weak.

The second important thing I remember was the acceptance of my friends. Not all of my friends, mind you. With some, the premise of our friendship was the integrity of my Christian life. When that began to wane, so did their friendship. Some of my friends' theology was very liberal and they had no problem with what I was doing, so I really liked to be with them. Since I've gotten back to my old self in many ways, though, these friends have also dropped away.

But one friend in particular stood by me during this difficult time. He loathed what I was doing, but there was no question that he loved me and that he was my friend. . . . His support and friendship was probably the single-most helpful thing in my recovery from depression. (in Hart 1978, pp. 161-62)

When it comes to unipolar depression, such *interpersonally mediated* experiences are vital for healing and recovery. We can only imagine what might happen if such connections were the norm rather than the exception in our fast-paced and increasingly self-absorbed society (Manning, 1994). Whatever could be done to improve our social networks would certainly be a wise and prudent investment.

Learning more about effective stress management techniques, and actually implementing them on a regular basis, would be another good investment. Helpful strategies include recognizing the cognitive patterns that precede and predict depression and those that seem to result from depression (Corey and Corey, 2002). Many of us harbor rather self-destructive attitudes and beliefs. From a faith perspective, we need to learn more about grace and experience forgiveness from God and those we have wronged (Smedes, 1993; Yancey, 1997). We need to act on what we believe and develop a more coherent (realistic) worldview (Garber, 1996). More fully realizing that life is full of losses and changes and finding better ways to face the fears so often associated with them (Sittser, 1996; Worden, 2002) seems foundational as well.

Finally, taking a closer look at our lifestyle and making changes as needed is another form of primary prevention. Mood disorders appear to be on the increase in both the church and the larger society and no doubt reflect some of the poor stewardship choices we make (Corey and Corey, 2002). We need to learn to recognize the cues of overarousal and choose healthy strategies to deactivate and avoid reliance on an adrenaline rush. If we have inherited or otherwise acquired a vulnerability to mood problems, we must find ways to reduce our dependence on self-medication (e.g., too much television or food) or other unhealthy forms of escape such as substance abuse.

Secondary prevention. By definition, secondary prevention seeks to identify individuals or groups who are at risk for developing mood disorders and intervene as soon as possible (Kruse and Canning, 2002). "Low-resourced" persons, especially those who are poor, friendless or feeling marginalized, need to understand (as do we) that mood symptoms are sometimes very understandable responses to difficult life circumstances or painful situational and developmental crises (Worden, 1996). Indeed, the historical emphasis on reactive or exogenous depression suggests as much. Imagine the strain on a new immigrant who has to learn new roles and new expectations. Imagine the college student who has never learned how to set realistic goals or use time wisely. Imagine the adult who is torn between caring for aging parents and finding sufficient time to care for his or her children (to say nothing about attending to his or her own needs).

In our own applied work, we have the privilege of participating in creative outreach programs that target often neglected or invisible populations of persons struggling with problems of mood. These programs are not limited to "talk therapy" but stress collaboration between providers and recipients of a variety of much-needed services—medical, legal, educational, social, therapeutic. Such diverse services can be synergistic, contributing to a greater sense of efficacy, purpose and social connectedness, all of which are known predictors of effective coping and adjustment (Pargament, 1997).

Tertiary prevention. Tertiary prevention is understood as the attempt to assist individuals in getting the right kind of care ASAP, or as any effort to reduce relapse or recidivism for those who have already sought treatment (Comer, 2003). Often this means educating the identified gatekeepers (e.g., pastors, teachers, mentors) of the community and encouraging them to make connections with specific programs and providers. Clinicians know how important advocacy can be; someone who is feeling helpless, hopeless and powerless needs to hear, "I believe in you, and I am wiling to help make the system work." Tertiary prevention may also include educating the gatekeepers about the latest research findings on treatment effectiveness. It may involve training in ways to improve compliance with prescribed medications and to report side effects so as to serve as a conduit of much-needed information between health care provider and client.

Since mood disorders tend to be of long duration, prevention should include periodic checkups with a trusted confidant. Not only can this help in assessing progress toward stated goals, but it might facilitate an immediate intervention if relapse or recidivism seems probable (e.g., if there are suicidal thoughts, interpersonal conflict, a pattern of withdrawal or social isolation). The need for careful follow-up seems obvious with former prisoners and those struggling with addictions, but it is no less necessary with the mood disorders. Our quick-fix mindset as a culture—reflected in the search for a formula for the "abundant life" in the church context—says more about the superficiality of our times than about how to meet the true, legitimate needs of hurting and broken persons.

Efforts toward prevention are an expression of what it means to incarnate truth in real life. As noted in both Kauffmann (2000) and Malony (1995) the church is a greatly underutilized resource for building more helpful (and therapeutic) community. As Jones and Butman (1991) remind us, we are to image the concerns of Christ in our work and relationships. Depression and mania are not always pretty, but facing up to the distasteful is an absolute biblical mandate (Wolterstorff, 1980) and the right thing to do.

INTEGRATIVE THEMES

To tie our discussion of problems of mood to the focal points of part one of this book, we need to consider their classification as a mental illness, the issue of disordered desires, and how problems of mood relate to sin and our fallen human condition.

Issues in classification. Depression is not a unitary phenomenon. Having told the very moving story of her recovery from a traumatic spinal cord injury, Joni Eareckson Tada writes:

Some of you that read this may be depressed. You need to realize that there are many different types of depression and many different reasons why people become depressed. Some of it is because of sin. Some of it has nothing to do with sin. Some of it is because of the chemical make-up of your body. Some of it is simply the Monday morning blues. I can't speak to depression as a whole, but I can speak about the depression that comes as a result of injury or illness or circumstances. I would encourage you to take up the advice of Paul when he said to weep with somebody else who can weep with you. You need to grieve, to cry, and perhaps even to express your anger to God. Better to get angry with Him then to walk away from Him. Give yourself time to sort through the emotions and to work through your feelings so you can begin to see your way through the insanity of your pain. Then share yourself with a small, intimate group of close friends. Allow them to minister to you in real and tangible ways. Then, with a group of friends, begin to reconstruct your faith from the pages of scripture. Let scripture be your light and especially your hope and comfort.

You also need to understand that your experiences of suffering are not out of keeping with the Christian life. . . . The writers of the New Testament make it abundantly clear that trials and tribulations are going to figure largely in what it means to grow in the grace and knowledge of the Lord. When we come to Christ, we don't have a guarantee that He is going to erase all our pain and problems. He does guarantee that He will see us through the middle of the pain and problems and the depression that comes as a natural result of facing those. . . . I think we need to be very clear that the cost of discipleship for some may mean the intimate fellowship of suffering. (in Hart, 1978, pp. 144-45)

Tada is an exemplar of a person seeking to make sense of what appears to be senseless suffering. Her candor is refreshing, and her insights are compelling.

What especially troubles us, however, is the assumption some make that the depressive experience can be easily generalized from one's own limited life experiences and exposure to the intense suffering of family members and friends. It can be tempting to use the *DSM* formulations (APA, 2000) formulaically, trying to make suffering persons fit some neat and tidy criteria. But as with the common cold, any of a number of "bacteria" and "viruses" can cause a mood disorder. Symptoms can wax and wane hourly, and relapse is quite common, especially in "flu season." Remember, depression is a biopsychosocial *process*, not just an *event*. The patterns that unfold may last for years and even decades. They are not easily fixed. Depression is a complex phenomenon, and we need to respect both its uniqueness and its complexity as we decide how best to respond.

Reductionistic tendencies are especially unhelpful when it comes to depression. Naive, simplistic formulations hardly do justice to the intense suffering that Joni Eareckson Tada describes in her moving narrative. It is not just sin or neurotransmitters or stress or negative self-talk or choice. It can be any or all of these and much more.

Pastoral care and disordered desires. One of the integrative challenges facing Christian mental health professionals lies in balancing the need to stand against suffering, injustice and evil with the awareness that there can be meaning in suffering.

Ben Patterson observes:

> Looking back over my own experiences with depression, I can see that I learned some lessons that will prepare me to deal more effectively with depression if and when it comes again. I would be willing to let go and let the depression come. I wouldn't try to fight it or ignore it or run away from it. I think my depression was worst when I was trying to fight it off. I think a lot of emotional problems I have had in my life have been intensified because I was afraid that if I really looked at them and let them come, they would devour me. When I was finally able to accept my depression as a part of life, it really helped me get over it.
>
> Now I think I'd say, here comes the depression—it's part of life, let it come. I would be quicker in yelling for help. I would cling to God and keep open the communication between us. I would ask my church and friends for help in very practical things—housecleaning, babysitting, and meals. I would not let pride dig us into a hole. In short, I would struggle to have some reference point outside myself. While we often talk about the centrifugal tendencies in a person's life, which split them apart, I think the opposite is just as bad—the tendency to turn everything in. That is depression with a capital "D." Whether it was the primary force of prayer, or the kind act of friends, or a

Beethoven symphony, these external reference points were critical in modifying the centripetal tendencies of my depression. I would work hard at developing and maintaining them in a future encounter.

Depression is by definition a movement away from growth. For many it is much more—it is a devastating experience, which can mark their lives with uncertainty and fear. I thank God that my depressions have been used by Him to move me in the direction of ultimate growth. (in Hart, 1978, p. 167)

We suspect that God ultimately cares more about what he can teach us through depression than about the ways depression can be relieved. This seems especially salient when people struggle with bouts of spiritual depression and questions about God's presence in their life. The "dark night of the soul" can be a particularly painful struggle with uncertainty about God's goodness and lovingkindness.

It can be so tempting to conclude that the presence of depressive or manic symptoms in someone's life reflects unfavorably on their Christian commitment. Yet depression should not cast doubt on one's faith. We can never know for sure what raw material a person brings into their experience of mood disturbance. Depression is seldom simply a willful act of disobedience. Mood disorders ultimately spring from the rift that sin has driven between Creator and creature (Grounds, 1976), but biological and sociocultural factors are usually the proximate causes. The spiritual world has an enormous influence on our day-to-day functioning, but the physical and social aspects of our existence are important as well (Jones and Butman, 1991). We are not disembodied spirits existing in a nonphysical world. We are called to be biblical realists and to see things for what they truly are. In the words of Smedes:

Our ultimate hope is not to escape a damned world, but that God's will shall be done in His redeemed world. We truly hope for the renewal of the earth only if we really wish for it. We actually hope for it only if we can imagine it. And we will hope for the renewal of our world only if we have reason to believe that God can and will make it happen. My own reason for believing that it will happen is God Himself, the God who "makes all things new." Believers are not optimists, they are people of hope. Their only reason for so huge a hope is the story of how the Maker of the world once came to His world, died, lived again, and still intends to come back and fix His world once and for good. (1998, p. 180)

In the interim, the problems of mood are yet one more painful reminder that we live in a broken, fallen and sinful world. They should awaken a deep yearning for something more than we can experience in this temporal existence (Ortberg, 1997). Meanwhile we are all imperfect image bearers, with widely differing vulnerabilities and stressors, so we should be exceedingly cautious about making any judgments about character, fully recognizing that we rarely have any clear sense of "the story behind the story" (Bilezikian, 1997). Those of us who are blessed to be "well resourced" with mental, emotional and physical well-being have a special responsibility to see things clearly and respond with compassion and understanding (Crabb, 1999).

While we believe that in most cases God's concern is less with symptom reduction than with what we can learn through experiences of depression, we do not wish to push the notion that great spiritual lessons can always be learned through our struggles with our fallenness and limitations. Yet there can be value in being "sadder but wiser." As long as we believe that we are masters of our life, pride is a serious issue (Kauffmann, 2000). Perhaps depression teaches that we are human *beings*, not human *doings*. Limits on our upward mobility can remind us of our utter dependence on God as the ultimate source of our strength and our need for the community of believers in the thick and thin of everyday existence (Hood et al., 1996). Perhaps only when we have experienced our painful limitations can we come to understand what it means to care for others and be cared for ourselves. For us as clinicians, our work with depressed individuals has greatly deepened our appreciation and awareness of God's steadfast love and faithfulness.

One lesson depression can teach us is that life is precious. Every day people kill themselves. Many of them are struggling with mood disorders. Far too many of us are "soldiers" and no longer "civilians"—we are the surviving family members and friends. Suicide is a national tragedy and an incredible waste of human talent. We would all be wise to become thoroughly familiar with the risk factors and have a contingency plan in place before our next encounter with a seriously distressed person.

Loss is one of the inevitable experiences of life, and it behooves all of us to learn more about what it means to do "good grief work"

(Worden, 2002). Our illusions about our own safety and security can be shattered dramatically when someone we know and care about takes their own life.

Learning to respond more effectively to a suicidal crisis may be part of what it means to confess Jesus Christ as Lord, seek after righteousness and love the brothers and sisters (Kauffmann, 2000). Making important information on "psychological first aid" available to the identified gatekeepers in our community is a most worthwhile investment: it can make the difference between life and death.

Not surprisingly, persons who contemplate taking their own life often lack adequate coping resources. They usually do not have a sense of being connected, nor do they feel efficacious or competent. Personal or situational stressors overwhelm them, and they feel extremely vulnerable. Helping them to find meaning and purpose and make life-affirming choices requires an exquisite sense of timing, tact and sensitivity (Haas, 1966).

Another lesson that is sometimes learned through struggles with problems of mood is that our worldview and lifestyle choices really matter. We find it fascinating that the nonpharmacological interventions that have proved to be most effective with mood disorders are the cognitive-behavioral and interpersonal approaches. This certainly calls for holistic and integrative care. What is needed is a balanced emphasis on thinking, feeling and behaving (cognitive-behavioral) and recognition of the importance of healthy relationships in the home and community (McLemore, 2003).

Self-defeating cognitive and behavioral patterns often speak loudly about our core values—what gets us up in the morning and keeps us going through the day (Garber, 1996). They force us to ask ourselves, *What do I truly love?* It ought to be more than money, sex or power. Clinicians who regularly work with mood-disordered persons know all too well how little attention people usually give to matters of meaning and purpose before their illusions are shattered.

Likewise with our decisions about how we really want to live (Corey and Corey, 2002): our choices need to be more deliberate and intentional. We need to reflect on the short-term and long-term consequences of how we think, feel and behave. Taking time to learn essential life skills and practicing them in our daily life is an expression of faithfulness (Smedes, 1998). We need to learn better ways to take care of ourselves in terms of body, mind and spirit (Kauffmann, 2000). Our gifts and talents cannot be used to accomplish the mission and task of the church if we are easily distracted by things that truly do not matter from the perspective of eternity. We need discipline and focus if we are to solve problems (Peck, 1978).

SIN AND PSYCHOPATHOLOGY

In part one of this book we discussed the many ways that sin can be understood in relation to the psychopathologies. Sin engenders a constant background noise within this fallen world and is reflected in the structures of society. But we are not left without help. For a person who suffers from mood disorders as one expression of the world's fallenness, psychotropic medications can help bring balance to neurotransmitters that are not functioning as they should.

A careful reading of the available evidence (e.g., Antony and Barlow, 2002) suggests that psychotropic medications are potent catalysts for change, even potentially life-saving (as was Zoloft in the account with which this chapter began). Both unipolar depression and bipolar disorders are difficult if not impossible to treat without chemical assistance. Although the exact reason for the effectiveness of psychotropic medications is not always understood, they often do work for even the most severe expressions of mood disorders.

These medications can, of course, be misused or abused. They can be treated as a substitute for the hard work of much-needed counseling or psychotherapy (Weyerhauser, 1980). They should be used carefully and responsibly and given only after careful assessment, ideally in an interdisciplinary fashion (Boivin, 2003).

On the one hand, there is the risk of expecting too much from medication, even personal transformation. On the other hand, there is the even more serious problem of avoiding medication or not even considering the option because of fear, ignorance or shame.

Mood disorders do respond well to the right type of medication and the best dosage. It is hard for us to understand how a mental health practitioner could proceed with a clear conscience without making this resource available when it could help. As compelling as the scientific research is, we are even more persuaded by the cumulative evidence of the stories told by afflicted persons who have been greatly helped by medication. Whether it is lithium carbonate for the bipolar disorder or an SSRI for unipolar depression, we believe these are good gifts from our Creator. Their proper use takes account of the biological bases of behavior and the important need of adjuncts or aids to more traditional forms of verbal therapy: they can open up conversation about the roots of one's suffering.

Christian mental health professionals should also take seriously sin in the structures of society. The problems of mood are far more prevalent among the poor and powerless. Most often in our culture we tend to assume within-the-person rather than external-to-the-person influences on human actions (Jones and Butman, 1991). This fundamental attributional error causes needless confusion and frustration. In our attempts to understand depression or mania, we rarely consider such factors as ageism, racism or sexism. Leibenluft (2001) warns us how naive and unhelpful this can be. Remember, for example, that women are twice as likely as men to be clinically depressed. The subtle, pervasive influence of socialization on gender roles and expectations can have profound implications for treatment and prevention (Van Leeuwen, 2002). Another example: throughout much of the developing world and even the most affluent societies there are many economically exploited farmworkers and persons who are involuntarily unemployed or underemployed (see Mt 26:38). If we take the stress-diathesis model of etiology and maintenance seriously, we need to consider the impact of such injustices (e.g., Kozol, 1995).

Several authors (e.g., Garber, 1996; Kauffmann, 2000; Paloutzian, 1996) argue convincingly that we need "immersion experiences" in (sustained exposure to) environments quite different from our own. Without some regular dissonance or disequilibrium, we tend to become too comfortable with the status quo and are little inclined to engage in altruistic activity. Dealing effectively with serious mood disturbance requires that we be willing to move beyond the safety and security of the familiar. It is not that we should stretch ourselves because it is "good for us," but cultural stretching helps us to see beyond the limitations of our biases and stereotypes. And without such regular exposure, we are not likely to develop a sufficiently complex Christian worldview to withstand the challenges of pluralism (Garber, 1996; Mouw, 2002). The authors of this book have chosen to do at least some of our work with under-served populations, and it often forces us to recognize how myopic and limited our understanding of a situational context has been (Kruse and Canning, 2002).

A CONCLUDING COMMENT

A prayer from the *Book of Common Prayer* expresses well our thoughts on how we ought to respond to the problems of mood:

O merciful Father, who hast taught us in the holy Word that
thou dost not willingly afflict or grieve the children of men: look
with pity on the sorrows of thy servant for whom our prayers are
offered. Remember him, O Lord, in mercy, nourish his soul
with patience, comfort him with a sense of thy goodness, lift up
thy countenance upon him, and give him peace; through Jesus
Christ our Lord. Amen. (1979, p. 831)

RECOMMENDED READING

Jamison, K. (1993). *Touched with fire: Manic-depressive illness and the artistic temperament.* New York: Simon & Schuster. This is a fascinating discussion by one of the most respected authorities on the bipolar condition. Kay Redfield Jamison has had a truly remarkable recovery herself. The narratives of gifted artists included here are powerful.

McGrath, E. (1998). *The complete idiot's guide to beating the blues.* New York: Simon & Schuster. Don't let the unfortunate title mislead you: this is one of the best self-help books on the market for dealing with mild to moderate levels of depression.

McLemore, C. (2003). *Toxic relationships and how to change them: Health and holiness in everyday life.* New York: Wiley-Interscience. Given the importance of healthy relationships for the prevention and treatment of mood disturbance, this book should be required reading for lay and professional audiences alike. Written from a robust faith perspective and full of wisdom and keen insights.

Pargament, K. (1997). *The psychology of religion and coping: Theory, research, practice.* New York: Guilford. This is the definitive work on coping and adjustment from a faith perspective. It offers fascinating insights into our needs for social support, a sense of efficacy, and meaning and purpose in life.

REFERENCES

American Psychiatric Association. (2000). *Diagnostic and statistical manual of mental disorders* (4th ed.). Washington, DC: Author.

Antony, M., and Barlow, D. (Eds.). (2002). *Handbook of assessment and treatment planning for psychological disorders.* New York: Guilford.

Barlow, D. (Ed.). (1993). *Clinical handbook of psychological disorders* (2nd ed.). New York: Guilford.

Bilezikian, G. (1997). *Community 101: Reclaiming the church as a community of oneness.* Grand Rapids, MI: Zondervan.

Boivin, M. (2003). Finding God in Prozac or finding Prozac in God. *Christian Scholar's Review, 33*(1), 159-76.

Carson, R., Butcher, J., and Mineka, S. (2002). *Fundamentals of abnormal psychology and modern life.* Boston: Allyn and Bacon.

Carter, R., and Golant, S. M. (1998). *Helping someone with mental illness.* New York: Random House.

Chave-Jones, M. (1995). Depression. In D. J. Atkinson, D. F. Field, A. Holmes and O. O'Donovan (Eds.), *New dictionary of Christian ethics and pastoral theology* (pp. 299-301). Downers Grove, IL: InterVarsity Press.

Collins, G. (1980). *Christian counseling: A comprehensive guide.* Waco, TX: Word.

Comer, R. (2003). *Abnormal psychology* (5th ed.). New York: Worth.

Corey, G., and Corey, M. (2002). *I never knew I had a choice* (7th ed.). Pacific Grove, CA: Brooks/Cole.

Crabb, L. (1999). *The safest place on earth.* Nashville: Word.

Episcopal Church. (1979). *Book of common prayer.* Washington, DC: Author.

Faiver, C., Eisengart, S., and Colona, R. (2003). *The counselor intern's handbook* (3rd ed.). Belmont, CA: Thomson/Brooks/Cole.

Francis, A., and First, M. (1998). *Your mental health: A layman's guide to the psychiatrist's Bible.* New York: Scribner.

Frederick, C. (1983). Suicide prevention procedures. In P. A. Kelly and L. G. Kitt (Eds.), *Innovations in clinical practice: A sourcebook* (2:161-73). Sarasota, FL: Professional Resource Exchange.

Garber, S. (1996). *The fabric of faithfulness: Weaving together beliefs and behavior during the university years.* Downers Grove, IL: InterVarsity Press.

Grayson, P., and Meilman, P. (1992). *Beating the college blues.* New York: Facts on File.

Grounds, V. (1976). *Emotional problems and the gospel.* Grand Rapids, MI: Zondervan.

Haas, H. (1966). *The Christian encounters mental illness.* St. Louis: Concordia.

Hart, A. (1978). *Depression: Coping and caring.* Arcadia, CA: Cope.

Hood, R., Spilka, B., Hunsberger, B., and Gorsuch, R. (1996). *The psychology of religion: An empirical approach* (2nd ed.). New York: Guilford.

Jamison, K. (1993). *Touched with fire: The manic-depressive illness and the artistic temperament.* New York: Simon & Schuster.

Jamison, K. (1995). *An unquiet mind.* New York: Vintage.

Jamison, K. (2001). Manic-depressive illness and creativity. In R. Comer (Ed.), *Scientific American: Psychology reader* (pp. 12-17). New York: Worth/Scientific American.

Jones, S., and Butman, R. (1991). *Modern psychotherapies: A comprehensive Christian appraisal.* Downers Grove, IL: InterVarsity Press.

Jongsma, A., and Peterson, M. (1995). *The complete psychotherapy treatment planner.* New York: Wiley-Interscience.

Kauffmann, D. (2000). *My faith's OK: Reflections in psychology and religion.* Goshen, IN: Goshen College Bookstore.

Korchin, S. (1976). *Modern clinical psychology.* New York: Basic Books.

Kozol, J. (1995). *Amazing grace: The lives of children and the conscience of a nation.* New York: HarperCollins.

Kruse, S., and Canning, S. (2002). Practitioner's perceptions of the vocational rewards in work with underserved groups: Implications for "rightsizing" the psychology workforce. *Professional Psychology: Research and Practice, 22*(1), 1-7.

Lazarus, A., and Lazarus, C. (1997). *The 60-second shrink: Over 100 strategies for staying sane in a crazy world.* New York: Barnes & Noble.

Leibenluft, E. (2001). Why are so many women depressed? In R. Comer (Ed.), *Scientific American: Psychology reader* (pp. 7-11). New York: Worth/Scientific American.

Manning, B. (1994). *Abba's child: The cry for intimate belonging.* Colorado Springs: NavPress.

Malony, N. (1995). *The psychology of religion for ministry.* New York: Paulist.

Maxmen, J., and Ward, N. (1995). *Essential psychopathology and its treatment.* New York: W. W. Norton.

McGrath, E. (1998). *The complete idiot's guide to beating the blues.* New York: Alpha.

McLemore, C. (1984). *Honest Christianity.* Philadelphia: Westminster Press.

McLemore, C. (2003). *Toxic relationships and how to change them.* New York: Wiley-Interscience.

Meyer, R., and Deitsch, S. (1996). *The clinician's handbook* (4th ed.). Boston: Allyn and Bacon.

Miller, W., and Jackson, K. (1995). *Practical psychology for pastors* (2nd ed.). Englewood Cliffs, NJ: Prentice-Hall.

Mouw, R. (2002). *The smell of the sawdust: What evangelicals can learn from their fundamentalist heritage.* Grand Rapids, MI: Eerdmans.

Nathan, P., and Gorman, J. (1998). *A guide to treatments that work.* New York: Oxford University Press.

Oden, T. C. (1987). *Pastoral counsel: Vol. 3. Classical pastoral care.* Grand Rapids, MI: Baker.

Oden, T. C. (1994). *Crisis ministries: Vol. 4. Classical pastoral care.* Grand Rapids, MI: Baker.

Ortberg, J. (1997). *The life you've always wanted: Spiritual disciplines for ordinary people.* Grand Rapids, MI: Zondervan.

Paloutzian, R. (1996). *Invitation to the psychology of religion* (2nd ed.). Boston: Allyn and Bacon.

Pargament, K. (1997). *The psychology of religion and coping.* New York: Guilford.

Peck, M. S. (1978). *The road less traveled.* New York: Touchstone.

Sanders, R. (Ed.). (1997). *Christian counseling ethics.* Downers Grove, IL: InterVarsity Press.

Schwartzberg, S. (2000). *Casebook of psychological disorders: The human face of emotional distress.* Boston: Allyn and Bacon.

Scully, J. (Ed.) (1990). *Psychiatry* (2nd ed.). Malvern, PA: Harwal.

Smedes, L. (1993). *Shame and grace: Healing the shame we don't deserve.* New York: HarperCollins.

Smedes, L. (1998). *Standing on the promises: Keeping hope alive for a tomorrow we cannot control.* Nashville: Thomas Nelson.

Sittser, G. (1996). *A grace disguised: How the soul grows through loss.* Grand Rapids, MI: Zondervan.

Stapert, K. (1994). Will pharmacological Calvinism protect me? *Perspectives,* June/July, pp. 9-10.

Sutker, P., and Adams, H. (1993). *Comprehensive handbook of psychopathology* (2nd ed.). New York: Plenum.

van der Kolk, B. (2002). Posttraumatic therapy in the age of neuroscience. *Psychoanalytic Dialogues, 12*(3), 381-92.

Van Leeuwen, M. (2002). *My brother's keeper.* Downers Grove, IL: InterVarsity Press.

Weyerhauser, W. (1980). The significance of John Finch for a Christian psychology. In N. Maloney (Ed.), *A Christian existential psychology* (pp. 3-14). Washington, DC: University Press of America.

Wolterstorff, N. (1980). *Until justice and mercy embrace.* Grand Rapids, MI: Eerdmans.

Worden, W. (1996). *Children and grief.* New York: Guilford.

Worden, W. (2002). *Grief counseling and grief therapy* (3rd ed.). New York: Springer.

Yancey, P. (1988). *Disappointment with God.* Grand Rapids, MI: Zondervan.

Yancey, P. (1997). *What's so amazing about grace?* Grand Rapids, MI: Zondervan.

Yarhouse, M. A., and Turcic, E. M. (2003). Depression, creativity, and religion: A pilot study of Christians in the visual arts. *Journal of Psychology and Theology, 31*(4), 348-55.

7

PROBLEMS OF
SOCIAL IMPACT

Alcoholism, substance use disorder and a variety of addictive behaviors are problems of social impact because they have reached a point of crisis in the United States. From an economic standpoint, an estimated $148 billion per year may be lost in productivity, unemployment and the increased cost of health care due to these disorders (Harwood, Fountain, Livermore and Lewin Group, 1998). From a psychosocial perspective, economic loss is only overshadowed by the strain on families and entire communities affected by destructive patterns of behavior and the lack of available resources to address such concerns.

The statistics on substance use disorders are astounding. Next to nicotine—where nearly one in four persons has a history of tobacco dependence (Anthony, Warner and Kessler, 1994)—alcohol is the most frequently abused substance in the United States. A conservative estimate is that ten million adults are alcoholics and an additional seven million adults are problem drinkers (Julien, 1992). In their National Comorbidity Survey, Anthony, Warner and Kessler (1994) reported that one in seven (14 percent) adults ages seventeen to fifty-four met criteria for alcohol dependence. The next most frequently abused substance is probably cannabis. Although the use of marijuana has decreased since its peak period of use in the late 1970s (Julien, 1992), 4.2 percent of respondents met the diagnostic criteria for cannabis dependence (Anthony et al., 1994). Julien (1992) estimates that between twenty and thirty million people in the United States have used cocaine and "crack" cocaine, and probably five million people use cocaine regularly. Heroin is abused by at least one-half million Americans, and an estimated 1.9 million have experimented with the drug (Uddo, Malow and Sutker, 1993). As alarming as these statistics are, they do not reflect the spread of HIV, which is associated with the abuse of substances (Kalichman, 1996).

THEMES IN PASTORAL CARE

People of the ancient Near East certainly knew that substances could be abused and that the misuse of substances could come with grave consequences. Cheydleur (1999) reminds us that Noah had become drunk at one point (Gen 9) and that a number of ancient cultures have written records of the use and abuse of alcohol. Scripture is clear in telling believers not to misuse alcohol (Prov 23:29-35).

At a broader theological and pastoral level, substance abuse and dependence or addiction are considered problems because people are created by God for the purpose of relating to him rather than being "subject to another controlling influence" (Vere, 1995, p. 298; see 1 Cor 6:12). Along these lines, our minds and bodies are not ours. We are stewards of the mind and body we have been given by God, and when we misuse substances we do an injustice to God's claim on our body (Vere, 1995; see Prov 23:19-21; 1 Cor 6:19-20).

Also, the short-term gains that come from substance abuse are fleeting and ultimately an illusion that keeps people from facing their circumstances. There is in substance abuse a longing for something else, for some completion. As Plantinga (1995, p. 135) observes, "Because they are human beings, addicts long for wholeness, for fulfillment, and for the final good that believers call God."

Augustine described this seeking for completion as a habitual giving away of the freedom to choose the better path. He conceptualized the struggle, as Paul does, as one between the spirit and the flesh, and one that was characterized by habit and, ultimately, enslavement:

> As in all tragedy, the enemy is within as well as without. We
> know we are doing wrong, we want not to do it, and still we do it.

The reason is that at some other level of our being we do want to do it. Giving in to that want at that level leaves a bondage we both create and resent. Each wrong choice forges a link in the chain that binds us. (Plantinga, 1995, p. 146)

We turn now to several themes from contemporary psychopathology. We will return to these pastoral and integrative themes, as the relationship between sin and addiction is a potentially enlightening one for Christian mental health professionals.

CONTEMPORARY CATEGORIZATION

The *DSM-IV* organizes what we are referring to as the problems of social impact into substance dependence and substance abuse. *Substance dependence* typically involves habituation, which refers to the process by which nerve cells become less sensitive to repeated stimuli, and cravings, which refer to physical urges that continue after an individual gives up a substance. *Substance abuse* typically refers to the use of a substance beyond safe levels for physical and/or psychological well-being (Johnson and McCown, 1993). *Addictions* refer to a broader class of behaviors of habit or compulsion, such as sex, gambling, eating and so on.

The problems of social impact share a number of common features. They all involve short-term gratification at the cost of long-term negative social and medical consequences. In the case of drug use, each substance associated with addiction produces an excitatory effect (by stimulating neurotransmitters in the brain), while several addictive drugs (e.g., alcohol) produce an inhibitory effect as well (by reducing anxiety) (Johnson and McCowen, 1993). Also, they are all remarkably resistant to traditional treatment approaches and show a high propensity for relapse. The abuse of some substances may also lead to a form of dependence at biological and chemical levels, which further complicates treatment.

The major categories of substances are (1) depressants (e.g., alcohol, sedatives), (2) stimulants (e.g., amphetamines, cocaine), (3) opiates (e.g., heroin, codeine), and (4) hallucinogens (e.g., LSD, marijuana). Additional substances, such as inhalants and over-the-counter medications, are commonly abused but do not fit into the other major categories.

Depressants. Depressants, such as alcohol, sedatives, hypnotics and anxiolytic drugs (e.g., barbiturates, benzodiazepines), reduce arousal by decreasing activity in the central nervous system. Alcohol tends to impair motor coordination and judgments. Long-term consequences of alcohol dependence can include tremors, hallucinations and delirium in addition to medical consequences such as liver disease and cardiovascular disease. About two-thirds of adults in America report report consuming alcohol at some point in their life, and about 45 percent currently use alcohol (Nathan, Skinstad and Dolan, 2001). Prevalence rates for alcohol dependence are estimated at about 13-14 percent (lifetime) and 4-5 percent (current) for the U.S. population (ibid.).

Sedatives, hypnotics and anxiolytics have a calming influence, relaxing muscles and reducing inhibitions. When combined with alcohol, these drugs have a synergistic effect. According to the *DSM-IV-TR* (APA, 2000), 15 percent or more of Americans use these medications (most often by prescription) in a given year. However, about 6 percent in a recent survey admitted to ever using sedatives or tranquilizers for reasons other than their intended purpose at some point. The typical course is to experiment with sedatives, hypnotics or anxiolytics during adolescence or young adulthood, and this experimentation typically increases to daily use and increased levels of tolerance.

Stimulants. Stimulants, such as caffeine, nicotine, cocaine and amphetamines, have an excitatory effect by increasing activity in the central nervous system. Caffeine is one of the most frequently used substances. Consistent caffeine use can lead to tolerance and dependence, and headaches are a common symptom of withdrawal. An estimated 85 percent of Americans use caffeine in a given year, and among those who use caffeine, about 85 percent consume a beverage with caffeine at least once a week, taking in an average of about 200 milligrams per day (APA, 2000). Those who use caffeine typically begin in mid-adolescence and increase their intake through young adulthood.

Nicotine can also lead to tolerance and dependence, and nicotine dependence is associated with depression. Symptoms of withdrawal include depression, insomnia and concentration difficulties. According to the *DSM-IV-TR* (APA, 2000), nearly three-fourths (72 percent) of adults in the United States have used cigarettes (lifetime prevalence rate), while nearly one-third (32 percent) smoked cigarettes in the previous year. Although smoking has significantly decreased in the United States over the past decades, there is increased interest in smoking among adolescents and young adults. In 1997 about 65 percent of seniors in high school reported "ever having used cigarettes," which is an increase in the three years prior to that study (p. 268).

Cocaine use leads to feelings of euphoria and increased alertness due to a blocking of dopamine reuptake. Cocaine is addictive, with gradual onset dependence evidenced by both tolerance and withdrawal. According to the *DSM-IV-TR* (APA, 2000), "cocaine smoking and intravenous use tend to be particularly associated with a rapid progression from use to abuse or dependence, often occurring over weeks to months" (p. 249). In contrast, intranasal use tends to lead to a more gradual course, over months to years. About 10 percent of the U.S. population has used cocaine (2 percent has used "crack" cocaine), with about 2 percent using cocaine in the previous year (0.6 percent having used "crack" in the previous year) (APA, 2000).

Amphetamines abuse stimulates the central nervous system, producing euphoria, anxiety and impaired judgment, followed by a "crash" characterized by tiredness and in some cases depression. Symptoms of amphetamine use disorder include increased heart rate and perspiration, weight loss, and nausea or vomiting. Depression is a common symptom of withdrawal.

Opiates. The most common opiates are opium, heroin, morphine and codeine. Opiates produce euphoria by activating enkephalins and endorphins in the body. They can be combined (e.g., combining cocaine and heroin to make "speedballs"), and those who abuse opiates are at increased risk of premature death, often by overdose. Prevalence estimates for the opiates vary considerably, but it is believed that nearly two million Americans have experimented with heroin and that at least one-half million abuse heroin (Uddo, Malow and Sutker, 1993). In terms of course, "problems with opioid use are most commonly first observed in the late teens or early 20s" (APA, 2000, p. 276), and although periods of abstinence may be practiced, relapse is common, with only about "20-30% of individuals with Opioid Dependence [achieving] long-term abstinence" (pp. 276-77).

Hallucinogens. Hallucinogens produce hallucinations and delusions and alter general sensory perception. Marijuana is a widely used hallucinogen that induces memory impairment, motivation impairment and heightened sensory perception. In a National Comorbidity Survey, Anthony, Warner and Kessler (1994) reported that about 4 percent of respondents were dependent on cannabis. There is some evidence for tolerance to marijuana, with mild withdrawal symptoms, though there is no evidence that those who abuse marijuana experience cravings. Dependence and abuse usually develop slowly, with a gradual increase in frequency and amount (APA, 2000).

LSD causes similar perceptual impairments as does marijuana, including hallucinations, increased heart rate, perspiration and blurred vision. LSD leads to tolerance and withdrawal. According to the *DSM-IV-TR* (APA, 2000), hallucinogen abuse or dependence rates are about 0.6 percent (lifetime) and 0.1 percent (previous year). Rates of use are particularly high among adolescents and young adults, with about 16 percent of those eighteen to twenty-five years old reporting having ever used a hallucinogen, and 7 percent having used a hallucinogen in the previous year (APA, 2000).

ANTECEDENTS TO PROBLEMS OF SOCIAL IMPACT

A number of factors play a role in whether a particular person's use of a substance will result in abuse or addiction by a particular individual. These factors include prior experience using drugs, genetic susceptibility, cognitive factors and attributions, environmental stressors and personality, exposure to substances, and reinforcement schedules. Rather than focusing on different etiological pathways for the different categories of substances, we will organize this section under the following four headings: biological, psychosocial, sociocultural and spiritual.

Biological factors. All people are not equally likely to become dependent on a substance. Many people consume alcohol without becoming dependent on it. Some individuals even use drugs without becoming dependent on them. Researchers have looked to heredity to explain a particular person's vulnerability to substance dependence.

Nathan, Skinstad and Dolan (2001) discuss evidence that biology contributes to a person's vulnerability to alcoholism or alcohol abuse. The evidence includes early studies comparing children of alcoholics with children of nonalcoholics and studies comparing adopted and nonadopted children of alcoholics (Cloninger 1987; Goodwin et al., 1974). These studies suggest that heritability may play a more significant role in later alcohol abuse than does family environment; however, the biological hypothesis raises a number of questions, and the nature and degree of influence of biology on alcoholism are yet to be determined.

Some researchers have hypothesized that there are at least two types of alcoholism (for a review of various conceptualizations of alcoholism, see Epstein and McCrady, 1994). One is manifest in persons who cannot abstain but drink steadily, while the other type is seen in those who can go without alcohol for long periods but cannot control themselves once they start drinking (Cloninger, 1987). The first type is referred to as *steady* drinking, which is associated with early onset, anxiety and depression; it may also be associated with antisocial characteristics such as impulsivity, lying, fighting and lack of remorse for antisocial behavior. Studies suggest that such drinking is strongly influenced by heredity (Nathan, Skinstad and Dolan, 2001). The second type of drinking is referred to as *binge* drinking, which is associated with emotional dependence, perfectionism, introversion and guilt. Research suggests that binge drinking is influenced by both heredity and environment, is associated with less severe pathology and responds better to treatment.

Additional evidence for a biological basis for addiction is the pleasure experienced with an increase of the neurotransmitter dopamine in a specific area of the brain. Addictive substances such as cocaine, amphetamines, nicotine, caffeine, THC (the active ingredient in marijuana), alcohol and barbiturates produce pleasurable feelings associated with the release of dopamine, which serves as a potent reinforcer for continued substance use. Substances such as alcohol and barbiturates, in addition to producing pleasurable feelings, decrease the discomfort of anxiety, which makes reinforcement both positive (increasing pleasure) and negative (decreasing anxiety).

Although there is evidence for a biological basis for vulnerability to alcoholism, Gallant notes "that the majority of offspring of alcoholics never develop alcoholism, and a significant number of alcoholics have no family history of alcoholism" (1987, p. 44). Alcoholism and other substance use disorders are complex, and it would be simplistic to conclude that they are exclusively genetic problems.

Psychosocial factors. One way to organize the various psychological factors implicated in addiction is to consider the three categories of motivation, personality and attachment. When substance abusers are interviewed, they tend to offer a number of predictable reasons for their use of particular drugs. These include the need to reduce tension, anxiety and depression, reduce aggressive and sexual drives, increase a sense of euphoria, pleasure and well-being, increase aggressive and sexual drives, avoid reality problems, satisfy curiosity, defy authority, gain spiritual insights, and reduce inhibitions (Van Wicklin, 1992; cf. Kayloe's 1993 discussion of antecedents to food addiction, including depression and anxiety).

In addition to motivation, research suggests a number of psychological features that make persons prone to develop substance dependency or to engage in compulsive eating or gambling or addictive sexual behavior. One core issue appears to be *impulsivity*. Some persons
are inclined to act on impulse rather than reflection, and their behavior can often be characterized as rash and impetuous and may be related to low attention span (Tarter and Vanyukov, 1994). A number of
other features are also associated with substance abuse and addictive
behaviors: emotional immaturity, excessive dependency, limited capacity to tolerate tension, limited capacity for delaying gratification, low
tolerance for frustration, limited problem-solving ability, and inability
to tolerate painful or unpleasant feelings (Miller and Jackson, 1995).

Depression is also associated with substance abuse and addictive
behaviors. Lifestyle deterioration, loss of meaningful relationships
and other failures related to patterns of addictive behavior all contribute to a depressive state. Further, many addicted individuals learn to
use such things as alcohol, food or sex habitually to reduce anxiety.
As Pincu observes, "Food and sex are important aspects of most people's lives, but when either is used to sublimate other needs . . . the
perception of the need becomes distorted and the patters of gratification become fixed, reinforced, and compulsive" (1989, p. 64). Excitement is another common feature of addictive behavior, and it is seen
especially in compulsive sexual behavior and gambling. Sometimes
the risk and fear involved in compulsive sexual behavior and gambling excite and reinforce the behavior itself: "Addictive gamblers are
not chasing the win. If the win [were] . . . important, gamblers would
stop when they won. They are chasing the action, the excitement, the
moment, and eventually they chase the losing, for this allows them a
reason to chase again" (Nakken, 1988, quoted in Pincu, 1989).

In addition to motivation and personality, May (1988) discusses *attachment* as a key psychological variable. Attachment involves the
three stages of learning, habit formation and struggle. The learning
stage simply involves associating a specific behavior with a feeling of
pleasure or relief from pain or anxiety; one can associate taking a
drug, consuming alcohol, or engaging in compulsive gambling or sexual behavior with feelings of pleasure or anxiety reduction. The second stage is associating the pattern of behavior with other experiences. Habits are formed as we seek out behaviors we believe will
provide either immediate enjoyment or some measure of comfort in
the midst of feeling disconnected, powerless or out of control. As a

habit becomes an integral part of our life, we find ourselves increasingly uncomfortable if we do not engage in the preferred behavior of attachment. Blocking behavior commonly leads to withdrawal.

Sociocultural factors. A number of sociocultural factors, including community-based values and shared experiences regarding substance abuse, are significant for determining the rate of abuse in a community. Sociological variables such as poverty, race, age, gender and social standing should inform the Christian counselor's understanding of addictions and substance use disorders.

Low socioeconomic status and urban residence are associated with the highest rates of alcohol abuse and other abused substances (Anthony, Warner and Kessler, 1994). Geographical areas with concentrated, persistent poverty and social dislocation are at greatest risk for long-term damage because of the hopelessness and meaninglessness experienced by families struggling with insufficient income, family violence and discord, inadequate housing, chronic hunger and poor health. Admittedly, the relationship between substance abuse, cultural identity and socioeconomic status can be confusing; for example, substance use disorders are believed to be of greater concern in Hispanic American communities than other communities (Anthony, Warner and Kessler, 1994), but these disorders are both the cause and result of numerous other problems, including unemployment, crime and broken families. Although it is difficult to say in a specific case which is the cause and which the effect, the chaotic struggle for survival faced by many families reflects the social, economic and political realities of our day.[1]

Cultural attitudes also play an important role in the acceptance or rejection of substances. Examples of cultural effects may be seen in the low rate of alcoholism among Jewish people and the high rate of opiate abuse but low rate of alcoholism among the Meo of Southeast Asia (Gallant, 1987). In this regard there are important questions to be asked: What kind of problem is a particular substance in a given community? How is it experienced and responded to in those communities? Without such an understanding, efforts to bring change will likely fail. For example, the assumption that Native Americans have a strong desire for alcohol complicated by an unfortunate ge-

---

[1]The government plays a profound role in shaping these social, economic and political realities. For example, significant segments of government-supported U.S. agriculture and industry are engaged in the production and marketing of substances that many Americans abuse, such as alcohol and nicotine.

netic vulnerability to it is simply naive (Green, 1982). From a sociocultural perspective, it is more accurate to say that substance use disorders among some Native Americans stem in part from individuals'
having no sense of belonging to either traditional Native American
communities or the dominant European American communities. As
Green reminds us, a sense of isolation associated with the pressure
of cultural contact is exacerbated when access to economic rewards
is obstructed.

Christian mental health professionals should also be careful not to
allow cultural stereotypes or myths to distort their assessment of a particular person. For example, television and other media tend to encourage the stereotype that substance use disorders are more common in the African American community; yet recent research
suggests that African Americans are less likely than European Americans and Hispanic Americans to have a history of chemical dependency (Anthony, Warner and Kessler, 1984). Mental health professionals should be informed consumers of empirical research and
should not be swayed by popular messages or cultural myths.

Cultural identity is also shaped by acculturation and social change.
Rapid social changes during the last several decades, including migra-
tion and the growth of mass media, have played a significant role in
blurring the distinctives of cultural groups. Gallant (1987) highlights a
number of circumstances where cultural changes have had an impact
on substance abuse. For example, Sioux and Navajo Indians have
shown an increased rate of death from alcohol-related illness, including cirrhosis of the liver, as many have moved from native tribal loca-
tions to what have been referred to as "White-Indian" towns. Also,
Jewish Yemenite immigrants to Israel have a much higher rate of alcohol abuse than do native Israelis; conversely, significantly more
second- and third-generation American Jews abuse alcohol than Jews
from the first generation. Certainly rapidly changing cultures and acculturation play a part in some experiences of substance abuse.

In terms of familial influences, the lowest rates of abuse are associated with clear norms of alcohol use, a neutral stance toward alcohol
consumption (but a negative view of excessive drinking), a positive
view of abstinence, and consistent parental modeling of moderate alcohol use. As might be expected, lack of family cohesiveness appears
to be associated with an increased likelihood of alcohol abuse (Burnside, Baer, McLaughlin and Pokorny, 1986). Children whose earliest
memories are of neglect, deprivation or brutality are in a poor position

to cope with the stressors of adolescence and adulthood, and it should come as no surprise that family chaos and discord leads many young people to alternative coping mechanisms. This appears to be true even in less extreme cases; one study found that disruption in families due to early death, divorce or separation of parents was correlated with alcohol-related problems in adolescents (ibid.). More recent research confirms the significance of the parent-child relationship in whether or not a young person will drink (e.g., Tarter et al., 1993).

Peer and media influence can also significantly shape a young person's decision to abuse substances. Negative peer influence may involve modeling, encouraging substance abuse and supplying drugs and can seriously impede efforts to prevent substance use (Botvin, Schinke and Orlandi, 1995). As Van Wicklin observes, the media provide ample opportunities for influence: "Social learning of drug use would include identification with movie and television heroes, musical lyrics, and what is observed and learned about personal drug habits of professional athletes, entertainers and other celebrities" (1992, p. 384).

Another way the media influences public perception is a result of efforts to frighten people away from substance abuse. Children and adolescents are constantly bombarded with drug news stories and anti-drug messages, but in a certain developmental context "just say no to drugs" may create an interest in drug experimentation, as young people may act out oppositionally in response to strong prohibitions (Botvin, Schinke and Orlandi, 1995). Also, sometimes the messages are sensational, so that warnings function as lures.

Spiritual factors. Spiritual variables also affect vulnerability to the problems of social impact, as addictions and compulsions reflect a significant void in a person's life, especially in regard to a sense of life's meaning and value. Those who abuse substances or become trapped in addictive patterns of behavior have often displaced onto other experiences and behaviors their fundamental yearning for relationship, connection and intimacy. Insofar as a desire implies the absence of its object, addictions and compulsions may imply the absence of a person's most fundamental object of desire: God. True recovery, then, may involve recognizing the gravity of sin and the necessity of atonement, being held responsible for behavior, becoming recommitted to the nurturing of one's spirit, and being a part of loving and accountable relationships over a lifetime. The concept of personal responsibility plays a significant part in this model, and a major strength of this view is its emphasis on prevention.

An appreciation of the spiritual variables in addiction recognizes that a psychology that proclaims half-truths about addiction and recovery will do tremendous damage to individuals and to society. A half-truth might take the form of misrepresenting a spiritual vacuum as a disease, thereby discounting the need for an existential encounter with God and replacing it with a "safe," materialistic account of cause and effect, disease course and treatment. (For a discussion of the relationship between materialism and interpretations of research on homosexuality, see Yarhouse and Jones, 1997.)

Each of these factors—biological, psychological, sociocultural and spiritual—plays a role to a different degree in each experience of addiction. And the existence of multiple factors in the origins of addiction calls for a holistic approach to treatment.

TREATING PROBLEMS OF SOCIAL IMPACT

Themes in treatment. One of the most significant general predictors of treatment outcome is the severity of the person's problems at the beginning of treatment. An additional predictor is the number of previous substance abuse treatments (McLellan et al., 1994). The person who has gone through more treatments will have a more difficult time successfully completing treatment. Interestingly, demographic characteristics such as age, race, gender and education have been shown to be least related to treatment outcome. The same study reported that a person's social adjustment at follow-up is related to his or her access to a greater number of psychiatric, medical, employment and family services.

Unfortunately, established treatment programs may not actually be designed to meet the treatment needs of the substance abuser. For example, the typical alcoholism treatment program in the United States combines detoxification, prescribed medication (e.g., Librium), group or individual psychotherapy, educational lectures and Alcoholics Anonymous (AA). Yet none of these elements has been found in empirical research to produce reliable long-term change in drinking behavior (see McLellan et al., 1994; Nathan, 1993).

Current trends in research and treatment of addictions and substance use disorders include an increased use of multiple models for understanding problem behaviors. These include issues such as personal susceptibility, a coming together of biological and psychological models for understanding addictive behaviors, neuropsychology, and the development of effective treatment strategies that incorporate cognitive-behavioral, family systems, psychopharmacological, self-help and preventative approaches.

Of course, the particular dimensions of any program must be selected carefully. As McLellan and colleagues observe, although there may be helpful rehabilitative effects associated with group therapy, alcohol and drug education, and twelve-step meetings, "there is a point of diminishing returns with regard to the provision of these services" for reducing alcohol and drug use (1994, p. 1156). Although many in the Christian community have turned to twelve-step meetings for treatment, there is little evidence that such programs help individuals beyond preliminary or superficial attempts at reducing alcohol and drug abuse (Nathan, 1993). In fact, the twelve-step approach has taken on a life of its own. Although many psychologists heartily endorse approaches that emphasize increased control over one's environment and interpersonally mediated support, we should be wary of any industry built on a single conceptualization that can profoundly affect *and limit* how people perceive and interpret their life experiences. Researchers are turning their attention toward approaches like family therapy, employment counseling and individual psychotherapy for improved psychological functioning (Edwards and Steinglass, 1995; Liddle and Dakof, 1985). In the case of alcohol abuse, aversion therapies, the teaching of alternative coping skills and, in the case of less severe problem drinking, self-control training may be the most effective interventions (Nathan, 1993).

Generally speaking, effective treatment of addictions and substance use disorders is long-term, is interpersonally mediated, and requires a high degree of accountability and self-confrontation. In addition, for any treatment to be effective, competing reinforcement must be found. If nothing replaces the behavior or substance, then the person is left with a large empty space in his or her life that may ultimately be filled with the same or worse.

The provider needs to carefully examine what motivates a specific addict. As was mentioned above, numerous motives can account for an addictive behavior. For example, those who are motivated by sensory experience appear to be drawn to risk-taking experiences and may find it helpful to replace the abused substance with a competing sensory experience, such as skydiving, mountaineering or various forms of exercise. The key is to identify what motivates the person and to provide a compelling alternative experience that can help prevent a relapse.

Effective treatment programs are also highly active and directive, helping the person to rework her or his entire lifestyle to replace the patterns surrounding the abused substance. The person must find new activities, new causes, new social circles, often a new job and even a new place to live. Obviously, such change requires a long-term commitment and the support of the community beyond the clinic that provides initial services. In short, positive social behavior must compete with prior self-destructive behavior.

In what contexts do such changes occur? For substance use disorders, a prevailing treatment option at present is residential care, which is considered by many to be advantageous as it removes the addict from the environment in which the addiction initially occurred. Of course many addicts are still seen on an outpatient basis because of financial restrictions, lack of adequate health insurance or other factors. Traditional outpatient therapy, however, is often ineffective in the face of serious, long-term patterns of substance abuse.

Emerging themes in treatment. Two emerging trends in addiction treatment involve an intensive approach to intervention. The first trend is toward creating a challenging, stretching experience, often for a week or a month or more, in a very different geographical location, not only removing individuals from their immediate environment but also exposing them to personal challenges that call for courage and instill confidence and self-esteem. Such an approach is exemplified by Outward Bound, an intensive wilderness-survival program for adolescents.

A second emerging trend in the literature on addiction treatment is intensive outpatient work offered in the community in which the person lives. Such an approach is an attempt to bridge the gap between residential treatment planning and traditional outpatient interventions. It involves several hours of treatment per week in a regularly scheduled, structured program. One advantage is that services can be provided over a longer period of time for less money. Also, recovering addicts are supported as they practice coping strategies within their daily living environment. Obviously they face numerous situations that may trigger relapse; however, many in the field of addiction research argue that success in the environment in which the addicted person lives is a realistic measure of recovery and that it is best to have professionals immediately available to respond to relapses as they occur.

No matter how cost efficient treatment programs become, however, no treatment program is a match for the cost effectiveness of prevention. It is widely recognized that the key to addressing problems of social impact is effective preventative programs.

PREVENTION

The family is clearly the most influential preventative influence in a young person's life. Yet a traditional family of two parents and two or three children is not a prerequisite for prevention. Rather, children need certain experiences in order to mature; these include consistent experiences of authority and love, stimulation and support, coherence, and an absence of chaos. These experiences should occur in a family context with clear boundaries and support for organizational or structural differences (e.g., the parental dyad and the sibling subsystem). When children experience a reasonably stable, protective, predictable and responsive environment and when they are taught the connection between actions and their consequences, a buffer is created between the child and anxiety and stress. Children from families such as these have ample financial, social and psychological resources.

However, many families do not have these resources. They are referred to as "at risk" because of the prevalence of addictions and substance use disorders among children of abusers of alcohol and other drugs; victims of physical, sexual or psychological abuse; families of low socioeconomic status; families with mental health problems; and the like (Kumpfer, 1989). When children grow up deprived of affection, stability and predictability, and when caregivers are consistently absent, they may have greater difficulty adhering to standards for responsible behavior at school and church and in the larger society. These children not only grow up with a feeling of unworthiness but also tend to withdraw to isolated sources of comfort and security.

But there is hope for these children. At-risk families can make use of preventative interventions focused directly on providing a reasonably stable environment that protects the child from hunger and harm. Preventative measures can be carried out by community centers or neighborhood agencies, which can provide or direct families to affordable pediatricians, daycare, and individual, couple and family counseling. Support groups can also be formed for those who experience sudden or extreme stressors, such as the death of an infant, the loss of a job or the dissolution of a marriage, as well as for those experiencing the long-term stressors of chronic illness (e.g., family caregivers of those with Alzheimer's disease). Community centers can provide home visitors trained to meet some needs of a family in their living environment.

Such creative, intensive programs have been implemented successfully. For example, Homebuilders in Tacoma and the Bronx offers intensive care at home through crisis intervention, an emphasis on preserving families and efforts to prevent out-of-home placement[2] (Schorr, 1989). For older children, community centers can provide positive competing experiences in the form of sports, music programs and after-school clubs. With the right leadership, such programs can provide daily lessons in coping with stress, delaying gratification, being accountable to others and connecting with authority figures and peers.

Many preventative measures can also be provided by the local church (or the church working in conjunction with a community center). This goes beyond offering space for AA meetings. The local church can play a vital role in mobilizing coping strategies and adaptive behaviors that reduce stress. One way to cultivate authentic and supportive relationships within the church is through active identification and participation in the community. The church can network with community centers or hospitals and provide support to at-risk families, especially during key periods of transition (e.g., pregnancy, childbirth, retirement). Obviously services work best if they are comprehensive enough to meet a wide range of a family's needs, but even limited, specific efforts to provide help (e.g., providing rides to pre- or postnatal care or watching a family member who is cognitively impaired) can set a foundation of trust on which to build structures of further support.

Perhaps the greatest strides toward prevention will be made if middle-class Americans identify with disadvantaged families, seeing the personal connection between their own needs and those of families of a lower socioeconomic class. One program designed to create such identification is the family-to-family program of the Outreach Community Center in Carol Stream, Illinois, through which selected church families and disadvantaged families in the community are brought into a supportive relationship with one another. More commitment is required when a middle-class family actually relocates to a

---

[2]Other examples include the New Haven program, created under the auspices of the Yale University Child Study Center, and the Prenatal/Early Infancy Project in Elmira, New York. Both of these programs are concerned with changing long-term outcomes by providing support to mothers and infants (see Schorr, 1989). See also Penney and Garfield's 1984 discussion of prevention through parents' groups.

disadvantaged neighborhood (Perkins, 1993). Such initiatives can have a profound impact, shoring up families with long-standing social, emotional and psychological needs, as well as shaping the character of the families that risk personal involvement and identification.

Although the best investment for prevention among at-risk populations is at the family level, research on other primary and secondary prevention programs suggests alternative ways for decreasing addictive behavior.[3] Taxation policies can help (or hinder) the primary prevention of alcohol abuse. Several researchers argue that significant increases in federal excise taxes on alcohol are associated with numerous benefits. These include decreased development of alcohol-related diseases and hospital admission rates, as well as decrease in violent deaths.

Another trend in primary prevention literature involves "driving while intoxicated" (DWI) laws. Numerous studies show that alcohol misuse results in a significantly increased risk of automobile accidents and loss of lives. Many strategies have been proposed for reducing incidences of drunk driving (e.g., policy recommendations from Mothers Against Drunk Driving and the Federal Railroad Administration). However, most primary prevention strategies are only recommendations at this time.

In addition to federal tax policies and DWI laws, studies showing a high correlation between the minimum legal drinking age and mortality rates in younger drivers has led to nationwide efforts to raise the minimum drinking age to twenty-one. Although there are numerous difficulties related to enforcing a minimum drinking age of twenty-one, many people recognize that sanctioning drinking at a younger age is neglectful.

Finally, educational programs are generally ineffective at preventing substance use and may stimulate curiosity (Botvin, Schinke and Orlandi, 1995). Research, however, does support preventative programs designed to inoculate teens against strong messages promoting substance use and to teach skills for countering them, as well as programs that provide positive peer influences and interventions that target kids' motivations to experiment with substances in the first place (ibid.).

---

[3] We agree with Parry (1999) that we need to think about how social policy changes might be viewed as a form of prevention. What follows is a summary of what Gallant (1987) discusses in greater detail (see pp. 221-45).

INTEGRATIVE THEMES

A Christian understanding of the problems of social impact must begin with a perspective on sin and how the experience of sin has certain parallels with what we refer to as the addictions.

Sin and psychopathology. As mentioned above, there are important parallels between a person's struggles with substance abuse and dependency and the broader human struggle with sin. Again, according to McMinn (2004), sin can be thought of with reference to (1) specific acts of sin, (2) sin as our fallen state or condition and (3) the consequences of sin. An understanding of these three points of reference and their relation to the experience of addiction is a particularly promising thread for the integration of Christian thought and contemporary psychopathology. An appreciation for the parallels between sin and addiction can illuminate our understanding and help us create alternative ways of approaching those who struggle with addictive patterns of behavior and substance abuse.

As Cornelius Plantiga Jr. observes, "Addictions often include sin—or, putting matters the other way around, . . . some sin displays the addictive syndrome" (1995, p. 144). Plantinga goes on to list dynamics of addiction that overlap with sin:

1. Repetition of pleasurable and therefore habit-forming behavior, with developing tolerance and escalating desire

2. Unpleasant after-effects of such behavior, including withdrawal symptoms and self-reproach

3. Vows to moderate or quit, followed by relapses, and by attendant feelings of guilt, shame, and general distress

4. Attempts to ease this distress with new rounds of the addictive behavior (or with the first rounds of a companion addiction)

5. Deterioration of work and relationships, with accompanying cognitive disturbances, including denial, delusions, and self-deceptions

6. Gradually increasing preoccupation, then obsession, with the addiction

7. Compulsivity in addictive behavior: evidence that one's will has become at least partly split, enfeebled, and enslaved

8. A tendency to draw others into the web of addiction, people who support and enable the primary addiction (p. 145)

Christians should be the first to recognize the remarkable parallel between sin and addiction. Even in cases were sin is not fully addictive, we find ourselves in a condition of inner conflict and turmoil. This condition reflects our fallen state, and it is out of this condition that we act or think in ways that are displeasing to God or fail to act or think in ways that God intends. We struggle: part of us wants to make choices that contribute to others' well-being and reflect obedience to God, while another part of us wants desperately to fulfill self-gratifying desires. As Plantinga observes, in both sin and addiction we are enslaved by our basic state, and our actions seem to be extensions of that core condition. Furthermore, in light of our core condition, attempts to change specific behaviors are often ineffective. The problem is more fundamental than what is suggested by changes in behavior. Even success with a given behavior in a specific circumstance touches only the tip of the iceberg.

A related consideration is whether Christian mental health professionals are able to see aspects of themselves in their clients. Although it may be helpful to see addicts as different for the purposes of diagnosis and treatment, it is unwise for Christians to ignore the areas of overlap between their own struggles with sinful habits of greed, sloth, lust, pride or gluttony and the struggles of addicted people. As Christians identify ways they fall into sinful patterns and find success in resisting temptation, they may identify with the person struggling with addiction, and they may also see more clearly how certain interventions will have a greater probability of success than others.

When examining the parallels between sin and addiction, we are reminded that although Christian doctrine attests to the inevitability of sin, we still hold people responsible for their behaviors. There is no compelling reason for Christians to adopt the contemporary myth that understanding a problem excuses it. Although Scripture certainly emphasizes our inevitable inheritance of sin, we are still treated as morally responsible. Responsibility can be diminished, but it is never obviated. No one is without excuse, despite the fact that we are "wired" to sin.

As has been suggested, a Christian account of addiction takes seriously the question of whether people are responsible for their choices. Christians assume that persons are—at some point in the history of their decision making—capable of apprehending principles regarding what they ought to do and not do. We also assume that persons can exert their will in a desired direction and have some success in doing so, even in the face of negative conditions: "Addiction may oppress our desire, erode our wills, confound our motivations, and contaminate our judgment, but its bondage is never absolute" (May 1988, p. 18).

What do we do then with antecedent physiological, neurological, psychological and environmental conditions that place a person at risk for addiction? These antecedents are the consequences of sin and reflections of our fallen human condition. We must come to appreciate the complexities of these antecedents in setting the stage for a potentially destructive drama. However, Christians are not forced to choose between determinism and a simplistic view that the addict has made a habit of sinful or harmful behavior. Plantinga appreciates the complexity of the issue: "The chaos of addiction comes out of particular human character and sin, but also out of the temptations and disorganizing forces resident in an addict's home and neighborhood and maybe even in her genes" (1995, p. 22). Christians must have an eye for the complexity of addiction, so that we can offer a meaningful account of personal responsibility and human agency in relation to physiological, environmental and other factors.

Addiction is the splitting of the will; it is ultimately about idolatry (Plantinga, 1995). One expression of personal responsibility is choosing to surrender. Addicts who succeed in recovery at some point surrender and take responsibility for the destruction that surrounds their addiction and for the hard work that constitutes recovery. Those who are recovering addicts will be the first to say that recovery begins with heartbreaking surrender—the surrender of one's ultimate concern and the present longing of one's heart (May, 1988). Recovery begins when one asks the question, To whom do I ultimately belong?

In the strictest sense, sin is ultimately alienation from God and is therefore not the same as addiction to substances or behaviors. Nevertheless, as we have seen, an understanding of sin can help us reach a better understanding of addiction, which couples an evasion of personal responsibility with the sociocultural effects of evil which are far beyond what an individual can control. The best understanding of both sin and addiction calls for a full awareness of personal limitations and for accountability and support in a community, which can enable struggling persons to do something about problems they were previously unable to solve.

Pastoral care and disordered desires. Several attitudes and values are confounding to those who seek to understand addictive behaviors from a distinctively Christian perspective. One value that challenges our understanding of addictive patterns of behavior is perfectionism—the pressure individuals feel to be perfect at any cost. Sometimes the church contributes to a person's feeling pressure to be perfect when leaders avoid talking about their own failures and disappointments. The danger of perfectionism, of course, is revealed when persons in its thrall are confronted with the fact that they are actually still imperfect.

Perfectionism can fuel an addict's tendency to exaggerate the extent to which she or he can solve the problem of addiction alone. This is the problem of individualism or human self-sufficiency. Addicts are caught in a dilemma that cannot be resolved by means of their own efforts, and their refusal to admit how much they need help is an indication of the basic problem of individualism.

Individualism can be fueled by denial. The defense mechanism of denial has been described by one writer as analogous to a racehorse's wearing blinders to decrease the excitement generated by various stimuli, so that the horse's concentration will be focused on the goal of crossing the finish line (Gallant, 1987). In the case of substance abuse or addictive sexual behavior, denial serves as the person's blinders and restricts the scope of vision, which facilitates his or her ability to minimize the severity of the addictive behavior.

The church sometimes contributes to the tendency toward isolation and individualism. We do this when we insist that God alone is the author of our healing and recovery. If this view limits access to helpful resources, the addict can experience further isolation. Also, if we hold the view that addictions are strictly the cumulative result of self-consciously chosen sinful behaviors, each of which the individual could have avoided, we will be inclined to argue that recovery too is a simple matter of free choice. However, not only does this view minimize the serious effects of neglectful upbringing, aberrant socialization, poverty and a complex range of psychological variables, but it also further isolates addicts. They are seen as especially sinful or as belonging to a different class of sinners. To refuse to identify at some level with the addict allows us to put considerable distance between ourselves and persons struggling with addictive patterns of behavior or substance abuse. Viewing the addict as especially sinful distances us from the human condition. We do not have to address our own propensity to sin.

The problems of social impact need to be examined from the perspective of the body of Christ. We are called to identify with the disenfranchised of our communities because God through Christ identified with us. But given the attitudes and values that can hinder our understanding, and in light of the similarities between our own experience of sin and the addict's experience, how should the church respond to those who struggle with problems of social impact? Recovery is constructive only in a community where confrontation and long-standing, supportive follow-through go hand in hand. A tension must be kept between external structure and accountability and internal realignment of the deepest longings of the heart. The level of support that is available to a person during treatment for addiction is a powerful predictor of the treatment's positive outcome (Havassy, Hall and Wasserman, 1989). And the church must do more than wait to hear about opportunities to help; we must pursue those who are inclined to withdraw and isolate themselves from support.

There are four themes to consider when offering support to a person who is undergoing treatment for substance abuse or another problem behavior: motivation, acceptance, commitment and support.

Motivation begins with specific feedback from others about what they see happening to the person and what they are concerned may happen. People struggling with addictions need to hear the concerns of others. Such feedback avoids argument and imposing a "guilt trip"; rather, it is a process characterized by active concern for the person's welfare. The church community can assist the person to become aware of the negative consequences of their actions and how those actions affect those who care about them (see Babor's 1994 study on the use of dissuasion or exhortation with *low-severity* alcohol abusers).

In addition to motivating an individual to change, it is important to express *acceptance*. Although one may express strong disapproval of another's behavior, it is important to still show respect for that person, which increases the likelihood that concerns will be heard. Acceptance is most clearly expressed by a sustained presence, which is crucial not only because of the time it takes to prove the genuineness of one's concern and acceptance but also because the interpersonal presence is competing with a rewarding addictive pattern. Abandoning an addictive pattern is an act of courage many of us have not had to undertake. It can seldom be done outside a context of sustained and supportive relationships.

Building a *commitment* to change is the next concern. A decision to change an addictive pattern seldom involves an immediate total commitment. Talking about "parts" of a person may be helpful here. There is probably one part of the person that wants to make a commitment to change, while another part wants to sabotage the process or is afraid of the ramifications of both success and failure. As commitment builds, it is essential that struggling persons have the opportunity to explore the options before them. This is where awareness of treatment interventions is important. At this point a joint exploration of options available in the community is most helpful, because it demonstrates freedom and respect for the individual.

With most addictive behaviors, the next step is primarily professionally mediated. Treatment can take many forms, including traditional outpatient care, inpatient residential care and intensive outpatient work. However treatment is pursued, the person will continue to need *support* and encouragement in addition to professional help. Visiting them in the hospital and spending time with the extended family can be crucial.

At some point immediate professional involvement will end, and the therapeutic setting may or may not be available for financial or other reasons. (The church community can also play a role in creatively providing for the financial needs of the person undergoing treatment, including treatment expenses, lost wages and so on.) What people need most at this point is positive encouragement for change. This kind of support should be consistent and sustained. It is important to recognize times when the temptation to rely on external "support" such as alcohol or a sexual outlet of some kind can be overwhelming. Temptations to relapse will likely come in cycles or waves, depending on internal and external stress levels. Often relational issues and other problems were placed on the "back burner" during intensive treatment but will resurface and need to be addressed. It is important to help the individual meet the challenges of everyday living and to recognize and address the occasional desire to escape the mounting pressures of life.

The majority of persons struggling with addictive behaviors are likely to relapse despite their best efforts and intentions. A person who is viewed as *good* does not necessarily become *bad* when he or she falls back into old patterns of behavior. It is important for the person to understand that one violation does not necessarily lead to a major relapse either. Backsliding is a concept that should be familiar to Christians. The only unpardonable sin is rejecting the Holy Spirit and so refusing to confess Jesus Christ as Lord. There is forgiveness for all other sins with confession and repentance. Relapse into addictive behaviors is normal, and it should be planned for. Support can be offered to assist the struggler to take one step at a time, day by day.

CONCLUSION

Addictive behaviors such as alcohol and drug abuse, addictive sexual behaviors, and compulsive eating and gambling are complex problems, resulting from and maintained by multiple forces, including human agency. An accurate understanding of the problems of social impact (as well as the best hope for change) will acknowledge the complexity of these overlapping influences. The call is for a creative, informed and deliberate response from the body of Christ. Our efforts should not work to isolate the addict further, whether by ignoring opportunities for prevention, intervention and treatment, viewing addicts as belonging to a different class of sinners, or sending the message that the church is a place for the "well" rather than for the "sick." The church, the body of Christ, is called to make plain the fullness of grace to persons who struggle with problems of social impact.

RECOMMENDED READING

May, G. G. (1988). *Addiction and grace: Love and spirituality in the healing of addictions.* New York: HarperCollins. This is a very helpful introduction to issues of addiction from a religiously sensitive perspective.

Plantinga, C., Jr. (1995). *Not the way it's supposed to be: A breviary of sin.* Grand Rapids, MI: Eerdmans. A terrific, thoughtful scholarly resource.

Schorr, L. (1989). *Within our reach: breaking the cycle of disadvantage.* New York: Doubleday. A helpful resource focusing on the needs of the underserved.

REFERENCES

American Psychiatric Association. (2000). *Diagnostic and statistical manual of mental disorders* (4th ed.). Washington, DC: Author.

Anthony, J. C., Warner, L. A., and Kessler, R. C. (1994). Comparative epidemiology of dependence on tobacco, alcohol, controlled substances and inhalants. *Experimental and Clinical Psychopharmacology, 2*(3), 244-68.

Babor, T. F. (1994). Avoiding the horrid and beastly sin of drunkenness: Does dissuasion make a difference? *Journal of Consulting and*

Clinical Psychology, 62(6), 1127-40.

Ball, J. C., and Coty, E. (1988). *Basic issues pertaining to the effectiveness of methadone maintenance treatment* (NIDA Research Monograph 86) (pp. 178-91). Washington, DC: Government Printing Office.

Botvin, G., Schinke, S., and Orlandi, M. (1995). School-based health promotion: Substance abuse and sexual behavior. *Applied and Preventive Psychology, 4,* 167-84.

Burnside, M. A., Baer, P. E., McLaughlin, R. J., and Pokorny, A. D. (1986). Alcohol use by adolescents in disrupted families. *Alcoholism: Clinical and Experimental Research, 10,* 274-78.

Cheydleur, J. R. (1999). Alcohol abuse and dependence. In D. G. Benner and P. C. Hill (Eds.), *Baker encyclopedia of psychology and counseling* (2nd ed.) (pp. 59-64). Grand Rapids, MI: Baker.

Cloninger, C. R. (1987). Neurogenetic adaptive mechanisms in alcoholism. *Science, 236,* 410-16.

Edwards, M., and Steinglass, P. (1995). Family therapy treatment outcomes for alcoholism. *Journal of Marital and Family Therapy, 21*(4), 475-509.

Epstein, E. E., and McCrady, B. S. (1994). Research on the nature and treatment of alcoholism: Does one inform the other? *Journal of Consulting and Clinical Psychology, 62*(6), 1091-95.

Gallant, D. M. (1987). *Alcoholism: A guide to diagnosis, intervention and treatment.* New York: W. W. Norton.

Goodwin, D. W., Schulsinger, F., Moller, N., Hermansen, L., Winokur, G., and Guze, S. B. (1974). Drinking problems in adopted and nonadopted sons of alcoholics. *Archives of General Psychiatry, 31,* 164-69.

Graedon, J., and Graedon, T. (1986). *The people's pharmacy.* New York: Avon.

Green, J. W. (1982). *Cultural awareness in the human services.* Englewood Cliffs, NJ: Prentice-Hall.

Harwood, H. J., Fountain, D., and Livermore, G. (1998). Economic costs of alcohol abuse and alcoholism. In M. Galanter (Ed.), *The consequences of alcoholism: Medical, neuropsychiatric, economic, crosscultural.* Vol. 14 of *Recent developments in alcoholism* (pp. 307-30). New York: Plenum.

Havassy, B. E., Hall, S. M., and Wasserman, D. A. (1989). Social support and relapse: Commonalities among alcoholics, opiate users and cigarette smokers. *Addictive Behaviors, 16,* 235-46.

Jaffe, J. (1990). Drug addiction and drug abuse. In A. Gilman, T. Rall, A. Nies and P. Taylor (Eds.), *Goodmand and Gilman's the pharmacolog-*

ical basis of therapeutics (8th ed.) (pp. 621-42). New York: Pergamon.

Johnson, J. L., and McCown, W. G. (1993). Addictive behaviors and substance abuse. In P. B. Sutker and H. E. Adams (Eds.), *Comprehensive handbook of psychopathology* (2nd ed.) (pp. 437-50). New York: Plenum.

Julien, R. M. (1992). *A primer of drug action* (6th ed.). New York: Freeman.

Kalichman, S. (1996). *Answering your questions about AIDS*. Washington, DC: American Psychological Association.

Kaplan, J. (1983). *The hardest drug: Heroin and public policy.* Chicago: University of Chicago Press.

Kayloe, J. C. (1993). Food addiction. *Psychotherapy, 30*(2), 269-75.

Kumpfer, K. L. (1989). Prevention of alcohol and drug abuse. In D. Shaffer, I. Philips and N. Enzer (Eds.), *Prevention of mental disorders, alcohol and other drug use in children and adolescents* (OSAP Prevention Monograph 2) (pp. 310-71). Rockville, MD: U.S. Department of Health and Human Services.

Lenters, W. (1985). *The freedom we crave: Addiction—the human condition.* Grand Rapids, MI: Eerdmans.

Liddle, H., and Dakof, G. (1985). Efficacy of family therapy for drug abuse: Promising but not definitive. *Journal of Marital and Family Therapy, 21*(4), 511-93.

May, G. G. (1988). *Addiction and grace: Love and spirituality in the healing of addictions.* New York: HarperCollins.

McLellan, A., Alterman, A., Metzger, D., Grissom, G., Woody, G., Luborsky, L., and O'Brien, C. (1994). Similarity of outcome predictors across opiate, cocaine and alcohol treatments. *Journal of Consulting and Clinical Psychology, 62*(6), 1141-58.

McMinn, M. R. (2004). *Why sin matters: The surprising relationship between our sin and God's grace.* Wheaton, IL: Tyndale House.

Miller, W., and Jackson, K. (1995). *Practical psychology for pastors* (2nd ed.). Englewood Cliffs, NJ: Prentice-Hall.

Nakken, C. (1988). *The addictive personality.* New York: Harper/ Hazelden.

Nathan, P. E. (1993). Alcoholism: Psychopathology, etiology and treatment. In P. B. Sutker and H. E. Adams (Eds.), *Comprehensive handbook of psychopathology* (2nd ed.) (pp. 451-76). New York: Plenum.

Nathan, P. E., Skinstad, A. H., and Dolan, S. (2001). Alcohol-related disorders: Psychopathology, diagnosis, etiology and treatment. In H. E. Adams and P. B. Sutker (Eds.), *Comprehensive handbook of psy-*

chopathology (3rd ed.) (pp. 595-622). New York: Plenum.

National Institute of Justice. (1989). *Fiscal year-1990 program plan.* NIJ Document 119318. Washington, DC: Author.

Newcomb, M. D., and Bentler, P. M. (1989). Substance use and abuse among children and teenagers. *American Psychologist, 44*(2), 242-48.

Parry, C. (1999). *Alcohol policy and public health in South Africa.* London: Oxford University Press.

Penney, A., and Garfield, E. (1984). Parent groups in drug abuse prevention: Is this the constituency we've been waiting for? *Journal of Primary Prevention, 4,* 173-97.

Perkins, J. M. (1993). *Beyond charity.* Grand Rapids, MI: Baker.

Pincu, L. (1989). Sexual compulsivity in gay men: Controversy and treatment. *Journal of Counseling and Development, 71,* 63-66.

Plantinga, C., Jr. (1995). *Not the way it's supposed to be: A breviary of sin.* Grand Rapids, MI: Eerdmans.

Schorr, L. (1989). *Within our reach: Breaking the cycle of disadvantage.* New York: Doubleday.

Tarter, R. E., Blackson, T., Martin, C., Loeber, R., and Moss, H. (1993). Characteristics and correlates of child discipline practices in substance abuse and normal families. *American Journal on Addiction, 2*(1), 18-25.

Tarter, R. E., and Vanyukov, M. (1994). Alcoholism: A developmental disorder. *Journal of Consulting and Clinical Psychology, 62*(6), 1096-107.

Uddo, M., Malow, R. M., and Sutker, P. B. (1993). Opioid and cocaine abuse and dependent disorders. In P. B. Sutker and H. E. Adams (Eds.), *Comprehensive handbook of psychopathology* (2nd ed.) (pp. 477-503). New York: Plenum.

Van Wicklin, J. (1992). Substance abuse. In C. DeSanto, Z. Lindblade and M. Poloma (Eds.), *Christian perspectives on social problems* (pp. 379-97). Indianapolis: Wesley.

Vere, D. W. (1995). Dependence. In D. J. Atkinson, D. F. Field, A. Holmes and O. O'Donovan (Eds.), *New dictionary of Christian ethics and pastoral theology* (pp. 298-99). Downers Grove, IL: InterVarsity Press.

Yarhouse, M. A., and Jones, S. L. (1997). A critique of materialist assumptions in interpretations of research on homosexuality. *Christian Scholar's Review, 26*(4), 478-95.

8

PROBLEMS OF
BODY AND MIND

A successful performance at a moment of crisis
rests largely and essentially upon the depths of
a self wisely and rigorously prepared
in the totality of its being—mind and body.

DALLAS WILLARD

*T*he relationship between the psychological and the physical—
between mind and body—is very complex. There have been and continue to be very diverse opinions regarding the nature of this relationship. Some contend that the two are so interrelated as to be
inseparable. For example, W. Miller Brown, in a discussion of ways to
conceptualize mental illness, states:

> If we reject, as I believe we must, any version of mind-body dual-
> ism, then any mental disease, indeed any mental condition at
> all, must be a manifestation of some bodily condition, presum-
> ably of the central nervous system. In particular, a mental condi-
> tion which we correctly deem to be *diseased* must correspond, it

seems, to a physical condition which, were it known, would also be considered to be *diseased* in some correspondingly appropriate manner. (1985, p. 555)

Others have asserted that the mind and body are separate—a position commonly referred to as *classical dualism* (see Cooper, 1989). Historically, the medical and psychological professions have focused their interest on physical and mental/emotional factors respectively, avoiding the areas of overlap between the two. Clinical and research efforts in medicine have concentrated on physiological and anatomical factors in bodily diseases, whereas psychology's focus has primarily been on addressing the psychosocial factors associated with mental, emotional and behavioral disorders. More recently, however, the narrowness of these perspectives has been recognized: "Although a disorder may be primarily physical or primarily psychological, it is always a disorder of the whole person—not just of the body or the psyche" (Carson and Butcher, 1992, p. 229).

Numerous studies have demonstrated a relationship between emotional states and physical states (e.g., Antoni et al., 1990; Dohrenwend and Dohrenwend, 1974, cf. articles on body and mind disorders; Rutter, 1981). Such studies suggest that positive emotions and optimistic attitudes can actually strengthen the body's immune system and ability to recover after illness or injury (Scheier and Carver, 1987; Jones, 1977; O'Leary, 1985). Similarly, chronic negative emotion or affect, attitudes of helplessness, multiple life changes and/or excessive stress may decrease the body's immune functioning and increase its susceptibility to physical disease or psychological distress (Peterson and Seligman, 1987; Elliott, 1989; Payne, 1975; Friedman and Booth-Kewley, 1987; Levor et al., 1986). For example, a direct relationship between extremely stressful life events and the development of mental and physical problems has been well documented (Holmes and Rahe, 1967; Geiser, 1989; Koranyi, 1989; Rogers, 1989; Jemmott and Locke, 1984; Antoni et al., 1990).

Virtually all problems addressed in this book (and by the study of psychopathology in general), though primarily psychological in nature, will manifest themselves with some physical symptomatology; however, some struggles manifest themselves with an especially complex combination of both. In this chapter we will consider problems that are characterized to a significant degree by both mental and physical symptoms—*problems of body and mind*. How are we to understand the relationship between problems of the body and problems of the mind? Does one precede or produce the other, or are they inherently interconnected? These are difficult questions that have been debated for centuries by philosophers, physicians, scientists *and* pastoral theologians.

THEMES IN PASTORAL CARE

The Bible does not support any notion of classical dualism which separates the mind and body or the spirit and body. Hoekema states that the Scriptures do "not teach any . . . sharp antithesis between spirit (or mind) and body. According to the Scriptures matter is not evil but has been created by God. The Bible never denigrates the human body as a necessary source of evil but describes it as an aspect of God's good creation" (1986, p. 206).[1] To suggest such would be to reassert the position of the Gnostic heresies that emerged sometime during the second century and held that the body and soul are separate and morally distinct. The body was viewed as evil and the spirit as good. The Scriptures clearly deal with human beings as a combination of two natures (physical and nonphysical), and to cease to be either is to be less than human (or, as in the intermediate state between death and resurrection, to await being made whole). The interchangeability of these concepts in the Scriptures suggests a direct correlation between them, such that impact to one nature will affect the other. However, the Scriptures do not infer a direct causal link, such that physical damage necessarily leads to mental or spiritual damage or vice versa.

To attempt to separate these aspects of humanity is clearly wrong, but to overstate their unity would be an equally futile and potentially misleading endeavor. The Scriptures speak of the "mystery" of God's creation (Groeschel, 1992). In Paul's theology, *mysterion* (mystery) is something that cannot be understood apart from divine revelation (O'Brien, 1993). One profound example of the mysteries of God is his very nature as triune yet one (see 2 Cor 13:14; Deut 6:4). Humankind was created in the image of God (Gen 1:27), and perhaps the incarnation (embodiment) of our souls/minds is a mystery we will not fully understand this side of heaven.

Though we may never fully understand how our mind and body relate to one another, pastoral writers have for centuries acknowledged

---

[1]For a helpful discussion of Gnostic thought in light of early Christian anthropology, see Burns (1981).

that they do relate to one another and that problems associated with one can affect the other. For example, Pope Gregory wrote in the sixth century about the discernment and varied skills necessary to minister to people in diverse circumstances and of differing temperaments and character qualities. In this context, he articulated the approach he believed most helpful in ministering to people who are ill.

The hale are to be admonished in one way, the sick in another. The hale are to be admonished to employ bodily health in behalf of mental health. . . . On the other hand, the sick . . . should be told that if they believe that the heavenly country is for them, they must needs endure labours in this country, as if it were an alien one. . . . The sick are to be admonished to consider what great health of the heart is bestowed by bodily affliction, for it recalls the mind to a knowledge of itself and renews the memory of our infirmity, which health commonly disregards. Thus the spirit which is carried out of itself to pride is made to remember the condition to which it is subject, owing to the ills of the flesh which it bears. (Gregory, 1950, pp. 120, 123)

According to Pope Gregory, the illnesses of the body are an occasion to remember our humble circumstances and be reoriented to a right relationship with God: there is a "health of the heart" that can come with "bodily affliction" as one gains a truer knowledge of oneself before a holy God.

At the heart of many of the disorders in this chapter is an inability to do just this. Sleeplessness, self-starvation and preoccupation with bodily ailments seem to share in common an inability to see ourselves as we really are—"harassed and helpless" (Mt 9:35-38) and in need of a physician of souls. We yearn to be whole—more whole than we have any right to expect to be. As fallen people in a fallen world, we are subject to imperfection, and we must be willing to accept this and see ourselves in this way. We suffer from afflictions that bombard our bodies and our minds with painful struggles. Mental and emotional pain is no less and sometimes more difficult to bear than physical pain.

What the pastoral writers encourage is that in the face of this reality we not lose hope, for God promises to give us comfort in the form of "patient endurance" to face our sufferings (2 Cor 1). Despair is perhaps the greatest danger in problems of the body and mind. When people are afflicted with suffering of both body and mind, they need strength to endure, and the pastoral writers acknowledge that this comes from the love of a merciful God.

When pain is to be borne, a little courage helps more than much knowledge, a little human sympathy more than much courage, and the least tincture of the love of God more than all. (Lewis, 1959, p. viii)

THEMES FROM PSYCHOPATHOLOGY

As problems of body and mind, we will consider four major categories of problems identified by the *DSM-IV* as manifesting themselves with significant psychological and physical symptoms: sleep disorders, eating disorders, somatoform disorders and mental disorders due to a general medical condition. In addition, we will discuss a fifth *DSM* category, dissociative disorders, in this chapter.[2] A central theme in problems of the mind and body is the relationship between psychological factors and physical health. Most diagnoses of psychological disorders anticipate the presence of physical symptoms such as changes in appetite and changes in sleep patterns; however, with this cluster of disorders, the relationship between psychological and physical is more intense. In them, psychological factors disrupt the person's ability to function and can lead to physical symptoms that may result in serious illness and even death.

Just as psychological factors can have an influence on physical health, so medical factors can have an impact on psychological health. A significant percentage of patients suffering from medical illness experience psychological symptoms in addition to physical symptoms. At the very least, the presence of physical symptoms often leads to emotional distress, which in itself can be disabling.

---

[2]We include the dissociative disorders with "problems of the mind and body" even though they do not meet our criteria for disorders that manifest themselves with significant physical as well as psychological symptoms. In general, the dissociative disorders are not well understood or clearly defined, and thus they do not fit well into any of our conceptual clusters for this book. However, they do share a striking similarity to a number of the disorders we discuss in this chapter. The dissociative disorders, like sleep disorders, eating disorders and somatoform disorders, involve *a process of intrapsychic separation*. During the course of any of these disorders, whether normally as in sleep or abnormally as in eating disorders, somatoform disorders and dissociative disorders, the struggling person separates themselves in some way from a truthful, conscious perception of reality. Their perception and experience of reality becomes fragmented, compartmentalized or distorted. Because of this shared phenomenology, we include the dissociative disorders in our category of "problems of mind and body."

Sleep disorders. Between 30 and 40 percent of adults in the United States in any given year will report some form of insomnia or other sleep disturbance (APA, 1994), and approximately 15 percent of U.S. adults will struggle with a period of chronic insomnia at some point in their life (Meyer and Deitsch, 1996; Harsh and Ogilvie, 1995, cf. articles on body and mind disorders; Hauri, 1991, cf. articles on body and mind disorders; Montplaisir and Godbout, 1991). Sleep disorders may contribute to emotional distress, social and occupational difficulties, elevated risks for injury and in some situations serious medical complications (Morin and Edinger, 2003). The *DSM-IV* classifies four major categories of sleep disorders according to their presumed etiology: primary sleep disorders, sleep disorders related to other mental disorders, sleep disorders due to general medical conditions, and substance-induced sleep disorders. We will focus on the primary sleep disorders, which are subdivided into two categories: dyssomnias (sleep problems related to the duration of sleep, the quality of sleep or the time when sleep occurs) and parasomnias (abnormal biological phenomena or behaviors that occur in connection with sleep, certain stages of sleep or transitions between sleep and wakefulness). These are considered primary sleep disorders because they are "presumed to arise from endogenous abnormalities in sleep-wake generating or timing mechanisms, often complicated by conditioning factors" (APA, 1994, p. 551). In other words, it is assumed that there is an identifiable pathology in the mechanisms that control either the transitions between sleep and wakefulness or the ability of a person to fall asleep or wake up in a timely manner that is appropriate to their life conditions. These mechanisms can be affected by biological, psychosocial or environmental factors.

The dyssomnias include primary insomnia (difficulty in falling asleep or staying asleep, or experiencing sleep that is restful and restorative regularly for at least one month), primary hypersomnia (excessive sleep), narcolepsy (unpredictable episodes of sleep and/or cataplexy, a sudden loss of muscle control), breathing-related sleep disorder (obstructive sleep apnea syndrome is the most common, in which breathing difficulties disrupt sleep repetitively, preventing rest and restoration), circadian rhythm sleep disorder (mismatch between a person's perceived natural cycle of sleep and wake and the expectations or demands of their environment) and dyssomnia not otherwise specified (NOS). The parasomnias include nightmare disorder (persistent nightmares that disrupt sleep), sleep terror disorder (repeated abrupt, terrifying awakenings from sleep, often accompanied by screams or crying), sleepwalking disorder (repeated episodes of moving about while still in a state of sleep) and parasomnia NOS.

The common element of all of these problems, of course, is their relation to sleep. Our ability to understand these struggles rests in large part on our understanding of the nature of sleep and its purpose. According to Hillstrom,

> Sleep is so familiar and universal that we seldom stop to think about its strangeness. Yet, when we sleep we enter a peculiar and vulnerable state in which we lose our awareness of the outside world and our ability to control our thoughts or actions. Mental events become surrealistic, distorted, and bizarre, and voluntary muscles are periodically paralyzed to prevent us from acting out our dreams and possibly injuring ourselves or others. Memory is altered, too. Most of the mental activity and vivid imagery of the night disappears without a trace, so insistently that it would seem that we are programmed to forget it. What is the purpose of this odd state called sleep? Scientists are still not sure. (1999, p. 1130)

Hillstrom summarizes a few of the significant research findings regarding the nature of sleep:

1. Sleep occurs in five distinct stages: rapid eye movement (REM)—characterized most often by increased heart rate, breathing and brain activity (often the vivid dream cycle of sleep), and movement of the eyes back and forth as if watching a tennis match—and four stages of nonrapid eye movement or slow-wave sleep (NREM).

2. The fourth NREM stage is believed to relate to brain restoration, because it typically involves a drop in the temperature of the brain accompanied by an approximately 75 percent reduction in the metabolism and blood flow of the brain (see Buschbaum et al., 1989). Others contend that REM sleep serves a similar function.

3. The body seems to be able to restore itself through rest without sleep, but sleep deprivation studies have shown that prolonged wakefulness can produce brain dysfunction resulting in problems with concentration, attention and, in some cases, rational thought.

Eating disorders. The *DSM-IV* names two categories of eating disorders and one potential category awaiting further research: anorexia nervosa (distortion in one's perception of one's own body weight and appearance accompanied by fear of weight gain and persistent weight loss behaviors such as starvation or excessive exercise), bulimia nervosa (cycles of binge eating followed by purging behaviors such as vomiting, diuretics, laxatives) and binge-eating disorder (recurrent compulsive binge eating for the purpose of numbing uncomfortable emotions; coded as an eating disorder NOS).

Eating disorders are among the most debilitating psychological disorders (Klein and Walsh, 2003). Estimates of their prevalence suggest that under 1.5-2 percent of people (predominantly women, though cases of eating disorders in males are on the rise, especially among males who identify themselves as gay) struggle with either anorexia (Willi and Grossman, 1983) or bulimia nervosa (Schotte and Stunkard, 1987) in the United States. Studies suggest that international prevalence rates range somewhere between 0.3 and 1 percent (Hoek and van Hoeken, 2003). However, the behaviors associated with bulimia may be more common than the disorder itself. The shocking fact is that these estimates represent a quadruple increase over only a twenty-year span (Williamson, Barker and Norris, 1993). Eating disorders are diagnosed primarily among middle and upper socioeconomic classes (Fornari et al., 1994; Bruch, Czyzewski and Suhr, 1988; Agras, 1987), more often among Caucasians than minorities (Striegel-Moore et al., 2003), and with onset most often during the teenage years. With anorexia nervosa, there is irrevocable damage to the patient's bone structure, and subsequent mortality rates have been estimated at between 5 and 15 percent (Fornari et al., 1994; Vitousek and Manke, 1994).

Somatoform disorders. Somatoform disorders can be severely incapacitating and cause much subjective distress, but they are rarely understood by either providers of health care services or well-meaning family members and friends. The *DSM-IV* classifies seven types of somatoform disorders in which physical symptoms suggestive of general medical conditions are described but no medical condition can be identified:

- somatization disorder—persistent physical complaints beginning before age thirty; medical treatment is continually sought for a combination of symptoms including pain, gastrointestinal discomfort, sexual problems and pseudoneurological problems

- undifferentiated somatoform disorder—unexplained physical symptoms for at least six months that do not meet the criteria for a somatization disorder

- conversion disorder—symptoms such as blindness, paralysis, uncontrolled vomiting, seizures or aphonia which suggest the presence of a neurological condition but are deemed to be of psychological origin

- pain disorder—persistent pain to whose onset, severity, exacerbation or maintenance psychological factors are deemed to contribute significantly

- hypochondriasis—persistent fear or belief that one has a serious medical disease, based on misinterpretation of one's own bodily functions or symptoms

- body dysmorphic disorder—exaggerated preoccupation with an imagined defect in appearance

- somatoform disorder NOS

There are no reliable prevalence statistics available for the somatoform disorders, as they are often difficult to diagnose, are most often handled by primary care physicians and are frequently left untreated. Some general statistics, however, warrant mention. On the average, 60-80 percent of the "normal" population will experience some physical symptom in a given week (Kellner, 1985). Studies report that anywhere from 20 to 80 percent of patients examined by primary care physicians complain of symptoms that are either somatic or considered idiopathic (origin unknown) by the physicians (Barsky and Klerman, 1983; Kellner, 1985). Between 50 and 70 percent of patients who are diagnosed with psychological disorders first seek help for physical symptoms. In addition, studies have found that hospitalization is lengthened for medical patients with a comorbid psychological problem (Katon, 1993).

Dissociative disorders. People who suffer from what are referred to today as dissociative disorders experience a kind of disconnect in either consciousness or personal identity. Typically this involves some kind of dissociation, depersonalization or loss of sense of reality. Considerable disagreement exists regarding the incidence rates of dissociative disorders (Kluft and Fine, 1993); however, in general these disorders are considered to be uncommon (Dunn, 1992). The *DSM-IV* states that the dissociative disorders are characterized by "a disruption in the usually integrated functions of consciousness, memory, identity, or perception of the environment" (APA, 1994, p. 477). Four types of dissociative disorders are classified, and one type is suggested for consideration in future revisions of the *DSM*.

Depersonalization disorder is rare and involves alarming feelings of unreality (involving both depersonalization and derealization) that significantly affect normal activities. Average age of onset is about age sixteen, and people who suffer from this condition often have difficulties with attention and concentration, as well as short-term memory.

Dissociative amnesia includes various presentations of psychogenic memory loss. For example, a person might suffer from generalized amnesia, being unable to recall anything. Another person might suffer from selected amnesia (or localized amnesia), being unable to recall a specific event.

Dissociative fugue is related in some ways to dissociative amnesia. Persons with dissociative fugue find themselves in strange and unfamiliar places, having no idea how they got there and who they are.

The validity of *dissociative identity disorder* (DID), formerly known by the label "Multiple Personality Disorder," as a diagnostic category has historically been challenged. Some suggest that DID should be seen as a constellation of symptoms associated with other disorders rather than a distinct category in itself (Fahey, 1988; North et al., 1993). Others contend that it is not only a valid category but an underdiagnosed one. For example, Rifkin et al. say, "In recent years reports have appeared suggesting that dissociative identity disorder is common, and there is concern that it is misdiagnosed as schizophrenia, borderline personality disorder, or major depression" (1998, p. 844). Though current research points to the validity of the diagnosis, Gleaves, May and Cardeña insist that "there is room for improvement in the specifics of the diagnostic criteria, including an empirically based, more precise description of the symptoms associated with DID" (2001, p. 603).

DID is characterized by the expression of various identities, each with its own idiosyncratic voices and behaviors. The average number of identities within a given individual is about fifteen, with impulsive, risk-taking alters and cross-gendered alters often being present. Clinicians refer to the transition from personality to personality as a "switch," and it can occur very quickly. Females are more likely to present with DID than males by a ratio of about nine to one, and it is estimated that between 3 and 6 percent of the population suffers from DID (Waller, 1997; Kihlstrom, 2001).

Dissociative trance disorder (under consideration for future revisions) is defined by *DSM-IV* as "an involuntary state of trance that is not accepted by the person's culture as a normal part of a collective cultural or religious practice and that causes clinically significant distress or functional impairment" (APA, 1994, p. 727). It varies significantly across cultures and is typically labeled as either a "trance" or "possession trance." In a "possession trance," the dissociative symptoms are attributed to spirits or possession of some kind that is recognized within that culture.

Mental disorders due to a general medical condition. The *DSM-IV* identifies a number of psychopathological symptoms that may originate from a physiological pathology. With these disorders, the "mental symptoms are judged to be the direct physiological consequence of a general medical condition" (APA, 1994, p. 165). These include catatonic disorder due to a general medical condition (GMC), personality change due to a GMC, delirium due to a GMC, dementia due to a GMC, amnestic disorder due to a GMC, psychotic disorder due to a GMC, mood disorder due to a GMC, anxiety disorder due to a GMC, sexual dysfunction due to a GMC, sleep disorder due to a GMC and mental disorder NOS due to a GMC. Estimates of mental disorders tied to chronic medical problems range from 30 to 60 percent for hospitalized medical patients and 50 to 80 percent for medical patients seen in outpatient facilities (Barrett et al., 1988; Lipowski, 1967).

The connection between medical problems and the development of mental and emotional problems is especially relevant in geriatric care. Statistical projections assume that by the year 2040 about one in five Americans will be over the age of sixty-five (Burch, 1985). Currently it is estimated that about 12 percent of Americans survive to this age (U.S. Bureau of the Census, 1992). This demographic change in the U.S. population will bring a need for better diagnosis and treatment of the mental health of the aging population. As medical science continually discovers ways to prolong life (and/or death), mental health providers will be increasingly challenged with the needs of patients who suffer from psychological symptoms accompanying their chronic medical illnesses. Much more understanding of the relationship between chronic medical illness and mental health is needed. At the very least, mental health care providers need to be prepared for increasing numbers of patients who will be suffering from both.

ANTECEDENTS TO PROBLEMS OF MIND AND BODY

When a person is suffering from any one of these problems of the mind and body (sleep disorder, eating disorder, somatoform disorder, dissociative disorder or psychological disorder associated with a chronic medical problem), it is unlikely that a single factor can be identified as the cause of the problem. It is sometimes hard to discern what might cause the disorder (etiology) and what may result from a self-defeating pattern of symptoms (maintenance). In almost all cases, a significant interaction of numerous factors leads to the development of the problem. These include biological, psychosocial, sociocultural and spiritual factors.

Biological factors. It has become generally accepted that our genetic makeup plays at least some role in the development of any psychological or physical problem, if only by the presence of an inherited vulnerability. However, the role of genetic factors has been implicated in the etiology of some disorders (e.g., schizophrenia) much more than others (e.g., adjustment disorder). With the cluster of disorders we are conceptualizing as problems of the mind and body, the role of biological factors is less clearly understood.

As has been mentioned, physiological studies have revealed a link between the immune system of the body and emotions (Antoni et al., 1990). The limbic system, which has centers in the amygdala and hippocampus of the brain, is involved in the regulation of both the immune system and the physiological production of emotions. Neuropeptides (e.g., endorphins) are produced by the limbic system and are involved in both of these physiological processes. Because of this direct link between these two systems, our immune system may reflect our emotional state and vice versa.

Some evidence suggests a genetic contribution to the development of somatoform disorders. Early neurophysiological studies suggested that conversion symptoms (physical symptoms that would point to a medical problem in the absence of any evidence of such medical problems) arose from corticofugal inhibition in the brain due to damage or malfunction (Whitlock, 1967; Ludwig, 1972). These studies proposed that inhibition of sensory stimulation at the level of the brain stem reticular formation results in selective inattention to certain bodily functions. Later studies lent some credibility to this and focused interest on the right cerebral hemisphere as the primary source of the alteration of affect and/or motivation in somatic symptoms (Galin, Diamond and Braff, 1977; Stern, 1977). Similar studies with somatization disorder suggest that bilateral frontal and right hemisphere dysfunction contributes to the development of the disorder (Flor-Henry et al., 1981; Gordon et al., 1986; James et al., 1987). Guze (1983) identified familial concordance for both somatization and sociopathy in women and attributed this to a shared behavior (assortative mating) in women of both disorder groups.

Twin studies with anorexia nervosa (spawned by high incidence rates of eating disorders within families of anorexics) have suggested concordance rates as high as 50 percent; however, the studies involved twins reared together, which limits the significance of the findings (Scott, 1986; Holland et al., 1984). Neurological and anatomical studies have suggested the involvement of the hypothalamus of the brain in regulating essential body functions or the influence of neurotransmitters like dopamine, serotonin or norepinephrine (e.g., Wakeling, 1985). It is not yet clear, however, whether these biological factors are precipitants of eating disorders or secondary effects of starvation.

At this point, our understanding of the biological contributions to this cluster of disorders is very limited and inconclusive.

Psychosocial factors. Numerous psychosocial factors have been identified as contributors to the etiology of each of the groups of disorders in this chapter. Common themes in discussions on the etiology of sleep disorders include intense anxiety and an inability to establish some order and consistency in daily schedules, especially at bedtime. The anxiety is often due to the presence of fears or overwhelming stress. The inability to establish consistency can also often be tied to the feeling of being overwhelmed, with not enough hours in the day to get everything done. The consequence is that the individual lacks any comfortable rituals to prepare for sleep and often ends up ruminating on stressful concerns in bed—perhaps the first moment of peace during the day (Bootzin et al., 1993). Fear and lack of control are also psychosocial explanations for the origins of eating disorders. Some have suggested that anxiety related to feelings of helplessness and powerlessness in puberty contributes to the adoption of starvation behaviors as an attempt to regain control (e.g., Gamer and Garfinkel, 1985). Others have suggested that the fear of fatness associated with eating disorders is in reality a fear of loss of control rooted in a passive and dependent personality (e.g., Goodsit, 1985).

Meyer and Deitsch (1996) identified lifestyle and family characteristics indicative of patients who somatize emotional stress and subsequently develop somatoform disorders, including the following:

• upbringing in an atmosphere of illness, with an invalid family member or a significant relationship with someone suffering from a somatoform disorder

• dependency in relationship to a family member who gave much attention and nurturing in times of illness but remained largely non-expressive or emotionally distant when the person was healthy

- tendency to mask psychological conflict and existential needs with somatic complaints, leaving the tensions and needs unresolved
- an inherited sensivity to bodily sensations and pain

With somatoform disorders, Kimball and Blindt (1982) suggest that conversion symptoms may be used by people as a way to receive special privileges or attention, manipulate others or avoid unwanted responsibilities. Brown and Vaillant (1981) propose that hypochondriasis is the result of repressed hostility. People who have been abandoned, hurt or unloved may displace their feelings of anger onto their own body. Other displacement theories have suggested that hypochondriasis results from an inability to tolerate one's feelings of inadequacy or worthlessness. Physical symptoms and complaints replace the intolerable emotional concerns (McCranie, 1979). In general, somatizers tend to blame their failings on physical symptoms.

Two distinct perspectives are currently debated regarding the etiology of DID: the iatrogenic and traumagenic theories (Gleaves, May and Cardeña, 2001). The iatrogenic theory maintains that DID is an artifact of psychotherapy and the media—its symptoms emerge in response to suggestion and not trauma. Though it has been well documented that false memories can be created in response to specific suggestions from therapists, there is little empirical support for iatrogenic theories. The traumagenic theory assumes that DID develops in response to trauma and sees its symptoms as a complex variant of PTSD. Proponents of this position explain the relative low incidence of DID among the population of persons abused in childhood by the assertion of a diathesis-stress model, in which those who eventually develop DID are believed to possess a disposition toward dissociative coping behaviors. Significant trauma (e.g., sexual or physical abuse) in early childhood is probably the single most consistent finding in the history of those who struggle with symptoms of dissociative disorders. Most experts in this area would view characteristic symptoms, such as dissociation, as a protective function that helps the child manage an experience that is otherwise unmanageable. Those who contend with symptoms of DID tend to have a rich fantasy life and tend to be rather suggestible. Some have even suggested that certain personality factors (e.g., "harm-avoidant temperament, immature defenses, and overconnection and disconnection cognitive schema") may be associated with dissociative pathology (Simeon et al., 2002, p. 490).

Strain and Grossman (1975) have identified seven different stresses that confront the medically ill patient and may contribute to the development of psychological problems. These are based on psychodynamic theory and include the following:

1. The illness/hospitalization may pose a fundamental threat to a person's sense of self (narcissistic integrity).

2. Forced to entrust their health and life to numerous hospital staff they don't know, they may suffer from a fear of strangers.

3. Anxiety may increase because of separation from family, friends and "normal" life.

4. As a result of the illness, they may fear a loss of the love and approval of those who are closest to them.

5. With debilitating illness, they may fear a loss of developmentally achieved functions (e.g., fear of becoming incontinent).

6. Similarly, they may fear a loss of or injury to their body parts.

7. They also may experience guilt over being ill and fear of retaliation by those they feel they are letting down.

Any or all of these may contribute to the development of or exacerbate already existing psychological problems.

In general, psychosocial themes in the etiology of problems of the mind and body include overwhelming external stresses (e.g., severe medical illness), intense fear and anxiety (e.g., with sleep and eating disorders), family backgrounds characterized by illness or unhealthy response patterns (e.g., with somatoform disorders), and/or lifestyle patterns of chronic overcommitment or lack of self-discipline. Persons may begin to feel that their life is getting out of control, which only intensifies their fear, anxiety and subsequent symptom patterns.

Sociocultural factors. Several striking sociocultural factors emerge with specific disorders from this cluster. They include factors related to socioeconomic status, cultural origin, age and family patterns.

Eating disorders (especially anorexia nervosa) are most prevalent in higher socioeconomic families (Crisp, Palmer and Kalucy, 1976). Preoccupation with image and overconcern with one's external appearance in the eyes of others are more common in people of this socioeconomic class. Family dynamics may revolve around the development of "appropriate" poise, beauty and body image. In addition, societal and peer pressures to be accepted often involve superficial definitions of beauty and popularity. Though it would be overly simplistic to attribute the etiology of eating disorders to issues of class alone, the prevalence of eating disorders in affluent settings is an indication of the presence of an overly materialistic view of individual worth.

In striking contrast, Goldberg and Bridges (1988) describe a "narcissistic idealization of the self" within Western cultures as a factor reducing the frequency of somatoform disorders. According to them, somatoform disorders are more prevalent in *non*-Western cultures (e.g., China), where the "luxuries" of narcissism and an overabundance of physicians are uncommon. Within cultures where emotional distress is unacceptable, somatization of psychological tension is more common. Subcultures within Western culture may hold similar values and be more likely to foster somatization (e.g., some Christian communities equate psychological problems with spiritual deficits). This will be discussed in more depth below.

In general, persons may use their symptoms as a means to communicate their sense of helplessness and to foster an environment that perpetuates this perception, thus relieving them of expectations of or opportunities for developing efficacy. In addition, others are inhibited from responding to them with assertiveness or anger. Sociocultural and familial reinforcement often perpetuates the "sick role" for these persons, initially exempting them from unwanted responsibilities and duties but eventually stripping them of any remnant of an active or enjoyable life. Perpetuating the role takes precedence even over wanted activities and relationships.

As stated above, changing social demographics suggest that the population of elderly persons will continue to expand throughout the next half-century in the United States. The needs associated with this population will become an increasing issue for both the mental and physical health professions. Our knowledge of the role of psychological distress in the process of healing and coping with chronic illness is growing but still limited. This will need to be a central concern in the years to come.

Spiritual factors. Spiritual issues also play a role in the development of problems of the body and mind. The Scriptures speak of the priority God places on balance and order in life. The meaning we ascribe to certain aspects of our life plays a very important role in our ability to foster or maintain such balance. Van Leeuwen and her colleagues (1993) contend, for example, that our culture ascribes gender-related meanings of worth based on body shape. Unquestionably ours is a highly sexualized society with an obsession with thinness, especially in women. Pathogenic weight-control behaviors reflect certain value assumptions about what it means to be an "ideal" man or woman. Change is possible only if we are willing to create other meanings for femininity and masculinity than those that are dominant in our affluent postmodern society. Our pattern of defining worth based on external appearance not only runs contrary to sound biblical and theological teaching but can lead to tragic and even fatal consequences.

With this cluster of disorders, balance is often lost as preoccupations and obsessions with symptoms take on a life of their own. Persons may lose perspective on the nature of their suffering and begin to isolate themselves from family and friends. In so doing, they lose the help that community affords on a psychological and spiritual level. Often it is necessary for family and friends to intervene and provide this perspective, although it is rarely willingly accepted. This process of isolation, denial and rejection of the perceptions and intentions of others is similar to the insidious wedge that sin can drive between persons and their family and friends. Prognosis is often contingent on the degree to which support systems are in place and family and friends are willing to be understanding and persevere despite the resistance of those suffering from disorders of the mind and body.

Perhaps one of the more controversial issues involves the spiritual dimensions that appear related to some dissociative disorders. It is not uncommon for those suffering from DID to have alters that have a demonic name or "presence" in relation to other alters. Some view all alters as aspects of a person's divided personality, while others distinguish among alters (as expressions of a client's personality) and demons, which may also be present. Relatively little has been written considering the overlap of psychopathology and demonic influence. Even Christian researchers and authors in the field of psychopathology tend to stay away from the idea of demonic involvement in the development of mental disorders. One notable exception, Bufford (1989), contends that demon possession and psychopathology are distinct phenomena that involve different dimensions of human functioning. He suggests that they may occur together or separately but that they do influence each other.

Virkler (1999) suggests that part of the challenge of discerning demonic influence in the development of psychopathology has to do with our worldview assumptions about the nature of the cosmos. Summarizing the ideas of C. Peter Wagner and Paul Hiebert, Virkler identifies three distinct views of the cosmos. First, some believe in a single-tiered universe, in which only "natural" phenomena are believed to exist and warrant consideration. Others believe in a two-tiered universe, in which God and other supernatural beings dwell in one level and humans in a lower level. A third option (which he argues is the view of most non-Western cultures and of the biblical world) is a belief in a three-tiered universe, in which there is a middle level where supernatural beings interact with humans (often on an intrapsychic level). According to this view, "much of what happens in human life is believed to occur in this middle story" (Virkler, 1999, p. 326). The *DSM* nosology is based on the assumption of a single-tiered universe, according to Virkler, while the common Christian worldview posits a three-tiered universe. The result is an inability to communicate across conflictual worldviews, compounded by the absence of substantive research and/or theoretical literature from Christians about psychopathology and the demonic. We will revisit this idea in our discussion of integrative themes below.

A model that accounts for a multiplicity of causal factors in the relationship between emotional distress and illness and the etiology of problems of the mind and body is needed. With any individual, it is crucial to acknowledge this multiplicity of contributing factors and to understand the theories associated with these factors which may prove instrumental in helping the person. At some level we all are vulnerable to the development of problems with our mind or body or both; however, some seem to be more susceptible than others, and the factors that may play the greatest role for any one person are highly idiographic. Biological, psychosocial, sociocultural *and* spiritual factors all must be considered in the care of any individual.

TREATMENT THEMES

Key themes emerging from this cluster of disorders include the need for careful assessment, the need to address the physical as well as psychological symptoms, the importance of rapport in the psychotherapeutic relationship, the need to help the patients develop a realistic perspective on their problems and on themselves, and the potential benefit of family involvement.

First, a careful assessment is crucial because of the often complex symptoms presented by patients. Collaborative efforts are often needed between physicians and mental health professionals to address these complex symptoms, and a thorough assessment can be invaluable. Assessment of the medically ill patient suffering from psychological symptoms needs to involve careful discernment, because these symptoms may be reactions to the stress of the illness or the hospitalization, or they may be direct psychological effects of the illness itself or the treatment regimen. Many who suffer from sleeping disorders also struggle with significant symptoms of depression, anxiety and/or obsessive-compulsive characteristics, which may complicate the treatment of their sleep difficulties (Meyer and Deitsch, 1996; Harsh and Ogilvie, 1995, cf. articles on body and mind disorders). Such determinations made during the assessment process will have a dramatic impact on the course chosen for treatment.

Second, it is important to address both the physical and psychological aspects of the patient's problems, as they likely have been suffering from the symptoms for a long time and have been to numerous professionals seeking help. A thorough physical exam will at the very least provide reassurance to the patient, allowing therapy to focus on the psychological issues. As just stated, a team effort with the patient's physician is ideal. Biofeedback may be a helpful auxiliary to psychological interventions, as it may provide the patient with incentive to accept the psychological aspects of their problems. With many of these disorders, the physical symptoms may be highly resistant to treatment, and realistic goals for treatment need to reflect this. For example, with chronic pain sufferers, the major emphases in treatment need to be on the enhancement of specific competencies (e.g., training in social skills and assertiveness; vocational rehabilitation) to facilitate independence rather than mere pain reduction (Love and Peck, 1987).

Third, rapport is an extremely crucial element of treatment. Often patients struggling with physical as well as psychological symptoms have had extensive, and seemingly unproductive, encounters with health professionals. They often seek help from mental health professionals as a last resort and are frustrated and skeptical at best, angry and cynical at worst. It is important to develop a relationship of trust based on genuine concern and empathy for their sufferings and trials. This does not necessitate validating their perceptions, but it does require communicating understanding and acceptance.

Table 8.1. Sample Guidelines for Treatment of Problems of the Mind and Body

Eating Disorders (adapted from APA, 2000)

Anorexia Nervosa

1. Treatment outcomes are most positive when a variety of modalities (including nutrition management and rehabilitation, psychotherapeutic interventions, and medication) are offered at progressive stages of the disorder.

2. The goals of treatment include
   - to regain a healthy weight
   - to restore healthy eating habits
   - to treat physical complications
   - to address dysfunctional beliefs
   - to approach those dysfunctional thoughts, feelings and beliefs
   - to deal with affective and behavioral issues
   - to deal with associated or contributory psychological difficulties
   - to include family therapy when appropriate and possible
   - to teach relapse prevention (Koocher, Norcross and Hill, 1998, p. 386)

3. Individual psychotherapy is most successful after the acute phase of treatment (refeeding and reestablishment of a minimally healthy body weight) and is typically focused on increasing the patient's understanding of
   - their experience of the disorder
   - the interaction of family, development and cultural factors on the etiology and maintenance of the disorder
   - the degree to which the disorder represents a "maladaptive attempt to cope and emotionally self-regulate"
   - relapse prevention strategies
   - healthy coping alternatives for the future

4. Family therapy and/or couples therapy may help with symptom reduction and maintenance of healthy eating patterns and to deal with any family patterns which may have contributed to the etiology of the disorder.

5. Support groups for patients and family members offer support, advice and education about the disorder.

6. Medication proves most helpful after a healthy weight has been restored to help maintain weight and manage emotions.

Bulimia Nervosa

1. Common treatment modalities include nutrition counseling and rehabilitation; individual, family and group psychotherapy; and medication.

2. Primary goals for nutrition counseling and rehabilitation include the reduction of binge eating and purging behaviors.

3. Primary goals for psychotherapeutic interventions include
   - reducing or eliminating binging and purging behaviors
   - improving perceptions of self related to the eating disorder
   - development of healthier eating behaviors and attitudes (e.g., increas-

ing variety in the diet, decreasing food restricting behaviors)
- teaching healthy exercise regimens
- treatment of any comorbid psychopathology

4. Antidepressant medications are most often prescribed to help reduce the frequency of binging and purging behaviors.

Sleep Disorders (Bootzin, Epstein and Wood, 1991; Schoicket, Bertelson and Lacks, 1988; Lacks and Morin, 1992)

Educate the patient on the following guidelines regarding good sleep hygiene:

1. Establish a regular bedtime and arousal time.
2. Avoiding naps during the day.
3. Develop a habit of morning or afternoon exercise (not evening).
4. Eat only a light snack at night, avoiding caffeine or other stimulants.
5. Sleep in a comfortable bed whenever possible.
6. Use the bed for sleep or sex only (i.e., no working or watching television in bed).
7. Lie down to sleep only when sleepy, and don't lie in bed ruminating if having trouble sleeping. After ten minutes of unsuccessful attempts to sleep, get up and engage in some other activity until sleepy.

Somatoform Disorders (Katon, 1993)

1. Acknowledge and accept the patient's suffering as true (this will counteract some of the anger that has likely built up over years of frustrating interactions with skeptical physicians and will be a strong step toward developing rapport with the patient)
2. Establish regular appointment times to avoid the perception that a symptom is required to come for an appointment.
3. Conduct a thorough physical exam, but not more than is needed.
4. Limit psychoactive and pain medications whenever possible except for possible antidepressants.
5. Be aware that these patients often come from environments where physical symptoms were used to express emotion and where a history of abuse is not uncommon.
6. Begin with interventions targeting physical symptoms (e.g., relaxation training or biofeedback), and progress to supportive and dynamic techniques.
7. Establish realistic treatment goals—stress coping and management strategies for the symptoms—realizing that they may not all diminish.
8. Stress activity (both physically and psychologically), since resting and inactivity are countertherapeutic for them
9. Involve the family in order to facilitate change in the system and to increase the likelihood that gains will be maintained.

In the case of eating disorders, for example, developing an empathic relationship with the individual and her family is crucial. The patterns surrounding eating or the avoidance of eating are difficult to change (as with any "addictive" behavior) and may have become deeply rooted in family dynamics. Attempts to effect change in these systems require high levels of trust from all family members. Behavior modification may be an essential step after any medical risks have been reduced (this may require inpatient treatment). Eventually, family therapy should be incorporated into the treatment plan to promote generalization and maintenance of any progress.

Most persons who struggle with eating disorders will not seek treatment on their own and will deny their illness. Close friends or family members need to insist on treatment. In both inpatient and outpatient settings, these same persons will usually test the limits of any treatment plan. The behavior can become an extremely vicious cycle. With eating disorders, it is clear that intervention is needed at multiple levels.[3]

With all of the disorders of the mind and body, distortions or misperceptions about oneself and the reality of one's problems are common. Therefore, a fourth need is to help establish a more realistic perspective. One way this can be achieved is by empowering the patient through the establishment of a structure in the therapy relationship and the treatment plan. Increased ability to function within the boundaries and expectations of a structured relationship and treatment regimen may reinstill feelings of self-efficacy. Some examples of treatment guidelines are offered in table 8.1.

Fifth, marital and family interactions may serve to provide secondary gain to persons with these disorders and should be considered for possible reinforcement patterns. Family therapy may be the only means of counteracting some of these patterns: family members can be taught "to give the person psychological reassurance and caring responses, while at the same time ignoring or otherwise avoiding the reinforcement of the concerns about physical disorder" (Meyer and Deitsch, 1996, p. 139).

Most people with specific dissociative disorders, such as dissocia-

---

[3]The National Anorexic Aid Society, the American Anorexia and Bulimia Association, the National Association of Anorexia Nervosa and Associated Disorders, and Anorexia Nervosa and Related Eating Disorders have all been especially visible in recent years. They offer hotlines, professional referrals, printed information, workshops and conferences. Self-help and support groups are active throughout North America.

tive amnesia or dissociative fugue, tend to experience a resolution of their condition over time. However, those who suffer from DID tend to be involved in more long-term therapy with a focus on self-control, stress management and, ultimately, reintegrating the fragmented identities. According to Barlow and Durand (2001), a key step is identifying and resolving specific experiences that might set off a traumatic memory. As in the treatment of posttraumatic stress disorder, clinicians often help the client relive some aspects of the traumatic event to come to terms with it.

Treatment with any of these disorders should emphasize balance and the ascription of meaning to different aspects of the person's life. Establishing balance is no easy task for persons suffering from problems of the mind and body. Their ability to see themselves and their life clearly is often significantly distorted, as is the meaning they ascribe to certain aspects of their life. To create more balance in their life, or at least to counteract feelings of helplessness and powerlessness, it will be necessary to help them identify some of the resources they have or need.

PREVENTION THEMES

As stated above, the family can be a central factor in the maintenance of symptoms associated with problems of the mind and body. On the other hand, it can serve as a critical preventive influence in children's lives. The experiences of childhood, especially in the family, contribute to the development and maturation of the self and often establish the patterns of interrelatedness and self-perception that become distorted in these disorders. Children need a stable environment in which they are taught, especially through modeling, how to handle responsibility, respond to limits, gain self-control, establish appropriate boundaries in relationships, live productively in community and value themselves and others. Children who grow up in such an environment develop the necessary resources to live productively and cope with negative events and emotions. When this type of environment is not present, children often grow up struggling with psychological conflict and uncertainty.

Adjusting to inevitable changes, losses and transitions in life can become a major developmental challenge. When facing stressful experiences, persons readily fall back on patterns learned within their family. Families that lack the resources or skills to teach their children good coping and relational skills are at risk, and the children from these families are especially at risk for the development of psychological problems. Such families are primary targets for preventive efforts. However, little has been written on this subject in relation to this group of disorders.

One clear area for preventive efforts is with families who have a member suffering chronic illness. We have already addressed the patterns of somatization that often arise within these families: emotional conflict is often expressed through physical symptoms. Inactivity associated with illness can become a family trait. Parents may lack the energy or incentive to encourage their children to develop the active life-style that is essential to healthy development, both physically and psychologically. Preventive efforts for such at-risk families can come from support groups, community centers, hospital or hospice volunteer organizations, or churches. Persons with basic training and skills in home visitation could assess the patterns developing within such families and encourage more healthy family interactions as well as involvement of the children in outside activities. Family therapy may also help to disrupt unhealthy patterns and prevent the children from suffering similar problems as they grow up.

Chronic illness often brings dramatic and permanent changes in lifestyle for the person who is ill. Treatment regimens may include restrictive medical schedules and many medications. The sufferer must often endure chronic pain and cope with increasing physical limitations. DeVries and Gallagher-Thompson address these issues:

> These demands are stressful, strain coping resources, and challenge the person's sense of self-worth and control. Assessing the individual's beliefs about changes in body image, competence, and sense of self is critical in identifying those at risk for psychological distress. . . . Those who hold negative beliefs about themselves and their ability to cope with their illness are likely to develop symptoms of depression. It is these persons who are at greatest risk for psychological crisis. (1994, p. 207)

Effective treatment with these individuals and their families may serve to prevent the development of comorbid psychological problems such as depression and anxiety.

Family patterns have been identified as an etiological factor in the development of eating disorders. These families often suppress emotional expression and lack cohesiveness. Emotional and relational conflict is often intense, but it is seldom addressed, as communication is difficult and considered threatening (Humphrey, 1986; Garfinkel et al., 1983). Such families are often void of any atmosphere of support, understanding or nurturance (Strober and Humphrey, 1987). In addition, socioeconomic status and its priority in the home may affect family communication and family values (Crisp, Palmer and Kalucy, 1976). Such families are difficult to identify, and preventive interventions pose many logistical problems. Perhaps the most feasible and accessible preventive strategy can come from local churches. Ministry, teaching and mentoring centered on the health and values of families are desperately needed and may serve to counteract some of the potentially devastating family patterns and messages that contribute to the etiology of eating disorders in adolescent girls.

In general, preventive efforts on individual, family and community levels can stress the importance of balance and a healthy, active lifestyle. For example, good sleep patterns are crucial to health and well-being. We spend up to a third of our life sleeping. Sleep disturbances are among the most common concerns presented to health care and human service providers. In general, about 30 percent of the population in America suffers from insomnia. Although we don't know for sure why humans need sleep, prominent theories suggest that sleep has a restorative function, cleanses our metabolism and/or serves an adaptive function to the stress of our daily life. Whatever its purpose may be, it is a necessary element of good health, and by association so is rest. It is crucial to incorporate periods of rest, relaxation and enjoyment into one's daily routine. As obvious as this sounds, few take seriously the need for a balanced, active lifestyle.

INTEGRATIVE THEMES
The problems addressed in this chapter raise several challenges for integration.

Pastoral care and disordered desires. "Flesh, history, and finite reality have been rescued from their former disparagement by the Logos that has come into them. They have now become dimensions in which truth is and which can thus be objects of scientific inquiry. As image they share the essence of supreme truth, the truth of God himself" (Thielicke, 1977, p. 163).

The interrelatedness of our body and mind is one of the miracles of God's creation. As we seek to bring comfort and healing to those suffering from afflictions of the body and mind, we must continually strive to understand this interrelatedness. Historically the health and mental health professions have addressed them separately. Only in recent times have efforts been made to understand the overlap between the two. Similarly, the history of theology is replete with attempts to separate issues related to the physical realm and the spiritual/mental realm. Distortions such as the Gnostic heresy of the second century attempted to separate the spirit from the flesh entirely and contended that activities associated with one had no relevance or impact on the other. Similar reasoning has reemerged continually throughout the theological history of the church. On some level we participate in such distortions of sound theology when we overemphasize the value of the spirit or mind in relation to the body.

In the above quote, Helmut Thielicke observes that the incarnation of Jesus Christ has profound implications for the value of the body. The incarnation elevated the status of material reality. When Christ took the form of a human, that form and the needs associated with it were demonstrated to be of significant concern to God—a concern that is reiterated throughout Scripture. For example, Jesus spoke often about and demonstrated the importance of ministering to the physical needs that people have, and Scripture teaches of a bodily, not just spiritual, resurrection. These truths have implications for the disorders addressed in this chapter.

First, we must not neglect the physical needs of people, especially people who are suffering. We have already discussed the need to address the physical symptoms of people who are suffering with problems of the mind and body; however, Jesus' example challenges us to an even more stringent application of this ideal. He continually demonstrated his concern for people by feeding and healing them—meeting their physical needs. Similarly, our concern for people could be expressed not only in our compassion for their physical suffering but also in concern for their family functioning, their socioeconomic well-being, their occupational functioning and so on. The literature of community psychology effectively addresses the need to bring preventive and therapeutic interventions to the whole context of people's lives in order to facilitate change that will last. This is a metaphor of the incarnation. God entered the whole context of our lives to bring healing and change.

Second, balance is needed in our understanding and application of the relationship between the mind and body. In many circles in the church today, we continue to react to psychological problems in polar ways. On one extreme, people suffering from psychological distress are often marginalized from the community. In his provocatively titled book *Why Do Christians Shoot Their Wounded?* Carlson (1994) suggests that some Christians who struggle with mental illness have been told by others in the church that their problems are solely the result of their sin or lack of spirituality. Whether this response arises from ignorance of the nature of psychopathology or an overly simplistic understanding of spiritual issues, he says, the results can be devastating. The same pattern of disengagement or insensitivity can be seen with just about any expression of serious mental illness. We fear that which we do not fully understand. A needless burden of guilt may be heaped on persons who already feel ashamed, isolated and depressed.

On the other extreme, medical and psychological interventions are often offered with little or no consideration of the spiritual dimensions of people's lives. Jones and Butman describe this overall trend toward polarization.

> Some so emphasize or exaggerate the immaterial side of our being as to deify humanity and deny that we are inevitably conditioned by our physical existence. . . . The other extreme is to emphasize or exaggerate our temporal existence so as to make us mere physical machines that are just another biological phenomenon caught up in the grand mechanistic universe. (1991, p. 46)

It is perhaps a characteristic of our nature (or at least our culture) to overly compartmentalize and attempt to reduce what was once whole to its constituent elements.

A similar split is evident in many places in society, with the mental or physical aspect of our being overly emphasized to the disregard of the other. Some segments of society do not value or attend to expressions of psychological distress. Denial of emotional and mental problems can lead to the somatization of psychological tension and an overemphasis on physical symptoms, which are considered acceptable. Physical pain becomes the only acceptable way to suffer. Balance in our understanding of psychological health and physical health is needed, and their relationship to spiritual health needs to be addressed. The need for this balance is reflected by a Christian psychiatrist who produced the following statement to give to his Christian patients who were reluctant to consider medication for their psychological struggles:

> The interaction of the brain and mind and soul is one of the most complexing questions on the minds of scientists, philoso-

phers and theologians. People continually ask me whether I think their problems are more likely to be "chemical" or "emotional." This is an excellent question with an extremely fuzzy answer. Every experience that we have as humans affects or is mediated in some way by our physiology. Sometimes this is pretty obvious, such as when someone steps on your foot. The pain you feel is very real and very physiological. But the extent of the pain depends not only on how hard your foot was stepped on, but on whether the injury was perceived as intentional or unintentional. If it appears to be intentional, then our pain seems to be worse. In other words, our system interprets events in such a way that the event's meaning will have great impact on the extent of harm perceived. Another common example occurs when you are having a great day and feeling your best, only to receive a very disheartening phone call that suddenly causes your system to crash, as if you went from fifth gear to reverse in three seconds. This is no less of a physiological process. However, it is clearly an emotional and intellectual process as well. So you can see that the question of "chemistry" versus "emotion" is neither a simple one nor a particularly helpful one.

The goal of medical treatment and medications is to attempt to reverse harmful changes that have occurred in a person's system, regardless of their source. Of course, the more clearly the underlying source is understood, the more precise and appropriate the treatment can be. Due to the complexity and individuality of each living person, attempts to use medications are an inexact science and are certainly not a "cure of souls." Nevertheless, if a patient and their physician are willing to patiently work together, medications can usually help to bring about a significant improvement in a person's symptoms and general sense of well-being. But there will usually continue to be other significant and deeper life issues that will be best dealt with nonmedically, such as with a therapist, friend, or spiritual adviser. Often, a person's progress is limited by deep wounds or fears that keep them from trusting or hoping. They may then tend to passively expect more from the medications than is realistic. So even though medications can be tremendously helpful and even life-saving, they have their limitations. As disappointing and unfair as this may seem to some people, it is due to the fact that we are much more than a physiological tangle of nerve cells and chemicals. There is some deeper, more profound part of every human that needs to courageously choose to live their life fully, boldly, responsibly in spite of all the obstacles before them or lack of encouraging support from others. But I am confident that if a person is willing to invest the necessary time and energy in addressing the full reality of their difficulties, they will eventually be rewarded for their ventures with a fuller and freer quality of life.

This leads to a third implication. Our theology needs to reflect this balance. Many theological traditions have lost sight of the importance of physical manifestations of our faith and relationship with God. Relatively few evangelical churches emphasize or even encourage such practices as kneeling in prayer, raising hands or dancing in praise. Expressions of emotion and spiritual movement are more commonly limited to cognitive or nonphysical expressions.[4] We need theologies that reflect the incarnation and elevate the material world back to an appropriate level. Such theologies would recognize our need to express our faith with our entire being—mind and body. They would stress balance in care for our mental, emotional, spiritual and physical needs. It is our belief that a Christian community environment reflecting such a balance would be an important preventive step to foster balance in the lives of families and individuals.

Sin and psychopathology. A related integrative challenge is to come to an accurate understanding of sin in relation to problems of body and mind. Again, as mentioned in part one, if we understand sin to include the fallen and incomplete aspects of humanness, as well as being embedded in the structures of society, there are real implications for the Christian community that exists within a given culture. The church often adopts the values of its surrounding culture, and if some disorders are constructed by an American social reality, then integration must take seriously ways in which that social reality might contribute to what is pathological.

Our society's preoccupation with youth and individualism fosters problems of the mind and body. Feelings of powerlessness and worthlessness may increase the risk of somatization of psychological distress or accelerate physical or cognitive impairment. Misplaced val-

---

[4]We recognize that these are generalizations and that exceptions to this are easily identifiable. However, it is a general trend that we have witnessed, and often the exceptions are more attributable to cultural or ethnic diversity than to theological ideology.

ues about the centrality of individual life versus the life of the community confuse our thinking and open the door to problems in the way we see ourselves and live our life.

Okholm summarizes the teachings of John Cassian, a Christian monk who wrote in the late fourth and early fifth century, about how we should approach even the task of feeding ourselves not as an individualistic activity but as an opportunity to value others: "Eating is to be ruled by concern for the community rather than for one's individual gustatory desires: one is to eat what is offered as it has been prepared, so as not to offend, shame, or annoy other members of the community" (Okholm, 1997, pp. 324-25; see Cassian *Conferences* 5.11). Okholm goes on to state, "This relational emphasis is crucial in our contemporary situation, for we have come to realize that disordered eating often promotes and is promoted by disordered relationships (with ourselves, others, the earth, God)" (ibid., p. 325).

> When I cannot, or do not, or will not eat with my fellow creatures—or, when conversely, I cannot or do not seem to be able to stop eating—I am bodying forth the brokenness of a fallen world and of a distorted will. . . . Not only am I refusing and defying companionship; I am also refusing the carnal medium through which these gifts of grace appear. (Bringle, 1992, quoted in Okholm, 1997, p. 325)

Societal values can perpetuate a disregard for the role of community and family in the life of individuals and may contribute to preoccupation with self and self-perception.

Seeing ourselves as we truly are—created in the image of the only God, stained with sin and helpless to cleanse or heal ourselves, yet beloved and valuable in the eyes of our loving Lord—is the basis for establishing realistic and appropriate priorities and goals; for assessing ourselves, our giftedness and our contribution to the community; for maintaining hope in the midst of the struggles and pains of life. Seeing ourselves as the world sees us often leads to adversarial relationships, self-doubt and self-deprecation, and misplaced priorities and goals, some of which may be at the root of some of the problems of the body and mind. "If standing 5' 10" and weighing 120 pounds is the only way for a woman to be beautiful and beloved (concepts which our image-conscious culture all too often conflates with one another), then many of us whose bodies refuse those contours are destined to a life of ugly lovelessness" (Bringle, 1994, p. 139). When we believe the lies of our society about what is beautiful, valuable, successful or acceptable, we open the door to many stresses that leave us feeling overwhelmed, ashamed and in despair.

Some, unable to face the truth of their emotional struggle, somatize it. "Patients who ought to be complaining of problems in daily living often focus on bodily sensations and seek a medical cure for these problems. For example, it is easier for these patients to say to a physician 'my back hurts' than it is to say 'I want to die because my life has no meaning'" (Iezzi, Duckworth and Adams, 2001, p. 212). And until they can say what they really mean, true healing may remain elusive.

Some who are stressed by the pressures of life cannot shut out the noise of the lies in their head even to sleep. The command in the Scriptures for sabbath rest is tied to God's teaching that right relationship with him involves a right perspective on ourselves, our work and our place in his creation. This perspective can be gained only through time set aside to be still before him and to know the limits of our control over our life and our world. It is a foreshadowing of the rest that awaits us in eternity with him (Heb 4). The Scriptures suggest that restful sleep is a gift from God (Ps 127), and for some, the inability to sleep may be tied to an inability to accept the gift of oneself and one's life as it truly is. For others, the challenges of sleepless nights arise from biological or environmental factors beyond their control. The inability to experience restful sleep and the restoration which comes from it can be a devastating pattern in people's lives. Acceptance of ourselves before God is not a guarantee of restful sleep; however, for some, it may represent a much-needed step toward inner peace.

We deceive ourselves, and that deceit may play a role in the development and maintenance of problems of the body and mind. As we seek to help people who struggle in any of these ways, our faith can help us to value the complexity of our created nature. God has created us in such a way that our psychological, physical and spiritual health are all related. Clark challenges Christian counselors to acknowledge this complexity in their work with people struggling with eating disorders:

> Christian counselors need to pay particular attention to the fact that the person with the eating disorder not only will treat people like they treat food (for example, anorexics resist letting people in in much the same way they disallow food—for fear of

becoming out of control or fat) but also will respond to God similarly (for example, anorexics may be fearful of "letting the Holy Spirit in" to lead their lives when the only one they trust to lead their lives is themselves). (1999, p. 378)

Science has for generations assumed that eventually it would be possible to identify an exact one-to-one causal relation between the mind and the brain. However, that has not happened:

In the first place, it is not even certain whether there is complete correlation between brain events and specific states of consciousness. . . . Furthermore, the sheer number of brain cells and complexity of the brain itself, as well as the complex interactions of brain cells connected with any particular mental state, make the mapping of mental states onto clearly defined brain states a practical impossibility. So the thesis that all mental events are correlated with specific kinds of brain events has not and may never be empirically demonstrated. (Cooper, 1989, p. 225; cf. MacKay, 1980)

Finally, there is need for further reflection on dissociative disorders and encounters with spiritual influences, such as the demonic, in human experience. Christian psychologists must be careful not to interpret dissociations as solely spiritual concerns that require spiritual interventions. At the same time, Christians affirm that the spiritual realm is real and that there are malevolent forces that impinge on our life and the lives of our clients. It may be helpful, then, to reflect more on differential diagnosis of dissociation and oppression in such a way that we take seriously resources from both psychology and pastoral care. It has been argued that in cases of oppression the person experiences a more automatic, persistent and consistent presentation of a new personality. The new personality often identifies itself as a demon, using titles or names, and makes use of personal pronouns, such as referring to the demon in first person and to the person being oppressed in the third person. Another consideration in differential diagnosis is evidence of sudden attainment of knowledge or ability not possessed by the person. An additional consideration is whether the presence of a demon is accompanied by moral decline.

The Scriptures acknowledge four levels of demonic participation in human experience (Virkler, 1999):

- no involvement (sin is a result of our own desires)

- demonic temptation (sin results from a direct introduction of thoughts and desires from a demonic origin)
- demonic oppression (a more intense version of demonic temptation)
- demonic possession (the actual indwelling of a person by a demon)

Virkler suggests that if we are to be serious about a biblical worldview that acknowledges multiple ways in which demonic forces can influence our behavior, then a Christian perspective on psychopathology needs to incorporate this in its consideration of the development of abnormal behavior. He offers a model with eight categories to consider in determining the development of psychopathology:

1. psychopathology due to genetic vulnerability or inheritance (e.g., schizophrenia)
2. psychopathology due to mistaken beliefs, interpretations or conclusions about human experiences
3. psychopathology due to inadequate coping or social skills
4. psychopathology due to lack of awareness of one's thoughts, goals or feelings
5. psychopathology due to our sin nature (e.g., self-centeredness)
6. psychopathology due to trauma
7. psychopathology due to demonic temptation or oppression
8. psychopathology due to demonic possession

Virkler challenges the Christian psychological community to strive toward models of psychopathology that will increase our understanding of the areas of connection between psychopathology and demonic involvement, enhance our ability to differentially diagnose and lead to more effective methods of treatment. This is an area that has been all but dismissed by contemporary work in psychopathology, but it must not be neglected by serious Christian scholars who recognize the reality of the spiritual realm.

CONCLUSION

There is little debate in modern health care that strong links exist between emotions and health. The nature of those links is not entirely understood, and it is dangerous to make strong causal connections before all the science is in. But clearly we are gaining new insights into what it means to be "fearfully and wonderfully made." Finding ways to more effectively regulate our arousal and responsiveness may be a matter of life and death. The stewardship of our minds and bodies is shown to be all the more important by this cutting-edge research. Choice and responsibility are important for each of us, and there is also the potential to be helpful to one another through giving intentional affirmation of and accountability for better lifestyle decisions.

There is no debate that a healing relationship between a patient and a physician plays a vital role in medical care. But the quality of relationships between family members and friends can be no less important for the maintenance of physical, emotional and perhaps even spiritual well-being. We suspect the best cognitive neuroscience will increasingly help us see that our simplistic and often naive notions about the mind-body connection need to be revised and updated. We can safely predict that this entire section of the *DSM* will be reworked and revised in the years and decades ahead. As we continue to progress in understanding the relationship between the body and mind, we must not accept any perspective that disregards or negates any part of our nature—physiological, psychological or spiritual—and we must pay close attention to the implications of each for the healing of the people for whom we provide care.

RECOMMENDED READINGS

Hoekema, A. (1986). *Created in God's image.* Grand Rapids, MI: Eerdmans. This book presents a readable and understandable overview of theological anthropology.

National Center on Sleep Disorders Research <www.nhlbi.nih.gov /about/ncsdr>.

National Eating Disorders Association <www.nationaleatingdisorders .org>.

Willard, D. (2002). *Renovation of the heart: Putting on the character of Christ.* Colorado Springs: NavPress. A helpful consideration of the nature of the soul and its transformation.

REFERENCES

Agras, W. (1987). *Eating disorders.* New York: Pergamon.

American Psychiatric Association. (1993). *Practice guidelines for eating disorders.* Washington, DC: American Psychiatric Press.

American Psychiatric Association. (1994). *Diagnostic and statistical man-*

ual of mental disorders (4th ed.). Washington, DC: Author.

Antoni, M. H., Schneiderman, N., Fletcher, M. A., and Goldstein, D. A. (1990). Psychoneuroimmunology and HIV-1. *Journal of Consulting and Clinical Psychology, 58,* 38-49.

Barch, E. A., Jr. (1993). Emotional disorders in chronic medical illness. In P. B. Sutker and H. E. Adams (Eds.), *Comprehensive handbook of psychopathology* (2nd ed.) (pp. 671-88). New York: Plenum.

Barlow, D. H., and Durand, V. M. (2001). *Abnormal psychology: An integrative approach* (2nd ed.). Belmont, CA: Wadsworth/Thomson Learning.

Barrett, J. E., Barrett, J. A., Oxman, T. E., and Gerber, P. D. (1988). The prevalence of psychiatric disorders in a primary care practice. *Archives of General Psychiatry, 45,* 1100-106.

Barsky, A. J., and Klerman, G. L. (1983). Overview: Hypochondriasis, bodily complaints and somatic styles. *American Journal of Psychiatry, 140,* 273-83.

Bootzin, R. R., Epstein, D., and Wood, J. M. (1991). Stimulus control instructions. In P. Hauri (Ed.), *Case studies in insomnia* (pp. 19-28). New York: Plenum.

Bootzin, R. R., Manber, R., Perlis, M. L., Salvio, M., and Wyatt, J. K. (1993). Sleep disorders. In P. B. Sutker and H. E. Adams (Eds.), *Comprehensive handbook of psychopathology* (2nd ed.) (pp. 531-62). New York: Plenum.

Bringle, M. L. (1992). *The god of thinness: Gluttony and other weighty matters.* Nashville: Abingdon.

Bringle, M. L. (1994). Swallowing the shame: Pastoral care issues in food abuse. *Journal of Pastoral Care, 48*(2), 135-44.

Brown, H. N., and Vaillant, G. E. (1981). Hypochondriasis. *Archives of Internal Medicine, 141,* 723-26.

Brown, W. M. (1985). A critique of three conceptions of mental illness. *Journal of Mind and Behavior, 6*(4), 553-76.

Bruch, H., Czyzewski, D., and Suhr, M. (1988). *Conversations with anorexics.* New York: Basic Books.

Bufford, R. K. (1989). Demonic influence and mental disorders. *Journal of Psychology and Christianity, 8*(2), 35-48.

Burch, E. A., Jr. (1985). *Psychopharmacological variables in the elderly.* Philadelphia: Wyeth Laboratories.

Burns, J. (Ed.). (1981). *Theological anthropology.* Philadelphia: Fortress.

Buschbaum, M. S., Gillin, J. C., Wu, J., Hazlett, E., Sicotte, N., Dupont, R. M., and Bunney, W. E. (1989). Regional cerebral glucose metabolic rate in human sleep assessed by position emission tomography. *Life Sciences, 45,* 1349-56.

Carlson, D. L. (1994). *Why do Christians shoot their wounded? Helping (not hurting) those with emotional difficulties.* Downers Grove, IL: InterVarsity Press.

Carson, R. C., and Butcher, J. N. (1992). *Abnormal psychology and modern life* (9th ed.). New York: HarperCollins.

Cassian, J. (1985). *Conferences* (Colin Luibheid, Trans.). New York: Paulist.

Clark, M. F. (1999). Eating disorders. In D. G. Benner and P. C. Hill (Eds.), *Baker encyclopedia of psychology and counseling* (p. 378). Grand Rapids, MI: Baker.

Cooper, J. (1989). *Body, soul and life everlasting: Biblical anthropology and the monism-dualism debate.* Grand Rapids, MI: Eerdmans.

Crisp, A. H., Palmer, R. L., and Kalucy, R. S. (1976). How common is anorexia nervosa? A prevalence study. *British Journal of Psychiatry, 128,* 549-54.

DeVries, H. M. (1996). Cognitive behavioral interventions. In J. E. Birren (Ed.), *Encyclopedia of gerontology* (vol. 1). San Diego: Academic Press.

DeVries, H. M., and Gallagher-Thompson, D. (1994). Older adults. In F. M. Dattilio and A. Freeman (Eds.), *Cognitive-behavioral strategies in crisis intervention* (pp. 200-218). New York: Guilford.

Dohrenwend, B., and Dohrenwend, B. (Eds.). (1974). *Stressful life events: Their nature and effects.* New York: Wiley.

Dunn, G. (1992). Multiple personality disorder. *Professional psychology: Research and practice, 23,* 8-23.

Elliott, G. (1989). Stress and illness. In S. Cheren (Ed.), *Psychosomatic medicine: Theory, physiology and practice* (pp. 45-90). Madison, CT: International Universities Press.

Fahy, T. (1988). The diagnosis of multiple personality disorder: A critical review. *British Journal of Psychiatry, 153,* 597-606.

Flor-Henry, P., Fromm-Auch, D., Tapper, M., and Schopflocher, D. (1981). A neuropsychological study of the stable syndrome of hysteria. *Biologic Psychiatry, 16,* 601-26.

Fornari, V., Kent, J., Kabo, L., and Goodman, B. (1994). Anorexia nervosa: Thirty something. *Journal of Substance Abuse Treatment, 11,* 45-54.

Friedman, H. S., and Booth-Kewley, S. (1987). The "disease-prone" personality: A meta-analytic view of the construct. *American Psychologist, 42,* 539-55.

Galin, D., Diamond, R., and Braff, D. (1977). Lateralization of conversion symptoms: More frequent on the left. *American Journal of Psychiatry, 134,* 578-80.

Gallagher-Thompson, D., and Thompson, L. W. (1995). Psychotherapy with older adults in theory and practice. In B. Bongar and L. E. Beutler (Eds.), *Comprehensive textbook of psychotherapy: Theory and practice* (pp. 359-79). New York: Oxford University Press.

Garfinkel, P. E., and Garner, D. M. (1982). *Anorexia nervosa: A multidimensional perspective.* New York: Brunner/Mazel.

Garfinkel, P. E., Garner, D. M., Rose, J., Darby, P. L., Brandes, J. S., O'Hanlon, J., and Walsh, N. (1983). A comparison of characteristics in families of patients with anorexia nervosa and normal controls. *Psychological Medicine, 13,* 821-28.

Gamer, D. M., and Garfinkel, P. E. (Eds.). (1985). *Handbook of psychotherapy for anorexia nervosa and bulimia.* New York: Guilford.

Geiser, D. S. (1989). Psychosocial influences on human immunity. *Clincal Psychology Review, 9,* 689-715.

Gleaves, D. H., May, M. C., and Cardeña, E. (2001). An examination of the diagnostic validity of dissociative identity disorder. *Clinical Psychology Review, 21*(4), 577-608.

Goldberg, D. P., and Bridges, K. (1988). Somatic presentations of psychiatric illness in primary care settings. *Journal of Psychosomatic Research, 32,* 137-44.

Goodsit, A. (1985). Self psychology and the treatment of anorexia nervosa. In D. M. Garner and P. E. Garfinkel (Eds.), *Handbook of psychotherapy for anorexia nervosa and bulimia* (pp. 55-82). New York: Guilford.

Gordon, E., Kraiuhin, C., Meares, R., and Howson, A. (1986). Auditory evoked response potentials in somatization disorder. *Journal of Psychiatric Research, 20,* 237-48.

Gregory I. (1950). *Ancient Christian Writers: The works of the fathers in translation (Vol. 11). Pastoral care* (Henry Davis, Trans. and Annotator). Westminster, MD: Newman Press.

Groeschel, B. (1992). *Spiritual passages: The psychology of spiritual development.* New York: Crossroad.

Guze, S. B. (1983). Studies in hysteria. *Canadian Journal of Psychiatry, 28,* 434-37.

Harsh, J., and Ogilvie, R. (Eds.). (1995). *Sleep onset: Normal and abnormal processes.* Washington, DC: American Psychological Association.

Hauri, P. (Ed.). (1991). *Case studies in insomnia.* New York: Plenum.

Hillstrom, E. L. (1999). Sleep and dreaming. In D. G. Benner and P. C. Hill (Eds.), *Baker encyclopedia of psychology and counseling* (2nd ed.) (pp. 1130-32). Grand Rapids, MI: Baker.

Hoek, H. W., and van Hoeken, D. (2003). Review of the prevalence and incidence of eating disorders. *International Journal of Eating Disorders, 34*(4), 383-96.

Hoekema, A. (1986). *Created in God's image*. Grand Rapids, MI: Eerdmans.

Holland, A. J., Hall, A., Murray, R., Russell, G. F. M., and Crisp, A. H. (1984). Anorexia nervosa: A study of thirty-four twin pairs and one set of triplets. *British Journal of Psychiatry, 145*, 414-19.

Holmes, T., and Rahe, R. (1967). The social readjustment rating scale. *Journal of Psychosomatic Research, 11*, 213-18.

Humphrey, L. L. (1986). Family relations in bulimic-anorexic and nondistressed families. *International Journal of Eating Disorders, 5*, 223-32.

Iezzi, T., Duckworth, M. P., and Adams, H. E. (2001). Somatoform and factitious disorders. In H. E. Adams and P. B. Sutker (Eds.), *Comprehensive handbook of psychopathology* (3rd ed.) (pp. 211-58). New York: Kluwer Academic/Plenum.

James, L., Singer, A., Zurynski, Y., Gordon, E., Kraiuhin, C., Harris, A., Howson, A., and Meares, R. (1987). Evoked response potentials and regional cerebral blood flow in somatization disorder. *Psychotherapy and Psychosomatics, 47*, 190-96.

Jemmott, J. B., III, and Locke, S. E. (1984). Psychosocial factors, immunologic mediation and human susceptibility to infectious diseases: How much do we know? *Psychological Bulletin, 95*, 78-108.

Jones, R. A. (1977). *Self-fulfilling prophecies: Social, psychological and physiological effects of expectancies*. Hillsdale, NJ: Erlbaum Associates.

Jones, S. L., and Butman, R. E. (1991). *Modern psychotherapies: A comprehensive Christian appraisal*. Downers Grove, IL: InterVarsity Press.

Katon, W. (1993). Somatization disorder, hypochondriasis and conversion disorder. In D. Dunner (Ed.), *Current psychiatric therapy*. Philadelphia: Saunders.

Kellner, R. (1985). Functional somatic symptoms and hypochondriasis: A survey of empirical studies. *Archives of General Psychiatry, 42*, 821-33.

Kimball, C. P., and Blindt, K. (1982). Some thoughts on conversion. *Psychosomatics, 23*, 647-49.

Klein, D. A., and Walsh, B. T. (2003). Eating disorders. *International Re-

view of Psychiatry, 15(3), 205-16.

Kluft, R., and Fine, C. (1993). *Clinical perspectives on multiple personality disorder.* Washington, DC: American Psychiatric Press.

Koranyi, E. K. (1989). Physiology of stress reviewed. In S. Cheren (Ed.), *Psychosomatic medicine: Theory, physiology and practice* (pp. 241-78). Madison, CT: International Universities Press.

Levor, R. M., Cohen, M. J., Naliboff, B. D., and McArthur, D. (1986). Psychosocial precursors and correlates of migraine headache. *Journal of Consulting and Clinical Psychology, 54,* 347-53.

Lewis, C. S. (1959). *The problem of pain.* New York: Macmillan.

Lipowski, Z. J. (1967). Review of consultation psychiatry and psychosomatic medicine, part 2: Clinical aspects. *Psychosomatic Medicine, 29,* 201-44.

Lipowski, Z. J. (1977). Psychiatric consultation: Concepts and controversies. *American Journal of Psychiatry, 134,* 523-28.

Love, A., and Peck, C. (1987). The MMPI and psychological factors in chronic low back pain: A review. *Pain, 28,* 1-12.

Ludwig, A. M. (1972). Hysteria: A neurobiological theory. *Archives of General Psychiatry, 27,* 771-77.

MacKay, D. (1980). *Brains, machines and persons.* Grand Rapids, MI: Eerdmans.

McCranie, E. J. (1979). Hypochondriacal neurosis. *Psychosomatics, 20,* 11-15.

Meyer, R. G., and Deitsch, S. E. (1996). *The clinician's handbook: Integrated diagnostics, assessment and intervention in adult and adolescent psychopathology* (4th ed.). Boston: Allyn and Bacon.

Montplaisir, J., and Godbout, R. (1991). *Sleep and biological rhythms: Basic mechanisms and applications to psychiatry.* New York: Oxford University Press.

Morin, C. M., and Edinger, J. D. (2003). Sleep disorders: Evaluation and diagnosis. In M. Hersen and S. M. Turner (Eds.), *Adult psychopathology and diagnosis* (4th ed.) (pp. 583-612). New York: John Wiley and Sons.

Mosbacher, R. A., Ortner, R., and Kincannon, C. L. (1989). *Statistical abstract of the United States, 1989.* Washington, DC: Government Printing Office.

North, C. S., Ryall, J. M., Ricci, D. A., and Wetzel, R. D. (1993). *Multiple personalities, multiple disorders: Psychiatric classification and media influence.* New York: Oxford University Press.

O'Brien, P. T. (1993). Mystery. In G. F. Hawthorne, R. P. Martin and

D. G. Reid (Eds.), *Dictionary of Paul and his letters* (pp. 621-23). Downers Grove, IL: InterVarsity Press.

Okholm, D. L. (1997). Being stuffed and being fulfilled. In R. C. Roberts and M. R. Talbot (Eds.), *Limning the psyche: Explorations in Christian psychology* (pp. 317-38). Grand Rapids, MI: Eerdmans.

O'Leary, A. (1985). Self-efficacy and health. *Behavior Research and Therapy, 23,* 437-51.

Payne, R. L. (1975). Recent life changes and the reporting of psychological states. *Journal of Psychosomatic Research, 19*(1), 99-103.

Peterson, C., and Seligman, M. E. P. (1987). Explanatory style and illness. *Journal of Personality, 55,* 237-65.

Rifkin, A., Ghisalbert, D., Dimatou, S., Jim, C., and Seth, M. (1998). Dissociative identity disorder in psychiatric patients. *American Journal of Psychiatry, 155*(6), 844-845.

Rogers, M. P. (1989). The interaction between brain behavior and immunity. In S. Cheren (Ed.), *Psychosomatic medicine: Theory, physiology and practice* (pp. 279-330). Madison, CT: International Universities Press.

Rutter, M. (1981). Stress, coping and development: Some issues and questions. *Journal of Child Psychology and Psychiatry and Allied Disciplines, 4,* 323-56.

Scheier, M. F., and Carver, C. S. (1987). Dispositional optimism and physical well-being: The influence of generalized outcome expectancies on health. *Journal of Personality, 55,* 169-210.

Schotte, D. E., and Stunkard, A. J. (1987). Bulimia vs. bulimic behaviors on a college campus. *Journal of the American Medical Association, 258,* 1213-15.

Scott, D. W. (1986). Anorexia nervosa: A review of possible genetic factors. *International Journal of Eating Disorders, 5,* 1-20.

Simeon, D., Guralnik, O., Knutelska, M., and Schmeidler, J. (2002). Personality factors associated with dissociation: Temperament, defenses and cognitive schemata. *American Journal of Psychiatry, 159*(3), 489-91.

Solomon, J. R., Faletti, M. V., and Yunik, S. S. (1982). The psychologist as geriatric clinician. In T. Millon, C. Green and R. Meagher (Eds.), *Handbook of clinical health psychology* (pp. 227-49). New York: Plenum.

Stern, D. B. (1977). Handedness and the lateral distribution of conversion reactions. *Journal of Nervous and Mental Disease, 164,* 122-28.

Strain, J. J., and Grossman, S. (1975). *Psychological care of the medically ill: A primer in liaison psychiatry.* New York: Appleton-Century-Crofts.

Striegel-Moore, R. H., Dohm, F. A., Kraemer, C., Taylor, C., Barr, C., et al. (2003). Eating disorders in white and black women. *American Journal of Psychiatry, 160*(7), 1326-31.

Strober, M., and Humphrey, L. L. (1987). Familial contribution to the etiology and course of anorexia nervosa and bulimia. *Journal of Consulting and Clinical Psychology, 55,* 654-59.

Sutker, P. B., and Adams, H. E. (Eds.). (1993). *Comprehensive handbook of psychopathology* (2nd ed.). New York: Plenum.

Thielicke, H. (1977). *The evangelical faith* (G. W. Bromiley, Trans.). Grand Rapids, MI: Eerdmans.

Van Leeuwen, M. S., Knoppers, A., Koch, M. L., Schuurman, D. J., and Sterk, H. M. (1993). *After Eden: Facing the challenge of gender reconciliation.* Grand Rapids, MI: Eerdmans.

Virkler, H. A. (1999). Demonic influence, sin and psychopathology. In D. G. Benner and P. C. Hill, *Baker encyclopedia of psychology and counseling* (2nd ed.) (pp. 326-32). Grand Rapids, MI: Baker.

Vitousek, K., and Manke, F. (1994). Personality variables and disorders in anorexia nervosa and bulimia nervosa. *Journal of Abnormal Psychology, 103,* 137-47.

Wakeling, A. (1985). Neurobiological aspects of food disorders. *Journal of Psychiatric Research, 19,* 191-201.

White, F. J. (1985). Adjustment disorders. In D. G. Benner (Ed.), *Baker encyclopedia of psychology* (pp. 21-22). Grand Rapids, MI: Baker.

Whitlock, F. A. (1967). The aetiology of hysterical. *Acta psychiatrica Scandinavia, 43,* 144-62.

Willard, D. (1991). *The Spirit of the disciplines: Understanding how God changes lives.* San Francisco: HarperCollins.

Willi, J., and Grossman, S. (1983). Epidemiology of anorexia nervosa in a defined region of Switzerland. *American Journal of Psychiatry, 140,* 564-67.

Williamson, D. A., Barker, S. E., and Norris, L. E. (1993). Etiology and management of eating disorders. In P. B. Sutker and H. E. Adams, *Comprehensive handbook of psychopathology* (2nd ed.) (pp. 505-30). New York: Plenum.

9

PROBLEMS OF PSYCHOSIS

*I*n a truly remarkable document, "Coping with schizophrenia," a clinical psychologist who recovered from psychosis—and now treats chronically mental ill individuals—states:

> I, too, am a person with schizophrenia. I am not currently psychotic but I have been in the state of psychosis frequently enough to become somewhat familiar with the trips there and back. After years of keeping my experiences with schizophrenia a secret, a few years ago I decided to become open about my condition. . . . I cannot tell you how difficult it is for a person to accept the fact that he or she is schizophrenic. Since the time when we were very young we all have been conditioned to accept that if something is crazy or insane, its worth to us is to be automatically dismissed. We live in a world that is held together by rational connections. That which is logical or reasonable is acceptable. That what is not reasonable is not acceptable.
>
> The nature of this disorder is that it affects the chemistry that controls your cognitive processes. It affects your belief system. It fools you into believing that what you are thinking or what you believe is true and correct, when others can usually tell that your thinking processes are not functioning well.

I have been hospitalized five times before I was willing to consider the possibility that there might be something wrong with me. We are all conditioned from birth not to accept that which is crazy or insane. That which is insane is beyond the pale of that which those in our human family will accept. We accept that which is logical, that which is rational and reasonable. That which is crazy is dismissed. Therefore it is very difficult for us to accept that what we are thinking is in fact crazy. Psychosis is a "catch 22." If you understand that you are insane then you are thinking properly and are therefore not insane. You can only be psychotic if in fact you believe you are not. Therefore almost everyone with this disorder initially denies that they have it. Some will deny it all their lives. Most of the 300 patients I have in the hospital where I work will tell you that they are not mentally ill. Denial of the disorders comes as part of the territory for most of us that have it. Some of those who have the disorder not only deny that they have it but also deny that it exists.

It is exceedingly difficult for you to admit to yourself that your mind does not function properly. It fools you. With this disorder you develop an epistemological structure that is not consonant with that of the vast majority of those in the larger, majority population. But if one does not acknowledge that they have the disorder, how can it be helped? Why would anyone want to be cured of a disorder that they do not believe they have? (Frese, 1993)

Persons who struggle with the problems of psychosis are generally frightened and confused. They pursue "reality" in very different ways (Miller and Jackson, 1995). This can be threatening to "normal" folks. Persons who suffer from schizophrenia can be very blunt and frank, and they often do not follow the rules of social convention. Frankly, we sometimes find such speech refreshingly honest, amid church and community settings that highly value compliance and conformity. But there is no denying that *psychosis*—a dramatic break with a person's sense of reality—is the ultimate psychological breakdown.

The most common form of breakdown is *schizophrenia,* a syndrome that has been recognized for at least two centuries throughout the world (Adams and Sutker, 2001). It is a *very* serious problem that demands professional attention. Without medication, it is almost impossible to help a person who has lost the ability to accurately perceive and effectively respond to the environment, and who often experiences hallucinations (false sensory perceptions) or delusions (false beliefs; Comer, 2003). Psychosis can be induced by substance abuse or traumatic brain injury, but its most common expression by far is schizophrenia, the focus of our attention in this chapter.

THEMES IN PASTORAL CARE

Throughout the centuries of church history, the bizarre behavior associated with schizophrenia and related disorders led many to diagnose sufferers as suffering from demonic influence. While we cannot say for certain in which cases pastoral care writers are referring to schizophrenia and in which cases demonic influences (or perhaps in some cases both), the descriptions themselves are fascinating. In the following case, the writer makes no strong commitment either way but appears to be describing hallucinations:

> For those who are beginning to be . . . disturbed in their minds, begin in this way. They are first carried away by fancies to some pleasant and delightful things, then they are poured out in vain and fond motions towards things which have no existence. Now this happens from a certain disease of mind, by reason of which they see not the things which are, but long to bring to their sight those which are not. But thus it happens also to those who are suffering phrenzy, and seem to themselves to see many images, because their soul, being torn and withdrawn from its place by excess of cold or of heat, suffers a failure of its natural service. But those also who are in distress through thirst, when they fall asleep, seem to themselves to see rivers and fountains, and to drink; but this befalls them through being distressed by that dryness of the unmoistened body. Wherefore it is certain that this occurs through some ailment either of the soul or body. (*Recognitions of Clement*, quoted in Oden, 1987, p. 261)

In another account, Athanasius describes what he diagnoses to be demonic influence:

> Another, a person of rank, came to [Antony], possessed by a demon; and the demon was so terrible that the man possessed did not know that he was coming to Antony. But he even ate the excreta from his body. So those who brought him besought Antony to pray for him. And Antony pitying the young man prayed and kept watch with him all the night. And about dawn the

young man suddenly attacked Antony and gave him a push. But when those who came with him were angry, Antony said, "Be not angry with the young man, for it is not he, but the demon which is in him. And being rebuked and commanded to go into dry places, the demon became raging mad, and he has done this. Wherefore give thanks to the Lord, for his attack on me thus is a sign of the departure of the evil spirit." When Antony had said this, straightway the young man had become whole, and having come at last to his right mind, knew where he was, and saluted the old man and gave thanks to God. (Athanasius *Life of Antony,* quoted in Oden, 1987, pp. 262-63)

What is particularly intriguing, as Oden (1987) observes, is that Athanasius has those with him focus not on the man's behavior but on the etiology of the behavior, so that they will not be angry with the man himself.

Most people today recognize schizophrenia as a mental, not spiritual, disorder, though there may be language to help us recognize spiritual dimensions as well. We will discuss this further in the integration section at the end of the chapter.

Schizophrenia is a remarkably common disorder. It affects approximately one in one hundred people in the world (Carter and Golant, 1998), and we suspect that it has been observed in all cultures throughout recorded history. In faith-based communities, it has often been misdiagnosed as "demon possession." As noted in part one of this text, we do not doubt the existence of "powers and principalities" as important factors in the etiology and maintenance of psychopathology. However, we fear the naive realism or spiritual reductionism that is often associated with well-intentioned but uninformed attempts to explain serious mental illness. This has especially unfortunate effects when it comes to schizophrenia, since the evidence seems overwhelming that psychosis has a strong biological diathesis, whether inherited or acquired (Adams and Sutker, 2001).

Perhaps some of the most tragic chapters in the history of pastoral care have involved individual and corporate attempts to respond to what was perceived as demon possession. Recent textbooks in psychopathology (e.g., Butcher, Mineka and Hooley, 2004) usually make reference to the *Malleus Maleficarum,* the medieval witch-hunting manual first released in 1484. Indisputably, its guidelines for determining who was (or was not) "demon possessed" directly led to the death of tens of thousands of innocent persons, a disproportionate number of them women. It is not surprising, then, that contemporary academicians, clinicians and researchers are rather cautious about using the designation today. As persons of faith, we should be appalled by the historical abuses and exceedingly careful when entering into similar conversations today about "differential diagnosis" (cf. Peck, 1983).

Certainly there are accounts of demon possession recorded in the Bible (Collins, 1980). We suggest that some of the afflicted persons may well have been suffering from what today would be perceived as schizophrenia or another form of psychosis. Obviously, the controversies have to do with how best to understand what actually is happening, how it developed and how best to respond to the afflicted persons (Roberts and Talbot, 1997, cf. chapter on psychosis). As noted in chapter two, we always need to be careful to avoid the sin of "nothing-but-ism."

Given the havoc wreaked on afflicted individuals and their loved ones, perhaps the more important question is what we can do to help. A number of recent efforts have been geared to equipping family members and friends to respond effectively to the needs of psychotic persons (Morrison, 2002; Norcross et al., 2003). Those who suffer from schizophrenia need continuing contact with persons who can handle the vicissitudes of "crazy talk" and offer support. Ideally, persons struggling with schizophrenia should be made to feel welcomed in our congregations and communities. With the right combination of structure, support and supervision, schizophrenic individuals can be made to feel that they are valued members of society. As with many other disorders, such social support is absolutely essential. As many authors note (e.g., Comer, 2003; Haas, 1966; Hood et al., 1996), special communities of concerned persons have committed significant portions of their lives and resources to caring for troubled persons who couldn't cope with the demands of everyday living. They were tolerant of often strange behaviors of individuals who suffer from schizophrenia and were not easily frightened by that which they could not yet fully understand. As Paloutzian (1996) comments, it takes a special kind of person to offer supportive community to those who have lost touch with reality (see also Pargament, 1997). They can be role models for us in building networks of social support for afflicted persons and their loved ones.

Undoubtedly the most powerful narrative of a descent into the depths of severe psychosis with a spiritual perspective is still Anton

Boisen's *Out of the depths* (1960). Active in ministry in the early twentieth century, Boisen suffered a severe mental breakdown. Eventually he recovered and founded Clinical Pastoral Education, perhaps the largest faith-based pastoral care movement in the mainline Christian tradition (Hood et al., 1996). Boisen was deeply convinced that his slow, arduous pilgrimage back to health was first and foremost a spiritual struggle, especially in his search for a sense of meaning and purpose in his life. Stripped bare of defenses, he was forced to ask himself what truly mattered from the perspective of faith. The sense of utter abandonment he felt in the private hell of his pain rings true for others who have also recovered from psychosis. Boisen raises the possibility that there are profound spiritual lessons to be learned through such suffering. We do not want to risk romanticizing schizophrenia, but we suggest that our notions of "sanity" may need to be challenged. And just possibly, we ourselves are a tad more confused, doubtful and frightened than we usually care to admit (Miller and Jackson, 1995). The raw humanity of those who are keenly aware of some of the absurdities and contradictions of life has much to teach us all about our own need for greater humanity and humility in daily living.

Schizophrenia, then, ought not to be confused with demon possession. As the ultimate psychological breakdown, schizophrenia powerfully reminds us that we are all biopsychosocial entities. Even in the midst of a horrific descent into madness, the needs for social support, self-efficacy and a sense of meaning or purpose remain important. But the wisdom of the centuries would suggest that a very specialized kind of care is needed both professionally and within our churches and communities. Sometimes that will include medication and hospitalization. Longitudinally, it usually means a special network of people who are comfortable with odd or eccentric behavior and can help normalize it when possible or absorb it when not. Finally, we always need to be receptive to what this kind of suffering has to teach all of us about what truly matters in life and what really doesn't.

THEMES FROM PSYCHOPATHOLOGY

As noted earlier, psychosis is usually defined as a loss of contact with reality. One's ability to accurately perceive and effectively respond to the environment is profoundly impaired. Although psychosis can be triggered by drug abuse or traumatic brain injury, it is most often the result of a slow and insidious process that reflects a synergistic combination of biological vulnerabilities (inherited or acquired) and stressors (personal and/or situational). More than any disorder in the entire *DSM-IV-TR* (APA, 2000), it is the ultimate psychological breakdown.

Currently at least 2.5 million American struggle with the troublesome symptoms of schizophrenia, the most common expression of psychosis. As noted, available research suggests that it afflicts approximately 1 percent of the adult population in all cultures and communities (Butcher, Mineka and Hooley, 2004). One can only imagine how many others are directly or indirectly affected by the pain and suffering (Carter and Golant, 1998).

Schizophrenia is a very costly disease in another sense as well. Recent estimates suggest that it affects the U.S. economy at the rate of $100 billion per year (Pliszka, 2003) and that it is a major contributing factor in a variety of other healthcare and human services concerns, including a significant risk of suicide. Afflicted individuals are likely to be unable to properly care for themselves on a daily basis, so "lifestyle diseases" are especially common (Morrison, 2002). In the midst of psychosis, few affected individuals know how to seek help or how to comply with a prescribed healthcare regimen even when it is offered (Adams and Sutker, 2001).

Schizophrenia has been observed in all socioeconomic groups, but it is especially common in the culture of poverty. Researchers assume that a lack of resources contributes greatly to the personal and situational stressors that pave the way for this disorder in already vulnerable persons (Comer, 2003). Interestingly, gender distribution seems to be approximately equal, but the course is strikingly different. With men, the symptoms are usually seen earlier and tend to be more severe. Persons going through major life changes, losses and transitions seem especially vulnerable (whether this is a cause or an effect is not clearly understood).

In examining the *DSM* (APA, 2000), it becomes readily apparent that psychosis ought to be viewed as a group of disorders; there are several subtypes of schizophrenia. Symptoms vary by subtype, and responses to pharmacological, psychotherapeutic and psychosocial interventions can be highly variable (Nathan and Gorman, 1998). Consequently, careful assessment is essential to determine the best treatment strategies to offer (Jongsma and Peterson, 1995).

There are a number of distinct clinical features among the various expressions of schizophrenia (after Adams and Sutker, 2001). One cluster is called *form of thought,* having to do with how one's thinking processes are expressed through nonverbal and verbal communica-

tion. Symptoms may include loose associations (speech is not linear
or logical), poverty of content (many words but little meaningful substance) and thought blocking (words get "stuck," so there are gaps in
a conversation). A second cluster is called *content of thought*. This usually means that the afflicted individual has fixed false beliefs (delusions) that seem impervious to logic. Especially fascinating about
these delusions is their content; they are almost always religious, sexual, political or philosophical. Most authors suggest that this reflects
the fact that we prize these areas of life most highly (Francis and First,
1998). A third cluster is called *perceptual disturbance*. This usually
means that sensory experiences and their interpretations may be distorted. In the *DSM-IV-TR* these are called "hallucinations" or "illusions" (changes in bodily perceptions). With references to the former,
the sensations can be visual, auditory, olfactory or even tactile-kines-
thetic (the person feels touched by unseen forces). Of these, auditory
and visual hallucinations are especially common, and often quite up-
setting to the afflicted persons or their loved ones. It is not surprising
that persons of faith throughout the centuries have viewed these as
expressions of demonic activity. In our own travels in the United
States and abroad, we have often heard such attributions.

A fourth cluster has to do with *affect*, how moods or emotions are
expressed in word and deed. Affect can be blunted or flat (greatly diminished), or it can be inappropriate to the situation (laughter instead of tears). Sometimes this can mean wide mood swings (emotional lability). Suffice it to say that schizophrenia can make it difficult
to express "normal" mood states or to modulate mood states according to the interpersonal or situational context.

A fifth cluster has to do with the *sense of self*. A person struggling
with psychosis doesn't usually feel a clear sense of identity; self-
esteem suffers greatly. Schizophrenic individuals do not feel efficacious; they believe that what they do does not really make a difference. Consequently, they tend to withdraw and disengage from the
tasks of everyday living.

This is closely related to a sixth cluster, usually called *volitional
symptoms*. Schizophrenic individuals tend to have great difficulty in
maintaining purposeful, goal-directed activity and interest. They tend
to become apathetic and lethargic. The drive and ambition that "normal" people take for granted are simply not there. The afflicted persons prefer the internal worlds of their own construction to the more
confusing and frightening world of external events, a process that

Hollywood certainly got right in movies like *A Beautiful Mind, Birdy, Shine* and *The Fisher King* (cf. discussion of media resources in Norcross et al., 2003).

The final cluster of symptoms has to do with *motor activity*. People struggling with schizophrenia often show some striking nonverbal behaviors, which along with the cognitive and affective symptoms seem most troubling to others. These may include long periods of rocking and stereotyped behaviors (repetitive gestures that seem to be self-soothing). Both fine and gross motor movements can be impaired and look rather rigid and inflexible.

The net result of all seven clusters is that important social and interactional skills are lost and the ability to care for self (or others) is greatly diminished. A significant portion of the homeless in our urban centers struggles with the effects of chronic mental illness, especially schizophrenia. Some authors put the rate as high as 50 percent (Comer, 2003).

It is hard to determine which symptoms trigger the break from reality and which are direct results of the schizophrenic person's gradual disengagement from reality. Still, the symptoms can be grouped into three categories: positive, negative and psychomotor symptoms. *Positive symptoms* include delusions, disordered thinking and speech, heightened perceptions and hallucinations—that is, pathological excesses that can best be viewed as bizarre additions to an individual's personality and temperament. *Negative symptoms* are what seems diminished or lacking in an individual's personality and temperament. This usually means diminished affect or speech and an overall pattern of withdrawal from the external world. Finally, *psychomotor symptoms* have to do with physical activity that is more, less or different when compared to the person's condition before the onset of psychosis.

Some authors make a distinction between two broad categories of schizophrenia (Scully et al., 1990; Sutker and Adams, 1993). Type I schizophrenia is dominated by positive symptoms. It is assumed that persons struggling with this disorder were better adjusted prior to the onset of symptoms. Further, age of onset was later. With respect to treatment, they tend to have a better prognosis, perhaps because the symptoms are related to aberrations in their neurochemistry. Type II schizophrenia is characterized by more negative and psychomotor symptoms. As you might expect, it is associated with an early onset, a less favorable premorbid condition and a less favorable outcome. Recent research (Pliszka, 2003) suggests that these symptoms may be associated with structural defects in the brain and nervous system.

As with all disorders, diagnosis can be challenging and difficult (Johnson, Snibbe and Evans, 1981). Other conditions, including a host of medical disorders, can mimic psychosis (cf. Morrison, 1997). The key issue is careful differential diagnosis, which involves paying attention to the intensity, duration and frequency of symptoms across time and in multiple settings. According to *DSM-IV-TR* standards, a diagnosis of schizophrenia should be given only after the symptoms have been evident for six months or more and there is marked impairment in multiple domains of the person's life. Five subtypes are discussed in the manual (disorganized, catatonic, paranoid, undifferentiated and residual), distinctions that are important for making therapeutic decisions (Meyer and Deitsch, 1996; Schwartzberg, 2000). It is our judgment that a diagnosis of schizophrenia should be made only by a highly trained mental health professional who has sufficient experience with persons who have lost touch with reality and extensive knowledge of what resources are needed and available (cf. Morrison, 1995; 1997; 2002).

ANTECEDENTS OF THE PROBLEMS OF PSYCHOSIS

There is no clear consensus about the etiology and maintenance of this group of disorders. In recent decades there has been a virtual explosion of research in cognitive neuroscience. Yet despite a bewildering array of correlates, there is no solution yet for the riddle of schizophrenia (Adams and Sutker, 2001). Perhaps more than with any other group of disorders discussed in this text, there is a need for responsible eclecticism (Jones and Butman, 1991) and a biopsychosocial perspective (cf. chapter four). Most reputable textbooks on psychopathology adopt a stress-diathesis perspective on etiology and maintenance (e.g., Butcher, Mineka and Hooley, 2004).

Probably the strongest research evidence available speaks to the biological basis of the psychoses. How exactly this might affect choice and responsibility is not yet fully understood (cf. Roberts and Talbot, 1997; cf. chapters on schizophrenia), but it does suggest at least somewhat diminished capacity and freedom. Genetic and biological studies have dominated our understanding of schizophrenia for decades.

With reference to genetic studies, the evidence strongly suggests that a significant percentage of the people who eventually develop schizophrenia have a biological predisposition (Comer, 2003). Not all people who are predisposed develop the disorder; it must be triggered by overwhelming personal or situational stressors. Especially compelling are the family pedigree studies (e.g., 1 percent in the general population versus 10 percent among first-degree relatives). Still, researchers are cautious with respect to causal attributions; correlation does not imply causation. Factors other than genetic predisposition may explain the data. Large questions remain: What is the nature of the genetic defect(s)? More specifically, how does the genetic predisposition affect the neuroanatomy and/or neurochemistry? The assumption is that genetic effects can be widely divergent among afflicted individuals (Pliszka, 2003). A careful review of twin and adoptive studies would suggest that we don't fully understand the many and complex ways in which nature (biology) and nurture (environment) interact across the lifespan. Schizophrenia is not a unitary phenomenon, and the symptoms wax and wane during the course of the disease; there are further mysteries to be more fully appreciated and understood. We suspect that future research will implicate defects on or damage to the chromosomes, that most foundational site for determining brain-behavior relationships. Chromosomal damage can affect the structure and functioning of the neuroanatomy and neurochemistry, which can be implicated in the etiology and maintenance of psychotic symptoms.

With reference to neurotransmitters and neuromodulators, most of the focus is on dopamine. The assumption is that the neurons using dopamine fire too often and this causes some of the symptoms of schizophrenia. There is growing evidence that antipsychotic medications bind to the neuron sites (dopamine receptors) and act as "dopamine antagonists" (Comer, 2003). Whether this is because persons predisposed to schizophrenia have too many sites to begin with or the sites are more active (or both) is not clearly understood. Work with recent medications seem to suggest that serotonin may also be involved (Adams and Sutker, 2001)—that schizophrenia may reflect abnormal combinations of dopamine and serotonin, leading to various combinations of positive, negative and psychomotor symptoms. Patients with Parkinson's disease who take too much L-dopa (a medication used to treat this degenerative disease) can develop complications that mimic schizophrenia (Morrison, 1997). Drug addicts who take too much amphetamine can also appear psychotic. This suggests that dopamine sites are critical for overall well-being and highly susceptible to insult and injury.

With growing sophistication in medical imaging techniques, there is also increased evidence that schizophrenia can often be correlated with an abnormal brain structure. Persons with schizophrenia often have smaller temporal and frontal lobes and abnormal blood flow to important brain regions. In other cases, enlarged ventricles have been observed. All of these findings suggest diminished capacities to be fully present to the demands of everyday living (Butcher, Mineka and Hooley, 2004).

A final biological theory posits that schizophrenia may be related to viral infections in the prenatal period. A disproportionate number of persons who develop schizophrenia were born in the winter months—and the pattern is reversed in the Southern Hemisphere. Some of the most important brain and nervous system (e.g., the frontal lobes) functions are believed to develop in the final months of pregnancy, when exposure to toxins such as an influenza virus can be especially damaging. Obviously, this would affect important brain-behavior connections.

What is not clear is why some people who have been exposed to viral infection (or any other predisposing factor) develop schizophrenia and others do not. Perhaps the biological variables can best be understood as varying degrees of vulnerability that pave the way for important psychosocial or sociocultural factors. Again, this reflects the importance of the stress-diathesis model.

Psychological views on the etiology and maintenance of schizophrenia have been offered for centuries. What is striking to us, however, is their diminishing influence on the thinking of laypersons and professional alike, especially after recent intensive cognitive neuroscience research on these most serious forms of mental illness (Pliszka, 2003). Psychodynamic theorists tend to view schizophrenia as a severe form of regression to a state of primary narcissism (extreme withdrawal and childish behavior). The assumption is that the familial or interpersonal network is harsh, punitive or toxic (damaging). There is little empirical evidence, however, that "schizophrenegenic environments" lead to the problems of psychosis.

Cognitive and behavioral theorists tend to focus on faulty thinking processes or the effects of conditioning and modeling. There is little doubt that these may be factors in *maintenance* of symptoms, but they are probably less directly implicated in etiology (cf. Jones and Butman, 1991).

Systemic and interpersonal theorists tend to focus on extreme patterns of disengagement or self-assertion (passivity). But these perhaps are more reflective of what schizophrenia does *to* a person than of what tends to make him or her disturbed initially (McLemore, 2003).

Finally, humanistic or existential theorists tend to see schizophrenia as a direct result of highly conditional loving or extreme self-deceit (inauthenticity).

Of all these approaches, only the cognitive and behavioral strategies have offered any real hope for dealing with the most troublesome symptoms of schizophrenia (Antony and Barlow, 2002, cf. chapters on schizophrenia; Jongsma and Peterson, 1995), and a systemic perspective can help facilitate much-needed family support.

In contrast, sociocultural views have been gaining attention. Sociocultural factors may be especially implicated in triggering or maintaining the symptoms of schizophrenia. People who are different tend to be quickly isolated or marginalized in most every culture or community (Paloutzian, 1996). Obviously, this can be an enormous stressor, especially in settings where compliance and conformity are exceedingly important (Hood et al., 1996). As we are all painfully aware, peers can be harsh and punitive, and social networks can be even more so.

Try to imagine what it might be like to be strikingly different from others and not know why. Then imagine how others who can't tolerate any deviance treat you unkindly and further contribute to your sense of hopelessness, helplessness and powerlessness. At some level, that is what it might feel like to be psychotic.

Once labels are applied to people who are different, they tend to become a self-fulfilling prophecy; it becomes harder to look and act "sane." Indeed, the cultural relativism hypothesis was once a major theory about schizophrenia—that every community needs a certain number of persons to be "crazy" or "insane." We can only wonder what this might mean at the level of the local church (Haas, 1966). Suffice it to say that our social networks can be the context in which our problems in living unfold, and any kind of dysfunction in roles and expectations can be enormously stressful and toxic (McLemore, 2003).

With reference to causation, we echo the words of Morrison:

> With so many threads in the tapestry left untied, it is clear that we are still far from completing our picture of what causes schizophrenia. Although chaotic, high-volume family life is undoubtedly stressful and may contribute to symptoms relapse, we can completely discredit old psychological theories that as re-

cently as a generation ago blamed families (especially mothers) for producing psychosis by inducing stress. The balance of the evidence has prompted some researchers to claim that schizophrenia is actually a neurological disorder. (2002, pp. 268-69)

Frances and First wisely add:

> In most clinical situations, the boundary between psychosis and normality is straightforward and easy to draw. Occasionally, however, each of the psychotic symptoms (delusions, hallucinations, disorganized speech) can blend into normal so that distinctions are not so clear-cut as might be expected. . . . Each of us operates according to an explicit or implicit set of assumptions about the meaning of life, what happens after death, how the world began, how we expect others to behave, and how we view ourselves. Undoubtedly, many of our most cherished beliefs are "false" or at least debatable and are based on very incomplete knowledge and possibly mistaken conceptions. One person's religious belief or strongly held political conviction might be someone else's delusion. A false belief is considered to be a delusion only if the person believes it so strongly, uncritically, and single-mindedly as to lose his grip on reality. . . .
>
> Philosophers and epistemologists have pondered for thousands of years on what is "reality," what is truth, how we know them, and how do we know when we know them. . . . We caution you against using your own belief system as the absolute yardstick for measuring everyone's else's. Cultural and religious mores play a tremendous role in laying the groundwork for one's sense of reality. . . . It is often impossible to distinguish a crisis of religious faith from a religious delusion unless you follow the person over time and see how things turn out.
>
> All of us can be very wrong about things . . . and still not be considered delusional. Being in touch with reality does not require capturing truth—this would be far too high a standard that few if any could attain. Instead, the question is whether the beliefs are sustained by a consensual validation of others. . . . Reality depends on social context. . . . It is often helpful to get the advice of someone in or closer to the person's cultural context in determining whether the beliefs or experiences make sense when corrected for cultural differences. (1998, pp. 319-20)

TREATMENT OF THE PROBLEMS OF PSYCHOSIS

Far too often, the treatment of persons who struggle with problems of psychosis is a scandal (Carter and Golant, 1998). Without a good insurance policy and access to high-quality mental health services and providers, it is highly improbable that afflicted individuals and their loved ones will get the services that they need. Sadly, good insurance and a good provider network are the main determinants of what services a schizophrenic individual will actually receive, whether psychotropic medications, psychotherapeutic services or adjunct treatments (Comer, 2003). If you are poor and psychotic in the United States, you are more likely to become homeless than to receive intensive multi-disciplinary treatment in a psychiatric hospital (Miller and Jackson, 1995). This is a justice issue; our system makes for extremely poor stewardship of human talents. Advocacy and empowerment are especially important when it comes to the responsible treatment of schizophrenia (Morrison, 2002).

Institutionalization. Historically, people who were assumed to be psychotic were considered beyond help and without hope (Comer, 2003). Truthfully, schizophrenia is hard to treat, but given the antipsychotic medications discovered in recent decades, many of the most troublesome symptoms can be controlled, if the right medication(s) for the individual can be found. Yet even with the greater availability of psychotropic medications, schizophrenia can have a devastating effect on family and friends. This strongly suggests that it should be viewed as a family disease and not just as the painful struggles of an afflicted individual (Norcross et al., 2003).[1]

Before the "first wave" of antipsychotic medications were developed in the 1950s and 1960s, persons with schizophrenia were likely to be placed in state hospitals or other institutional settings. It was generally assumed that they were incurable because they were "insane." In the first half of the twentieth century, more beds were devoted to the treatment of "mental illness" than to all the other physical diseases (e.g., cancer, heart disease) *combined* (Sutker and Adams,

---

[1]Try to imagine what it might like to observe firsthand a person's process of deterioration in the late teens and early twenties (the usual onset of the symptoms). As Torrey (2001) has noted in an excellent work, *Surviving schizophrenia: A manual for families, consumers and providers*, the effects can be simply overwhelming, not unlike a process of continual grief and bereavement. Torrey really seems to "get it," which is not surprising: he is a highly regarded research psychiatrist who has a brother who struggles with schizophrenia.

1993). The assumption was that hospitalization would remove sufferers from the stressors of everyday life and provide a safe environment. Sadly, well-intentioned efforts quickly went awry. The institutions often became overcrowded and understaffed, and little quality care was actually offered. The "back wards" of most public facilities in those days were "human warehouses filled with hopelessness" (Comer, 2003), and patients rarely improved under such horrific conditions (Gotkin and Gotkin, 1992). The usual pattern following hospitalization was called the "social breakdown syndrome": patients became increasingly apathetic, angry, disengaged, odd and withdrawn, often abandoned by family and friends alike (Butcher, Mineka and Hooley, 2004).

In the second half of the twentieth century, there were some signs of hope. The development of *milieu therapy* (efforts to create a positive social climate on the ward) and *token economies* (behavior management programs to teach essential life skills) helped to make life in these settings more humane and tolerable. Staff become more consistent, predictable and reinforcing toward patients, and patients were more motivated to engage with others and take responsibility for relearning the tasks of everyday living (Meyer and Deitsch, 1996). At their best, these approaches have improved the social support system, helped to develop a greater sense of efficacy, and offered potential for a greater sense of meaning and purpose—all known predictors of more effective coping (Hood et al., 1996; Paloutzian, 1996; Pargament, 1997).

Psychopharmacology. What really revolutionized the care of the chronically mentally ill was the discovery of the phenothiazines, a group of antihistamine drugs, in the 1950s. Perhaps the best known of the first group of antipsychotic drugs was Thorazine, which was first approved for sale in the United States in 1954.

In the decades that followed, other groups of drugs were discovered to have psychoactive properties. Today these are usually called the *conventional* antipsychotic or neuroleptic drugs; they tend to cause certain undesirable neurological side effects (e.g., Parkinsonian "shakes"), though they can reduce some of the most troublesome psychotic symptoms. More than a dozen of these medications are available today.

In recent years a third group, usually called the *atypical* antipsychotic medications, has been introduced; these appear to have some of the same active benefits with fewer side effects. Medications available today include Thorazine, Mellaril, Clozaril, Serentil, Seroquel,

Moban, Trilafon, Loxitane, Stelazine, Prolixin, Navane, Haldo, Orap, Risperdal, Zypexa, Geodon and Abilify (brand names).[2]

The decision about which medication(s) to use seems to be as much an art as it is a science. Drug effectiveness and side effects vary considerably from person to person and across time. There is no perfect drug for the problems of psychosis, providing active benefits without any risks. Responsible clinicians assert that the process is almost always a quest for *titration*—just enough medication to control troublesome symptoms but not enough to cause side effects. It can take weeks, even months, to find the right drug and dosage combination—an often long and arduous process for afflicted individuals (and their loved ones). As with any serious condition, getting the right kind of help as soon as possible is crucial. But with a condition like schizophrenia, where much denial and avoidance are involved, this can be an especially daunting challenge (cf. helpful suggestions in Torrey, 2001).[3]

In recent years, we have seen incredible improvement in afflicted individuals within just days or weeks with some of the newer antipsychotic agents like Clozaril, Resperidal, Seroquel and Zyprexa. With Faiver et al. (2003), we think it is simply irresponsible to attempt to treat the problems of psychosis *without* psychopharmacological intervention. When schizophrenia is suspected, a physician (ideally a psychiatrist) should be immediately consulted to do a thorough and careful medical evaluation. Medication is almost always needed, and the newer antipsychotic medications, which have far fewer side effects than phenothiazines or conventional antipsychotic drugs, can make all the difference in the world. This can be a matter of life or death—both literally and symbolically.

Before discussing the various psychotherapeutic options, we need to mention the problem of noncompliance with prescribed medication(s). Anyone well acquainted with the urban poor who are mentally ill knows that persons who struggle with psychosis tend to take their medication only when they "feel the need." Obviously, this can have disastrous consequences for mental health. Only when the most troublesome symptoms are effectively controlled can there be any

---

[2]See Morrison (2002) for a helpful lay discussion or Purselle, Nemeroff & Jongsma (2004) for a superb professional presentation. A wonderful website <www.PsyD-fx.com> can be easily downloaded for up-to-date information for consumers and providers alike.

[3]We also recommend <www.schizophrenia.com> or <www.menthealth.com> for additional information (cf. Norcross et al., 2003).

possibility of a "normal" life. Learning to give accurate feedback to medical personnel can be one very tangible expression of a commitment to be an advocate for the mentally ill (Carter and Golant, 1998). Indeed, it has been argued that one of the reasons the community mental health movement did not more fully realize the dreams formulated in the 1960s and 1970s was noncompliance with prescribed medication (see also Miller and Jackson, 1995). In retrospect, it did not make sense to deinstitutionalize long-term residents of state hospitals and release them into the community when they would not take their prescribed medications and when adequate psychotherapeutic services weren't in place for them (Adams and Sutker, 2001).

It is hard to find the right type of physician and the right type(s) of medication and to ensure compliance with the prescription(s). Without a good social network of providers and advocates, it hardly even makes sense to talk about gaining access to good psychotherapeutic and community resources. Far too often, there is a large gap between what could be and what is.

Psychotherapeutic options. Probably every type of counseling and psychotherapy ever proposed has been used with schizophrenic individuals. A fair read of the available literature, we believe, would suggest that unless the person is somewhat in touch with reality and can make interpersonal connections, verbal psychotherapies make little sense at all (Jones and Butman, 1991). Careful research in the past two or three decades has made it increasingly clear what approaches are potentially helpful and which are not (Antony and Barlow, 2002, cf. chapters on schizophrenia; Barlow, 1993, cf. chapters on schizophrenia; Jongsma and Peterson, 1995; Meyer and Deitsch, 1996; Morrison, 2002; Nathan and Gorman, 1998).

Perhaps more important than the *type* of psychotherapeutic approach utilized are the interpersonal skills and sensitivities of the clinician working with the afflicted person and with family members and friends. Effective agents of change are comfortable with the often-bizarre beliefs and eccentric behaviors of schizophrenic persons; they have been sufficiently "field tested." They learn to take an active role in treatment, set realistic goals and offer gentle, corrective feedback; this therapy goes far beyond just listening. Cognitive and behavioral strategies that model, prompt, shape and reinforce interactional and self-help skills are absolutely essential (Torrey, 2001). The clinicians must be willing to collaborate with family members and friends so that important changes can be generalized and maintained beyond the consulting room. Effective change agents are not only well informed about the realities of serious mental illness but patient and hopeful persons.

Good treatment approaches with schizophrenia combine teaching essential coping skills with forming a strong interpersonal bond. This means focusing on the here and now and talking about specific, concrete *realities* and not reinforcing delusions or "crazy talk." The clinician must be an especially skilled observer and willing to provide a safe, predictable and controlled environment.

Especially encouraging of late has been the work done in family and interpersonal therapy (McLemore, 2003). Clearly, persons struggling with the problems of psychosis have a strong tendency to withdraw or to assume a position of "learned helplessness" (inability to appropriately assert themselves). Helping family members and friends engage schizophrenic persons, and vice versa, is vitally important (Torrey, 2001). Interventions may include teaching how to better modulate strong emotions, creating realistic expectations (goal setting) or dealing with the differences of opinion that occur in any human relationship (conflict management). At their best, family and interpersonal strategies teach more than problem-solving skills; they provide much-needed education, support and understanding (Morrison, 2002). Recent evidence suggests that such strategies are also *preventative* in that they help reduce the possibility of relapse and recidivism (Comer, 2003).

Community strategies. Like a number of the problems of social impact (cf. chapter seven), the problems of psychosis must also be treated at the level of the broader social environment, beyond immediate family members and friends. The Community Mental Health Act of 1963 was a well-intentioned effort to deinstitutionalize tens of thousands of people with serious mental illness and treat them in the community rather than in often-impoverished institutional settings. Ambitious strategies were proposed, including coordinated services, short-term hospitalization when needed, psychoeducation programs geared toward increasing public awareness, a focus on prevention rather than remediation (cf. chapter four), and supervised residences and worksites for persons in transition (Carson, Butcher and Mineka, 2002). Ideally, the movement would have greatly improved social support networks for afflicted individuals, assisted them in developing a greater sense of efficacy and provided some meaning and purpose in their lives (Pargament, 1997).

But the movement failed (Comer, 2003). Adequate resources and personnel were not made available, and the majority of people with schizophrenia received no services at all. This was no doubt compounded by poor coordination of existing services. The painful reality today is that even "treated" persons seldom receive more than medication. Their families tend to feel overwhelmed by what it means to care for them on a daily basis (Torrey, 2001). When family members can no longer care for them, they may end up in nursing homes or jails or on the streets (Comer, 2003). Most major urban centers in the United States have at least a few single-room occupancy hotels in run-down neighborhoods that are full of men and women who have severe mental illness (Miller and Jackson, 1995).

But what is the case on a national level is not always so at the local level. Several organizations seem especially adept at providing the kind of care that was first envisioned when the Community Mental Health Act was introduced. Some of these are faith-based; others are not. Groups like the National Alliance for the Mentally Ill (NAMI) have done some incredible things to not only raise awareness but also prompt necessary action. Not only are these services needed, but they are cost effective in helping growing numbers of seriously mental ill persons return to a more normal life (Carter and Golant, 1998). For a reader wanting to learn more about these possibilities, we suggest Francis and First, 1998; Norcross et al., 2003; Torrey, 2001; and some of the Internet sites mentioned in the previous section.

The treatment of the problems of psychosis must go beyond simply offering medication when the symptoms are most troublesome or providing cognitive-behavioral therapy when a sufferer needs to be stabilized. Long-term hospitalization doesn't work (Comer, 2003). What is truly needed is better aftercare when the persons are discharged. Much more could be done by persons of faith in this area, if only providing good friendship to the suffering person (Haas, 1966). As was suggested in chapter four, "If the church was truly the church, who would need counseling?" (Warren, 1972). There will always be brokenness and fallenness this side of Eden, especially with the problems of psychosis, but the need for social support is especially foundational for schizophrenic persons.

PREVENTION OF THE PROBLEMS OF PSYCHOSIS

Until we have a greater understanding of the biological bases of schizophrenia, there is little that we can do to *prevent* schizophrenia.

As stated earlier, there is little debate that biological diatheses (acquired or inherited) are involved in the problems of psychosis. Perhaps within our lifetime, a child predisposed to develop schizophrenia will be able to receive help prior to birth, or soon thereafter, through interventions such as genetic engineering or altering neurotransmitter sites (Pliszka, 2003). In the interim, we encourage our readers to pay close attention to the findings of the Human Genome Project, especially as they relate to cognitive neuroscience (Schwartzberg, 2000). *Primary prevention,* taking steps to prevent problems from developing in the first place, will have to remain a dream for the foreseeable future.

We can be more encouraged when it comes to *secondary prevention,* or efforts to intervene early with high-risk persons (Maxmen and Ward, 1995). Though there is little we can probably do to alter neuroanatomy (structure) or neurochemistry (biochemical processes), much can be done to reduce internal and/or external stressors for persons who might be predisposed. Biology is not destiny! A person who has a first-degree relative with schizophrenia, for example, needs to find stress-management techniques that work for him or her and use these strategies regularly (Jongsma and Peterson, 1995). Given what we know about coping and adjustment, finding effective ways to "deactivate" or self-soothe when one is overaroused seems absolutely imperative. The need is much like that of a person who knows there is a history of alcoholism in his or her family. Certainly this presupposes sufficient self-awareness and knowledge what can and should be done. This could be viewed as a form of appropriate and necessary self-care and as a matter of good and responsible stewardship of body, mind and spirit (Torrey, 2001).

At the level of structures and systems, it is *at least* as important to pay close attention to environmental and situational stressors that can trigger the problems of psychosis or keep an afflicted person in a vicious cycle of isolation and withdrawal. Lack of social support and limited coping resources can definitely add to the risk that an individual will develop schizophrenia. In the prodromal (building) phase of psychosis, any barriers to health and well-being—injustices of any sort—can become risk factors. Well-resourced communities have the *potential* to be more therapeutic communities where fewer individuals fall between the cracks (Paloutzian, 1996; Hood et al., 1996). When life circumstances become overwhelming, psychosis is always a possibility, especially for "high-risk" individuals (Scully et al., 1990). We applaud the efforts of those who have given serious thought to what it might mean to make our communities and churches better spaces for vulnerable persons (e.g., Carter and Golant, 1998; Smedes, 1998; Hood et al., 1996; Torrey, 2001).

Perhaps the area in which we can stretch the most is *tertiary prevention*, or strategies to gain access to the right types of services and to reduce dependency on individuals or organizations that are not committed to helping the suffering person realize his or her potential. At the most basic level, this means educating the "gatekeepers" of the community, those who are usually first approached in a time of crisis. For persons of faith, this often means the pastor or a key lay leader in a local congregation (Miller and Jackson, 1995). "Equipping the saints" through programs like Stephen Ministries or Clinical Pastoral Education (Hood et al., 1996) makes tremendous sense to us. Given that schizophrenia usually first develops in adolescence or young adulthood, it would make sense to train high school and college teachers to recognize both obvious and subtle signs of serious mental illness.

We dream of the day when all communities and churches will have access to information on schizophrenia (like Torrey, 2001) and be knowledgeable about the options for treatment. Collaboration will help concerned church and community leaders know which providers and organizations are helpful (like NAMI) and which are not. As with most any health care concern, knowledge can be used to empower others. Since many myths and stereotypes surround the problems of psychosis, accurate information is especially important; we often fear that which we don't understand.

The history of pastoral care (cf. chapter one) shows that there have always been men and women of faith with a vision for providing safe and supportive places where troubled souls could get help. When it comes to the problems of psychosis, this might mean developing more alternative treatment facilities that can welcome persons who are trying to regain their sanity and stay in touch with reality (Collins, 1980). As anyone who works in healthcare or human services knows all too well, finding such places at present can be a tremendous challenge. Helping someone find the right type of treatment with the right type of person(s) is at the heart of tertiary prevention.

Finally, in light of the failure of the Community Mental Health Act, we need to raise our voices to call for social justice. The great majority of afflicted individuals seldom get more than minimal attention, and that often means only phenothiazines or neuroleptic medication, since atypical antipsychotic medications are quite expensive. In our urban settings, it is not uncommon for a single caseworker to be "responsible" for scores if not hundreds of chronically mental ill individuals living in Third World conditions. That we even tolerate this as a society speaks volumes about what we truly value: it does not include severely impaired individuals who don't quite fit in. But the biblical exhortation to offer compassion to "the least of these" must surely apply to those struggling with the problems of psychosis (Boisen, 1960).

INTEGRATIVE THEMES AND CHALLENGES

Certain themes are foundational in our attempts to respond to the problems of psychosis from the perspective of a Christian worldview and lifestyle. Of particular importance is the classification of schizophrenia as a mental illness, the issue of disordered desires and how problems of psychosis relate to sin and our fallen human condition.

Pastoral care and disordered desires. One of the integrative challenges facing Christian mental health professionals lies in recognizing the common humanity among those with even the most severe expressions of psychopathology. We must stand against a view of those who suffer from problems of psychosis as "other," as it leads to a diminished view of the image of God in them and of our responsibility for the care of the weak and vulnerable.

Christians must cultivate a profound appreciation for the value of being human and of individual human beings (cf. Jones and Butman, 1991, chap. 2). Even in the midst of severe psychosis, the worth and dignity of the afflicted person is in no way diminished; the *imago Dei* may be tainted but is never removed. Given our own humanity, surely we can find some empathy for those who appear to us to be deluded or who have lost touch with reality. Christian philosopher and psychiatrist A. A. Howsepian (1997) argues persuasively that we all have disordered thinking and appetites (desires) to at least some degree. Thus there is room for some humility in this conversation.

Though we live in an increasingly complex and pluralistic society, many kinds of deviance are not often tolerated. We all have our cherished beliefs and strong convictions. For schizophrenic individuals, these can become especially troublesome and cause significant distress. For generations, prophets and priests have told us that we find the ambiguities, contradictions and absurdities of life difficult to tolerate, and this seems especially true regarding psychotic persons (Miller and Jackson, 1995). Far too easily a respect for authority and tradition can lead to dogmatism and rigidity, and blind obedience to people in positions of power can replace careful discernment and true wisdom (Hood et al., 1996). We often struggle with expressing our convictions with the "convicted civility" we are called to demonstrate in word and deed in our churches and communities (Jones and Butman, 1991).

With Howsepian (1997), we suggest that we are all deluded and "psychoticlike" to at least some extent; we can easily lose touch with reality. Without our defenses and supports we too might struggle with schizophrenia. Staying in touch with reality and not losing one's grip is surely one of the major challenges of being a Christian in the thoroughly postmodern world of today.

We all need discerning and supportive communities. Ideally, these should be representative groups of individuals (not all like-minded) who are willing to "speak the truth in love." Schizophrenic individuals have a profound disorder of beliefs and desires and need considerable assistance in finding a sense of meaning and purpose in their life (Howsepian, 1997). Rather than simply labeling their symptoms as "evidence" of their psychosis, we would do well to reflect deeply on what their beliefs and desires might be telling *us* about the nature of reality and the search for significance and truth (Torrey, 2001). Their cognitive and affective disturbances can be profoundly troubling, but they are not without potential meaning and significance for *us,* for example in offering us a painful awareness of our own fears and vulnerabilities.

The witness of history (e.g., the *Malleus maleficarum*) is that we are almost always far too quick to judge and label difference without understanding what that difference might *mean.* The historical (and contemporary) abuse of deviance and noncompliance is appalling. As Paloutzian (1996) has noted, it is much easier for us to internalize ways we are different than ways we are alike—our shared humanity. We have to get better at tolerating, sometimes even accepting, beliefs and behaviors that are unconventional, if only to become more effective in working with afflicted individuals.

The Christian community can be at the forefront of demonstrating utmost respect for the person suffering from schizophrenia. Here we draw on the keen insights of Lara Jefferson, a woman who was institutionalized for "insanity" yet whose insightful commentary constitutes one of the most highly regarded narratives about psychosis prior to the widespread availability of psychotropic medication:

The doctor was through just now and flattered the extent of my intelligence and education by discussing me in some long-handled, technical words I suppose were the labels of my phobias. For all I know of what he said, he might have been swearing at me in Yiddish. . . .

Oh, he is a good Doctor all right. An excellent Doctor. All his conclusions are founded on excellent logic; the things he tells me are true—nauseatingly true. He is right, sickeningly right. In fact, he is the very embodiment of all the virtue and wisdom in the world. For that reason, I detest him—passionately. But knowing these things does not keep me from the impulse to smack him down and that very impulse confirms the things he has told me.

I wish I could put a bell on him—so I would be aware when he starts probing around in the crooks and crannies of my crooked brain, hunting for phobias. He can do nothing with them when he finds them, so what is the use of hunting? Phobias are sensitive little critters—and it's like having a boil lanced, to have them probed into. He cannot cure them. All he does is go prowling around them among them, knocking them over. When he finds an extra fine specimen he is as thrilled with his discovery as some be-spectacled bug-hunter who captures a rare type of beetle.

Oh, how I wish, that I had the genius to take some of the smug complacency out of him. He calls me Egotistical—and I am—but he suffers most bumptiously from it too. I do not see how he can fail to observe the symptoms in himself, when he can see them in others so clearly. (Kaplan, 1964, pp. 5, 14-15)

Again, we are challenged at the level of *application* of our theological anthropology. Do we always see persons struggling with the problems of psychosis as created in the image and likeliness of God? Do we treat them with the utmost respect? Or do we too quickly give in to our reductionistic tendencies and treat these persons in a patronizing, condescending manner? Do we really believe that broken and hurting persons, including those suffering from schizophrenia, have nothing to teach us about the nature of God's creation and our well-intentioned (but uninformed) attempts to do "justice and mercy"? As Lara Jefferson might tell us if she were alive today, perhaps nothing is more toxic than consulting a technician when you are in pain. The

call on all of us, laypersons and professionals, is to image God in all
our work in terms of *his* character, *his* concerns and *his* compassion
(cf. Jones and Butman, 1991, chap. 15).

A related challenge lies in discerning "reality." Earlier we quoted
Francis and First (1998) on the ongoing challenge of discerning "reality," what is truth, how do we know it and how do we know when we
know it. A major challenge in making sense of the problems of psychosis is determining what indeed is truthful and what is not. The interpretive debate certainly has a lot to do with the social, cultural and
religious context.

Our work with schizophrenic individuals has shown us how easily
it is for even "normal" people to become arrogant, confused and even
deluded. Our senses are certainly not inerrant or authoritative in all
matters of faith and practice. We have a deep respect for human freedom and agency, but there are significant limitations on reason, science and experience. So how can we best determine truth?

Working with "crazy" people has potential epistemological implications for "sane" folks. It might get us, like Boisen, to think about what
things are "immutable" and what things are *not* essential for well-
being. It might enable us (like Lara Jefferson) to see more of the ambiguities, contradictions and absurdities of "normal" life. It can remind us, however painfully, that there can be meaning in suffering
and that the pursuit of self-gratification can lead to a hellish existence
(Howsepian, 1997). In short, study of the problems of psychosis
should bring us back to basics.

But it is not always easy to remain thoroughly biblical and faithful
to the orthodox Christian faith. Throughout Scripture this search
seems as much collective as individual. Perhaps psychosis has something to teach us about the need to look for consensual validation beyond our own immediate thoughts, feelings and experiences. No person in isolation can *fully* grasp reality or truth. This demands more
epistemic humility than is often found in community or church settings, even among those with an ecumenical spirit

Psychotic persons hold on to their delusions with great passion
(Howsepian, 1997), perhaps feeling these are needed to help them
cope with an external reality they can't understand. They prefer a
world of their own construction. If we are truly honest, perhaps we
can acknowledge some of the same distorting bias in ourselves. To
whom do we want to be accountable? Or are we only looking for con-
firmation of our own pathologies?

SIN AND PSYCHOPATHOLOGY

Our brokenness, deceit and fallenness are evident in any expression of human psychopathology, but perhaps somewhat less so in the problems of psychosis. Perhaps more than in any other group of disorders in the *DSM-IV-TR*, in schizophrenia the physical aspects of our existence have certainly gone awry. How else can you explain the often encouraging response to psychotropic medications? It is hard to see how the afflicted person has a full capacity for choice and responsibility when his or her body and mind have become so obviously disconnected (Jones and Butman, 1991). Schizophrenia is a disease of the body and mind, not just an expression of a disembodied spirit. If there is any better case for the need for Christians to embrace a more holistic view of the person, we don't know one (see also Pliszka, 2003).

In regard to schizophrenia, we would argue that sin's effects are evident in the underlying human condition, much more than in the overt symptoms (Howsepian, 1997). With reference to the stress-diathesis perspective, genetic predispositions or faulty neurochemical processes could *ultimately* be attributed to effects of sin and the Fall, whereas structural and systemic evil could be more overt expressions of deception, evil or even the demonic (Peck, 1983). Although we can never know with certainty what raw material a person brings into his or her experience of the world, we do well to be attentive to what obstacles the world might place before that person to in the course of his or her formative years (cf. chapter two, "Sociocultural and Biological Foundations of Mental Illness" section).

There can be meaning within our fallen and incomplete condition, even in the midst of madness. We were profoundly moved when we read the autobiography of Anton Boisen, *Out of the depths* (1960). It reminded us that Scripture offers no promise of complete relief from pain and suffering in this world, only the promise of God's presence in the midst of suffering. Boisen writes of the "crucible" of his pain and suffering, the "refiner's fire" mentioned in the Bible; we shudder to think what this might mean for us in a similar situation. Boisen does not romanticize his pain; he is brutally frank and honest. He had to decide anew what was truly important and what he really believed. The Christian, then, can cultivate a vision for a life in which suffering can have meaning. Exemplars like Boisen show us by word and deed that something more important that money, sex and power (or any other self-gratification) is worth pursuing.

Consider these words from Lara Jefferson, written on pieces of scrap paper while she was institutionalized for psychosis in the mid-twentieth century:

> Something has happened to me—I do not know what. All that was my former self has crumbled and fallen together and a creature has emerged of whom I know nothing. She is a stranger to me—and has an egotism that makes the egotism that I had look like skimmed milk; and she thinks thoughts that are—heresies. Her name is insanity. She is the daughter of madness—and according to the doctor, they each know the genesis in my own brain. I do not know—and I doubt if the doctors are as sure of what they think they know as they would like others to believe—or would like to believe themselves. I know nothing of these things, at least not in the way their knowledge runs. (quoted in Kaplan, 1964, p. 6)

Eventually an entire book of Jefferson's reflections was published, with very few editorial changes (Jefferson, 1948). It is especially striking that her acute insights were offered prior to the availability of modern psychopharmacological and psychotherapeutic treatments, suggesting that there might be some "sanity" even in the midst of insanity.

This brings us to the biblical concept of hope. A generation ago, schizophrenia was assumed to be hopeless, incurable. Considering the fact that one out of a hundred persons in any culture eventually develops schizophrenia or another form of psychosis, this realization could easily be demoralizing. No wonder there is much denial of this painful reality. Life would be easier if we could pretend that the problems of psychosis simply did not exist.

We may not have consensus about the etiology and maintenance of schizophrenia, but we do seem to know what makes a difference in treatment. Tremendous progress that has been made in the development of a new generation of antipsychotic medications. When appropriately prescribed, these should be properly viewed as gifts from God, one more fruit of the hard work that has been done in the area of general revelation (reason and science). Likewise there is good news regarding psychotherapeutic and community options (Nathan and Gorman, 1998; Torrey, 2001). Once a sufferer is stabilized on psychotropic medication and amenable to psychosocial interventions, much can be done to increase their social support system, their sense of efficacy, and their sense of meaning and purpose (Pargament,

1997). As Smedes (1998) has argued, there *is* reason to keep hope alive in a world we cannot control.

AN ADDITIONAL CONSIDERATION

Unfortunately, safe spaces are hard to find. The issues are similar to those involved in trying to care for a parent with Alzheimer's disease in the home setting. You may feel that you are watching a part of someone you love die each day, with no prospect of relief or recovery on the near or distant horizon. Schizophrenia is most certainly a family disease, and all members are affected in significant and profound ways. Obviously, the immediate family needs help with the burdens and responsibilities. Churches and communities could certainly offer assistance in practical and tangible ways as an expression of Christian charity and concern.

Even if the family can find a good mental health provider who will take their loved one seriously, the battle is far from over. Dealing with schizophrenia is a long-term process that can last years and even decades. Medications and psychotherapeutic services can offer much valuable assistance. But beyond stabilization, an alternative placement may be needed to aid the person with integration into society. With the right support, structure and supervision, there is a much higher probability of integration into the broader social and vocational world. Finding these resources can be a time-consuming affair, however, for family members and friends (Torrey, 2001).

A CONCLUDING THOUGHT

Schizophrenia is the ultimate psychological breakdown. It is humanity in an especially raw form. Initially, it should be treated as a psychiatric and medical emergency. A thorough and careful assessment of overall functioning is indicated. Most likely psychotropic medication and professional intervention, including cognitive-behavioral and interpersonal strategies, will be required. Beyond that, much more needs to be done, including finding settings that can help absorb or normalize certain beliefs and behaviors and contain others. Besides an understanding family and supportive group of friends, what is needed most from a longitudinal or developmental perspective is a safe, healing and purposeful community, one that can help set realistic expectations as well as model, shape, prompt and reinforce adaptive coping behaviors. Concerned persons of faith need to be vitally and actively involved in promoting this much-needed healing for broken and hurting persons.

RECOMMENDED READING

Morrison, J. (2002). *Straight talk about your mental health.* New York: Guilford. One of the best available no-nonsense discussions of serious mental illness, from a highly respected author and psychiatrist.

Norcross, J., et al. (2004). *Authoritative guide to self-help resources in mental health.* New York: Guilford. This is an outstanding resource for laypersons on every major type of mental disorder.

Torrey, E. (2001). *Surviving schizophrenia: A manual for families, consumers and providers.* 4th ed. New York: Harper Perennial. If you could buy just one book on the subject from the most credible source, this would be the one.

REFERENCES

Adams, H., and Sutker, P. (2001). *Comprehensive handbook of psychopathology* (3rd ed.). New York: Kluwer Academic/Plenum.

American Psychiatric Association. (2000). *Diagnostic and statistical manual of mental disorders* (4th ed.). Washington, DC: Author.

Antony, M., and Barlow, D. (Eds.). (2002). *Handbook of assessment and treatment planning for psychological disorders.* New York: Guilford.

Barlow, D., ed. (1993). *Clinical handbook of psychological disorders* (2nd ed.). New York: Guilford.

Boisen, A. (1960). *Out of the depths.* New York: Harper & Brothers.

Butcher, J., Mineka, S., and Hooley, J. (2004). *Abnormal psychology* (12th ed.). Boston: Pearson.

Carson, R., Butcher, J., and Mineka, S. (2002). *Fundamentals of abnormal psychology and modern life.* Boston: Allyn and Bacon.

Carter, R., and Golant, S. M. (1998). *Helping someone with mental illness.* New York: Random House.

Collins, G. (1980). *Christian counseling: A comprehensive guide.* Waco, TX: Word.

Comer, R. (2003). *Abnormal Psychology* (5th ed.). New York: Worth.

Faiver, C., Eisengart, S., and Colona, R. (2003). *The counselor intern's handbook* (3rd ed.). Belmont, CA: Thomson/Brooks Cole.

Francis, A., and First, M. (1998). *Your mental health: A layman's guide to the psychiatrist's bible.* New York: Scribner.

Frese, F. (1993). Coping with schizophrenia. *Innovations and Research, 2.* Available online at <http://www.mentalhealth.com/story/p52-sc04.html>.

Gotkin, J., and Gotkin, P. (1992). *Too much anger, too many tears: A personal triumph over psychiatry.* New York: Harper Perennial.

Haas, H. (1966). *The Christian encounters mental illness.* St. Louis: Concordia.

Hood, R., Spilka, B., Hunsberger, B., and Gorsuch, R. (1996). *The psychology of religion: An empirical approach* (2nd ed.). New York: Guilford.

Howsepian, A. (1997). Sin and psychosis. In R. Roberts and M. Talbot (Eds.), *Limning the psyche: Explorations in Christian psychology* (pp. 264-81). Grand Rapids, MI: Eerdmans.

Jefferson, L. (1948). *These are my sisters.* Tulsa, OK: Vickers.

Johnson, C., Snibbe, J., and Evans, L. (1981). *Basic psychopathology: A programmed text* (2nd ed.). New York: SP Medical Books.

Jones, S., and Butman, R. (1991). *Modern psychotherapies: A comprehensive Christian appraisal.* Downers Grove, IL: InterVarsity.

Jongsma, A., and Peterson, M. (1995). *The complete psychotherapy treatment planner.* New York: Wiley-Interscience.

Kaplan, B. (1964). *The inner world of mental illness.* New York: Harper & Row.

Maxmen, J., and Ward, N. (1995). *Essential psychopathology and its treatment.* New York: Plenum.

McLemore, C. (2003). *Toxic relationships and how to change them.* San Francisco: Jossey-Bass.

Meyer, R., and Deitsch, S. (1996). *The clinician's handbook* (4th ed.). Boston: Allyn and Bacon.

Miller, W., and Jackson, K. (1995). *Practical psychology for pastors* (2nd ed.). Englewood Cliffs, NJ: Prentice-Hall.

Morrison, J. (1995). *DSM-IV made easy: The clinician's guide to diagnosis.* New York: Guilford.

Morrison, J. (1997). *When psychological problems mask medical disorders: A guide for psychotherapists.* New York: Guilford.

Morrison, J. (2002). *Straight talk about your mental health.* New York: Guilford.

Nathan, P., and Gorman, J. (1998). *A guide to treatments that work.* New York: Oxford.

Norcross, J., Santrock, J., Campbell, L., Smith, T., Sommer, R., and Zuckerman, E. (2003). *Authoritative guide to self-help resources in mental health.* New York: Guilford.

Oden, T. C. (1987). *Classical pastoral care: Vol. 3. Pastoral counsel.* Grand Rapids, MI: Baker.

Paloutzian, R. (1996). *Invitation to the psychology of religion* (2nd ed.). Boston: Allyn and Bacon.

Pargament, K. (1997). *The psychology of religion and coping.* New York: Guilford.

Peck, M. S. (1983). *People of the lie.* New York: Simon & Schuster.

Pliszka, S. (2003). *Neuroscience for the mental health clinician.* New York: Guilford.

Purselle, D., Nemeroff, C., and Jongsma, A. (2004). *The psychopharmacology treatment planner.* New York: Wiley.

Roberts, R., and Talbot, M. (1997). *Limning the psyche: Explorations in Christian psychology.* Grand Rapids, MI: Eerdmans.

Schwartzberg, S. (2000). *Casebook of psychological disorders: The human face of emotional distress.* Boston: Allyn and Bacon.

Scully, J., Bechtold, D., Bell, J., Dubovsky, S., Neligh, G., and Peterson, J. (1990). *Psychiatry* (2nd ed.). Malvern, PA: Harwal.

Smedes, L. (1998). *Standing on the promises: Keeping hope alive for a tomorrow we cannot control.* Nashville: Thomas Nelson.

Sutker, P. and Adams, H. (1993). *Comprehensive handbook of psychopathology* (2nd ed.). New York: Plenum.

Torrey, E. (2001). *Surviving schizophrenia: A manual for families, consumers and providers* (4th ed.). New York: Harper Perennial.

Warren, N. (1972). If the church was truly the church, who would need counseling? Typescript, Fuller Theological Seminary, Pasadena, CA.

10

PROBLEMS
OF PERSONALITY

*W*e all know people who are difficult to understand and even harder to love. Sometimes this has to do with differences in our worldviews and lifestyles; in other cases it has more to do with our personalities or interactional styles, or both. As Christians, we are called to confess Jesus Christ as Lord, seek after righteousness and love the brothers and sisters. If the latter commandment were to simply love those with whom we felt comfortable, it would not be so hard. But we are also called to love those who are difficult to love, including our "enemies," and that does not come easy for any of us. As Smedes (1998) has observed, living out our commitments and forgiving those who have hurt us when we did not deserve it are two of the most difficult commandments set before disciples of Jesus Christ.

The *DSM* lists a group of disorders pertaining to persons who have enduring patterns of maladaptive behavior. Their symptoms do not wax and wane as do those of some other major mental disorders (e.g., schizophrenia or serious mood disturbance). They cannot be directly attributed to exposure to overwhelming stressors or traumatic life events, as with PTSD. Rather, the *DSM* defines them as a consistent pattern of behavior that impairs social functioning, causes significant distress to self or others, and has been evident since early childhood or adolescence (Miller and Jackson, 1995). Collectively, these are called the *personality disorders*. They are best understood as enduring traits of persons that have been observed since their formative years.

Learning to set realistic expectations for relationships can become a major personal or professional challenge for people with these disorders (Cloud and Townsend, 2002). Forming loving, healthy relationships with others in our family and community is an awesome responsibility for men and women of faith, so finding effective strategies for coping and change ought to be of intense interest to all Christians. Fortunately, helpful resources are now available (e.g., McLemore, 2003). But recognizing that there may be some significant barriers to begin with is foundational for implementing more effective strategies.

Personality disorders have been hotly debated in mental health circles for decades. Throughout the different editions of the *DSM* the typology has changed, often reflecting shifts in clinical and theoretical understandings of these enduring patterns of social interaction. It has been assumed that personality disorders are difficult to treat. Until recently, careful research on etiology or maintenance or the effectiveness of various treatment strategies has been somewhat lacking. But that is changing (Benjamin, 2003; Bockian and Jongsma, 2001). Our feelings about dealing with "toxic" people (those who are hard to understand or love) can be strong and confusing, especially when our notions of healthy interdependence and responsible self-assertion are fuzzy (McLemore, 2003).

THEMES FROM PASTORAL CARE

Gregory the Great in his work *Pastoral Care* reflects on many categories of persons and how to respond to each. He shows a remarkable understanding of personalities and the need to meet each individual with an appropriate pastoral response. For example, he distinguishes between those who are prone to humility and those who are prone to haughtiness:

> The humble are to be admonished in one way, the haughty in another. The former should be told how genuine is that excellence which they have by hoping for it; the haughty, how worthless is the temporal glory which is not retained even when in their grasp. Let the humble be told of the eternal nature of the things which they strive after, and of the transitoriness of the

things which they despise. Let the haughty be told how transitory the things which they set themselves to acquire, how eternal the things which they forfeit. (1978, p. 141)

The traits of our fallen humanity (e.g., kindly/envious, sincere/insincere, taciturn/talkative, obstinate/fickle) can make interpersonal relationships quite difficult. In fact, there is general consensus that throughout Christian history it has never been easy to form healthy friendships (Griffin, 1987), develop strong marriages and families (Worthington, 1993), or reduce conflict and stress at home, at work and at church (Malony, 1989). A veteran of the church in conflict observes, "Believers ought to be deeply concerned about the animosities, antagonisms and bitter conflicts so prevalent within the family of God. For what can unbelievers think of us when, as Joe Bayly suggested, our theme song seems to be: 'The strife is o'er, the battle done. Our church has split, and our side won'?" (Fenton 1987, p. 10).

Effective pastoral care takes the formation of healthy relationships and good community very seriously. Further, it recognizes that conflict is inevitable and that effective conflict management skills are essential for promoting health and holiness in everyday life (McLemore, 2003). Our theological anthropology tells us that good relationships not only reflect our creation in the image and likeness of God but are involved in our exercise of responsible dominion, using our gifts and talents in worship, fellowship and service (Kauffmann, 1999).

But our faith also tells us that we are all broken, fallen and sinful creatures, prone to biases, distortions and stereotypes. When it comes to the formation of healthy relationships and learning effective conflict management skills, we all have much to learn about forgiveness and reconciliation. McLemore notes:

Human actions are so subtle and multilayered that it is not always possible even to distinguish sharply between what is holy and what is sinful. . . . Christians who prefer simplicity to truth do not like this. They would prefer to sort everything into two discrete categories, the totally good and the totally bad. Yet many things in life are ambiguous mixtures of good and bad, which is why we should pray earnestly for wisdom, and fall continuously on God's mercy, lest we make tragic mistakes about others and the meanings of what they do. (2003, pp. 16-17)

Offering pastoral care to difficult or demanding people requires a prayerful approach to divine leading. Persons with deeply ingrained patterns of relating to self and others in self-defeating or destructive ways take huge amounts of time and energy. Offering them a "soft answer" (speaking the truth in love) in a way that does not seriously damage their self-esteem requires not only compassion and grace but great measures of wisdom and discernment as well (Kauffmann, 1999). Timing, tact and sensitivity are enormously important in giving (and receiving) helpful feedback.

Persons in ministry know that there are striking differences between people. In social science, *personality* is usually defined as a unique, long-term pattern of inner experience and outward behavior (Comer, 2004). The assumption is that each of us has certain *traits* that are consistent across time and evident in most settings. There are endless debates in the field about the "roots" (origins) of these "shoots" (overt expressions), but it is generally assumed that these characteristics are both inherited and learned.

Normally, we learn to "flex" in new environments and situations. Sadly, lack of flexibility is one of the hallmarks of the personality disorders. The implications for ministry are obvious. Rigid patterns of inner experience and outward behavior make the formation of healthy, interdependent relationships extremely difficult. When the inevitable conflict occurs, an inability to adapt makes it difficult to clearly communicate or collaborate, to say nothing about offering forgiveness or reconciliation (Malony, 1989). Such rigidity makes it difficult for the person to really listen to others, perhaps because their own inner experience is confusing and overwhelming or they are totally absorbed by their perceived needs or wants. Consequently they tend to struggle in attempts to affiliate with others and to express their needs in a direct but noncoercive manner (McLemore, 2003). They are either moving toward or away from others to unhealthy extremes or seeking to compete rather than collaborate in decision making. One can readily see the difficulties this can create in home, work or community settings.

Not surprisingly, people who struggle with personality disorders often have great difficulty in being warm or assertive. Their rigidity makes it hard for them to collaborate or work in small groups. When given the opportunity to lead, they tend to impose their agenda on others rather than to seek consensus. In contrast, servant leadership seeks to lead without power (DePree, 1997); it is about empowering others rather than simply imposing one's will. The focus is on responsible stewardship and a shared sense of values and vision (which in and of itself requires flexible commitments). Sufficient time is taken for team building or collaboration *before* making important decisions—which requires a kind of attentive and respectful listening that comes hard for a person struggling with a personality disorder.

Ultimately, effective ministry is about helping people to develop their gifts and talents, encouraging their spiritual development and formation, and equipping them to carry out the mission and task of the church (Kauffmann, 1999). For some persons, this is especially hard, perhaps because they have a personality disorder. Their rigidity may have less to do with a lack of faith commitment and more to do with potentially serious psychopathology. Unless sufficient attention is given, it is unlikely that these significant obstacles can be removed so that they can move in the direction of greater health and holiness (McLemore, 2003). Helping such persons move beyond their impression-management tendencies (Jones and Butman, 1991) and toward better stewardship of the gifts they have been given should be a shared concern for all in ministry. As we will see shortly, this often means setting clear limits and boundaries and sticking to them consistently. The pastoral or leadership team also needs to be fully informed about problematic behaviors so there will be no manipulation or conning (Miller and Jackson, 1995). Processing (debriefing and defusing) strong feelings of ambivalence and confusion, even anger and intense frustration, is often necessary. Further education about personality disorders, coupled with good professional consultation, can also be helpful. Ideally, this can help the pastoral or leadership team attack the problem(s) rather than the person (which would alienate or isolate those most directly affected). In the long run, such an approach is much more helpful than to spiritualize the problem or to offer religious interventions that are misinformed about the painful realities of rigid, inflexible patterns of relating.

THEMES FROM PSYCHOPATHOLOGY

There are ten major personality disorders discussed in the *Diagnostic and Statistical Manual of Mental Disorders (DSM-IV-TR)*. These are organized into three major categories or "clusters." Again, the common definition is that there are enduring patterns of inner experience and outward behavior that have been evident in most interactions for years (or even decades).

As noted, onset is usually adolescence or early adulthood. Generally the affected person does not see his or her interactional style as problematic; the symptoms are *ego-dystonic*. Family members and friends, however, usually do see the inflexibility and rigidity of their interpersonal communications and are painfully aware of how it causes significant impairment in social and occupational functioning. It is assumed that about 10 percent of the adult population fits the *DSM-IV-TR* criteria for a personality disorder (Adams and Sutker, 2001). Countless more persons are indirectly or directly affected by these troublesome patterns.

The "odd or eccentric" cluster includes the paranoid, schizoid and schizotypal personality disorders (also called *cluster A*). The "dramatic, emotional or erratic" cluster includes the antisocial, borderline, narcissistic and histrionic personality disorders (also called *cluster B*). Finally, the "anxious or fearful" cluster includes the avoidant, dependent and obsessive-compulsive personality disorders (also called *cluster C*). Unlike the majority of the disorders discussed in this book, all these are considered "Axis II" disorders, along with the developmental disorders and mental retardation.

These disorders are hard to diagnose and easy to misdiagnose (Comer, 2004). External behaviors can often be directly observed, but internal experiences can only be inferred, so clinical judgment is required. Changed criteria in almost every new addition of the *DSM* adds to the challenge of making accurate judgments about persons with problems in living. It is often hard to decide when a "normal" personality style becomes pathological or even merits professional attention. Most of the personality disorders can be understood as exaggerated expressions of adaptive coping strategies that have gone seriously awry (McLemore, 2003).

Unfortunately, many persons with a personality disorder have at least one "Axis I" concern as well, such as an anxiety or mood disorder. This simultaneity of conditions, called *comorbidity* (Benjamin, 2003), naturally complicates the assessment and treatment process.

Cluster A personality disorders. These disorders tend to leave the afflicted person socially disengaged and isolated. In a number of striking ways, these sufferers are not unlike persons who struggle with schizophrenia: they tend to be suspicious, socially withdrawn and idiosyncratic in their thinking. But they do not have the same degree of break with reality that you see in psychosis—the intensity, duration and frequency of the symptoms. Rarely do these individuals seek help, for their symptoms usually don't trouble them. To use the helpful typology of Benjamin (2003) and McLemore (2003), they rarely move *toward* people and seldom assert themselves in social situations. They greatly prefer a world of escape and fantasy to the demands of active engagement with others.

The core issue in the *paranoid* personality disorder is a deep suspicion or mistrust of others. When reading social cues, these persons tend to be hypersensitive, vigilant and cautious. It is less that they are delusional and more that they tend to mistrust nearly everyone and everything. Consequently, relationships are troublesome, so they tend to be avoidant whenever possible. The *schizoid* individual bears the added burden of severely limited emotional expression; they tend to look and act in a *very* constricted manner. If trust issues are central to the paranoid personality disorder, the core issue with the schizoid person is a lack of desire to be in relationship with anyone. Finally, *schizotypal* persons have many of these same problems but also struggle with what others judge to be bizarre ways of thinking and perceiving the world. Of the three disorders in this cluster, it is usually thought to be the most severe disturbance. Trying to interact with a schizotypal person can be enormously difficult, since they struggle with staying focused and on task. When they speak, which is rare, their speech tends to be vague and confusing to others.

Again, these disorders look a lot like the prodromal (building) phases of schizophrenia—moving away from people in thought, word and deed. The assumption of mental health professionals is that "warm assertion" in our interpersonal relationships is healthy (McLemore, 2003). By definition, persons with a cluster A disorder are neither warm nor assertive. Therein lies the problem.

Cluster B personality disorders. In any volume on personality disorders, this group of disorders gets the bulk of the attention, perhaps because they create much distress for laypersons and professionals alike. For a person with an antisocial, borderline, histrionic or narcissistic personality disorder, it is almost impossible to develop a mutually satisfying and truly reciprocal relationship. Of the four, we suspect the majority of our readers have heard about the antisocial personality disorder (persons often judged to be criminals in our society) or perhaps the borderline personality disorder (explored in the 1987 movie *Fatal Attraction*).

The *DSM-IV-TR* criteria for the *antisocial* personality disorder suggest the lay understanding of "psychopaths" or "sociopaths." These persons persistently disregard and violate the rights of others (Comer, 2004). Given their patterns of misbehavior (e.g., lying, stealing, impulsivity) it is usually only a matter of time before they get in trouble with the law (they must be at least eighteen to meet the *DSM* criteria). Perhaps the single most common personality disorder (up to 3.5 percent of the adult population), it results in incredible suffering for victims and costs billions in law enforcement and corrections. What is striking when one meets such a person is a lack of empathy and apparent "gaping holes" in the moral conscience (Adams and Sutker, 2001). Obviously something went seriously awry in their development.

The *borderline* personality disorder creates havoc of a different sort. Not only are these people dramatic in their self-presentation, but they tend to be notoriously unstable, impulsive and unpredictable (Benjamin, 2003). Especially frightening to others is their emotional lability, including angry, aggressive outbursts directed toward others or turned inward in self-destructive acts like "cutting" or suicidal gestures. Many emergency-room personnel have had painful experiences of dealing with a borderline individual in crisis. Normal development tends to be arrested. Emotions are difficult to modulate, and impulsive actions are exceedingly common and often life threatening. Attempts to nurture these persons, however well intentioned, tend to set up unrealistic expectations. When they are disappointed, they tend to act out verbally and physically, producing great fear and confusion in their family members and friends.

The other two personality disorders, *histrionic and narcissistic,* have many of the same dramatic features. Both tend to want to be the center of attention in their social relationships. Histrionic people are usually described as vain, self-centered and demanding. They are "social junkies" (McLemore, 2003), always looking for approval from others. Narcissistic persons also tend to be grandiose and constantly demand attention; they are highly manipulative and exploitive of others. They tend to focus on their accomplishments, exaggerating their achievements and talents (Comer, 2004). They are extremely arrogant and self-absorbed, like an adolescent who can never get enough attention. With both disorders, the dramatic tendencies go considerably beyond what is seen as normal for adults. In the terminology of Van Leeuwen (2002), it is as if the mandate for responsible dominion has degenerated in an overwhelming desire to control, manipulate or exploit others for personal gain and satisfaction. All of us harbor such wishes and sometimes act on them, but normally not to the extent that they become a whole worldview and lifestyle.

Cluster C personality disorders. The anxious group of personality disorders is characterized first and foremost by an overwhelming sense of fear. In a number of ways they are like anxiety or mood disorders, but they are still distinct entities.

Avoidant disorders are suffered by people who tend to be very uncomfortable and restrained in social situations. This goes far beyond shyness. Their fear is so strong that they assume nobody would find them to be adequate or attractive, so they seldom risk being vulnerable. In time they develop a pattern of social withdrawal. It is less that they fear social circumstances (as with a social phobia) and more that they fear social relationships. Like clinically anxious people, they fear humiliation, and this tends to incapacitate them in social situations.

Dependent persons are stuck in different ways: they want others to tell them how to think, feel and behave. At a somewhat deeper level, they rely far too much on others to take care of them, and they are unable or unwilling to make even the most basic decisions for themselves. The thought of needing to assume full adult responsibilities is simply overwhelming to them.

Finally, with the *obsessive-compulsive* personality disorder, inordinate attention is focused on maintaining control, order or perfection. These persons can lose all spontaneity, openness and simple joy in living. Consequently, they tend to be seen as formal, rigid and stiff, unable to see beyond the task at hand that consumes their time and energy. Order is their modus operandi and perfectionism their life script. Sadly, their relationships suffer tremendously, since they tend to set equally high expectations for others and simply cannot let go of them. More than a few Christian clinicians have noted that cluster C disorders may reflect a legalism or moralism gone badly awry (Jones and Butman, 1991)—a kind of sin management, if you will, pretending that we can somehow deny our humanity and brokenness.

ANTECEDENTS OF THE PROBLEMS OF PERSONALITY

There has been an explosion of helpful research on the etiology and maintenance of personality disorders from a biopsychosocial perspective (e.g., Adams and Sutker, 2001; Benjamin, 2003; Comer, 2004; McLemore, 2003). Historically, all three clusters of disorders were assumed to be problems with nurture rather than nature, more reflective of environmental and situational factors than either biology or culture. It is not that clear anymore—a powerful realization that raises important questions about choice and responsibility. Personality disorders almost always are multiply determined and multiply maintained.

Cluster A disorders. As noted earlier, not much systemic research is available on paranoid, schizoid and schizotypal personality disorders. It was assumed that the trust issues of paranoid persons could be traced back to problematic relationships with demanding or hostile parents. Recent research, however, focuses on cognitive or biological roots. Efforts have been made to look for a genetic predisposition (Adams and Sutker, 2001). More promising, however, is to see these disorders as an expression of cognitive distortions or maladaptive assumptions that have been interpersonally mediated (imprinted) through important relationships in the formative years (Benjamin, 2003). As in the person struggling with a phobia, an avoidant pattern of conditioning unfolds, and it becomes a vicious, self-defeating pattern of coping and responding.

Schizoid and *schizotypal* personality disorders may have somewhat similar etiologies. The focus of much attention is on faulty patterns of communication in the formative years, unsatisfied needs for human contact when attachment issues are most important, or serious deficiencies is the cognitive thinking processes (Pliszka, 2003). These persons have great difficulty reading social cues and consequently tend to withdraw and isolate themselves, so much so that "reality testing" begins to suffer. Having lacked an experience of healthy attachment when it truly mattered, they are cautious about initiating an encounter with someone they do not know or trust. In time, emotional impoverishment and lack of cognitive stimulation from external sources become intertwined, and the process of disengagement and escape becomes all too predictable. Since many of the symptoms of these disorders seem like those of the prodromal (building) phase of psychosis, it can be assumed that a link with certain biological diatheses will be discovered in the near future (Adams and Sutker, 2001).

Cluster B disorders. In contrast, some clear trends are emerging in our understanding of specific cluster B disorders, especially with the antisocial and borderline conditions. For example, there is little debate among clinicians and researchers that there are biological factors undergirding the *antisocial* personality disorder (Pliszka, 2003). Generally speaking, antisocial individuals are far more likely than other persons to take risks and seek thrills; their arousal levels are different. When it comes to learning important tasks, there are also striking differences in how they think and respond, making conditioning more challenging. Further, their cognitive-perceptual style leads them to interpret social situations in a vastly different manner, more to do with their immediate wants and less with the needs (or concerns) of others. Where there has been a pathogenic environment of poor parenting, inconsistent or nonexistent discipline, minimal accountability, exposure to unhealthy role models, or a synergistic combination of all these factors, it is not surprising that antisocial tendencies eventually emerge. Even when we take full account of possible biological vulnerabilities, it is impossible to minimize the importance of reinforcement, modeling (conditioning) and crazy living situations that offer few viable alternatives to being "one up" in social relationships, especially those in which there is a possibility of personal gain or exploitation.

It may be helpful to think of the *borderline* disorder as biopsychosocial as well. There is evidence that these persons have different levels of brain serotonin activity and that there is a strong genetic predisposition (Pliszka, 2003). When this is coupled with a lack of acceptance by parents in the formative years, it is not surprising that many of these persons have an intense fear of abandonment (Benjamin, 2003). This might be especially true for a person going through an unusual number of changes, losses and transitions (McLemore, 2003), who will find it tempting to latch on to anybody who seems safe, stable or supportive, such as warm Christians who care deeply (Cloud and Townsend, 2002).

In contrast, there is no clear evidence for a biological predisposition for either the *histrionic* or *narcissistic* personality disorder (Adams and Sutker, 2001). With both disorders, psychosocial and sociocultural theories are posited. We are especially impressed with some cognitive-behavioral and interpersonal formulations. Especially with narcissists, the real problem may be that they think too highly of themselves (they overvalue their self-worth). Ours is often seen as a "culture of narcissism" and extreme self-absorption (Francis and First, 1998). It is assumed therefore that some persons are shaped, prompted and reinforced to act and behave in a dramatic and demanding manner, always needing to be at the center of attention.

Lest we fault our culture only, it should be noted that persons who develop either disorder tend to have an overarching need to convince themselves (and others) that they *are* truly self-sufficient and *not* in need of more mutually satisfying reciprocal relationships. Rather than coming to grips with the possibility that they truly need others and want to be cared for in a less dramatic or exploitive manner, they engage in dramatic, vain and selfish means of meeting their most urgent and pressing *wants* (but not their deeper *needs* for true intimacy). Beneath what can often appear to be arrogant optimism is a less acknowledged desire to be truly cared for by others (McLemore, 2003). The dramatic cry for help may reflect a deeply held belief that they are inadequate, incompetent or unworthy in their own eyes and desperately want others to care for them, notice them and protect them (Benjamin, 2003).

Cluster C disorders. As with the disorders in cluster A, cognitive-behavioral and interpersonal theories are usually offered for the avoidant, dependent and obsessive-compulsive personality disorders. Cognitive neuroscience certainly has something to offer us in our attempts to make sense of the antisocial and borderline conditions (Pliszka, 2003), but not regarding the anxious or fearful disorders. With the *avoidant* personality disorder, there is evidence to suggest that persons who were raised in harsh, judgmental home situations tend to assume that others will always treat them the same. A shame-based identity can result, making it far more difficult to experience grace and forgiveness (Smedes, 1993). It is assumed that early trauma or conditioned fears can make a person feel especially vulnerable, and when current stressors overwhelm that person, unresolved fears or hurts can impair interpersonal effectiveness.

When we look at the data on the *dependent* personality disorder, we are persuaded that cognitive, behavioral or interpersonal factors are likewise implicated. For anyone it is hard to assume full adult responsibilities, especially in a culture that tends to prolong the adolescent process of attachment and separation (Benjamin, 2003). Compliance with parental requests will look vastly different in a home that is either permissive or authoritarian rather than authoritative (love with limits). Children and adolescents who are not increasingly given appropriate choices and responsibilities learn to defer to others or even expect others to protect them far beyond what is appropriate. Especially when parents have been overinvolved and overprotective, their almost grown adolescents learn to fear accepting full responsibility and tend to stay *foreclosed* on important life decisions. They may borrow ideas but do not really internalize them. In the more extreme cases, as with dependent personality disorder, this can leave the person feeling helpless, hopeless and powerless. Dependent persons have an all too predictable set of assumptions and beliefs that contribute to an unhealthy passivity and disengagement from the challenges of everyday living.

Of the three disorders in this group, we probably know the least about the *obsessive-compulsive personality* disorder (OCP). As was noted earlier, this is *not* the same as the obsessive-compulsive disorder (OCD), which is dominated by obsessions (thoughts) and compulsions (behaviors) used to control an overwhelming sense of anxiety. OCP involves a rigid, inflexible way of trying to impose order on important life tasks to the point of losing all efficiency, flexibility and openness to change. This impairs the development of warm assertion in interpersonal relationships. Again, there is no evidence for a biological diathesis with OCP, and cognitive, behavioral or interpersonal factors are usually implicated by clinicians (Comer, 2004). Often relationships suffer with a lack of spontaneity and joy; controlling the unpredictable is the modus operandi. Being orderly and restrained does in some sense, at least, make life seem "safe." But control tends to become an all-consuming mindset; any deviation from the script is intolerable. In time, this leads to a host of beliefs about the way life should be and a stiffness and superficiality in relationships, with no tolerance of disequilibrium, dissonance or doubt. Once again, certain beliefs about the nature of life (or even faith) can become self-defeating and even abusive.

TREATMENT CONSIDERATIONS

Neither situational factors alone nor such factors in combination with biological variables can explain this often-bewildering group of disorders. What is clear is that rigid personality traits can wreak tremendous havoc in interpersonal relationships within families, communities and churches. Considering the fact that as many as one out of ten adults in the United States may be afflicted, there is a lot of suffering involved for family members and friends.

Not every challenging or difficult person we interact with has a personality disorder. And whether they do or not, we do well to recognize our own angry, dependent, fearful or intimate impulses in the often tragic choices of persons who may be particularly vulnerable and limited in their options to enjoy kindness, understanding and grace (Yancey, 1997). We must never forget the *human face* of emotional distress—a clinical maxim that is especially important with the problems of personality (Schwartzberg, 2000).

Before addressing treatment of each personality disorder, it is important to stress some *treatment principles*. Obviously, careful assessment is imperative. The behavioral manifestations of the personality disorders are overt, but the inner experiences of afflicted persons are far more hidden and usually have to be inferred. This should lead us to proceed carefully and cautiously and with appropriate humility and respect. It is also important to recognize that some of these individuals can be *very* difficult, unpleasant or manipulative (Miller and Jackson, 1995). The more aware we are of this truth, the more we can set appropriate and realistic expectations. Further, we need to remember that personality disorders by definition are of long duration. Years and even decades of interactional and coping styles are not likely to change in short periods; faithfulness, hope and steadiness will be required. As Cloud and Townsend have noted in their important 2002 work, setting personal and professional boundaries is crucial. Becoming oversocial or overresponsible does neither the helper nor the recipient of help much good in the long run and may even thwart growth toward further health (McLemore, 2003). Not unlike the parent who needs to be authoritative—firm yet fair—with a son or daughter, those who want to help someone with a personality disorder need to set clear guidelines regarding what they will and will not do. Especially with persons who struggle with a cluster B disorder, inappropriate disclosure or offering more than you can possibly deliver can be disastrous. As with all challenging disorders, seeking support from professional colleagues is important, if only to help us when we begin to lose our sense of perspective. Some hurting persons are especially equally draining for the helper, especially if we have strong rescuing tendencies, a need to fix or solve intransigent problems for others. Progress will be slow and painful, making it hard to remain faithful, hopeful and steadfast (Smedes, 1998). When working with personality-disordered persons, we will need to learn much from the client and from our own mistakes (Casement, 2002).

Cluster A disorders. The long-terms goals of working with *paranoid* individuals include the reduction of suspiciousness and distrust, the development of more reality-based beliefs, the development of essential interpersonal skills, and increased flexibility in thinking and problem solving (Bockian and Jongsma, 2001). Therapy tends to proceed very slowly, if it is sought at all. Learning to express anger in healthy and constructive ways (warm assertion) is often central to the helping and healing process. As the trust level increases, there is the possibility of greater intimacy and lessened feelings of rejection and vulnerability (Meyer, 2004). There is no proven medication for the treatment of the disorder (Comer, 2004).

The goals in working with *schizoid* persons include increasing social interaction, improving emotional responsiveness and reactivity, strengthening cognitive and interpretive processes, and raising levels of enthusiasm and energy overall (Bockian and Jongsma, 2001). Again, psychopharmacology hasn't proved to be effective (Adams and Sutker, 2001), so cognitive-behavioral and interpersonal interventions target much-needed social and interactional skills that can be modeled, prompted, shaped and reinforced. Sadly, treatment is rarely sought; for the afflicted person the symptoms are usually ego-syntonic. In time, group work can be helpful if the person feels it is safe, supportive and nonthreatening. Remember, the desire to move away from others can be overwhelming (McLemore, 2003).

The goals for working with *schizotypal* persons include bringing clarity to vague cognitions, reducing odd, idiosyncratic thinking, enhancing the pleasure of social activities and relationships, and improving interpersonal skills (Bockian and Jongsma, 2001). Medication *has* proved to be of some limited value for these persons, especially in reducing certain cognitive aberrations and distortions (Meyer, 2004). If treatment is sought, its focus is almost entirely on providing a safe and supportive environment for teaching essential communication and interaction skills, a task not easily accomplished when there is little perceived need (Benjamin, 2003). As with all disorders in this cluster, helping afflicted persons learn for themselves that relationships can be satisfying and safe is at the heart of effective treatment (McLemore, 2003).

Cluster B disorders. Much has been written about what can be done to help persons who struggle with the dramatic personality disorders (Adams and Sutker, 2001), especially for the borderline and antisocial conditions. As nearly everyone in a leadership or ministry position knows, these disorders are especially toxic and troublesome (Francis and First, 1998).

The goals for working with *antisocial* persons include increasing sensitivity to the needs of others, reducing harmful and impulsive behavior, teaching effective anger management strategies, learning to be more interpersonally aware and responsible, and accepting the rules of law and conduct that apply to all members of our society (Bockian and Jongsma, 2001). Only a portion (25 percent) of those with the diagnosis receive professional treatment for the most troublesome symptoms, and that is usually within the most progressive and well-resourced correctional facilities (Comer, 2004). Calls for prison reform have become increasingly common in the church and society (Smarto, 1993; Van Ness, 1986), but funding has been inconsistent or nonexistent. Fortunately, the number of prison-based ministries has expanded significantly in recent decades, especially with the advocacy and consciousness raising of Chuck Colson and others (cf. Institute for Prison Ministries at Wheaton College or links at <www.wheaton.edu>). Sadly, even intensive treatment programs have had only limited success; prevention makes much more sense. Treatment in settings that control the contingencies of the person's environment and where healthy behaviors can be modeled and reinforced are more successful than traditional outpatient work. Cognitive-behavioral and interpersonal strategies for developing greater empathy and moral sensitivity are assumed to be foundational. Beyond that, it is imperative to address the antecedents and consequences of antisocial behaviors so that the vicious, self-destructive patterns of coping and relating can be addressed (Meyer, 2004). Faith-based approaches that have had some limited success tend to stress mentorship, peer accountability, job training and values—again, the common predictors for coping and adjustment (Pargament, 1997).

The *borderline* personality disorder is probably equally difficult to treat. Treatment goals usually include a reduction of suicidal or self-destructive behaviors, stabilization of personal relationships, decreasing emotional reactivity and lability, development of a strong sense of self, and improvement of problem-solving and communication skills (Bockian and Jongsma, 2001). Treatment may involve psychopharmacology to target some of the most troublesome cognitive and emotional symptoms (Adams and Sutker, 2001; Schwartzberg, 2000). Psychotherapy tends to be intensive and long term and either interpersonal or cognitive-behavioral (Meyer, 2004). Within any approach to treatment, sufficient attention must be given to the therapist-client relationship, since it often becomes a microcosm of all the painful thoughts and feelings that must be worked through in order to learn more effective ways of coping and relating. Suicidal ideation and self-destructive tendencies must be constantly monitored. The work tends to be difficult and demanding, rife with modest success and periodic setbacks (Benjamin, 2003). Perhaps with no other personality disorder is the *corrective emotional experience* assumed to have such central importance.

With *histrionic* individuals the focus of therapy tends to be on the reduction of demands, temper tantrums or seductiveness (also called "grooming the therapist"). These persons need to learn ways to reduce their focus on gaining attention for the wrong reasons while finding more satisfying ways to strengthen their self-awareness and self-image (Bockian and Jongsma, 2001). Learning to form more authentic, reciprocal relationships is at the heart of treatment, as is stabilizing erratic moods and dramatic displays of emotion. Again, this requires great care and careful attention on the part of the therapist, and a sufficient knowledge base (McLemore, 2003).

With *narcissistic* persons the goals of treatment include improving empathy and awareness, reducing arrogant attitudes and beliefs, moderating the tendency to see self as perfect and invulnerable, and decreasing exploitive and manipulative behavior (Bockian and Jongsma, 2001). This degree of grandiosity or false pride is difficult to treat. There is no available medication, even if afflicted persons were willing to seek treatment. The narcissistic interactional style is assumed to be a factor in many domestic disputes and marital failures (Comer, 2004). It is especially difficult for the therapist to avoid being manipulated into supporting the false sense of superiority in a narcissistic client (McLemore, 2003).

Cluster C disorders. For persons who have an *avoidant* personality disorder, treatment is difficult for other reasons. Often they come to therapy looking for affection and attention, unable to find it in everyday interactions. As noted before, trust issues are huge; those who suffer with this disorder avoid others due to fears of criticism, disapproval or rejection (Bockian and Jongsma, 2001). The goals of therapy include reduction of the social isolation and loneliness, development of communication and conflict management skills, encouraging risk-taking and initiative, and decreasing fears and ruminations regarding rejection and humiliation (ibid., p. 46). Cognitive and behavioral strategies for teaching essential life skills are foundational for treatment success (Meyer, 2004). If medication is used at all, it is for specific targeted symptoms of overarousal and excessive anxiety (Adams and Sutker, 2001).

Dependent individuals need to work on such important treatment goals as improving self-confidence, decreasing submissive and obsequious behavior, increasing responsible self-assertion, initiating social interactions, and improving the repertoire of coping and communication skills (Bockian and Jongsma, 2001). Medication may be used to target related symptoms of anxiety or depression. Group work may be an opportunity to observe effective interpersonal skills and strategies (modeling). Central to effective treatment strategies is teaching the importance of responsible self-assertion and reducing passive or clinging behaviors. Especially for women, this may involve finding their own voice and practicing it in safe and supportive settings until it becomes congruent with their deeply internalized values.

Finally, persons who struggle with the *obsessive-compulsive personality* disorder need to reduce their preoccupation with rules, details and minutiae. Treatment goals usually include the reduction of perfectionism, guilt and self-criticism and an improved capacity to "flex" in problem solving and interpersonal relationships (Bockian and Jongsma, 2001). Persons with OCP may have lost the ability to relax and enjoy life, so effective treatment focuses on the importance of self-care and "responsible hedonism"—enjoying God and all of his creation. As with OCD, psychopharmacology may be used to target specific symptoms of overarousal or excessive worry (Adams and Sutker, 2001). Still, treatment needs to focus first and foremost on the teaching of coping and interactional skills. Toward that end, cognitive or dynamic strategies have proved to be essential (Meyer, 2004).

THE CHALLENGE OF PREVENTION

Academicians, clinicians and researchers agree that it is hard to change rigid and inflexible interactional and coping styles. The ultimate antidote to interpersonal toxicity is finding more effective ways to model, prompt, shape and reinforce "warm assertion" in a variety of private and public settings (McLemore, 2003). That means finding better ways to affiliate with others (warmth) and more honestly express one's true needs (assertion). Learning to do this without engulfing or attacking (pathological extremes of assertion) or retreating and submerging (pathological extremes of submission) is the really important developmental challenge.

Primary prevention. Ultimately, primary prevention includes strategies that attempt to reduce the intensity, duration and frequency of problematic behaviors. There is probably very little that can be done to reduce any biological predisposition for a personality disorder. Still, recognizing a predisposition in either genetics or neurochemistry should prompt us to think of ways to reduce internal or external stressors, again applying the diathesis-stress model of mental illness. Recent research suggests that this is especially apropos for the antisocial, borderline and schizotypal personality disorders (Meyer, 2004). In the interim, medication may be the best defense when the cognitive and affective systems become strained to the breaking point (Pliszka, 2003).

On the psychosocial or interpersonal level, the best prevention is teaching more effective ways for people to be intimate with family members and friends (Lerner, 2001). In time, that must include training in conflict management skills (Malony, 1989). These life skills are essential if we want to develop stronger families and communities (Kauffmann, 1999). Obviously, there is an important cognitive component to such instruction, but training must include opportunities to practice these skills in settings that are safe and supportive. Resources now exist that break these skills into their component steps, making such training realistic and practical (Bockian and Jongsma, 2001).

In addition to teaching intimacy and conflict management skills, sufficient energies need to be devoted to encouraging moral development (cluster B), risk-taking and initiative (cluster A) and responsible self-assertion (cluster C). Throughout the lifespan, we need to teach such important virtues as altruism, empathy and respect, if only to counter society's growing obsession with power, prestige and profit (Jones and Butman, 1991). For persons of faith, this would include the development of depth and substance of character, potential antidotes to some of the excesses of cluster B.

Further, a sharper focus on promoting shalom—the "embrace" of justice and mercy—can potentially reduce disengagement (cluster A), self-absorption (cluster B) and overwhelming fear (cluster C). Ultimately, healthy communities will promote stronger families, and vice versa. Access to exemplars of the virtues, or credible role models, can prompt the thoughtful discipleship that is needed in this thoroughly postmodern world. People would be seen as our most precious resource, not first and foremost as means to an end (cluster B) or something to be avoided at all costs (cluster A). Positive mental health begins with a respect for all persons, who are created in the image and likeness of God (Jones and Butman, 1991). We should all become "insatiably curious" about people, persons and processes (Malony, 1989).

Secondary prevention. Here the challenge lies in finding ways to intervene early with high-risk individuals. With reference to cluster A, we should be alarmed when we see a pattern of overall disengagement and passivity emerging in the formative years (Benjamin, 2003). From an early age, children who appear to be loners or friendless merit our special attention. For potential cluster A persons, opportunities for positive peer and parental interaction must be encouraged.

If disengagement and passivity become the preferred coping and interactional style, the prognosis for developing good intimacy and conflict management skills is not positive.

With reference to cluster B, we should be concerned when we see children growing up with unhealthy peer groups or few models of healthy, prosocial behavior. Indeed, negative socialization experiences are one of the most powerful predictors of juvenile delinquency, along with too-limited opportunities for recreational and avocational pursuits (Adams and Sutker, 2001). To counter the growing sense of entitlement and self-absorption in the culture, children and adolescents must be taught the importance of perspective taking—seeing beyond themselves. Ideally, education for responsible action does this well, but too often it gets lost in the busyness of everyday life (Smedes, 1998). Those prone to being histrionic or narcissistic need to have appropriate limits set on them at home or in the community, so that their exhibitionistic tendencies can be titrated (modulated). Learning to set realistic goals and appropriate expectations is a life skill that is essential for assuming full adult responsibilities (Griffin, 1987). Friendship formation that is based on what others do to make you feel good or satisfy your immediate impulses seldom teaches responsible self-control or delay of gratification. Credible role models have much to teach today's youth about sacrifice and servanthood (Kauffmann, 1999).

With reference to cluster C, the focus needs to be on modeling, prompting, shaping and reinforcing affiliation and assertion in anxious and fearful persons (McLemore, 2003). Obviously, there are important changes and losses throughout the lifespan. Teaching our youth to expect these things and find ways to negotiate them effectively can be a worthwhile investment in reducing serious pathology in adulthood. At the most basic level, this requires authoritative parenting and assertive discipline in the primary and middle school years; these elements foster healthy attachment and teach responsible assertion. At a deeper level, it means helping youth to face their difficulties rather than disengage and escape from pressures (Pargament, 1997). When coupled with a sense of meaning and purpose in life and with a strong support system in the home and community, this will help develop a sense of efficacy (i.e., *I believe that what I do makes a difference*). Without such structure, support and supervision, a person's coping and interactional styles are much less likely to be successful (Kauffmann, 1999).

Tertiary prevention. The core challenge here is helping afflicted persons (and often their loved ones) find quality treatment in the community as soon as possible. This requires knowledge of what treatment options are available and which ones are most effective with specific personality disorders. Fortunately, excellent resources are available on treatment options (Adams and Sutker, 2001; Francis and First, 1998; Meyer, 2004) as well as problem-specific treatment planners (Bockian and Jongsma, 2001). McLemore's *Toxic Relationships and How to Change Them: Health and Holiness in Everyday Life* (2003) is especially helpful for faith-based communities that want to work on prevention. Not only does it present a model of wholeness and maturity, but also it offers many practical suggestions on how best to reduce disordered tendencies in ourselves and those we care about or have to interact with on a regular basis. A work by Norcross et al. (2003) describes wonderful self-help resources in mental health (books, films, Internet, support groups) that can help those of us most directly affected.

We need to remember that it is rare for individuals struggling with cluster A or cluster B disorders to seek professional help (Miller and Jackson, 1995). Unless treatment is mandated (as with the antisocial personality disorder) or strongly suggested because of pressing concerns or crises (as with the histrionic or narcissistic personality disorder), the problems tend to remain insidious and chronic. In contrast, cluster C individuals often will seek help for their many fears and anxieties, so knowledge of treatment options and resources can be crucial. Treatment is most likely to be a slow and difficult process, in any case, so helping to build determination and motivation for change can be of the utmost importance (Miller and Jackson, 1995).

We suspect that we will see a rise in the number of persons in our churches and communities who receive these diagnoses in the twenty-first century. This is more than a fad in psychiatric nomenclature; growing numbers of persons are finding it hard to connect interpersonally. As a culture, we seem more disengaged from families and communities and less willing to collaborate in decision-making; competition is far more enticing. We need to be more intentional about the formation of community (social support), much more willing to ask ourselves what things truly matter (meaning and purpose), and far more committed to strengthening our problem-solving and interpersonal skills (sense of efficacy). No doubt, this will help us all cope with the demands of everyday living (Pargament, 1997).

INTEGRATIVE THEMES

Pastoral care and disordered desires. Christians are exhorted to "be angry but sin not" (see Eph 4:26), and this is certainly an issue on which we should reflect in integration. Learning to deal effectively with anger is an ongoing challenge for many persons struggling with a personality disorder, especially for those with a cluster B or cluster C disorder. For those in cluster B, the issue is most often a tendency to try to be one-up (overly competitive) in social situations, even to the point of becoming hostile and abusive (Lerner, 2001). Power, control and status become more important than an authentic connection. Winning is more important than understanding, which makes it almost impossible to think seriously about forgiveness and reconciliation (Worthington, 1993).

We find it fascinating that training in responsible assertiveness is a given in almost all treatment protocols for personality disorders (Bockian and Jongsma, 2001). Let's face it: dealing with strong emotions like anger can be a real challenge, especially when there is not a shared value of working through the differences of opinion that occur in any intimate or important relationship. Peacemaking is a biblical mandate. We simply do not have the option of avoiding all persons who make us feel uncomfortable (Kauffmann, 1999). How we deal with conflict, especially with our "enemies," speaks volumes about the nature of our character and our Christian commitment (Fenton, 1987).

As Van Leeuwen (2002) has noted, a capacity for healthy relatedness and responsible dominion (the creational mandate) degenerates in enmeshment and symbiosis or exploitation and manipulation. Such dynamics are especially manifest in certain cluster B and cluster C disorders. Whether the psychopathology is expressed in passivity or aggressiveness (or both), "getting even" and winning become more important than speaking truthfully and in love (Kauffmann, 1999). Perhaps more than any other group of disorders, personality disorders are painful reminders of what can go wrong when we are unable to be angry without sinning.

Intimate, authentic relationships are really hard work. If managing anger is a major challenge for personality-disordered individuals, so is learning how to make meaningful interpersonal connections (Lerner, 2001). Our faith tells us as much. In part, we were created for intimate communion, to "know as we are known" (Jones and Butman, 1991). Yet it is hard for us to acknowledge what we do not like or respect in ourselves—or fears others will disparage (McLemore, 2003). This is especially true for persons with rigid and inflexible coping styles.

We are called to truthfulness in our relationships, but our pride often gets in the way. For personality-disordered persons, other obstacles to truth may include arrogance, confusion, denial or fear (Benjamin, 2003). Certainly we can all relate to fear of making ourselves vulnerable. As McLemore (2003) has observed, it would be much easier, at least in the moment, to deny the existence of anything distasteful. So the pattern of avoidance and the reinforcement that often entails sets up vicious patterns of withdrawal, passivity, enmeshment or aggression (Malony, 1989). Our lives in community will thrive only to the extent that we face truth about ourselves and others and are willing to commit ourselves to the hard work of forgiveness and reconciliation (Smedes, 1998).

Sin and psychopathology. Others' sins can have effects in our clients' lives. Many personality-disordered individuals did not have healthy role models or mentors in their formative years. This seems especially true of individuals who struggle with cluster B disorders. Sadly, our culture doesn't have a clear vision for the importance of healthy mentors in critical periods throughout the lifespan. In the suburbs of Chicago, for example, it can take up to two years to find a Big Brother or Sister for a needy child or adolescent. In the absence of such a positive force, the gap can be filled with negative peer experiences that can profoundly shape identity formation, choices and moral character.

The research on moral development is abundantly clear that strong social support and opportunities to interact with good role models are powerful predictors of the quality of one's moral reasoning and ethical behavior (Garber, 1996; Paloutzian, 1996). Careful developmental histories of persons struggling with personality disorders suggest that significant others, whether peers or adults, were largely absent or disinterested. Abandonment of any sort, whether real or symbolic, is a major obstacle for holistic development. In the sense that personality disorders can be viewed as developmental disorders, such losses are huge and no doubt a significant factor in etiology and maintenance (Lerner, 2001).

As parents we are daily reminded of the awesome responsibility it is to shape the character, convictions and commitments of the next generation. Good parenting is *really* hard work, especially since we Christians are called to image God's character, God's concerns and God's compassion (Jones and Butman, 1991). We are called to faithfulness and steadiness in this work, but how easy it would be abrogate our parental responsibilities (Garber, 1996; Smedes, 1998). In the words of the contemporary Christian vocal artist Donnie McClurkin (www.donniemcclurkin.com), "We fall down—and we get up—we fall down—and we get up. . . . The difference between a sinner and a saint is that we fall down—and we get up . . ." That "long obedience in the same direction" is at the heart of our faith; it gives us a great measure of realistic—and we believe biblical—hope.

In our work with persons who struggle with the problems of personality, we have noted often profound deficits in "image bearing" (Jones and Butman, 1991) on the part of those who were charged with their care in formative years. This has helped us be more compassionate and understanding. It grieves us to see how often persons who should know better make choices that have profound harmful consequences for their children when they need them the most. Essential life skills were not modeled and shaped in critical periods of development, so it is not surprising if in adulthood their offspring become stuck in cyclical, maladaptive patterns—enmeshment or disengagement, aggression or passivity.

In our discussion of sin and psychopathology we also posited that grace and hope must play a more prominent role in the work of Christians interested in integration. In working with those struggling with personality disorders, we maintain that treatment can make a difference. Even a decade ago, it was not uncommon to hear even Christian mental health professionals disparage anyone with a serious personality disorder—at least behind a closed office door. When reviewing theory and research for this chapter, we were greatly encouraged by advances in understanding of the etiology and development of these disorders and the surprisingly large number of treatment options that are now available (Benjamin, 2003; Bockian, 2001; McLemore, 2003; Meyer, 2004). There is no debate that the work can be hard and demanding and that relapse and recidivism are remarkably common. Indeed, Adams and Sutker (2001) contend that working with personality-disordered persons is not unlike working with seriously addicted persons (cf. chapter three on sin and psychopathology). Even self-defeating interpersonal strategies may "work" in the short run but are clearly destructive and limiting in the long run. Still, it becomes incredibly difficult for the personality-disorder sufferer, as for the addicted person, to see beyond the craving for immediate gratification and release from stress.

Today, for a competent, compassionate Christian mental health professional or layperson to say that there is *no* hope for these individuals would be simply irresponsible. McLemore (2003) explores striking parallels between our coping and interactional styles and those evidenced in some narratives of Scripture. Drawing on the best of social science research and a well-reasoned faith commitment, he helps us to see parts of ourselves in more than a few of these styles and offers practical suggestions for bringing about change. He helps us to see where we ourselves are vulnerable in interpersonal attractions and how best to respond to others when there are deficiencies in intimacy or conflict management skills. So we say with Smedes (1998), "Never give up. . . . Keep hope alive."

Miller and Jackson certainly got it right: "The pronouncement of the diagnosis can ring in the ears like a death sentence, conveying chronicity, hopelessness, disapproval, rejection. These labels do not help people. They may momentarily assuage frustration as they cross the lips, but the attitudes they can convey are not healing" (1995, pp. 356-57).

Dealing with difficult people has always been a special challenge of religion. Yancey (1997) writes movingly about how important it is to show grace to even "unlovable" people. By definition, personality-disordered individuals are "different" and often demanding and difficult to understand. There is *no* debate about the need to set appropriate boundaries and realistic expectations (Cloud and Townsend, 2002). Again, we draw on the keen insights of Miller and Jackson:

> The challenge is to minister in a healing way without being consumed in the process—like the swimmer who caries a struggling, drowning person for some distance without being pulled under along the way. It's easier if you are not alone. It takes time. You will feel worn out at times. The person may fight against you. You need to keep a clear eye on where you are headed. You must hold the person firmly and lovingly but in a way that does not allow you to be pulled down. You will get tired and will need to rest. You will pray. Sometimes the shoreline seems impossibly far away. Sometimes there are waves, sometimes big ones. You will need to call for help. Still the task is to keep the person moving slowly towards the firm ground. (1995, p. 357)

This analogy makes a lot of sense and constitutes wise counsel on what it means to be fully present to a "victim" without drowning in the process. As image bearers of our Creator God, we are not called only to do what makes us feel comfortable but also to do the right thing, even when it costs us dearly. But again, costly discipleship and sustained altruism can be nurtured and developed only within healthy communities that know how to balance affirmation with accountability, and the priestly and prophetic witness of the truly committed (Kauffmann, 1999).

People can change their day-to-day behavior more easily than their underlying (long-term) personality (McLemore, 2003, p. 262). But the key is early detection and intervention; change becomes much harder with age. It is the witness of Scripture and convincing social science research that change *can* occur throughout the lifespan, but deeply ingrained habits often die hard. Motivation is certainly important, as is context—access to the right structures, social supports, supervision and "scaffolding" (Kauffmann, 1999; Pargament, 1997). But choice and responsibility are vital, and the drive eventually has to come from within; it must be voluntary.

The research on the change process is striking to us (Casement, 2002). Interpersonal and contextual variables are far more important than technique, and hope is absolutely essential (Smedes, 1998). McLemore adds:

> A person is more likely to change if he or she has made a public commitment to do so; church services are wonderful opportunities for this. But again, if the commitment is not voluntary, it won't do any good and may even do harm. Major emotional events are typically what cause people to make major changes. These are life experiences that often rock people to their foundation and therefore have lasting impact. There is no greater event than repentance and conversion. So before you try anything else, make sure that you are consistently praying for that person. (2003, p. 263)

"Our God can heal and redeem us from anything. No human actions are beyond the reach of His redeeming intent and capability" (Jones and Jones, 1993, p. 251). We all make mistakes and poor choices—and we must take the Christian disciplines of confession, repentance, forgiveness and reconciliation *very* seriously. Some of the most effective work with the antisocial personality disorder is done in the context of faith-based ministries that take these spiritual resources to heart (Smarto, p. 1993).

A Concluding Thought

In closing, we offer a prayer from *The Covenant Hymnal* of the Evangelical Covenant Church of America (1973):

> We confess to you, Lord, what we are: we are not the people we like others to think we are; we are afraid to admit even to ourselves what lies in the depths of our souls. But we do not want to hide our true selves from you. We believe that you know us as we are, and yet you love us. Help us not to shrink from self-knowledge; teach us to respect ourselves for your sake; give us courage to put our trust in your guiding and power.
>
> We also confess to you, Lord, the unrest of the world, to which we contribute and in which we share. Forgive us that so many of us are indifferent to the need of [others]. Forgive our reliance on weapons of terror, our discrimination against people of different races, and our total preoccupation with material standards, And forgive us Christians for being so unsure of our good news, and so unready to tell it.
>
> Raise us out of the paralysis of guilt into the freedom and energy of forgiven people. And for those who through long habit find forgiveness hard to accept, we ask you to break their bondage and set them free. Through Jesus Christ our Lord. Amen.

Recommended Reading

Benjamin, L. (2003). *Interpersonal diagnosis and treatment of personality disorders* (2nd ed.). New York: Guilford. The best professional treatment on personality disorders offered from a contemporary dynamic perspective.

Bockian, N., and Jongsma, A. (2001). *The personality disorder treatment planner.* New York: Wiley. An enormously helpful resource for laypersons and professionals who want to know how to set realistic treatment goals and expectations.

Cloud, H., and Townsend, J. (2002). *Boundaries* (Rev. ed.). Grand Rapids, MI: Zondervan. An updated edition of one of the bestselling books in Christian publishing in the 1990s.

Lerner, H. (2001). *The dance of connection.* New York: HarperCollins. This is a very user-friendly resource for those wanting to strengthen their ability to interact with difficult persons in stressful situations.

Malony, N. (1989). *When getting along seems impossible.* Old Tappan, NJ:

Fleming H. Revell. This is a helpful book from a highly respected clinical psychologist and ordained United Methodist minister.

McLemore, C. (2003). *Toxic relationships and how to change them: Health and holiness in everyday life.* San Francisco: Jossey-Bass. We think this is the single most important book on the subject for lay or professional readers.

Meyer, R. (2004). *The clinician's handbook* (4th ed.). Long Grove, IL: Waveland. One of the most widely used textbooks on psychopathology in graduate and professional training programs.

REFERENCES

Adams, H., and Sutker, P. (Eds.). (2001). *Comprehensive handbook of psychopathology* (3rd ed.). New York: Kluwer Academic/Plenum.

Benjamin, L. (2003). *Interpersonal diagnosis and treatment of personality disorders* (2nd ed.). New York: Guilford.

Bockian, N., and Jongsma, A. (2001). *The personality disorder treatment planner.* New York: Wiley.

Casement, P. (2002). *Learning from our mistakes.* New York: Guilford.

Cloud, H., and Townsend, J. (2002). *Boundaries* (Rev. ed.). Grand Rapids, MI: Zondervan.

Comer, R. (2004). *Abnormal psychology* (5th ed.). New York: Worth.

Covenant Hymnal, The. (1973). Chicago: Covenant Press.

Dupree, M. (1997). *Leading without power: Finding hope in serving community.* San Francisco: Jossey-Bass.

Fenton, H. (1987). *When Christians clash: How to prevent and resolve the pain of conflict.* Downers Grove, IL: InterVarsity Press.

Francis, A., and First, M. (1998). *Your mental health.* New York: Scribner.

Garber, S. (1996). *The fabric of faithfulness.* Downers Grove, IL: InterVarsity Press.

Gregory the Great. (1978). *Pastoral care* (H. Davis, Trans.). In J. Quasten and J. Plumpe (Eds.), *Ancient Christian Writers* (Vol. 11). New York: Newman. (Original work published 591.)

Griffin, E. (1987). *Making friends and making them count.* Downers Grove, IL: InterVarsity Press.

Jones, S., and Butman, R. (1991). *Modern psychotherapies: A comprehensive Christian appraisal.* Downers Grove, IL: InterVarsity Press.

Jones, S., and Jones, B. (1993). *How and when to tell you kids about sex.* Colorado Springs: NavPress.

Kauffmann, D. (1999). *My faith's OK: Reflections on psychology and reli-

gion. Goshen, IN: Goshen College Bookstore.

Lerner, H. (2001). *The dance of connection*. New York: HarperCollins.

Malony, N. (1989). *When getting along seems impossible*. Old Tappan, NJ: Fleming H. Revell.

McLemore, C. (2003). *Toxic relationships and how to change them: Health and holiness in everyday life*. San Francisco: Jossey-Bass.

Meyer, R. (2004). *The clinician's handbook* (4th ed.). Long Grove, IL: Waveland.

Miller, W., and Jackson, K. (1995). *Practical psychology for pastors* (2nd ed.). Englewood Cliffs, NJ: Prentice-Hall.

Norcross, J., Santrock, J., Campbell, L., Smith, T., Sommer, R., and Zuckerman, E. (2003). *Authoritative guide to self-help resources in mental health*. New York: Guilford.

Pargament, K. (1997). *The psychology of religion for coping*. New York: Guilford.

Paloutzian, R. (1996). *Invitation to the psychology of religion*. Boston: Allyn and Bacon.

Pliszka, S. (2003). *Neuroscience for the mental health clinician*. New York: Guilford.

Schwartzberg, S. (2000). *Casebook of psychological disorders: The human face of emotional distress*. Boston: Allyn and Bacon.

Smarto, D. (Ed.). (1993). *Setting the captives free!* Grand Rapids, MI: Baker.

Smedes, L. (1993). *Shame and grace: Healing the shame we don't deserve*. New York: HarperCollins/Zondervan.

Smedes, L. (1998). *Standing on the promises: Keeping hope alive for a tomorrow we cannot control*. Nashville: Thomas Nelson.

Van Leeuwen, M. (2002). *My brother's keeper: What the social sciences do (and don't) tell us about masculinity*. Downers Grove, IL: InterVarsity Press.

Van Ness, D. (1986). *Crime and its victims: What we can do*. Downers Grove, IL: InterVarsity Press.

Worthington, E. (1993). *Hope for troubled marriages*. Downers Grove, IL: InterVarsity Press.

Yancey, P. (1997). *What's so amazing about grace?* New York: HarperCollins/Zondervan.

11

PROBLEMS OF
SEXUALITY

*A*Christian perspective on the problems of sexuality begins with
a Christian view of human sexuality.[1] Although Scripture does not
neatly lay out an explicit theology of sexuality, it does give us a reasonably explicit set of ethical guidelines that can inform Christian
moral reasoning and sexual ethics. These guidelines can be organized around the four acts of the biblical drama: creation, Fall, redemption and glorification.

In creation God establishes marriage between one man and one
woman, identifying them as now being "one flesh." An affirmation of
the goodness of creation and a positive view of human sexuality are
seen elsewhere in the Old and New Testaments (e.g., Song 4:1-15; Eph
5:21-33). In contrast to messages from contemporary culture, in the biblical view sexuality is not the most important dimension of personhood.
However, Christians affirm that sexuality is a vital and irreducible aspect of personhood. To be human is to be intrinsically sexual, but this

---

[1]This section draws on material from Stanton L. Jones and Brenna B. Jones (1993), *How
and When to Tell Your Kids About Sex*, and Stanton L. Jones and Mark A. Yarhouse (2002),
"Anthropology, Sexuality and Sexual Ethics: The Ecclesiastical Challenge."

should not lead us to reductionism about the meaning of our humanity.

Christians recognize that although we bear God's image, we are fallen, and the Fall affects every aspect of our humanness, including our sexuality. This is evident in varying ways and to varying degrees. Not everyone struggles with sexuality or with a particular sexual desire. But sexuality is often an area in which people struggle as an expression of their fallen condition. Though we retain a capacity for relationships, love and delight in one another, our sexuality is distorted by selfishness and sensuality. We are capable of relating to others in a fundamentally disconnected way by separating physical desires from the transcendent purposes to which they are connected. In our fallen state we may see others as objects for our short-term gratification. This is an example of our tendency to struggle with lust, as we will discuss below.

Rather than leave us in our fallen condition, God steps into this fallen world through the incarnate Jesus and offers us redemption and glorification. It is only through this relationship that God is able to redeem us, to sanctify us, setting us apart for his purposes and his glory.

One key thread running through these four acts of the biblical drama is the value God places on physical existence as part of his creation. Physical existence is affirmed in creation and again through the incarnation, as God enters the world with a physical body. Scripture also affirms that we will have physical bodies in eternity. So through creation, the incarnation and the anticipation of glorification we see again and again the value God places on our physical bodies, our inherent physicality. This physicality, of course, includes our sexuality. As we have suggested, to be human is to be inherently physical, inherently sexual. Our sexuality, like every other aspect of our personhood, is affected by the Fall but is in the process of being redeemed.

THEMES IN PASTORAL CARE

The topic of lust is perhaps the most readily accessible point of contact between contemporary categorization of problems of sexuality and historic pastoral care. Historically, Christian leaders have focused on lust and related disordered desires in the pastoral care of believers. Lust is defined as "inordinate passion or unintegrated desire for pleasure, often sexual pleasure" (Olthuis, 1995, p. 558). Lust has been viewed as one of the seven deadly sins, to be countered with emphasis on temperance and chastity.

From a pastoral care perspective, problems of sexuality may stem from a person's seeking momentary gratification, even if it means exploiting others by relating to them as objects for their own sexual satisfaction. This depersonalizing is particularly devastating: "The perpetrator loses his or her sense of self to some unbridled fixation. Instead of integrating one's energies (including sexual) in a personal reaching out for mutuality and connection, one becomes a victim of one's own energies and is driven in any way to have needs met" (Olthuis, 1995, p. 559). Lust is contrasted with chastity and temperance in being "fundamentally a stance of hostility, alien to intimacy and an isolating, asocial attitude" (ibid; see Schimmel, 1997). Lust is so self-focused, then, that it is essentially hostile to intimacy and interpersonal connections characterized by love and mutuality.

From a Christian pastoral care perspective, lust should be distinguished from healthy sexual desire and attractions. Lust may not be an issue in sexual attraction, unless the attraction is disordered and leads to depersonalization and objectification of another for one's own gratification.[2]

CONTEMPORARY CATEGORIZATION

The *DSM-IV* organizes problems of sexuality into three major categories: sexual dysfunctions, paraphilias and gender identity disorders. Additional sexual issues are grouped as "sexual disorders not otherwise specified"; these include inadequate feelings about sexual performance, driven sexual behavior and distress regarding one's sexual orientation.

Sexual dysfunctions. Contemporary models of psychopathology generally conceptualize the sexual dysfunctions as problems at some stage in the sexual response cycle. The sexual response cycle is thought of as beginning with desire and proceeding through the stages of excitement, plateau, orgasm and resolution. The most common sexual dysfunctions, then, are sexual desire disorders, sexual

---

[2]*Saint Augustine's Prayer Book* (West Park, N.Y.: Holy Cross Publications, 1996) identifies several indicators that a person may struggle with lust:
- unchastity, which may be expressed in "sexual indulgence outside of matrimony, in thought or act, alone or with others"
- immodesty, or "stimulation of sexual desire in others by word, dress or actions . . . or in oneself by reading, pictures, or fantasies"
- prudery, or "fear of sex or condemnation of it as an evil in itself . . . repression of sex"
- cruelty, the "deliberate infliction of pain, mental or physical" (p. 120)

arousal disorders, orgasmic disorders and sexual pain disorders. The sexual dysfunctions can be lifelong (have always been a concern) or acquired (have become a concern after a specific event), generalized (in all circumstances or relationships) or situational (in specific circumstances or relationships). Mental health professionals also distinguish between dysfunctions that are due to psychological factors alone and dysfunctions that are due to both psychological and medical factors.

Sexual desire disorders include hypoactive desire disorder and sexual aversion disorder. Hypoactive desire disorder is a condition in which the person has no interest in sexual activity. This is a problem more common among women, as it affects about 33 percent of women compared to 16 percent of men.[3] In sexual aversion disorder, sexual stimuli evoke strong negative reactions, such as disgust, fear or panic.

In sexual arousal disorders the person has a desire for sexual activity but is unable to experience sufficient arousal. Male erectile disorder involves difficulty achieving or maintaining an erection; as many as 50 percent of males report some difficulty with erections at some time, and about 10 percent report complete erectile disorder. Female sexual arousal disorder refers to difficulty achieving or maintaining adequate lubrication; about 20 percent of women report lubrication difficulties, and this rises to about 40 percent of women following menopause.

Orgasmic disorders include inhibited orgasm (or anorgasmia) and premature ejaculation. Inhibited orgasm is much more common in women than men, and it is diagnosed when a person has sexual desire and arousal but is unable to achieve orgasm (about 25 percent of women report having difficulty reaching orgasm). About 30 percent of men report difficulty with premature ejaculation—ejaculation that occurs too soon in the sexual response cycle.

Sexual pain disorders are reported more often by women than men. These disorders include dyspareunia, or painful intercourse. Dyspareunia is reported by about 10 to 15 percent of women. Vaginismus, which is reported by about 15 percent of women in clinical samples, is characterized by an involuntary clamping down of the muscles surrounding the outer third of the vagina in response to penile, finger or object penetration.

---

[3]The largest sexuality study conducted to date was by Edward Laumann and his colleagues (1994) and is referred to as the National Health Social Life Survey. Most prevalence estimates in this section are drawn from this work.

Paraphilias. The paraphilias are conceptualized in contemporary models of psychopathology as sexual stimulation that requires unusual objects, imagery/fantasy or specific acts. They are unusual in being deviations from the norm in our society. The paraphilias include fetishism, pedophilia, sexual masochism or sadism, transvestic fetishism, voyeurism, frotteurism and exhibitionism.

Fetishism refers to sexual attraction to objects. Typically these are inanimate objects (e.g., panties) or parts of the body (e.g., feet). *Exhibitionism* refers to the practice of exposing one's genitals to strangers. *Voyeurism* refers to watching strangers who are undressing or are naked.

Persons diagnosed with *transvestic fetishism* are commonly referred to as "cross-dressers" if they experience sexual arousal from dressing in the clothes of the opposite sex. *Sexual sadism* refers to sexual arousal by inflicting pain or humiliation on another, while *sexual masochism* refers to sexual arousal from suffering pain or humiliation. *Pedophilia* refers to sexual attraction to children. Other less common paraphilias include *frotteurism* (arousal by rubbing up against another), *necrophilia* (arousal from corpses) and *scatologia* (arousal from obscene phone calls).

Gender identity disorders. People who are diagnosed with a gender identity disorder may be referred to as *transsexual* or *transgendered* persons. They often report feeling trapped in the body of the other sex (e.g., the biological female who believes she is a man trapped in a woman's body). The *DSM-IV* describes these disorders as involving "strong and persistent cross-gender identification accompanied by persistent discomfort with one's assigned sex" (APA, 1994, p. 493). The most common presentations are the

- female-to-male gender dysphoric: females who typically report a history of masculine appearance and behavior since childhood and often develop an attraction to males

- male-to-female gender dysphoric, androphilic type: males who report being effeminate in childhood and who develop an attraction to males

- male-to-female gender dysphoric, autogynephilic type: normal history, attraction to females, and an interest in dressing in women's clothing and imagining themselves as a female

The autogynephilic type is the most common among men seeking treatment.

Gender identity disorder is a rare clinical condition, with the best prevalence estimates suggesting that about one in eleven thousand men and one in thirty thousand women seek treatment for gender dysphoria. It is believed, however, that many more people experience some gender identity concerns but do not seek treatment (Carroll, 2000). The childhood manifestation of gender identity disorder, while rare, appears to be more common than what is found in adulthood. Transsexuals have no physical abnormalities, and their experience of gender identity confusion is independent of their experience of sexual attraction. That is, a person can be diagnosed with gender identity disorder and report either heterosexual or homosexual attractions. Some experts believe that many children diagnosed with gender identity disorder grow out of it, though there has been little systematic study of this. Prevention and early intervention are offered and will be discussed further below.

Other problems of sexuality. The *DSM-IV* also recognizes that a number of other problems of sexuality or sexual functioning may lead a person to seek mental health services. Specific examples of presenting problems that are mentioned in the *DSM-IV* include feelings of inadequacy about one's sexual performance, distress about serial relationships and concern that one is "using" others, and distress about one's sexual orientation. We discuss two of these concerns throughout this chapter. The first problem is essentially a paraphilia-related disorder commonly referred to as *sexual addiction* or *sexual compulsion.*[4] This behavior can be evidenced in compulsive masturbation, sexual promiscuity, pornography dependence, telephone sex dependence and cybersex (Kafka, 2000). The other is homosexuality, a clinical problem that is no longer officially included as a mental illness but that still leads many people to seek professional help.

ANTECEDENTS TO PROBLEMS OF SEXUALITY

It should come as no surprise that there is no one antecedent to sexual problems, given the range of problems addressed in this chapter. We consider a number of these factors, paying special attention to biological and psychosocial factors and how they might play a role in sexual dysfunctions, the paraphilias, gender identity concerns and other sexual problems.

---

[4]There is debate in the field as to whether the proper term is sexual *addiction* or sexual *compulsion.* Neither term is recognized as a mental disorder in *DSM-IV;* however, most professionals recognize a condition characterized by driven sexual behavior. See Goodman (2001) for a discussion of the name and some of the arguments for and against referring to the condition as an "addiction."

Sexual dysfunctions. Some of the earliest conceptualizations of sexual dysfunctions supposed deep-seated conflicts in the person's psyche. Long-term psychotherapy to resolve intrapsychic conflicts was the norm. However, following Masters and Johnson and other pioneers of sexology, clinicians began to conceptualize many dysfunctions as related to anxiety and favored approaches that would lead to symptom reduction. Current conceptualizations are rather eclectic and often draw on depth psychology, second-generation cognitive underpinnings and a concern for shorter-term interventions.

Biological. Biological factors appear to play a greater role in some sexual dysfunctions than in others. Assessment of sexual dysfunctions typically involves a referral for a thorough medical evaluation from a gynecologist or urologist. Medical evaluations help to rule out vascular and hormonal factors that may be related to disease or illness, such as diabetes mellitus, as well as normal changes in aging (see chapter thirteen), the impact of common medications, and/or the impact of alcohol and drug use. For example, sexual pain disorders such as dyspareunia may be related to biological factors, like insufficient vaginal lubrication following a reduction in hormones associated with menopause. Likewise, erectile dysfunction can be caused by vascular and hormonal factors.

Psychosocial. Key psychosocial factors appear to be past sexual trauma and other negative events that become associated with sexual activity in some way. When clinicians consider the role of anxiety in sexual dysfunctions, they are actually considering a variety of factors, including cognitive processes such as self-defeating thoughts or irrational cognitions and negative effects such as guilt or shame. Many therapists believe, for example, that some struggles with premature ejaculation are due to association with past hurried experiences of intercourse. A man who as a teen experienced sexual intercourse in encounters in which he was trying not to get caught might have difficulty letting go of those associations.

It has often been thought that religion is a negative predisposing influence that leads many people to struggle with sexual problems. The research to support this view is equivocal. Although clinical accounts often speak of a religious upbringing and negative or restrictive attitudes toward sex, research suggests that religion is often associated with sexual satisfaction among married couples (Hart, 1994; Hart, Weber and Taylor, 1998).

Paraphilias.

Biology. Biology has not been viewed as a direct causal factor in the development of atypical sexual behaviors. However, many experts do view biology as a predisposing factor in the later development of atypical sexual behavior. In other words, although there is no known biological marker for the paraphilias, there may be indirect pathways via temperamental and personality differences related to sexual risk-taking behavior, a variation on a tendency among some people to be low on inhibition in general (Wincze, 2000). People low on inhibition are at greater risk for engaging in behaviors that are contrary to social standards, such as the behaviors associated with the paraphilias.

Psychosocial. Most experts believe that several psychosocial factors may contribute to atypical sexual behaviors. These include poor social skills, an inability to form meaningful relationships, and early "atypical" sexual fantasies and experiences, including sexual abuse. For example, according to Wincze (2000), a child may be exposed directly or indirectly to sexual stimulation. The child may then experiment with the behavior and may receive either positive or negative consequences for doing so. Based on these experiences, the child may then repeat, vary and shape the behavior into any of a variety of expressions that may lead to stronger reinforcement.

Gender identity disorders.

Biology. Research to date has found no differences between people with gender identity disorder and the normal population in hormonal levels or genetic inheritance (Carroll, 2000). Researchers have considered whether prenatal hormonal exposure has an influence on gender identity disorders, but no significant findings have as yet been reported.

Psychosocial. Psychoanalytic and contemporary object relations approaches theorize that gender identity disorder is a psychotic disorder reflecting intrapsychic conflict (psychoanalytic) or that it reflects the development of an "all-good image" of the opposite sex, "which becomes merged with [his or her] self image and becomes split off" (object relations; Carroll, 2000, p. 378). Behavioral theorists believe that learning history leads to the development of gender identity disorder. Essentially, it is believed that cross-gender behavior in dress and play was reinforced and gender-stereotypic behavior was not.

Other problems of sexuality.

Paraphilia-related disorders. Although there are no particularly compelling studies suggesting a link to biology, there are studies suggesting that temperament or personality may place a particular person at risk for symptoms of sexual addiction. Psychosocial models typically point to prior physical or sexual abuse, early exposure to inappropriate sexual stimuli (e.g., pornography), early sexual debut and overly restrictive attitudes toward sexual expression and intimacy (Kafka, 2000).

Homosexuality. Although biology has been implicated in the etiology of homosexuality, the existing research on genetic factors, such as twin studies and studies of chromosomal markers (e.g., Bailey and Pillard, 1991; 1993; Hamer et al., 1993; Hu et al., 1995), is suggestive but hardly conclusive. The most recent research has not found nearly as great a genetic contribution (e.g., Bailey, Dunne and Martin, 2000; Rice et al., 1999).

Similar concerns are raised by the research on possible prenatal hormonal influences. Although some studies have been heralded as evidence in support of the prenatal hormonal hypothesis (e.g., Allen and Gorski, 1992; LeVay, 1991; Swaab and Hofman, 1990), these studies often conflict with other studies (cf. Demeter, Ringo and Doty, 1988), are unreplicated or suffer from significant methodological flaws (for a detailed review of this literature, see Jones and Yarhouse, 2000).

Some theorists believe that same-sex attraction is the result of various psychological and environmental factors. Proponents of this view typically implicate early child development, problems in parent-child relationships, childhood sexual abuse and early same-sex sexual debut. Research cited in support of the psychological or environmental hypothesis includes memory recall studies in which adults report having had engaged in cross-sex-typed behaviors (e.g., cross-dressing, toys, activities, role models) at higher rates than adults who do not identify as homosexual (Bailey and Zucker, 1995). Other studies suggest problems in parent-child relationships (e.g., Bieber et al., 1962; Evans, 1969; van den Aardweg, 1984) and childhood sexual trauma (Doll et al., 1992; Laumann et al., 1994).

There are a number of methodological limitations to the existing studies, and there seems to be a growing consensus that no one factor determines a person's sexual orientation. Rather, both nature and nurture may play a part to varying degrees in influencing whether a particular person will experience same-sex attraction.

TREATMENT

Sexual dysfunctions. Treatment for sexual dysfunctions originally followed the psychoanalytic theory that symptoms represent an underlying intrapsychic conflict. With the rise of behavioral theory, sex therapy went through a major paradigm shift that involved applying social learning theory to concrete sex therapy interventions. Perhaps no team was more influential during this period of time than William Masters and Virginia Johnson, who pioneered clinical research on professional interventions to treat the sexual dysfunctions.

Many of the interventions developed under Masters and Johnson are still widely used today (see Heiman and Meston, 1997; Segraves and Althof, 2002), though often in conjunction with pharmacotherapy. Typically sessions begin with assessment and psychoeducation and then lead to behavioral exercises. Psychoeducation may include information on sexual functioning, sexual anatomy, physiology, normal aging changes that influence sexual functioning, and individual differences in desire and responsiveness. Common structured behavior exercises include sofa sessions for couples to discuss relevant topics, such as their sexual script or foreplay; sensate focus (a form of nondemand sensual massage); relaxation exercises; and various body-awareness exercises, including genital examinations and directed masturbation.

Skills training is also an important dimension of sex therapy. Therapists will help clients learn things that range from social and communication skills to specific techniques for pleasuring one's partner, such as direct stimulation of the clitoris or variations in positioning during intercourse. This is accomplished through homework assignments the couple engages in throughout the week.

With respect to specific interventions and specific sexual dysfunctions, empirically supported treatments for sexual dysfunctions include directed masturbation alone and in conjunction with sensate focus for primary anorgasmia (Heiman and Meston, 1997). There is good research support for the use of vaginal dilators in conjunction with relaxation exercises and Kegel exercises in the treatment of vaginismus. For common sexual dysfunctions in males, there is research support for the use of systematic desensitization in the treatment of erectile disorder and the squeeze technique in the treatment of premature ejaculation.

Medical interventions are also promising and have been the focus of attention in the past several years. For example, treatment of erectile dysfunction includes pharmacological treatment, such as the introduction of vasodilating drugs (e.g., sildenafil [Viagra]), to increase blood flow in the smooth muscles of the penis. Pharmacological treatment is widely preferred to other medical interventions for erectile dysfunction, such as surgical implants and the use of vacuum constriction devices.

Paraphilias. The major approaches to intervening with those presenting with a paraphilic disorder are (1) individual behavioral interventions, (2) group therapy and (3) pharmacological interventions. Behavioral therapy tends to focus on reducing deviant arousal and increasing normal patterns of arousal. Early on in treatment, emphasis is typically placed on suppressing deviant sexual behavior, using either pharmacological or behavioral approaches or both (Wincze, 2000). Behavioral interventions include environment purging, orgasmic reconditioning, alternative behavioral completion, aversion therapy and relapse prevention. Environmental purging involves removal of sexual stimuli such as magazines and videos. Orgasmic reconditioning (or masturbatory retraining) involves changing deviant fantasies to appropriate sexual fantasies at the time when orgasm is imminent. Alternative behavioral completion involves imaginal desensitization: establishing a hierarchy of anxiety-producing sexual experiences and then desensitizing the client to these scenarios as played out in his imagination. This approach is coupled with imagery exercises of engaging in appropriate behavioral alternatives in the fantasy script (Maletzky, 2002; McConaghy, 1993). Aversion therapy has taken many forms and is somewhat controversial today. Based on classical conditioning models, aversion therapy may involve electric shock or covert sensitization (visualized deviant behavior followed by visualized aversive consequences for engaging in the behavior). Relapse prevention is a hallmark of behavioral interventions for the paraphilias; it involves identifying and avoiding high-risk situations, as well as preparing specific coping behaviors to head off tendencies to rationalize behaviors that place one at further risk of reoffending.

Group therapy is common for sex offenders. It is believed that the group format allows patients to have accountability and to learn and practice some social skills. Group therapy is typically offered alongside individual behavior therapy and pharmacological interventions, as indicated.

Pharmacological interventions usually involve chemical control (often referred to as "chemical castration"). This refers to temporarily suppressing testosterone and reducing sex drive by introducing anti-androgens, such as cyproterone acetate, into the system.

Gender identity disorders. There are four typical outcomes for adult gender identity disorder: (1) unresolved outcome, (2) accept biological sex and gender role, (3) engage in cross-gender behavior intermittently or (4) adopt cross-gender role through gender reassignment (Carroll, 2000). It is very common for a person with gender identity disorder to drop out of treatment. This has been attributed to the ambivalence she or he must feel in the face of such a distressing condition and given the alternatives for intervention. It is unclear what happens to most of the people who drop out of treatment.

People may accept their biological sex and come to terms with their gender role. It is unclear how often psychological intervention is successful in resolving gender identity disorder, but it appears that it is rare, though perhaps more likely among those who report autogynephilic transsexuality.

Many people resolve to engage in cross-dressing behavior on a part-time basis. According to Carroll (2000), the typical part-time or episodic cross-dresser is male, heterosexual and married. Although the cross-dressing behavior is often associated in his mind with sexual arousal, the person does not tend to have any other signs of psychopathology.

Adopting the full cross-gender role is a fourth possible outcome. Gender reassignment follows the Harry Benjamin International Gender Dysphoria Standards of Care (HBIGDA, 1998), which sets up specific guidelines for pursuing the full cross-gender role, including a psychological evaluation by a specialist, three months of therapy or three months of real-life experience in the other gender role, evaluation for appropriate hormones, one year living full time in cross-gender role, a second evaluation, and then gender reassignment surgery and follow-up care as needed.

About 8 percent of patients say they regret the surgery. Predictors of poor outcome include failure to make a differential diagnosis (e.g., there may be a comorbid major depressive disorder), failure to live through the trial period in a full-time cross-gender role, and "poor surgical results" from the actual sex reassignment procedure (Carroll, 2000, p. 386). Those who seem to be better candidates are patients seeking female-to-male sex reassignment and males who are androphilic transsexuals (male transsexuals who are attracted to males).

Other sexual problems. Treatment of paraphilia-related disorders, such as driven sexual behavior, are typically eclectic and focus on helping clients gain control over the symptoms of their sexual struggles. Interventions are often psychoeducational and practical, so that environment management helps reduce exposure to certain sexual stimuli. For example, clients typically discard pornography, use an Internet filter and work closely with an accountability partner or group to help them work toward stated goals. Therapy itself often focuses on managing thoughts and feelings associated with acting-out behavior, as well as social skills training, assertiveness training, and the learning and rehearsal of new coping skills to manage stressful events.

Some of the earliest treatment approaches for homosexuality involved behavioral interventions (e.g., Freeman and Meyer, 1975; Schwartz and Masters, 1984), aversion treatments (e.g., MacCulloch and Feldman, 1967; McConaghy, 1970) and psychoanalysis (e.g., Hatterer, 1970). Group therapy has also been found to be successful (e.g., Birk, 1974; Munzer, 1965; Pittman and DeYoung, 1971; Truax and Tourney, 1971). The major methodological concern with these studies was that the measures of success varied considerably from study to study (Haldeman, 1994). Some studies focused more on increasing heterosexual behavior, fantasy or desire, while others focused on decreasing homosexual behavior, fantasy or desire. But nearly every study ever conducted reported that some people experienced successful change of some kind.

More recent surveys of people who say they experience change of orientation (e.g., Schaeffer et al., 1999; Schaeffer et al., 2000) or who have worked with patients or clients who they believe changed their sexual orientation (e.g., MacIntosh, 1994) also support the view that some people can experience a change in their sexual orientation.

Emerging trends. Emerging trends in intervention are moving in two different but complementary directions. One direction is toward greater appreciation of sexual physiology. This can be seen in perspectives on premature ejaculation, for example. Some have argued that the man may be reaching orgasm at a low stimulation threshold due to differences in the nervous system (either hypersensitive or decreased sensitivity), such that the man cannot distinguish ejaculation and "inevitability." Critics question whether the differences are the cause or the physiological indicator (measure) of what is happening.

The other direction is toward a greater appreciation of systems theory. Systems theory brings several considerations to the table. For example, sexual dysfunctions may sometimes be symptomatic of a larger power struggle: partner conflicts may reflect ways one partner punishes the other for not meeting their needs.

Notably, evolutionary psychology has captured the imagination of many in the field of sexology. This has not led to particularly innovative treatment or prevention strategies, but it has produced fascinating explanatory models. For example, evolutionary psychologists claim that rapid ejaculation may originally have been protective, since a male could be vulnerable to attack during intercourse. In light of this notion, it is interesting that historically not much attention was paid to the duration of intercourse until recently (the 1960s and 1970s). More emphasis has historically been placed on reproduction than on sexual pleasure.

Evolutionary psychology's account includes theories of gender typing, the process of acquiring behavior that is deemed by culture to be appropriate to one's gender. For example, evolutionary psychologists might see men's traditional roles as hunters and warriors and women's roles as caregivers and gatherers as the result of our genes. Men have physical attributes that make them better suited to fight and hunt (upper-body strength and better visual-motor skills to aid in throwing spears, for example). Women are more predisposed to be empathic and nurturing, having historically responded to children's needs; this allows children to develop and eventually reproduce, which passes on one's genetic material.

Some evolutionary psychologists believe that the core human drive is survival. But the goal of survival does not focus on oneself as a person or on the survival of humanity; rather, emphasis is on survival of one's genes. In this view, structures that have developed over time help to promote the transfer of genetic material. For example, marriage increases the likelihood of stability and thus promotes the likelihood of passing on genes. Similarly, monogamy, at least for women, is the best structure for survival. We will discuss below a Christian response to evolutionary psychology, but for now we want to draw attention to it as an influential emerging trend in the study of human sexuality and sexual behavior.

PREVENTION

Sexual dysfunctions. Prevention of sexual dysfunctions typically focuses on sex education. Sex education that has as its goal the prevention of sexual problems is essentially lifespan education beginning in childhood. Parents play a critical role, modeling for their children a healthy view of sexuality. This includes identifying teachable moments for the discussion of sexual anatomy, behavior and values for sexual expression. Teachable moments include predictable occasions such as potty training and bath time, as well as unanticipated encounters, such as when a parent comes across their young child masturbating.

Puberty leads to increased sexual interest. Because teens receive most of their sex education from their peers, it is important for parents to play a more active role in discussing sex education and sexual health. If sex education and character formation have begun in childhood, later discussions are natural extensions of what has gone before.

Most secular sex education programs focus on transmitting facts about sex. This makes intuitive sense; a typical sex education curriculum covers male and female anatomy, the endocrine system, the impact of hormones on sexuality, sexually transmitted diseases, birth control and so on. This approach fails, however, to place sex education in the context of character formation; it fails to relate knowledge of facts to who someone is as a person.

In our view, preventive sex education cannot occur effectively outside of character formation. According to Jones and Jones (1993), this includes identifying and meeting a child's needs, teaching values, recognizing core beliefs, providing parental and peer support, and training in specific skills.

The two most significant *needs* children have are for relatedness and significance. Many sexual problems may develop because the need for relatedness was not met in childhood. Children need to feel loved and connected to others. Likewise, when children do not feel they partake in something meaningful, which could involve even small tasks of sharing household responsibility, they lack a sense of significance.

Children learn *values* from their parents. Values can be communicated verbally, but the most powerful way parents teach their children about values is by the choices parents make that reflect their own values. If parents value work more than relationships or material possessions more than serving others, children will learn these values. Concerning sexuality, parents can model for their children the values of chastity, self-control and fidelity.

Core beliefs are those basic beliefs we hold, live by and pass on to our children. They can be distorted, such as "It's best not to show weakness" or "You cannot trust others." They can also be consistent with a Christian worldview, as when we think and communicate to our children, "Your choices matter," or "Actions have consequences." As Jones and Jones (1993) observe, these core beliefs are crucial for sexual education.

Many of what we think are inborn traits may be more accurately understood as *skills* we have learned. Important skills include empathy for others, interpersonal strength and assertiveness, decision making, delayed gratification and self-control.

Because what children and teens do is often influenced by their environment, it is important that character formation occur in a context of broader *supports.* These include the family environment and whether family relationships are characterized by love, affirmation and respect, as well as the broader influences of a child's peer group and church environment.

Although this emphasis on sex education as lifelong character formation does not directly address some of the issues couples face with sexual dysfunctions, this approach leads to a positive view of sexuality, relationships out of which accurate information can be conveyed about sexual anatomy and functioning, the clear teaching of values, and opportunities for questions to be raised regarding any topic in the area of sexuality.

Paraphilias and paraphilia-related disorders. Very little has been done in the area of preventing the paraphilias and paraphilia-related disorders. One suggestion has been to pursue education tailored to areas of particular susceptibility. For example, McConaghy (1993) suggests that in light of some men's propensity to be sexually aroused by female children, efforts should be made to educate men (through school and media programs already in place) of this propensity and to teach skills for avoiding compromising circumstances and coping with unwanted sexual attractions. McConaghy sees this as especially important since many first offenses against children occur "in response to an unexpected opportunity in which they experience this arousal, of which they were previously unaware they were capable" (1993, p. 362). This is education that aims at helping potential offenders control deviant sexual arousal. This approach may be applicable to a number of atypical sexual behaviors, and proper education may remove the stigma that has kept people from learning skills that might aid in prevention.

Gender identity disorders and homosexuality. For prevention, psychological interventions are viewed as especially important when working with children, primarily because the vast majority of children who report gender identity concerns do not experience gender identity disorder (GID) as adults. Some experts believe that children can grow out of their gender identity disorder in childhood, while others believe that early intervention prevents adult gender identity disorder.

Adolescent expressions of gender identity disorder are typically viewed as more similar to adult manifestations of the disorder than childhood manifestations (Carroll, 2000). This has led to debates on whether teens should be allowed to pursue physical (surgical) gender reassignment or whether they should receive psychological interventions. Despite a push from some to allow for surgical reassignment, the standard of care is to recommend against the procedure until the adolescent turns eighteen.

Research on the prevention of gender identity disorder has dealt with factors that may contribute to the etiology of homosexuality. This has led to the question of whether homosexuality can be prevented. Experts agree that gender nonconformity in childhood is one of the best predictors of homosexual identification later in life. About 75 percent of children accurately diagnosed with GID will later self-identify as homosexual. (Adult GID—or transsexuality—is not the same as homosexuality. Homosexuality is a *sexual* identity concern, but it is not thought of as a *gender* identity concern by many experts despite the apparent link between sexual and gender identity seen in the high percentage of persons with GID who later self-identify as homosexual.) Those who believe that homosexuality can and should be prevented tend to focus on early intervention targeting gender confusion in childhood.

From a psychodynamic perspective, the fundamental problem experienced by homosexuals is that legitimate developmental needs were not met in childhood (Nicolosi and Nicolosi, 2002). According to this view, the adult homosexual essentially sexualizes members of the same sex because of a failure to identify with them earlier in life. Prevention, then, involves working with parents to prevent the gender identity confusion that some theorists believe could lead to homosexuality.

INTEGRATIVE THEMES

This chapter began with a Christian perspective on human sexuality. We turn now to several related integrative themes, tying our present discussion of sexual problems to the major focal points discussed in detail in part one of this book. Of particular importance are issues of classification as a mental illness, disordered desires, and how sexual problems relate to sin and our fallen human condition.

Disordered desires. The historic pastoral care emphasis on lust may initially seem to have an obvious connection to the problems of sexuality. But our understanding of the various sexual problems suggests that they are more complex than a simple appeal to lust would suppose. Lust does not seem to play a direct role in a number of sexual problems, including many of the sexual dysfunctions and the gender identity disorders, though it may figure more prominently in some of the paraphilias (e.g., pedophilia, sexual masochism and sadism) and paraphilia-related disorders (e.g., compulsive masturbation, sexual promiscuity and struggles with pornography). Lust is probably most accurately understood not as the single cause of any of these disorders but as a feature of the disorders, and a prominent feature in several of them.

Interventions that incorporate insights from historic pastoral care emphasize temperance and chastity by helping people habituate themselves to greater self-control in thoughts, fantasy and behavior. In addition, pastoral reflection on the sin of lust involves raising questions about one's moral obligations to others and the ethical implications of one's behavior. Both of these considerations are often overlooked in the individually focused world of professional psychology and counseling.

Issues in classification. In his discussion of the term *disease,* Wakefield (1992) made the point that "disease" is properly understood as "harmful dysfunction." From this point of view, a condition is a disease if it is *harmful,* meaning it leads to negative consequences,[5] and a *dysfunction* when relevant processes of the human organism fail to perform their natural functions (Goodman, 2001). As we discussed in chapter three, we see Wakefield's perspective as a reasonable starting point, but we believe it is insufficiently *Christian* in its understanding of disease.

A Christian understanding would not be satisfied with negative

---

[5]The focus on negative consequences led to a controversy over whether "subjective distress" had to be present to warrant diagnosis of a paraphilia. When the *DSM-IV* was first published, it was noted that the diagnostic criteria for the paraphilias had changed so that "subjective distress" or "impairment" had to be present to warrant diagnosis. Many were outraged by this change and viewed it as an indication that some wanted to treat as potentially healthy what had been previously considered ipso facto pathological (e.g., pedophilia). As Hilliard and Spitzer (2002) observe, however, this change in language was probably an embarrassing oversight by the editors of *DSM-IV,* and it was corrected in *DSM-IV-TR* (Text Revision).

consequences if these are limited only to symptoms the behavioral sciences purport to measure, such as elevations in measures of depression or anxiety. Negative consequences must be understood within a broader Christian worldview, and this cannot be understood apart from a Christian view of dysfunction. Whereas Wakefield sees dysfunction as related to the natural functions of organismic processes, we see function as related to God's design for a specific organismic process. Sexuality theorists typically take what *is* as evidence for what *ought* to be, but any undergraduate who has taken Introduction to Philosophy recognizes this as the naturalistic fallacy. The fact that behavior occurs tells us nothing about whether the behavior ought to occur—whether we should continue to engage in it. Christians look beyond the observed state of human sexuality and sexual behavior to ask questions about human nature and healthy functioning. Our reference point is not what occurs in a given setting but what God's intention is for our behavior, so that we can live in a way that reflects his purposes for our sexuality.

When considering God's design for specific organismic processes, Christians might reflect, for example, on cognitive faculties. Where an experience of psychopathology is rooted in problems of cognitive functioning—that is, tied to irrational beliefs—the person might be said to be evidencing cognitive malfunction, or "failure of the relevant cognitive faculties to function properly, to function as they ought to" (Plantinga, 1993, p. 4).

Healthy sexuality in the Christian perspective, then, means that a person's faculties pertaining to mental health and sexual functioning are free from malfunction. Much of this is established in common-sense contexts as we consider the proper function of our thoughts and feelings. However, there will be several points of dispute. How do we know that our sexual desires are functioning properly? Should we experience sexual attraction to a limited number of persons? to the same or opposite sex? If we engage in sexual behavior, do we know whether the behavior is right or wrong simply based on our sexual desires? Do our desires speak to proper sexual functioning?

Christians might take issue, then, with the exclusion of homosexuality from the *DSM,* as same-sex intercourse is seen as falling outside of what God intends for human sexuality and sexual expression. However, an additional consideration in classification is the role of a *public* psychology. Are the modern psychopathologies best understood as reflecting a public psychology, the common ground with respect to what is deemed a mental health concern within a society? Or are the modern psychopathologies best understood within the context of moral communities? We suspect there will be reasoned disagreement on this point. Perhaps we should expect that some clinical concerns and not others will land in the *DSM* because of the public dimension of the behavioral sciences, and clinical concerns tied specifically to Christian considerations might include others.

Maybe the best example among the modern psychopathologies is the etiological history of homosexuality, which had been considered a mental illness but was removed from the *DSM* in 1973.[6] However the removal of homosexuality came about, many Christians today seem to want homosexuality to be treated by our culture not only as immoral but as illegal and as a mental illness. For them it is not enough to view homosexual conduct as immoral; they want the full weight of the law and of the mental health professions behind them.

If we follow our analysis of organismic processes and design function, it is difficult to see how homosexuality can be anything other than a psychopathology. However, if we reflect on what it means to have a *public* psychology, an understanding of mental health that is steeped in a particular culture at a particular time, then we should not be surprised to find a public psychology at odds with a Christian sexual ethic.

This raises the issue of whether we sometimes label as *pathological* certain sexual behaviors that are more accurately understood as *sinful*. It is in this sense that Christians might resist the idea that homosexuality is a mental illness, because they might conclude that such a designation serves to pathologize behaviors that are better understood as sinful. A related concern is whether clinicians view people as responsible for their sexual behavior if that behavior constitutes a diagnosable pathology. All these questions have to do with the relation of sin and psychopathology, particularly pertaining to human sexuality and sexual behavior.

Sin and psychopathology. In what ways can a Christian perspective inform our understanding of the kinds of problems of sexuality that

---

[6]Bayer's (1981) analysis of this process suggests that it occurred at a time of significant social change and under the watchful eye of gay rights groups that had made explicit threats to disrupt the APA conventions, and that the removal of homosexuality occurred with unconventional speed that circumvented normal channels for consideration of the issues.

are discussed in the *DSM*?[7] For example, does a Christian perspective on gender inform our understanding of the gender identity disorders? Given that sin can be thought of broadly with respect to discrete thoughts and actions, a fallen state or condition, and the consequences of sin, we can see how struggles with gender identity disorder may reflect our fallen condition. Christians affirm that God created humanity as male and female and that God viewed as good our maleness and femaleness and experiences of complementary relationality. But gender is a complex and multifaceted construct, and the various dimensions of gender are usually but not always concordant. When they are not, one possible outcome is a gender identity disorder. Christians would not see GID as a natural human variation but as an unintended outcome that distorts God's intention for gender identity, enacted gender role and sometimes erotic preference, thus often compromising or constraining the fundamental need for relationality. Though some mental health professionals are pushing to remove gender identity disorder from the *DSM*, Christians at this point in time share with the broader mental health community the perspective that gender identity disorder is a psychopathology.

To return to the fallen condition and the impact of the Fall on human sexuality, we turn to a frequent theme in Scripture: the human tendency toward idolatry (see Yarhouse and Burkett, 2003). Richard Lints (2002) discusses the relationship between idolatry and the image of God, and we will summarize some of his points. In Scripture, concern expressed over idolatry is aimed directly at Israel, God's chosen people, rather than other nations. God reacted to the idolatry of his people, as they were prone to turn away from him and toward other gods. Idolatry, distilled to its essence, is really about subverting one's relationship with God.

We see this tendency most clearly in decisions people make about their sexual identity. For example, when people experience same-sex attraction, they can choose to integrate their experiences into a gay identity, or they can disidentify with their experiences of same-sex attraction and pursue a sexual identity organized around other dimensions of what it means to be human (Yarhouse, 2001). The fallen state or condition sets the stage on which a person chooses his or her actions, but the actions are volitional despite the fallen condition. In the area of sexual identity, then, some people focus mainly on their sex as

---

[7]This section is adapted from Jones and Yarhouse (2002).

male or female, while others find it best to focus on their identity in Christ (Yarhouse and Burkett, 2003). A biblical understanding of idolatry and of sexual identity helps keep Christians from foreclosing prematurely on their sexual identity and on the broader question of who they are as a person. Even for those who experience persistent same-sex attractions and would say that they experience a homosexual orientation, there remains a freedom to worship God on his terms, as we understand them, within a traditional Christian sexual ethic.

When people integrate their experiences of same-sex attraction into a "gay" identity, it seems inescapable that they are making their identity as gay primary and that they then relate to God on these terms. This does not constitute a failure to relate to God. People who take on a gay identity may very well relate to God, but the question is, on whose terms? We become who or what we worship, but the terms of agreement also shape the experience and outcome of worship. As Lints observes, "It is not merely 'giving yourself away' that is at stake in proper worship, but also 'whom you are giving yourself away to and in what manner are you giving yourself up'" (2002, p. 13). Citing Martin Buber, Lints reminds us that we can even worship God idolatrously, that is, "as an object for one's own purposes" (ibid.).

Sexuality and singleness. Sexuality and singleness is not addressed in most discussions of "problems of sexuality," at least if the *DSM* is our guide. However, many Christians today struggle to sort out how to live faithfully before God in the single state. Most churches cater to married couples, designing programs for them and recruiting them to lead various ministries. It is more difficult, in our experience, for singles to feel at home within a faith community beyond the stage of a college-age class. Furthermore, there is very little discussion of singles as sexual beings. This can lead to further problems for singles. The church ought to be providing a Christian vision for all persons in the body of Christ.

We affirm that neither the marital state nor the single state is necessarily superior. Both states can teach us about different facets of what it means to be a Christian and to have a relationship with God. Some recent resources provide valuable information and are written in a tone that is sensitive to what it feels like to be alone and "non-partnered." McMinn (2003), for example, makes a strong case for celibacy while recognizing how hard it can be to practice it in a culture that is as preoccupied with sexuality as ours is.

Also, Van Leeuwen (2002) addresses a number of issues including "nonrelational sexuality," especially in regard to pornography, the Internet and treating others like objects. The Christian community is certainly not immune to the sexual issues shaping our culture. We have seen many people get caught in sexual addictions after making poor choices about Internet pornography, which often functions as a "gateway drug" or "disinhibiting agent" with respect to sexual addiction.

Evolutionary psychology. Earlier we mentioned evolutionary psychology as an emerging theme in the "scientific" study of sexuality,[8] and here we offer a few observations on it from a Christian perspective.

Unfortunately, evolutionary psychology is utterly reductive in its understanding of gender and sexuality.[9] Humans do have a drive to reproduce, and this drive may be a powerfully motivating force in human relations. But we oppose the view that this drive is the primary and most fundamental human motivation and that it can explain all facets of human sexuality and sexual behavior. Evolutionary psychology interprets all the varied dimensions of human sexuality as based on the drive to reproduce. From a Christian perspective the drive to reproduce, while important, is properly placed in relation to other motives, including a desire to love, experience pleasure, and delight in oneself, others and God. So this particular motivation should be seen in relation to broader questions of what it means to live in response to transcendent reality and the claims of that reality on our lives.

A Christian critique raises a second and related concern—that the explanatory model found in evolutionary psychology is so flexible that it can explain anything, including seemingly contradictory findings:

> Why are mothers willing to die for their children? Of course, to maximize reproductive fitness (by protecting the presumably good genes they've passed on). Well then, why do some mothers kill their children? Of course, to maximize reproductive fitness (by getting rid of the presumably bad genes they've passed on). Why do adults invest more resources in children the more closely they are related to them biologically? Of course, the closer the relationship, the greater the number of one's own genes that are shared! Well then, why would people ever adopt biologically unrelated children? Of course, because of the more

---

[8]We join Mary Stewart Van Leeuwen (2002) in questioning whether evolutionary psychology is anything like science, primarily because of its capacity to explain away whatever data runs contrary to the main theory.

[9]Portions of this critique are adapted from Jones and Yarhouse (2002), "Anthropology, Sexuality, and Sexual Ethics."

generic gene for reciprocal altruism. (Van Leeuwen, 2002, p. 104)

These concerns are consistent with critiques of Freudian psycho-analytic theory: it is too comprehensive to permit a truly scientific ex-amination of the data. "Auxiliary concepts are multiplied to explain away whatever data are embarrassing to the main theory" (ibid.).

In offering this critique, we acknowledge that Christians do not have to reject all of evolutionary psychology or evolutionary thought. Christians may be drawn to versions of microevolutionary thought that provide testable hypotheses, theories that may explain subtle spe-cies adaptation without a worldview or philosophy or explanation for morality. This is similar to how Christians may draw on behavioral theory in their clinical practice by utilizing empirically validated inter-ventions while rejecting the utterly reductionistic and deterministic worldview found in broader models of behavioral theory (Jones and Butman, 1991).

CONCLUSION

Problems of sexuality encompass a wide range of clinical problems. In this chapter we have discussed sexual dysfunctions, paraphilias, gender identity disorders and several clinical concerns, including driven sexual behavior and homosexuality. A Christian perspective af-firms the goodness of our inherent physicality, as well as the place of sexuality in our physical being. A proper understanding of human sexuality is to see people as engendered beings who are profoundly relational: we were designed by God to be in relation to him, to oth-ers and to ourselves. Although we relate to others as gendered crea-tures, as Christians we do not reduce our understanding of what it means to be human to our sexuality but see sexuality in relation to transcendence.

RECOMMENDED READING

Jones, S. L., and Yarhouse, M. A. (2000). *Homosexuality: The use of scien-tific research in the church's moral debate.* Downers Grove, IL: InterVar-sity Press. A review of research on prevalence, etiology, status as a pathology and change, as well as the relevance of this research to the church's debate about homosexuality.

McMinn, L. (2003). *Sexuality and holy longing: Embracing intimacy in a broken world.* San Francisco: Jossey-Bass. This is an excellent re-source, particularly on the topic of sexuality and singleness.

Rosenau, D. (2002). *A celebration of sex* (2nd ed.). Nashville: Thomas Nelson. A very helpful resource for couples, with additional chapters on a range of topics in human sexuality.

Smedes, L. (1990). *Sex for Christians* (Rev. ed.). Grand Rapids, MI: Eerdmans. A thoughtful and—in its treatment of some topics—provocative book from a Christian scholar.

Van Leeuwen, M. S. (2002). *My brother's keeper.* Downers Grove, IL: InterVarsity Press. This is a fine resource—see especially her discussion of "nonrelational sexuality" as it relates to pornography, the Internet and treating others like objects (chap. 11).

Yarhouse, M. A., and Burkett, L. A. (2003). *Sexual identity: A guide to living in the time between the times.* Lanham, MD: University Press of America. This is a practical book for people who contend with same-sex attraction and seek to live in a way that is consistent with the traditional Christian sexual ethic.

REFERENCES

Allen, L., and Gorski, R. (1992). Sexual orientation and the size of the anterior commissure in the human brain. *Proceedings of the National Academy of Sciences, USA, 89,* 7199-202.

American Psychiatric Association. (1994). *Diagnostic and statistical manual of mental disorders* (4th ed.). Washington, DC: Author.

Augustine. (1996). *Saint Augustine's Prayer Book* (Rev. ed.) (L. Gavitt, Ed.). West Park, NY: Holy Cross.

Bailey, J. M., Dunn, M. P., and Martin, N. G. (2000). Genetic and environmental influences on sexual orientation and its correlates in an Australian twin sample. *Journal of Personality and Social Psychology, 78,* 524-36.

Bailey, J. M., and Pillard, R. (1991). A genetic study of male sexual orientation. *Archives of General Psychiatry, 48,* 1089-96.

Bailey, J. M., and Zucker, K. J. (1995). Childhood sex-typed behavior and sexual orientation: A conceptual analysis and quantitative review. *Developmental Psychology, 31,* 43-55.

Bayer, R. (1981). *Homosexuality and American psychiatry: The politics of diagnosis.* New York: Basic Books.

Bieber, I., Dain, H. J., Dince, P. R., Drellich, M. G., Grand, H. G., Gundlach, R. H., Kremer, M. W., Rifkin, A. H., Wilber, C. B., and Bieber, T. B. (1962). *Homosexuality: A psychoanalytic study.* New York: Basic Books.

Birk, L. (1974). Group psychotherapy for men who are homosexual.

Journal of Sex and Marital Therapy, 1, 29-52.

Byne, W., and Parsons, B. (1993). Human sexual orientation: The biologic theories reappraised. *Archives of General Psychiatry, 50,* 228-39.

Carroll, R. A. (2000). Assessment and treatment of gender dysphoria. In S. R. Leiblum and R. C. Rosen (Eds.), *Principles and practice of sex therapy* (3rd ed.) (pp. 368-97). New York: Guilford.

Demeter, S., Ringo, J. L., and Doty, R. W. (1988). Morphometric analysis of the human corpus callosum and the anterior commissure. *Human Neurobiology, 6,* 219-26.

Doll, L. S., Joy, D., Bartholow, B. N., Harrison, J. S., Bolan, G., Douglas, J. M., Saltzman, L. E., Moss, P. M., and Delgado, W. (1992). Self-reported childhood and adolescent sexual abuse among adult homosexual and bisexual men. *Child Abuse and Neglect, 16,* 855-64.

Evans, R. B. (1969). Childhood parental relationships of homosexual men. *Journal of Consulting and Clinical Psychology, 33,* 129-35.

Freeman, W., and Meyer, R. G. (1975). A behavioral alteration of sexual preferences in the human male. *Behavior Therapy, 6,* 206-12.

Goodman, A. (2001). What's in a name? Terminology for designating a syndrome of driven sexual behavior. *Sexual Addiction and Compulsivity, 8,* 191-213.

Haldeman, D. C. (1994). The practice and ethics of sexual orientation conversion therapy. *Journal of Consulting and Clinical Psychology, 62,* 221-27.

Hamer, D., Hu, S., Magnuson, V., Hu, N., and Pattatuci, A. (1993). A linkage between DNA markers on the X chromosome and male sexual orientation. *Science, 261,* 321-27.

Harry Benjamin International Gender Dysphoria Standards of Care. (1998). *The standards of care of gender identity disorders* (5th ed.). Dusseldorf: Symposion.

Hart, A. D. (1994). *The sexual man: Masculinity without guilt.* Dallas: Word.

Hart, A. D., Weber, C., and Taylor, D. L. (1998). *Secrets of Eve: Understanding the mystery of female sexuality.* Dallas: Word.

Hatterer, L. (1970). *Changing heterosexuality in the male: Treatment for men troubled by homosexuality.* New York: McGraw-Hill.

Heiman, J. R., and Meston, C. M. (1997). Empirically validated treatment for sexual dysfunction. *Annual Review of Sex Research, 8,* 148-94.

Hilliard, R. B., and Spitzer, R. L. (2002). Change in criterion for paraphilias in *DSM-IV-TR. Psychiatry, 159*(70), 1249.

Hu, S., Pattatuci, A., Patterson, C., Li, L., Fulker, D., Cherny, S., Krug-

Iyak, L., and Hamer, D. (1995). Linkage between sexual orientation and chromosome Xq28 in males but not in females. *Nature Genetics, 11*, 248-56.

Jones, S. L., and Butman, R. E. (1991). *Modern psychotherapies: A comprehensive Christian appraisal.* Downers Grove, IL: InterVarsity Press.

Jones, S., and Jones, B. (1993). *How and when to tell your kids about sex.* Grand Rapids, MI: Baker.

Jones, S. L., and Yarhouse, M. A. (2000). *Homosexuality: The use of scientific research in the church's moral debate.* Downers Grove, IL: InterVarsity Press.

Jones, S. L., and Yarhouse, M. A. (2002). Anthropology, sexuality and sexual ethics: The ecclesiastical challenge. Paper presented to the Alliance of Confessing Evangelicals, Colorado Springs, CO, June.

Kafka, M. P. (2000). The paraphilia-related disorders: Nonparaphilic hypersexuality and sexual compulsivity/addiction. In S. R. Leiblum and R. C. Rosen (Eds.), *Principles and practice of sex therapy* (3rd ed.) (pp. 471-503). New York: Guilford.

Laumann, E., Gagnon, J., Michael, R., and Michaels, S. (1994). *The social organization of sexuality.* Chicago: University of Chicago Press.

LeVay, S. (1991). A difference in the hypothalamic structure between heterosexual and homosexual men. *Science, 253*, 1034-37.

Lints, R. (2002). Imaging and idolatry: The sociality of personhood and the ironic reversals of the canon. Paper presented to the Alliance of Confessing Evangelicals, Colorado Springs, CO, June.

MacCulloch, M. J., and Feldman, M. P. (1967). Aversion therapy in management of 43 homosexuals. *British Medical Journal, 2*, 594-97.

MacIntosh, H. (1994). Attitudes and experiences of psychoanalysts. *Journal of the American Psychoanalytic Association, 42*, 1183-207.

Maletzky, B. M. (2002). The paraphilias: Research and treatment. In P. E. Nathan and J. M. Gorman (Eds.), *A guide to treatments that work* (2nd ed.) (pp. 525-57). New York: Oxford University Press.

McConaghy, N. (1970). Subjective and penile plethysmograph responses to aversion therapy for homosexuality: A follow-up study. *British Journal of Psychiatry, 117*, 555-60.

McConaghy, N. (1993). *Sexual behavior: Problems and management.* New York: Plenum.

Munzer, J. (1965). Treatment of the homosexual in group psychotherapy. *Topical Problems of Psychotherapy, 5*, 164-69.

Nicolosi, J., and Nicolosi, L. A. (2002). *A parent's guide to preventing homosexuality.* Downers Grove, IL: InterVarsity Press.

Olthuis, J. H. (1995). Lust. In D. J. Atkinson, D. F. Field, A. Holmes, and O. O'Donovan (Eds.), *New dictionary of Christian ethics and pastoral theology* (pp. 558-59). Downers Grove, IL: InterVarsity Press.

Pittman, F., and DeYoung, C. (1971). The treatment of homosexuals in heterogeneous groups. *International Journal of Group Psychotherapy*, *21*, 62-73.

Plantinga, A. (1993). *Warrant and proper function*. Oxford: Oxford University Press.

Rice, G., Anderson, C., Risch, N., and Ebers, G. (1999, April 23). Male homosexuality: Absence of linkage to microsatellite markers at Xq28. *Science*, *284*, 665-67.

Schaeffer, K. W., Hyde, R. A., Kroencke, T., McCormick, B., and Nottebaum, L. (2000). Religiously-motivated sexual orientation change. *Journal of Psychology and Christianity*, *19*, 61-70.

Schaeffer, K. W., Nottebaum, L., Smith, P., Dech, K., and Krawczyk, J. (1999). Religiously-motivated sexual orientation change: A follow-up study. *Journal of Psychology and Theology*, *27*, 329-37.

Schimmel, S. (1997). *The seven deadly sins: Jewish, Christian and classical reflections on human psychology*. New York: Oxford University Press.

Schwartz, M. F., and Masters, W. H. (1984). The Masters and Johnson treatment program for dissatisfied homosexual men. *American Journal of Psychiatry*, *141*, 173-81.

Segraves, T., and Althof, S. (2002). Psychotherapy and pharmacotherapy for sexual dysfunctions. In P. E. Nathan and J. M. Gorman (Eds.), *A guide to treatments that work* (2nd ed.) (pp. 497-524). New York: Oxford University Press.

Swaab, D., and Hofman, M. (1990). An enlarged suprachiasmatic nucleus in homosexual men. *Brain Research*, *537*, 141-48.

Truax, R. A., and Tourney, G. (1971). Male homosexuals in group psychotherapy. *Diseases of the Nervous System*, *32*, 707-11.

van den Aardweg, G. J. M. (1984). Parents of homosexuals—not guilty? Interpretation of childhood psychological data. *American Journal of Psychotherapy*, *38*, 180-89.

van den Aardweg, G. J. M. (1986). *On the origins and treatment of homosexuality*. New York: Praeger.

Van Leeuwen, M. S. (2001). Of hoggamus and hogwash: Evolutionary psychology and gender relations. *Journal of Psychology and Theology*, *30*(2), 101-11.

Van Leeuwen, M. S. (2002). *My brother's keeper*. Downers Grove, IL: InterVarsity Press.

Wakefield, J. C. (1992). The concept of mental disorder: On the boundary between biological facts and social values. *American Psychologist, 47,* 373-88.

Wincze, J. P. (2000). Assessment and treatment of atypical sexual behavior. In S. R. Leiblum and R. C. Rosen (Eds.), *Principles and practice of sex therapy* (3rd ed.) (pp. 449-70). New York: Guilford.

Yarhouse, M. A. (2001). Sexual identity development: The influence of valuative frameworks on identity synthesis. *Psychotherapy, 38*(3), 331-41.

Yarhouse, M. A., and Burkett, L. A. (2003). *Sexual identity: A guide to living in the time between the times.* Lanham, MD: University Press of America.

Part Three

PROBLEMS IN LIFE STAGES

12

PROBLEMS IN CHILDHOOD AND ADOLESCENCE

People were bringing little children to Jesus to have him touch them, but the disciples rebuked them. When Jesus saw this, he was indignant. He said to them, "Let the little children come to me, and do not hinder them, for the kingdom of God belongs to such as these. I tell you the truth, anyone who will not receive the kingdom of God like a little child will never enter it." And he took the children in his arms, put his hands on them and blessed them. (Mk 10:13-16)

*T*oo often children are viewed and treated as the disciples would have and not as Jesus did. The old adage "Children are to be seen and not heard" reflects the opinion of many and, sadly, the historic treatment of children in many cultures. Only since the modern era have societal standards and legislation emerged to protect children and provide standards of education and care.

The problems of childhood and adolescence are some of the most heart-wrenching of the disorders we describe in this book, because they are manifest in the lives of those who often don't understand what is happening to them and who don't have a voice within society to advocate for themselves. Their cries for help may take on forms that are misunderstood by those whose help they need. Too little attention has been paid to the experiences and needs of children historically, both within the church and in the larger society.

THEMES IN PASTORAL CARE

The struggles of childhood and adolescence were not a specific focus of the writers of the Scriptures or of much literature of the Christian church until the modern era. Historically, most references to children have centered on either their eternal state (discussions of original sin and baptism) or their spiritual formation (catechetical instruction). There has been little reference to their developmental processes or factors that can contribute to difficulties in their abilities to function. In part this has been due to a general disregard for the lives of children in the theological deliberations of the church. Becker (1979) suggests that within the church, teachings about how to live and believe have been limited to adult categories of understanding and experience.

> Adults of almost every Christian tradition assume that belonging to the Church is a matter of believing certain things and doing certain things. But the things to believe are mostly things only adults can understand, the things to do are mostly things only adults can do. So these adult categories of faith and conduct do not provide a suitable theological framework for interpreting the place of the child in the church. Childhood requires a theology of its own. (British Council of Churches, quoted in Becker, 1979, p. 237; see also Bunge, 2001)

For the majority of Christian history, life within the community of faith has centered on ways of living that reflect adult ways of being. In nearly all current theologies, human beings are conceptualized as having the characteristics of adults, and this assumption has led to a disregard for the experiences of children within the life of the church (Becker, 1979). The faith of children has been regarded as unimportant in contrast to adult faith, and worship typically reflects this attitude. According to Becker, life within the church has been conducted in a decidedly adult manner to the disadvantage of children, whose own fundamental experiences and interests, as well as particular ways of living and believing, are ignored.

In the biblical world, according to Perkin, "children were generally well loved, but their childhood was short and they were often regarded as laborers for the house or fields" (1988, p. 771). Though the Scriptures do not speak directly to the lives and struggles of children, they do give us some indication of their place in God's plan and in his kingdom. As Grassi points out: "In the Old Testament, children are a gift from God, instruments of God's activity, and symbolically a guarantee of the covenant between God and the people of Israel. In the New Testament, children are principally a model or image for the believer to emulate" (1992, p. 904).

Often God chose to accomplish his purposes through children. The covenant with Abraham (and thus the establishment of a chosen nation through which God incarnate would bring salvation) was to be through his child (Gen 12; 17). This covenant was to be signified from generation to generation through the birth and experience (circumcision) of children (Gen 17:6-7, 10). In addition, God chose to use young persons to bring about important historical events in the fulfillment of his purpose (e.g., Joseph, Samuel, David). Finally, the prophetic messianic expectation of the Old Testament focused on the coming of a child: "Therefore the Lord himself will give you a sign: The virgin will be with child and will give birth to a son, and will call him Immanuel [God with us]" (Is 7:14).

These Old Testament references reveal the important role children have played to further God's purposes. In the fulfillment of his providential plan, God chose not only to use children but to place the hopes of his people in the birth of a child who would be his saving grace. In the New Testament, the faith of children is held up as the example for faith in God: "He called a little child and had him stand among them. And he said: 'I tell you the truth, unless you change and become like little children, you will never enter the kingdom of heaven. Therefore, whoever humbles himself like this child is the greatest in the kingdom of heaven" (Mt 18:2-4).

In his Word, the Lord has seen fit to give children a place of honor in the kingdom of heaven. Unfortunately, this has not always been the case within the church. Though a significant body of literature exists regarding the education of children within the church (e.g., Luther's and Calvin's catechisms) and references to the moral responsibility of parents in training them up in the instruction of the Lord (Bunge, 2001), little has been written about the particular struggles children face in their development and in response to mistreatment, neglect, poverty and oppression.

THEMES FROM PSYCHOPATHOLOGY

Children have received equally little attention historically in the health and mental health fields. The neglect has been due in part to prejudicial attitudes within the mental health field toward children, beliefs that the problems of childhood are more transient or even "normal," and ultimately reflect the fact that children and adolescents lack any influence as a constituency in society to voice their need for attention (Mash and Barkley, 1996). Only in recent decades has specific focus been given to the emotional, behavioral and learning difficulties of children and adolescents.

As interest in child psychopathology has rocketed into the mainstream of the field over the past several decades, researchers have come to realize just how complex an undertaking it is. Distinguishing normal from deviant or dysfunctional developmental processes, functional from dysfunctional systems, shared symptoms, comorbidity of disorders, contextual influences, and on and on is an extremely difficult task due to the ever-changing landscape of child and adolescent life. Current conceptualizations of the nature of child and adolescent psychopathology must therefore account for the

> multidirectional, reciprocal, and dynamic interactions among genetic, neural, behavioral, and environmental influences over time. . . . In short then, current approaches view the roots of developmental and psychiatric disturbances in children as the result of complex interactions over the course of development between the biology of brain maturation and the multidimensional nature of experience. (Mash and Dozois, 1996, p. 5; see also Cicchetti and Tucker, 1994)

The *DSM-IV* includes as a separate section "Disorders Usually First Diagnosed in Infancy, Childhood or Adolescence." Though the disorders listed in this section are typically first evidenced during childhood and adolescence, they are by no means the only disorders with which children or adolescents struggle. This section in the *DSM-IV* begins with an important disclaimer:

> The provision of a separate section for disorders that are usually first diagnosed in infancy, childhood, or adolescence is for convenience only and is not meant to suggest that there is any clear distinction between "childhood" and "adult" disorders. Al-

though most individuals with these disorders present for clinical attention during childhood or adolescence, the disorders sometimes are not diagnosed until adulthood. Moreover, many disorders included in other sections of the manual often have an onset during childhood or adolescence. (APA, 1994, p. 39)

In this section, the *DSM-IV* identifies nine categories of problems that are typically first identified and diagnosed during childhood or adolescence:

- *mental retardation:* mild, moderate, severe, profound and severity unspecified

- *learning disorders:* reading disorder, mathematics disorder, disorder of written expression and learning disorder NOS

- *motor skills disorder:* developmental coordination disorder

- *communication disorders:* expressive language disorder, mixed receptive-expressive language disorder, phonological disorder, stuttering and communication disorder NOS

- *pervasive developmental disorders:* autistic disorder, Rhett's disorder, childhood disintegrative disorder, Asperger's disorder and pervasive developmental disorder NOS

- *attention-deficit and disruptive behavior disorders:* ADHD combined type, ADHD predominantly inattentive type, ADHD predominantly hyperactive-impulsive type, ADHD NOS, conduct disorder, oppositional defiant disorder and disruptive behavior disorder NOS

- *feeding and eating disorders of infancy or early childhood:* pica, rumination disorder, and feeding disorder of infancy or early childhood

- *tic disorders:* Tourette's disorder, chronic motor or vocal tic disorder, transient tic disorder and tic disorder NOS

- *elimination disorders:* encopresis with constipation and overflow incontinence, encopresis without constipation and overflow incontinence, and enuresis

The *DSM-IV* also includes five disorders not categorized under any of the above headings: separation anxiety disorder, selective mutism, reactive attachment disorder of infancy or early childhood, stereotypic movement disorder, and disorder of infancy, childhood or adolescence NOS.

As the *DSM-IV* acknowledges, many other disorders addressed in other sections of the *DSM-IV* may manifest themselves during childhood or adolescence, and these need to be addressed according to

Table 12.1 Diagnostic Questions for Child and Adolescent Disorders
(adapted from Goldman, 1998, pp. 100-103)

---

1. What is the primary location of the problem?

✓ If within the child (e.g., attention-deficit/hyperactivity disorder [ADHD], *proceed to question 2.*

✓ If not within the child, is it in the parent-child relationship? *V-codes*

✓ If not within the child, is it in the parent? Consider an *adjustment disorder* for the child and possibly a *diagnosis* for the parent.

✓ If not within the child, is it between the child and the school? Consider *systemic causes* and interventions.

2. Is the problem a reaction to an identifiable stressor or event?

NO: *Proceed to question 3.*

YES: Consider *adjustment disorder, posttraumatic stress disorder* or *acute stress disorder.*

3. What basic area or areas of the child's life are affected? (With each of the following criteria, a decision tree is provided in the article to aid in reaching a diagnosis.)

Behavior: Consider *conduct disorder, oppositional defiant disorder* or *ADHD.*

Mood:

Anxiety—Consider *generalized anxiety disorder, separation anxiety disorder, agoraphobia, panic attacks, obsessive-compulsive disorder* or *simple phobia.*

Depression—Consider *dysthymic disorder, major depressive disorder, cyclothymic disorder* or *bipolar disorder.*

Body parts or functions: Consider *eating disorders, pica, rumination disorder, enuresis, encopresis, tic disorders, sleep disorders, gender identity disorder, conversion disorder, somatiform disorders, language disorders, learning disorders* or *mental retardation.*

Disconnection: Consider *dissociative disorders.*

Relation to others: Consider *autism, Asperger's syndrome.*

Bizarre behaviors: Consider *childhood schizophrenia, major depressive disorder* or *bipolar disorder.*

4. Are the symptoms in question longstanding and ego-syntonic?

YES: Consider *Axis II disorders.*

the developmental needs and capacities of children and adolescents. For example, children with depression may manifest symptoms that are dissimilar to the expected symptom cluster for adults with the same diagnosis.

Ideally, a discussion of disorders of childhood and adolescence would include all disorders that bear any significance for children or adolescents. Realistically, however, it is beyond the scope of this chapter to reconsider every disorder in the *DSM-IV* with regard to its implications for diagnosis and treatment with children and adolescents. We do not want to be misunderstood as contributing to the historic disregard for the needs of children and adolescents; however, in order to do any justice to so broad a category of psychopathology, we must limit our discussion in this chapter to a select group of the more prevalent disorders identified in the *DSM-IV* section entitled "Disorders Usually First Diagnosed in Infancy, Childhood or Adolescence."[1] We will discuss these under the following broad headings:

- attention-deficit disorders
- disruptive behavior disorders
- mental retardation and learning disorders
- pervasive developmental disorders
- tic disorders
- elimination disorders

We will not be able to discuss the implications of any of the disorders covered in other chapters of this book for children or adolescents, nor the following disorders identified in this section of the *DSM-IV:* motor skills disorder, communication disorders, feeding and eating disorders of infancy or early childhood, separation anxiety disorder, selective mutism, reactive attachment disorder of infancy or early childhood, and stereotypic movement disorder.

The *DSM* nosology is predicated on the idea that psychopathology in childhood and adolescence is primarily distinguishable from normal functioning on the basis of identifiable impairment to the child or adolescent's ability to function in daily life activities at home or school. Accurate diagnosis, then, depends on the clinician's ability to identify the impairment and to distinguish it from other forms of im-

---

[1]We recommend Mash and Barkley 1996 and 1998 for more comprehensive considerations of diagnostic and treatment issues related to work with children.

pairment and "normal" childhood or adolescent behavior and experience. Goldman (1998) offered a series of diagnostic questions in the
form of a decision tree for accurate diagnosis of child and adolescent
disorders (see table 12.1). However, this is not the only way to conceptualize childhood psychopathology. It is but one of two approaches to
understanding psychopathology in children.

A second approach, referred to as *multivariate, psychometric* or *empirical,* relies heavily on statistical studies and the assumption that psychopathology exists on a continuum from normal to abnormal functioning. "Normative" samples are used for comparison, and emotional and
behavioral problems are determined on the basis of the degree of deviance from the experience of children and adolescents in the general
population. This viewpoint has resulted in the identification of two dimensions of psychopathology. Frick and Silverthorn briefly define
these dimensions, stating that the first "has been labeled undercon-
trolled or externalizing and includes various acting out, disruptive, de-
linquent, hyperactive, and aggressive behaviors. The second broad dimension of childhood behavior problems has been labeled
overcontrolled or internalizing and includes such behaviors as social
withdrawal, anxiety, and depression" (2001, pp. 881-82).

Ideally these two approaches to childhood and adolescent psychopathology would not be viewed as competing paradigms but rather as
complementary perspectives from which to draw a more holistic understanding of the capacities and needs of struggling children and
adolescents (see Kamphaus and Frick, 1996). Sadly, there has been a
disparity in research of childhood and adolescent psychopathology,
between the two areas of the second paradigm. More research has
been focused on the "externalizing" disorders than the "internalizing" disorders, perhaps in part because the externalizing disorders
tend to be more disruptive to the lives of children, their peers and
their families. However, according to Frick and Silverthorn, "it is becoming increasingly clear that internalizing disorders, such as anxiety
and depression, are more chronic and impairing in children than was
once thought, making research on these disorders an important goal
of child psychologists" (2001, p. 909).

Attention-deficit disorders. During the 1980s and 1990s, approximately 50 percent of all children referred to outpatient mental health
clinics were referred for concerns about possible attention-deficit hyperactivity disorder (ADHD; Frick and Silverthorn, 2001; Cantwell,
1996; Resnick, 1998). According to the *DSM-IV,* 3-5 percent of school-

age children in the United States struggle with ADHD. Frick and Silverthorn (2001) cite epidemiological studies suggesting childhood prevalence rates of 2-9 percent (Anderson et al., 1987; Cohen et al., 1993; Costello et al., 1996; 1997; Offord, Boyle and Racine, 1989; Verhulst et al., 1997) and adolescent prevalence rates of 2-4.5 percent (Kashani et al., 1987; Lewinsohn et al., 1993; McGee et al., 1990). It is not only one of the most common disorders among children and adolescents but one of the most controversial as well.

ADHD is generally considered to be a lifelong disorder; approximately 70 percent of children diagnosed with ADHD will struggle with symptoms into their adult life (Resnick, 1998). It is diagnosed far more frequently in boys than girls (ratios are as high as four to one), and the general symptom and behavior patterns for boys and girls seem to differ. Boys tend to exhibit more externalizing behaviors and symptoms and girls more internalizing (Resnick, 1998). However, some studies are beginning to question the validity of gender differences with ADHD (Silverthorn et al., 1996).

Two essential symptom clusters form the basis for a diagnosis of ADHD: inattention and hyperactivity/impulsivity. According to the *DSM-IV* criteria for diagnosis, symptoms must be evident before age seven, have been present for at least six months, be observable in at least two settings (e.g., home, school, church), represent developmentally inappropriate behavior and cause significant impairment.

Disruptive behavior disorders. Aggressive and antisocial behavior in children and adolescents is another source of concern and focus of mental health treatment. These problems may be evident in early childhood, and studies suggest that they increase in severity and prevalence by adolescence (Cohen et al., 1993). The *DSM-IV* identifies two major disruptive behavior disorders: conduct disorder (CD) and oppositional defiant disorder (ODD).

CD is diagnosed when a child or adolescent violates the basic rights of others and/or disregards rules or norms in one of four ways: (1) aggressive behavior toward others or animals, (2) destruction of property, (3) stealing or abnormal deceitful behaviors and (4) seriously breaking established standards or rules. ODD is often diagnosed before CD and represents less severe disruptive behaviors. In general ODD is diagnosed when children or adolescents develop behavior patterns that are significantly hostile, defiant or negative. Most children who are diagnosed with CD have previously been diagnosed with ODD. However, only about 47 percent of children who are diagnosed with ODD subsequently progress to a diagnosis of CD (Lahey et al., 1995). The *DSM-IV* recognizes a subtype of CD in which the symptoms become evident before age ten, because there appears to be a qualitative difference between CD which progressively develops from early childhood and that which is first evident only in adolescence (Frick and Silverthorn, 2001).

Each of these disorders is diagnosed significantly more in boys than in girls. *DSM-IV* estimates range from 6 to 16 percent for boys and 2 to 9 percent for girls. Cohen et al. (1993) suggest that prevalence rates with boys outnumber those with girls by as much as four to one during elementary school years, but by adolescence these are closer to two to one. The primary differences between boys and girls with these disorders seem to center on higher prevalence of aggressive and violent behavior in boys (McGee et al., 1992), whereas girls manifest these disorders more through relational aggressive behaviors such as excluding other children from social groups or spreading rumors about them (Frick and Silverthorn, 2001; Crick and Grotpeter, 1995). As Van Leeuwen (2002) observes, males tend to develop the pathologies of aggression or "acting out," whereas females are more likely to struggle with the pathologies of constriction, such as anxiety and depressive disorders.

Some, arguing that these categories are insufficient to classify the disruptive behavior struggles of children and adolescents, recommend subtypes of these classifications. For example, as noted, the *DSM-IV* recognizes a difference between CD with onset during childhood (before age ten), with an accompanying expectation that the severity by adolescence will be worse than for those with a later onset. Others have argued for further subtypes based on such distinctions as whether the disruptive behavior is exhibited alone or in groups (Quay, 1986), whether the behavior is aggressive or nonaggressive (Hinshaw, Lahey and Hart, 1993), whether the CD occurs in conjunction with ADHD (Lynam, 1996) or anxiety disorders (McBurnett et al., 1991; Walker et al., 1991), or whether the child exhibits an almost psychopathic lack of remorse or emotion in relation to his or her behavior (Christian et al., 1997).

Mental retardation and learning disorders. Three criteria form the basis of common conceptualizations of mental retardation: (1) significantly subaverage intellectual functioning, (2) deficits in abilities to perform daily activities of adaptive functioning such as communicating needs, eating, dressing oneself, following rules, playing with others, and (3) onset before age eighteen (Hodapp and Dykens, 1996).

Classification of mental retardation may be based on symptom severity (degree of intellectual impairment), etiological factors (such as chromosomal abnormalities) or symptom constellation; however, the most common classification approach is that adopted by the APA *(DSM-IV)* and the American Association of Mental Deficiency (AAMD): degree of intellectual impairment (see Grossman, 1973).

Classification of mental retardation is typically based on intelligence testing and the IQ (intelligence quotient) scores that result from these tests. The most common IQ scoring system sets a score of 100 for the mean (50th percentile) and a 15-point range for the standard deviation. Children and adolescents whose scores range below two standard deviations from the mean (or a score of less than seventy) are considered in the range of mental retardation. The *DSM-IV* diagnostic criteria distinguish severity of mental retardation according to the number of standard deviations below the mean a child scores:

- between 2 and 3 standard deviations = IQ score of 69-55 = *mild* mental retardation

- between 3 and 4 standard deviations = IQ score of 54-40 = *moderate* mental retardation

- between 4 and 5 standard deviations = IQ score of 39-25 = *severe* mental retardation

- above 5 standard deviations = IQ score of below 25 = *profound* mental retardation

Most researchers and clinicians agree on a basic definition of learning disorders. Frick and Silverthorn summarize that consensus definition thus: "A learning disorder, or learning disability, is a disorder in one or more of the basic psychological processes involved in understanding or in using language (spoken or written) that may manifest itself in an impaired ability to listen, speak, read, write, spell, or perform mathematical calculations" (2001, p. 903). Disagreement, however, exists regarding the best way to classify children according to this definition (Culbertson, 1998; Beitchman and Young, 1997). Some, for example, focus on the cognitive processes that disrupt learning (e.g., language-based vs. perceptual-organizational difficulties). Others focus on the academic deficits that result from learning disabilities. This is the approach of the *DSM-IV.* Three specific academic deficits are identified as learning disorders: reading disorder, mathematics disorder and disorder of written expression. Prevalence studies report that anywhere from 2 to 15 percent of children struggle with learning disorders (APA, 1994; Gaddes and Edgell, 1993). These numbers are confounded by the disparity in approaches to classifying childhood learning disabilities. Often learning disorders are diagnosed within school systems on the basis of assessed discrepancies between a child's intellectual capacities (as assessed by intelligence testing) and academic achievement (as assessed by achievement testing). This practice may be problematic, since the processes involved in a learning disorder may confound both types of testing and therefore decrease the validity of conclusions drawn from the variance between the scores (Frick and Silverthorn, 2001; Culbertson, 1998).

Interestingly enough, the problem of low intelligence—when it includes mental retardation and the range of mental deficiency—is one of the most common problems described in the entire *DSM*. Taken together, nearly one out of five adults struggle with basic and often essential life skills. Malony and Ward (1976) contend that they are often exploited, coerced and manipulated (e.g., "last to be hired and first to be fired" in difficult economic times). No doubt this strains their capacity to deal with the tasks of everyday living.

Pervasive developmental disorders. The *DSM-IV* identifies four distinct categories of pervasive developmental disorders: autistic disorder, Asperger's disorder, Rhett's disorder and childhood disintegrative disorder. These categories share some common features (e.g., language skills deficits, social skills deficits), which has led some to argue that they should all be seen as variations along an autistic spectrum of disorder (Szatmari, 1997). Of the four, autistic disorder is the most pervasive and debilitating. Its diagnosis requires onset of symptoms before age three, though some studies report onset as early as twelve months (Osterling and Dawson, 1994). These symptoms include impairment in social interaction; impairment in communication; and restricted, repetitive and stereotyped patterns of behavior, interests and activities. Most epidemiological studies with this classification of disorders have related to autism. The *DSM-IV* reports that autistic disorder affects 0.02-0.05 percent of children. Studies also indicate that more males than females struggle with this disorder; ratios range from three to one to four to one (Frick and Silverthorn, 2001).

Asperger's disorder is the most similar to autistic disorder. Children diagnosed with this disorder struggle with similar social impairments and restricted range of interests and activities, but they do not evidence any delay in cognitive or language development.

Rhett's disorder is distinct from the other two in that girls with this disorder develop normally for the first five months of life (Rhett's is diagnosed only in females, and the exact reason for this gender difference is not entirely understood). At five months, they suddenly begin to deteriorate in previously acquired competencies (e.g., language skills, trunk and hand movements). Head growth begins to deteriorate sometime after five months and before forty-eight months, and they develop stereotypical hand movements.

Childhood disintegrative disorder is distinct in that normal development continues until age two, at which point significant decline and loss of competencies follows until about age ten. The areas of deterioration identified must include two of the following five: social skills, language skills, elimination functions, play and motor skills.

Tic disorders. Parent surveys in the United States have indicated that as many as 11 percent of girls and 18 percent of boys at some point during their developmental years display tics or other nervous movements. Such potentially high prevalence estimates may indicate that tics in some form represent normal developmental phenomena (Evans, King and Leckman, 1996); however, most often the presence of tics is experienced as disruptive and distressing to children and their parents. Tics have been defined as "involuntary, sudden, rapid, repetitive, nonrhythmic, unexpected, and purposeless muscular movements or vocal utterances" (Frick and Silverthorn, 2001, p. 907; see table 12.2 for examples). The *DSM-IV* identifies three specific disorders in which children and adolescents exhibit tics: Tourette's disorder, chronic motor or vocal tic disorder, and transient tic disorder. These are conceptualized on a continuum of severity, from the milder transient tic disorder to the more severe Tourette's disorder (Leckman and Cohen, 1991).

Transient tic disorder is diagnosed when a child exhibits motor and/ or vocal tics—either a singular distinct tic or multiple tics—numerous times throughout the day for a period of at least four weeks. But by definition, they do not last for more than one year without a period of remission of symptoms. The tics must be evident almost every day during that period. Transient tic disorder is the most common and most benign of the tic disorders, and the tics frequently dissipate without the need of treatment (Lerer, 1987). Chronic motor or vocal tic disorder is slightly more severe than transient tic disorder, because its symptoms continue beyond one year. The most severe tic disorder is Tourette's disorder, which is diagnosed only when both motor and vocal tics are evident for a period of more than one year. The *DSM-IV* reports the prevalence of Tourette's disorder at between 0.04 and 0.05 percent of children.

Table 12.2 Commonly Diagnosed Tics
(adapted from Evans, King & Leckman, 1996)

Motor Tics

head & facial movements may include
head jerks, eye blinking or movements, nose twitching, mouth and jaw
movements, teeth clicking

body movements may include
shoulder shrugs, arm jerks, kicking, stomach tensing, jerking of any
body part

complex motor tics may include
prolongued stares, aggressive actions (e.g., biting, banging, hitting),
repetitive touches, throwing objects, hand gestures (including obscene gesturing)

Vocal Tics

simple sounds may include
grunts, hisses, growls, barks, screeches, coughs, sniffles, clearing the
throat, sucking, spitting

complex sounds may include
atypical tones, accents, rhythms or intensity of speech; repetition of
own or other's words; random syllables, words or phrases; or obscene,
aggressive or inappropriate words or statements (coprolalia)

Elimination disorders. The *DSM-IV* identifies two elimination disorders: enuresis and encopresis. Enuresis is diagnosed when a child who
is five years old or older experiences repeated urinary incontinence—
at least twice per week for a period of three months or more—in the
absence of any organic pathology that might explain the incontinence. Two forms are distinguished. Primary enuresis is diagnosed
when a child reaches five years without ever having experienced a period of bladder control. Secondary enuresis is diagnosed when a child
experiences a loss of previously attained bladder control. Enuresis is
most common during the night. Studies report that anywhere from 15
to 20 percent of five-year-olds struggle with nocturnal enuresis. As one
would imagine, the prevalence decreases with age, with only about 2-4
percent of early adolescents experiencing nocturnal enuresis (Costello
et al., 1996; Shaffer et al., 1996; Frick and Silverthorn, 2001). The prevalence of diurnal enuresis is significantly less.

Encopresis is diagnosed when a child of four years or older experiences fecal incontinence at least once per month for a period of

three months, in the absence of any organic pathology that might explain the incontinence. Encopresis may also be distinguished as primary or secondary and as diurnal or nocturnal. With encopresis, diurnal is the most common form (Frick and Silverthorn, 2001). Three forms of encopresis have been labeled:

- manipulative soiling: voluntary fecal incontinence that functions to manipulate a desired outcome (e.g., avoidance of school or punishment)

- irritable bowel syndrome: diarrhea resulting from stress or emotional discomfort

- retentive encopresis: staining of undergarments due to constipation, impacted intestines and subsequent seepage

Retentive encopresis is by far the most common form of encopresis, representing 80-95 percent of all cases. Prevalence estimates report that only approximately 0.3-0.8 percent of children struggle with some form of encopresis (Costello et al., 1996).

It is worth restating that the above list represents only a select group of disorders suffered by children and adolescents. Many other disorders could (and probably should) be addressed in order to do justice to the nature of psychopathology in the lives of children and adolescents. A separate volume is needed to explore the unique developmental issues related to child and adolescent psychopathology and to explore integrative themes related to their experience.

ANTECEDENTS TO PROBLEMS OF CHILDHOOD AND ADOLESCENCE

Attention-deficit disorders. Myths abound regarding the "causes" of ADHD. Some of these include diet (especially excess sugar or caffeine), an inadequate school environment and poor parenting. None of these have been verified as direct causal explanations for ADHD; however, each of them may serve to complicate or exacerbate the symptoms and behaviors (Resnick, 1998). No universally accepted cause for the development of ADHD has as yet been identified. Theories have considered neurobiological mechanisms (e.g., abnormal brain functioning), neurochemical irregularities, environmental toxins (e.g., lead), diet and family factors (Zametkin and Liotta, 1998; Barkley, 1998). It is clear that neurological deficits are part of the symptom pattern in children with ADHD (Frick and Silverthorn, 2001). What is not clear is what leads to these neurological deficits.

According to Frick and Silverthorn, "The same neurological deficit can result from multiple causal pathways. It is also unclear what the core deficit is that results from the neurological dysfunction and underlies the behavioral symptomatology associated with ADHD" (2001, p. 884).

One theory of note is that of Barkley (1997), who suggests that behavioral inhibition is the central area of deficit and dysfunction with ADHD combined type. According to his theory, "Impairments in delayed response lead to difficulties with self-regulation, which lead to the symptoms of hyperactivity, impulsivity, distractibility, and secondary symptoms of inattention and executive dysfunctions" (Frick and Silverthorn, 2001, p. 884).

Disruptive behavior disorders. Numerous factors have been identified which seem to have some relation to the development of ODD and CD in children and adolescents. These can be divided into factors within the child or adolescent and factors within their psychosocial environment (Frick and Silverthorn, 2001). Factors within the individual child or adolescent include neurochemical irregularities (e.g., lower levels of serotonin or epinephrine and higher levels of testosterone; see Kreusi et al., 1990; Magnusson, 1988; Olweus et al., 1988; Scerbo and Kolko, 1994) and central nervous system abnormalities (Lahey, McBurnett, Loeber and Hart, 1995). Factors within the context of the child include certain family dynamics (e.g., psychopathology in the parents, parental conflict and divorce, minimal parental involvement and supervision in the child's life, and inconsistent or overly critical discipline), peer isolation and rejection, association with other children with behavior problems, and lower socioeconomic status with limited opportunities for social and educational growth (Coie, Dodge and Kupersmidt, 1990; Wilson, 1987).

Other factors associated with the presence of ODD or CD include impulse control response inhibition problems, tendencies to respond behaviorally to rewards more often than to punishments, certain cognitive deficits (verbal abilities, executive functions and overall IQ), and deficits in social information processing, leading to aggressive interpersonal behaviors (Frick and Silverthorn, 2001).

It is unclear whether any of these factors represent direct causal links to the symptom behaviors of ODD and CD. They may only represent factors associated with the presence of these symptoms and perhaps even resulting from those symptoms. The most widely accepted perspective on the relationship of these factors to the development of ODD or CD is that the risk of developing one of these disorders increases with the cumulative effect of the presence of multiple factors. Recent studies have gone further, suggesting that different causal pathways may exist for childhood-onset and adolescent-onset, because those who develop symptoms in childhood seem to have more significant cognitive and neuropsychological deficits and greater family dysfunction. Moffitt (1993) suggests that this represents a more severe form of psychopathology (perhaps even characterological) than that present in those who develop symptoms in adolescence. Moffitt therefore views adolescent-onset CD as "more of an exaggeration of the normative developmental process of separation and individuation that characterizes adolescence" (Frick and Silverthorn, 2001, p. 889).

Mental retardation and learning disorders. The antecedents of mental retardation are typically thought of in terms of three major categories: genetic, physical and psychosocial. Chromosomal abnormalities lead to a number of syndromes that may manifest mental retardation as a common symptom. Down syndrome is the most common of these. It involves a third chromosome in the twenty-first of the twenty-three normal chromosome pairs and results in a myriad of symptoms including moderate to severe mental retardation. Physical problems associated with the normal developmental process may result in mental retardation. These can occur before, during and after birth. These include prenatal infection and trauma (e.g., drug abuse by the mother), premature birth, oxygen deprivation or head injury during birth, or any of various tragedies during childhood development (e.g., infection, malnutrition, poisons, oxygen deprivation, head injury). Psychosocial causes include emotional disturbance or a psychosocial environment grossly lacking in care, nutrition, intellectual stimulation and daily life skills instruction (Ferguson, 1999).

Theories regarding the origins of learning disorders are diverse, in part because of the varying approaches to understanding and classifying them. Frick and Silverthorn (2001) identify four emphases in the literature on etiology of learning disorders:

* family factors

* genetics (Pennington and Smith, 1988)

* neuroanatomy—physiological abnormalities that lead to problems in cognitive processing (Hynd and Willis, 1988; Beitchman and Young, 1997)

- psycholinguistic functioning—difficulties in processing sounds or producing them (Torgesen, 1986)

According to Frick and Silverthorn, "advances in our understanding of learning disorders have been limited by the lack of agreement on classifying children with these disorders" (2001, p. 904).

Pervasive developmental disorders. Current conceptualizations seem to favor neurobiological origins to pervasive developmental disorders. Neurochemical abnormalities (primarily elevated levels of serotonin, although some studies have identified abnormalities in noradrenergic, dopaminergic and opioid systems; McBride et al., 1998; Smalley, Levitt and Bauman, 1998) and neuroanatomical abnormalities (cerebellum, limbic system, cerebral cortex and overall brain size; Mesibov, Adams and Klinger, 1997) are a common focus of study. Twin concordance rate studies suggest that genetic factors play a significant role in the development of pervasive developmental disorders (Klinger and Dawson, 1996; Mesibov, Adams and Klinger, 1997). Some studies have found that as many as 25 percent of siblings of autistic children struggle with some form of cognitive developmental delay, which suggests that "autistic disorder may be on a continuum with other cognitive deficits" (Frick and Silverthorn, 2001, p. 900; see also Klinger and Dawson, 1996; Schreibman and Charlop-Christy, 1998).

Some studies have suggested a link between maternal health during pregnancy and autistic disorder (Mesibov, Adams and Klinger, 1997; Smalley, Levitt and Bauman, 1998).

Tic disorders. The precise origin of the pathology of tic disorders is still unknown. However, most current conceptualizations accept an interactive model that focuses on four factors in the etiology of tic disorders, especially Tourette's disorder. This model assumes that a genetic predisposition is required for the possibility of the disorder. These genes affect the development of the central nervous system and result in a particular neurobiological substrate within that system that affects the channeling of information regarding planning and monitoring motor functioning in the body. This substrate may also affect the circuits in the central nervous system that process cognitive and emotional information and regulate stress. Over the course of the child's development, a clinical phenotype begins to emerge that is further shaped by environmental factors, leading ultimately to the symptom patterns evident in the disorder (Evans, King and Leckman, 1996).

Some evidence suggests that the genetic predisposition associated with Tourette's disorder may be one shared by obsessive-compulsive disorder, and there is also some evidence for neurochemical irregularities in children with Tourette's disorder (Frick and Silverthorn, 2001).

Elimination disorders. Numerous biological factors may lead to difficulties with bladder and bowel control (e.g., infections, diabetes, neurological problems); however, enuresis and encopresis, by definition, are not diagnosed when such pathology is evident. Various factors have been considered as potential contributors to the development of these disorders, and these typically fall into six categories of theories. These theory categories are biological, developmental, psychopathological, psychodynamic, behavioral and family systems (Carr, 1999). Table 12.3 presents the basic tenets of these theories. It is worth noting that controlled studies fail to find any causal relationship between psychological disturbance and enuresis or encopresis (Frick and Silverthorn, 2001; see Ondersma and Walker, 1998; Walker, Milling and Bonner, 1988; Werry, 1986).

TREATMENT THEMES

In general, studies report significant positive effects with treatment of psychopathology in children and adolescents (Carr, 1999). Weisz and Weiss (1993) reviewed four meta-analyses of more than two hundred research studies encompassing over eleven thousand cases of psychopathology. They concluded that children receiving direct therapeutic interventions showed greater reduction of symptoms on assessment measures than 75 percent of untreated children in control groups. In addition, they reported that this improvement was still evident at follow-up assessments. Meta-analyses and narrative reviews of family therapy with children showed similar positive gains as a result of treatment (Shadish et al., 1993; Lebow and Gurman, 1995).

Carr (1999) reviewed the literature of child and family psychotherapy identifying key variables in effective treatment of children and adolescents. He presented these factors in a table, which we have reproduced as table 12.4 (see p. 362).

Attention-deficit disorders. Treatment for ADHD in childhood has lifelong ramifications. Studies have indicated that anywhere from 30 to 50 percent of children who are diagnosed with ADHD in childhood will exhibit symptoms into adulthood, and as many as 50 to 80 percent of them will exhibit symptoms during adolescence (Biederman, 1998; Barkley, 1998).

Treatment strategies for children and adolescents with ADHD typically include medication and behavior management training for par-

Table 12.3 Theories and Treatments of Elimination Disorders (Adapted from Carr, 1999, p. 207. Used by permission.)

Theory Type	Theoretical Principles	Principles of Treatment
Biological	Elimination problems are due to genetic factors or to urinary or anorectal structural or functional abnormalities.	Medication or surgery to rectify abnormalities or training in how to cope with them
Developmental	Elimination disorders are part of a specific or general developmental delay.	Reassurance and behavioral training
Psycho-pathological	Elimination disorders are part of a broader set of psychological problems. Psychopathology may cause elimination disorders. Psychopathology may arise from elimination disorders. Behavior problems and elimination problems may both be an expression of underlying psychopathology.	Psychological treatment for both the elimination problem and the psychopathology
Psychodynamic	Elimination problems are an expression of unconscious conflicts associated with neglectful or coercive parental toilet training during the anal stage of development.	Psychodynamic play therapy to help resolve conflicts underpinning elimination problems
Behavioral	Lack of positive reinforcement for appropriate toileting, or the association of toileting with pain or other aversive experiences, prevents the development or maintenance of appropriate toileting habits.	Behavioral program to learn appropriate toileting habits

Theory Type	Theoretical Principles	Principles of Treatment
Family Systems	Primary elimination problems may be due to living in a chaotic family environment. Secondary elimination problems may arise from acute stressful life events and family lifecycle transitions. Elimination problems may be maintained by coercive, intrusive, or triangulating interaction patterns with parents or caregivers.	Family therapy to alter interaction patterns that maintain the elimination problems

ents and teachers. The most widely used medications focus on central nervous system stimulation. These include methylphenidate (Ritalin), dextroamphetamine (Dexedrin), Pemoline (Cylert), methamphetamine (Desoxyn) or amphetamine salts (Adderall; Pelham, 1987; Sallee and Gill, 1998). To many, the use of stimulants for children who struggle with being still seems counterintuitive. The stimulant appears, however, to increase the child's ability to stay focused and direct his or her energy toward a specified goal, such as an academic task in school (Pelham et al., 1985). As many as 70 percent of children will show an immediate improvement on stimulant medications (Frick and Silverthorn, 2001); however, the medications alone do not seem to change the long-term course and prognosis of the disorder (Findling and Dogin, 1998).

Parent and teacher training programs aim to teach them how to "design and implement very structured and consistent behavioral management programs that (1) set clear behavioral goals for the child, (2) have a clear monitoring system to assess progress toward these goals, and (3) have a structured set of consequences designed to encourage behavioral goals and discourage negative behaviors" (Frick and Silverthorn, 2001, p. 885; see Barkley, 1997; Pfiffner and O'Leary, 1993). Psychotherapeutic interventions with the child have demonstrated some improvement in laboratory measures of attention and impulsivity in controlled studies but have not demonstrated any significant change in home and school behaviors (Frick and Silverthorn, 2001; Richters et al., 1995; Abikoff, 1985).

Table 12.4 Factors Influencing the Outcome of Psychological Treatment of Children (Adapted from Carr, 1999, pp. 82-83. Used by permission.)

Domain	Variable	Good treatment response	Poor treatment response
Child	Diagnosis	Internalizing and externalizing disorders	Pervasive developmental disorders
	Comorbidity	Single diagnosis	Comorbid diagnoses
	Severity	Mild problems	Severe problems
	Chronicity	Later age of onset and briefer duration	Chronic cases with early onset
	Age	Younger cases	Older cases
	Gender	Female	Male
Family	Parental adjustment	Good health and adjustment	Psychological or physical health problems
	Marital satisfaction	Marital satisfaction	Marital discord
	Family functioning	Flexible family functioning	Family disorganization
	Father absence	Father is involved	Father is not involved
	Socioeconomic status	High socioeconomic status	Low socioeconomic status
Professional network	Agency involvement	Single agency involvement	Multiagency involvement
	Coercive referral	Regular referral	Coercive referral
	Solicited referral	Solicited referral	Regular referral

Domain	Variable	Good treatment response	Poor treatment response
Treatment System	Therapeutic alliance	Positive alliance	Poor alliance
	Therapeutic model	Cognitive-behavioral better than systemic, humanistic and psychodynamic models	—
	Therapeutic modality for internalizing behavior problems	Individual, group and family modalities	—
	Therapy modality for externalizing and severe debilitating problems	Extensive family involvement	Individual or group formats
	Therapy duration	10 sessions and booster sessions	Fewer than 10 sessions without follow-up
	Therapist commitment to the model	Therapist is committed to the model	Therapist is not committed to the model
	Treatment manuals	Flexible use of manualized treatments	Rigid use of treatment manuals or non-manualized therapies
Evaluation system	Outcome measure	Specific measures of goal attainment	General measures
	Outcome rater	Independent observers, therapists and parents	Children receiving treatment, their peers and their teachers

Source: Based on data reviewed in Weisz and Weiss (1993); Kazdin (1994); Lebow and Gurman (1995); Carr (1997); Shadish et al. (1993)

The most effective treatment approach appears to be a multimodal strategy incorporating both medication and behavioral intervention. Some studies have reported results of such programs, in which children diagnosed with ADHD are indistinguishable from non-ADHD-impaired children following treatment (e.g., Gittelman-Klein et al., 1980).

Disruptive behavior disorders. Treatment for ODD and CD is a critical issue not only for the children and adolescents involved but for society as well. The symptoms of CD, in particular, seem to be remarkably stable over time, with a high rate of adult psychopathology and disruptive behavior problems among persons who were diagnosed with CD in childhood or adolescence. "Longitudinal studies that followed children with CD into adulthood found that from 43-60% of boys and approximately 17% of girls with CD were arrested for criminal behavior by adulthood and about 31% of boys and 17% of girls were diagnosed with antisocial personalities as adults" (Frick and Silverthorn, 2001, p. 890; see Krazter and Hodgins, 1997).

Frick and Silverthorn (2001) identify four categories of treatment which have been demonstrated in controlled outcome studies to be effective in treating children with ODD and CD:

1. behavioral strategies using basic operant conditioning to develop structured contingency management programs

2. parent management training (PMT) focused on teaching in-home structured contingency management and more effective supervision and discipline

3. cognitive behavioral strategies focused on empowering children to deal with deficits in social cognition and social problem-solving

4. stimulant medication—because of the high rate of comorbidity with ADHD (2001, p. 890)

Some of the more promising emerging approaches involve simultaneous intervention in multiple contexts, focused on multiple processes in the child (e.g., Families and Schools Together Program). Significant success has been reported by those that are designed to be flexible to the specific needs of the individual child (e.g., multisystemic therapy; Frick and Silverthorn, 2001; see Conduct Problems Prevention Research Group, 1992; Henggeler and Borduin, 1990; Borduin et al., 1995; Henggeler, Melton and Smith, 1992; Henggeler, Schoenwald and Pickrel, 1995).

Pervasive developmental disorders. Sadly, the prognosis is often not good for children diagnosed with these developmental disorders.

Werry (1996) indicates that as many as 90 percent of children diagnosed with autistic disorder will continue to struggle intellectually and socially throughout the remainder of their life and that only 10 percent or fewer become symptom free. Medications have proved less effective than was hoped, given the common neurobiological theories for the etiology of these disorders (Smalley, Levitt and Bauman, 1998). The most common treatment approaches are behavioral and comprehensive in scope, including emphases on symptom reduction and social and intellectual skill development (Rogers, 1998).

Perhaps the best known of these comprehensive behavioral programs is the approach of Lovaas (1987). This program involves direct, one-to-one supervision by a trained treatment provider thirty to forty hours per week, focusing on social skills, daily life skills and cognitive skills in an intensive operant-reinforcement model. Significant gains in these areas have been reported when this program has been implemented (Rogers, 1998). Those who have done this work often describe it as some of the most demanding, exhausting work they have ever done. It is not uncommon to see requests for help in college or university psychology departments from overwhelmed parents or caregivers.

Mental retardation and learning disorders. Educational services centered within the school system are the most common treatment interventions available to children with mental retardation. Treatments aim to discern realistic goals for progress in light of the degree of impairment and to offer training in the personal skills that are lacking.

One area of focus in recent years has been "mainstreaming" or "normalization." This strategy involves enabling mentally retarded children and adolescents to enter the mainstream of the educational system with "normal" children and to participate in all aspects of "normal" child and adolescent educational and social life within their capabilities. This concept is based on the idea that mentally challenged children possess the same rights as nonimpaired children and ought to be able to benefit from opportunities available in mainstream society.

Behavior modification is often incorporated in the treatment of mentally retarded children and adolescents. The focus most often is on basic behavior and personality challenges. These may be addressed through individual and family therapy, special educational programming, or institutionalization in extreme cases. Education and training for parents of these children is critical, and in many cases a therapy or support group is beneficial. Accepting the limitations of their child and learning the basic skills necessary to manage their child's care and provide continuity of treatment goals at home are important goals of this level of care. A key in all of these strategies is fostering an environment of care that facilitates "self-sufficiency and self-respect" (Ferguson, 1999).

Treatment approaches for *learning disorders* vary along the lines of conceptualization and classification approaches (Ingersol and Goldstein, 1993). Treatment strategies include neuropsychological assessment and targeted education intended to overcome difficulties in processing information; language skills training to address reading deficits; and cognitive interventions targeting issues like self-monitoring and problem-solving skills (Frick and Silverthorn, 2001).

Tic disorders. With the more severe of these disorders, psychopharmacological treatments are the most common and effective intervention. Tourette's disorder has been linked to the dopaminergic pathways of the body's neurochemistry, and studies of medications targeting these neurochemicals evidence a reduction of symptoms in 70 to 80 percent of children with Tourette's disorder (Towbin and Cohen, 1996; Shapiro et al., 1988). However, side effects with these medications are unpleasant and in some cases permanent. Psychotherapy treatments include self-monitoring, contingency management, massed negative practice, relaxation training and habit reversal (Schroder and Gordon, 1991).

Elimination disorders. Although a small percentage of enuretic children will gain bladder control without intervention, the vast majority will require some treatment in order to avoid prolonged urinary incontinence. Psychopharmacological treatments have had some success, with the most common being the use of a tricyclic antidepressant (imipramine). Frick and Silverthorn (2001) reported that 85 percent of children in controlled studies improve within two weeks; however, significant side effects and high recidivism rates when the medication is discontinued make this a less than ideal intervention. Behavioral treatments are the preferred approach. The most common approach remains a technique first developed in the 1930s by Mowrer and Mowrer (1938), which involves the use of a urine-sensitive pad placed in the child's pajamas or bed sheets which emits an alarm when wet. Some 60-90 percent of children experience successful remission of the disorder through a two-phase use of this technique (Ondersma and Walker, 1998).

The literature on treatment of enuresis is much more extensive

Table 12.5 Common Treatment Approaches for Encopresis
(adapted from Frick & Silverthorn, 2001, p. 906)

Type of Encopresis	Treatment Approach
Manipulative Soiling	Treatments most often focus on teaching parents how to extinguish any reinforcement to the soiling behavior experienced by the child, to provide positive reinforcement for appropriate toileting behaviors, and to teach appropriate ways for the child to control aspects of his or her environment that are distressing.
Irritable Bowel Syndrome or Chronic Diarrhea	This condition is most often related to stress and anxiety, and treatment strategies therefore focus on changing the environmental situations that are producing this stress or on teaching the child techniques to reduce or cope with anxiety.
Retentive Encopresis	The most promising treatment involves combining medical (to evacuate the impacted area) and behavioral strategies.

than that for encopresis—a disturbing fact, given the stress and shame often associated with encopresis in children (Frick and Silverthorn, 2001). Treatment for encopresis largely depends on the specific type of encopresis with which the child struggles. These are briefly outlined in table 12.5. For a more comprehensive discussion of treatment strategies, see Walker, Milling and Bonner, 1988.

INTEGRATIVE THEMES

Psychopathology during childhood and adolescence is a relatively recent focus of theory, research and treatment. Many myths and much misinformation have characterized that brief history. For example, during the mid-nineteenth century, many believed that "insanity" in children was caused by overstimulation in school, and during the mid-twentieth century, autism was believed to be caused by inadequate parenting practices (Mash and Barkley, 1996). The study of child and adolescent psychopathology is still a young discipline; however, it is evident that "psychopathology during childhood represents a frequently occurring and significant societal concern" (Mash and

Barkley, 1996, p. 9), and it ought to be a significant concern for us all. Mash and Barkley offer six reasons society ought to pay particular attention to the struggles of children and adolescents, and these offer a helpful framework for us to consider some integrative themes related to these struggles.

Many children suffer from the effects of psychopathology. Estimates run as high as 14-22 percent of all children suffering a diagnosable disorder at some time during their childhood (Brandenberg, Friedman and Silver, 1990). In reality, given the number of children who grow up in an environment lacking the resources or care to be diagnosed and treated, the prevalence is probably higher. At first glance, the prevalence of "disordered" children seems staggering and tragic; however, it should not come as a surprise to Christians. At the core of all psychopathology is sin. Whether we speak of sin as the condition of things in this world due to the work of Satan and the disobedience of Adam and Eve or as the willful choices to do evil that every human being makes, we all are disordered. The effects of sin are more devastating to the lives of some than to the lives of others, however, and suffering due to sin in the lives of children seldom reflects consequences of their own sinful choices. Rather, the suffering of children due to volitional sin is almost always a consequence of the choices of others.

Children who suffer from diagnosable psychopathology are not responsible for their own suffering. As they develop and gain the capacity to be responsible for their own behavior, it is still important to discern whether they have ever experienced a solid enough foundation for learning how to make healthy and moral choices. Thus much of the assessment and treatment of children needs to focus on the family—the system out of which they have come. Treatment of children, at its most fundamental level, needs to be viewed as treatment of the family, with recognition of intergenerational patterns of disorder and sin that may be the source of a child's psychopathology.

In addition, it is critical that the church take a more active role in seeking understanding of the developmental processes of childhood and their impact on the behaviors, thoughts and emotions of children. These issues need to be a focus of ministry training and parent education. It is paramount that those involved on any level with the education and spiritual formation of children be aware of developmental issues that lead children to behave in ways that are *appropriately* different from what is expected from adults. There is an important difference, for example, between egocentrism and selfishness. At the same time, those involved in the mental health care of children need to be aware of the spiritual issues that may be at work in children's developmental struggles. Christian mental health professionals are uniquely qualified (or they ought to be) to address this integrative task.

Most children don't "outgrow" their symptoms. The problems that children and adolescents face are real, and the symptoms can bring tragic consequences on into their adulthood. The challenges for appropriate diagnosis of psychopathology in children and adolescents are many. Experts in the field disagree on how best to conceptualize and respond to the many and diverse problems that face the young among us, and the consequences of overdiagnosis or underdiagnosis of these problems can be devastating in the lives of children and their families. Sadly, popular opinion and responses to psychopathology in children often swing dramatically between these extremes—underpathologizing (denial that the problem exists) and overpathologizing (inaccurately attributing "normal" childhood experience and behavior to pathology). In his provocatively titled book *Why Do Christians Shoot Their Wounded?* Dwight Carlson (1994) addresses the first of these—the reluctance in many groups within Christian subcultures to acknowledge the reality of psychopathology. The second is equally devastating.

A contemporary example of this can be seen in the dramatic increase in societal attention given to ADHD within recent years. The pathology of attention deficit hyperactivity disorder is very real, and the symptoms can be profoundly debilitating in extreme cases. However, some children are diagnosed with ADHD inappropriately; in such cases a systemic intervention with the family would be more helpful and less stigmatizing for the child. Careful assessment is extremely important, and the process of the assessment needs to be carried out in a way that fosters the confidence and self-respect of the child or adolescent.

Within the church, responses to children who have been identified with special needs or problems of psychopathology need to reflect the best of our integrative endeavors. Being involved in the spiritual formation of children constitutes a profound responsibility, and those who undertake this ministry need to pay attention to the best information available about the care of children who are suffering. Where possible, those in Christian ministries ought to work together with Christians in mental health fields to understand how to respond to these children's needs in ways that foster their relationship with

God and their place within the community of faith.

Innovative approaches to ministry with children have much to contribute to our understanding of the functioning of children within the community of faith. For example, Scottie May, in a research project titled "A Study of the Effect of Pace, Space and Volume on the Attitudes and Behaviors of Young Children," is exploring the learning environments of children within the church as well as the impact that an intentional, multigenerational, multiage learning environment has on the spiritual formation of children. Christian psychologists need to be aware of such research and how it can aid our understanding of children labeled with "behavior problems."

The problems of children are real. Without intentional care, their symptoms usually don't spontaneously disappear, and it is the collective responsibility of the community of faith to prioritize our care for them. Jesus himself said, "Whoever welcomes a little child like this in my name welcomes me. But if anyone causes one of these little ones who believe in me to sin, it would be better for him to have a large millstone hung around his neck and to be drowned in the depths of the sea" (Mt 18:5-6).

Societal changes may be placing children at increasing risk of psychopathology. Citing the National Commission on Children (1991), Mash and Dozois list these social stresses as

> multigenerational adversity in inner cities, chronic poverty in women and children, pressures of family break-up, single parenting, homelessness, problems of the rural poor, difficulties of North American Native American children, adjustment problems of children in immigrant families, and conditions associated with the impact of prematurity, HIV, cocaine, and alcohol on children's growth and development. (1996, p. 9)

The Scriptures speak of the response of God to such conditions as these:

> The LORD is a refuge for the oppressed,
>   a stronghold in times of trouble. (Ps 9:9)

> You hear, O LORD, the desire of the afflicted;
>   you encourage them, and you listen to their cry,
> defending the fatherless and the oppressed,
>   in order that man, who is of the earth, may terrify no more.
>   (Ps 10:17-18)

It is the work of the church in this world to respond as God would to injustice. Paul says that we are "Christ's ambassadors, as though God were making his appeal through us" (2 Cor 5:20). Who will advocate for the children if not the church?

The conditions of our society are worsening, and the church's voice needs to rise to the forefront in a call for repentance. Christians whose ministry it is to care for the souls of those who are struggling must let their voices be heard—not just within the Christian community but within the society at large. This is particularly true when it comes to the suffering of children and adolescents, who lack the ability to rise up as a collective group and advocate for themselves.

The changes of society are not limited to the devastating conditions mentioned above and highlighted in secular research.[2] Many of them may be symptomatic of deeper value shifts within the fabric of our society—away from foundational assumptions about right and wrong, truth and falsehood, hope and denial. As collective moral consciousness erodes, the bases on which we determine the limits of personal responsibility, appropriate behavior and our general concept of mental health become relativistic ideals open to interpretation. These shifts make it increasingly difficult to establish standards of conduct as a society, and they make it difficult to establish clear markers for the development of morally and societally acceptable behavior in children and adolescents.

Adolescence itself is becoming increasingly difficult to define. The concept has no origins in premodern cultures; there are no conclusive biological or psychosocial markers to delineate its beginning or ending, nor are there clear societal standards of responsibility expected at a time of rite of passage into adulthood. Today we are witnessing the inevitable lengthening of this ambiguous developmental period. Increasing numbers of "adults" don't want to give up the perceived carefree existence of "adolescence." We are becoming somewhat confused as a society about what adolescence means. While we are convicting children as "adults" in our courtrooms, many adults in their thirties are living at home with their parents.

Adolescence is not a concept that emerges from the Scriptures or that is evident in the biblical world. The Mosaic law recognized a rite

---

[2]We use the term *secular* without any intended derogatory meaning. We use it simply to denote research that does not arise from faith-based assumptions or agendas.

of passage from childhood to adulthood around the time of puberty. Paul acknowledges the difference between reasoning that is childlike and that which is adult. Wherever the Scriptures speak of the onset of adult categories of faith and life, ideas of maturity and responsibility are implicit. These qualities seem to be increasingly absent from our concepts of adolescence. Voices of reason grounded in a view of human beings that calls for right behavior, moral responsibility and personal maturity need to be heard.

The number of children suffering abusive treatment is staggering. Abuse is at least one factor in the development of childhood and adolescent psychopathology that is clearly rooted in the presence of evil in this world. The volumes used to research this chapter discuss many aspects of our world which diminish the ability of children and adolescents to develop in a healthy way and to live adjusted and fulfilling lives. However, few of these consider the reality of sin and evil. It is not within the scope of work for the vast majority of clinical psychologists, psychiatrists or mental health professionals to consider the impact of sin and evil on the development of psychopathology in children. Yet as believers, we know that this is the root of the problem.

Children not only live in a world in which evil exists, many are the victims of horrible experiences of evil: horrific abuse, violence, abject poverty. There is great need for theory formulation, research and treatment planning that acknowledges the reality of evil and sin and the impact of these on the developmental processes of childhood and adolescence. If this work does not emerge from Christians in the field of mental health, it will not likely be done.

Childhood psychopathology results in devastating lifelong consequences for the child, family and community. There is a very important stewardship issue to be considered as we discuss problems of childhood and adolescence. To the degree that we neglect the struggles of our children and adolescents, we only postpone the inevitable. The problems of childhood and adolescence become the problems of adulthood, and with that development they often become more costly on many levels. The pathologies become more difficult to treat, as they are entrenched in the developmental process of the person and become lifelong patterns of behavior and relating. The disruptive behavior of children may become the criminal behavior of adults. As disordered children become disordered adults, the suffering is more likely to multiply to family members, succeeding generations and society. Financial costs for society also increase in terms of treatment, disability, unemployment, litigation and the like.

Though this stewardship issue is an important one to recognize, it is not the primary reason for society to pay attention to the struggles of childhood and adolescence. The primary reason is that we should value the experience of our children, recognize their vulnerability and dependence on the goodwill of society to respond to their suffering, and respond to the call of God to care for those who are suffering, oppressed and unable to care for themselves.

"As many as 70% of children in need of special attention do not receive services." Children are an underserved population. For many of the reasons already mentioned, children as a constituency don't receive the care that they need. In addition, empirically validated programs of prevention and treatment are still as yet unavailable for many of the disorders of childhood and adolescence (Mash and Barkley, 1986). As a society, on one level we are preoccupied with the experience of adolescence. One merely has to tune in to radio or TV or scan film reviews to see the degree to which we cater to the adolescent audience. However, our attention as a society is not on the suffering of our young. This is a profound statement of our society's values—one for which we as Christians ought to feel discomfort, if not shame.

Those of us working with children and adolescents face some rather difficult challenges. One painful reality is that we cannot control all the contingencies of their lives (or even our own). Being a consistent, firm and supportive caregiver requires extra measures of wisdom, discernment and compassion and should drive us once again to our worshiping and fellowshiping communities of faith. None of us can respond effectively in the long run apart from a supportive context that helps give us a sense of efficacy, meaning and purpose.

The church as a whole, and especially Christians within the field of mental health, can stand against the tide by intentionally attending to the issues that face children and adolescents who struggle with psychopathology. In so doing, we will reflect the compassionate call of Jesus:

> Let the little children come to me, and do not hinder them, for the kingdom of God belongs to such as these. (Mt 19:14; Mk 10:14; Lk 18:16)

RECOMMENDED READING

Frick, P. J., and Silverthorn, P. (2001). Psychopathology in children. In P. B. Sutker and H. E. Adams (Eds.), *Comprehensive handbook of psychopathology* (3rd ed.) (pp. 881-920). New York: Kluwer Academic/ Plenum. A thorough consideration of clinical research and treatment on psychopathology in children.

Parrott, L. (1993). *Helping the struggling adolescent: A guide to thirty-six common problems for counselors, pastors, and youth workers.* Grand Rapids, MI: Zondervan. This book offers in the first half a helpful framework for thinking about how to communicate fundamentals of adolescent psychopathology and treatment to a nonprofessional audience.

Ratcliff, D. (2004). *Children's spirituality: Christian perspectives, research, and applications.* Eugene, OR: Cascade Books. This book represents some of the most current research and discussion on the nature of spirituality in children.

REFERENCES

Abikoff, H. (1985). Efficacy of cognitive training interventions in hyperactive children: A critical review. *Clinical Psychology Review, 5,* 479-512.

American Psychiatric Association. (1994). *Diagnostic and statistical manual of mental disorders* (4th ed.). Washington, DC: Author.

Anderson, J. C., Williams, S., McGee, R., and Silva, P. (1987). *DSM-III* disorders in preadolescent children. *Archives of General Psychiatry, 44,* 69-76.

Arnold, L. E., Abikoff, H. B., Cantwell, D. P., Conners, C. K., Elliot, G., Greenhill, L. L., Hechtman, L., Hinshaw, S. P., Hoza, B., Jensen, P. S., Kraemer, H. C., March, J. S., Newcorn, J. H., Pelham, W. E., Richters, J. E., Schiller, E., Severe, J. B., Swanson, J. M., Vereen, D., and Wells, K. C. (1997). National institute of mental health collaborative multimodal treatment study of children with ADHD (the MTA). *Archives of General Psychiatry, 54,* 865-70.

Barkley, R. A. (1997). Behavioral inhibition, sustained attention and executive functions: Constructing a unifying theory of ADHD. *Psychological Bulletin, 121,* 65-94.

Barkley, R. A. (1998). Attention-deficit/hyperactivity disorder. In E. J. Mash and R. A. Barkley (Eds.), *Child psychopathology* (pp. 63-112). New York: Guilford.

Becker, U. (1979). The child in theology and church. *Ecumenical Review, 31*(3), 234-40.

Beitchman, J. H., and Young, A. R. (1997). Learning disorders with a special emphasis on reading disorders: A review of the past 10 years. *Journal of the American Academy of Child and Adolescent Psychiatry, 36,* 1020-32.

Biederman, J. (1998). Attention-deficit/hyperactivity disorder: A lifespan perspective. *Journal of Clinical Psychiatry, 59*(suppl. 7), 4-16.

Borduin, C. M., Mann, B. J., Cone, L. T., Henggeler, S. W., Fucci, B. R., Blaske, D. M., and Williams, R. A. (1995). Multisystemic treatment of serious juvenile offenders: Long term prevention of criminality and violence. *Journal of Consulting and Clinical Psychology, 63,* 569-78.

Brandenburg, N. A., Friedman, R. M., and Silver, S. E. (1990). The epidemiology of childhood psychiatric disorders: Prevalence findings from recent studies. *Journal of the American Academy of Child and Adolescent Psychiatry, 29,* 76-83.

Bunge, M. J. (2001). *The child in Christian thought.* Grand Rapids, MI: Eerdmans.

Cantwell, D. P. (1996). Attention deficit disorder: A review of the past 10 years. *Journal of American Academy of Child and Adolescent Psychiatry, 35,* 978-87.

Carlson, D. L. (1994). *Why do Christians shoot their wounded? Helping (not hurting) those with emotional difficulties.* Downers Grove, IL: InterVarsity Press.

Carr, A. (1997). *Family therapy and systemic consultation.* Lanham, MD: University Press of America.

Carr, A. (1999). *The handbook of child and adolescent clinical psychology: A contextual approach.* London: Routledge.

Christian, R., Frick, P. J., Hill, N., Tyler, L. A., and Frazer, D. (1997). Psychopathy and conduct problems in children, part 2: Subtyping children with conduct problems based on their interpersonal and affective style. *Journal of the American Academy of Child and Adolescent Psychiatry, 36,* 233-41.

Cicchetti, D., and Tucker, D. (1994). Development and self-regulatory structures of the mind. *Development and Psychopathology, 6,* 533-49.

Clark, S. M. (1998). Child and adolescent diagnosis with *DSM-IV.* In G. P. Koocher, J. C. Norcross and S. S. Hill (Eds.), *Psychologists' desk reference* (pp. 100-103). New York: Oxford University Press.

Cohen, P., Cohen, J., Dasen, S., Velez, C. N., Hartmark, C., Johnson, J., Rojas, M., Brook, J., and Streuning, E. L. (1993). An epidemiological study of disorders in late childhood and adolescence, part 1:

Age- and gender-specific prevalence. *Journal of Child Psychology and Psychiatry, 34,* 851-67.

Coie, J. D., Dodge, K. A., and Kupersmidt, J. B. (1990). Peer group behavior and social status. In S. R. Asher and J. D. Coie (Eds.), *Peer rejection in childhood: Cambridge studies in social and emotional development* (pp. 17-59). New York: Cambridge University Press.

Conduct Problems Prevention Research Group. (1992). A developmental and clinical model for the prevention of conduct disorder: The FAST Track Program. *Development and Psychopathology, 4,* 509-27.

Costello, E. J., Angold, A., Burns, B. J., Stangl, D. K., Tweed, D. L., Erkanli, A., and Worthman, C. M. (1996). The Great Smoky Mountains Study of Youth: Goals, design, methods and the prevalence of *DSM-III-R* disorders. *Archives of General Psychiatry, 53,* 1129-36.

Crick, N. R., and Grotpeter, J. K. (1995). Relational aggression, gender and social-psychological adjustment. *Child Development, 66,* 710-22.

Culbertson, J. L. (1998). Learning disabilities. In T. H. Ollendick and M. Hersen (Eds.), *Handbook of child psychopathology* (3rd ed.) (pp. 117-56). New York: Plenum.

Evans, D. W., King, R. A., and Leckman, J. F. (1996). Tic disorders. In E. J. Mash and R. A. Barkley (Eds.), *Child psychopathology* (pp. 436-54). New York: Guilford.

Ferguson, L. N. (1999). Mental retardation. In D. G. Benner and P. C. Hill (Eds.), *Baker encyclopedia of psychology and counseling* (2nd ed.) (pp. 744-50). Grand Rapids, MI: Baker.

Findling, R. L., and Dogin, J. W. (1998). Psychopharmacology of ADHD: Children and adolescents. *Journal of Clinical Psychiatry, 59*(suppl. 7), 42-49.

Frick, P. J., and Silverthorn, P. (2001). Psychopathology in children. In P. B. Sutker and H. E. Adams (Eds.), *Comprehensive handbook of psychopathology* (pp. 881-920). New York: Kluwer Academic/Plenum.

Gaddes, W. H., and Edgell, D. (1993). *Learning disabilities and brain function* (3rd ed.). New York: Springer Verlag.

Gittelman-Klein, R., Abikoff, H., Pollack, E., Klein, D. F., Katz, S., and Mattes, J. (1980). A controlled trial of behavior modification and methylphenidate in hyperactive children. In C. Whalen and B. Henker (Eds.), *Hyperactive children: The social ecology of identification and treatment* (pp. 221-43). New York: Academic Press.

Goldman, S. M. (1998). Child and adolescent diagnosis with *DSM-IV.* In G. P. Kocher, J. C. Norcross and S. S. Hill III (Eds.), *Psychologist's desk reference* (pp. 100-102). New York: Oxford University Press.

Grassi, J. A. (1992). Child, children. In D. N. Freedman (Ed.), *The anchor Bible dictionary*. New York: Doubleday.

Grossman, H. (Ed.). (1973). *Manual on terminology and classification in mental retardation* (Rev. ed.). Washington, DC: American Association of Mental Deficiency.

Henggeler, S. W., and Borduin, C. M. (1990). *Family therapy and beyond: A multisystemic approach to teaching the behavior problems of children and adolescents*. Pacific Grove, CA: Brooks/Cole.

Henggeler, S. W., Melton, G. B., and Smith, L. A. (1992). Family preservation using multisystemic therapy: An effective alternative to incarcerating juvenile offenders. *Journal of Consulting and Clinical Psychology, 60,* 953-61.

Henggeler, S. W., Schoenwald, S. K., and Pickrel, S. G. (1995). Multisystemic therapy: Bridging the gap between university- and community-based treatment. *Journal of Consulting and Clinical Psychology, 63,* 709-18.

Hinshaw, S. P., Lahey, B. B., and Hart, E. L. (1993). Issues of taxonomy and comorbidity in the development of conduct disorder. *Development and Psychopathology, 5,* 31-49.

Hodapp, R. M., and Dykens, E. M. (1996). Mental retardation. In E. J. Mash and R. A. Barkley (Eds.), *Child psychopathology* (pp. 362-89). New York: Guilford.

Horn, W. E., and Ialongo, N. (1988). Multimodal treatment of attention deficit hyperactivity disorder in children. In H. E. Fitzgerald, B. M. Lester and M. W. Yogman (Eds.), *Theory and research in behavioral pediatrics* (4:175-220). New York: Plenum.

Hynd, G. W., and Willis, W. G. (1988). *Pediatric neuropsychology*. New York: Grune and Stratton.

Ingersol, B. D., and Goldstein, S. (1993). *Attention deficit disorder and learning disabilities: Realities, myths and controversial treatments*. New York: Doubleday.

Kamphaus, R. W., and Frick, P. J. (1996). *The clinical assessment of children's emotion, behavior and personality*. Boston: Allyn and Bacon.

Kashani, J. H., Beck, N. C., Hoeper, E. W., Fallahi, C., Corcoran, C. M., MacAllister, J. A., Rosenberg, T. K., and Reid, J. C. (1987). Psychiatric disorders in a community sample of adolescents. *American Journal of Psychiatry, 144,* 584-89.

Kazdin, A. E. (1994). Psychotherapy for children and adolescents. In S. Bergin and S. Garfield (Eds.), *Handbook of psychotherapy and be-*

havior change (4th ed.) (pp. 543-94). New York: Wiley.

Kazdin, A. E. (1988). *Child psychotherapy: Developing and identifying effective treatments.* Elmsford, NY: Pergamon.

Klinger, L. G., and Dawson, G. (1996). Autistic disorder. In E. J. Mash and R. A. Barkley (Eds.), *Child psychopathology* (pp. 311-39). New York: Guilford.

Krazter, L., and Hodgins, S. (1997). Adult outcomes of child conduct problems: A cohort study. *Journal of Abnormal Child Psychology, 25,* 65-81.

Kreusi, M. J. P., Rappaport, J. L., Hamburger, S., Hibbs, E., Potter, W. Z., Lenane, M., and Brown, G. L. (1990). Cerebrospinal fluid monamine metabolites, aggression and impulsivity in disruptive behavior disorders of children and adolescents. *Archives of General Psychiatry, 47,* 419-26.

Lahey, B. B., Loeber, R., Hart, E. L., Frick, P. J., Applegate, B., Zhang, Q., Green, S. M., and Russo, M. F. (1995). Four-year longitudinal study of conduct disorder in boys: Patterns and predictors of persistence. *Journal of Abnormal Psychology, 104,* 83-93.

Lahey, B. B., McBurnett, K., Loeber, R., and Hart, E. L. (1995). Psychobiology of conduct disorder. In G. P. Sholevar (Ed.), *Conduct disorders in children and adolescents: Assessments and interventions* (pp. 27-44). Washington, DC: American Psychiatric Press.

Lebow, J., and Gurman, A. (1995). Research assessing couple and family therapy. *Annual Review of Psychology, 46,* 27-57.

Leckman, J. F., and Cohen, D. J. (1991). Clonidine treatment of Gilles de la Tourette's syndrome. *Archives of General Psychiatry, 48,* 324-28.

Lerer, R. J. (1987). Motor tics, Tourette's syndrome, and learning disabilities. *Journal of Learning Disabilities, 20,* 266-67.

Lewinsohn, P. M., Hops, H., Roberts, R. E., Seeley, J. R., and Andrews, J. A. (1993). Adolescent psychopathology, part 1: Prevalence and incidence of depression and other *DSM-III-R* disorders in high school students. *Journal of Abnormal Psychology, 102,* 133-44.

Lovaas, O. I. (1987). Behavioral treatment and normal education and intellectual functioning in young autistic children. *Journal of Consulting and Clinical Psychology, 55,* 3-9.

Lynam, D. R. (1996). Early identification of chronic offenders: Who is the fledgling psychopath? *Psychological Bulletin, 120,* 209-34.

Magnusson, D. (1988). Aggressiveness, hyperactivity and autonomic activity/reactivity in the development of social maladjustment. In D. Magnusson (Ed.), *Individual development from an interactional per-*

spective: A longitudinal study (pp. 152-72). Hillsdale, NJ: Erlbaum.

Mash, E. J., and Barkley, R. A. (Eds.). (1996). *Child psychopathology.* New York: Guilford.

Mash, E. J., and Barkley, R. A. (Eds.). (1998). *Treatment of childhood disorders* (2nd ed.). New York: Guilford.

Mash, E. J., and Dozois, D. J. A. (1996). Child psychopathology: A developmental-systems perspective. In E. J. Mash and R. A. Barkley (Eds.), *Child psychopathology* (pp. 3-60). New York: Guilford.

McBride, P. A., Anderson, G. M., Hertzig, M. E., Snow, M. E., Thompson, S. M., Khait, V. D., Shapiro, T., and Cohen, D. J. (1998). Effects of diagnosis, race and puberty on platelet serotonin levels in autism and mental retardation. *Journal of the American Academy of Child and Adolescent Psychiatry, 37,* 767-76.

McBurnett, K., Lahey, B. B., Frick, P. J., Risch, C., Loeber, R., Hart, E. L., Christ, M. A. G., and Hanson, K. S. (1991). Anxiety, inhibition and conduct disorder in children, part 1: Relation to salivary cortisol. *Journal of the American Academy of Child and Adolescent Psychiatry, 30,* 192-96.

McGee, R., Feehan, M., Williams, S., Partridge, F., Silva, P. A., and Kelly, J. (1990). DSM-III disorders in a large sample of adolescents. *Journal of the American Academy of Child and Adolescent Psychiatry, 29,* 611-19.

McGee, R., Feehan, M., Williams, S., and Anderson, J. (1992). *DSM-III* disorders from age 11 to age 15 years. *Journal of the American Academy of Child and Adolescent Psychiatry, 31,* 50-59.

Mesibov, G. B., Adams, L. W., and Klinger, L. G. (1997). *Autism: Understanding the disorder.* New York: Plenum.

Moffitt, T. E. (1993). Adolescence-limited and life-course-persistent antisocial behavior: A developmental taxonomy. *Psychological Review, 10,* 674-701.

Mowrer, O. H., and Mowrer, W. M. (1938). Enuresis: A method for its study and treatment. *American Journal of Orthopsychiatry, 8,* 436-459.

National Commission on Children. (1991). *Beyond rhetoric: A new American agenda for children and families; The final report of the National Commission on Children.* Washington, DC: U.S. Government Printing Office.

Offord, D. R., Boyle, M. H., and Racine, Y. (1989). Ontario child health study: Correlates of disorder. *Journal of the American Academy of Child and Adolescent Psychiatry, 28,* 856-60.

Olweus, D., Mattesson, A., Schalling, D., and Low, H. (1988). Circulating testosterone levels and aggression in adolescent males: A causal analysis. *Psychosomatic Medicine, 50,* 261-72.

Ondersma, S. J., and Walker, C. E. (1998). Elimination disorders. In T. H. Ollendick and M. Hersen (Eds.), *Handbook of child psychopathology* (3rd ed.) (pp. 355-78). New York: Plenum.

Osterling, J., and Dawson, G. (1994). Early recognition of children with autism: A study of the first birthday home videotapes. *Journal of Autism and Developmental Disorders, 24,* 247-57.

Pelham, W. E. (1987). What do we know about the use and effects of CNS stimulants in the treatment of ADD? In J. Loney (Ed.), *The young hyperactive child: Answers to questions about diagnosis, prognosis and treatment.* New York: Haworth.

Pelham, W. E., Bender, M. E., Caddell, J., Booth, S., and Moorer, S. H. (1985). Methylphenidate and children with attention deficit disorder: Dose effects on classroom academic and social behavior. *Archives of General Psychiatry, 42,* 948-52.

Pennington, B. E., and Smith, S. D. (1988). Genetic influences on learning disabilities: An update. *Journal of Consulting and Clinical Psychology, 56,* 817-23.

Perkin, H. W. (1988). Family life and relations. In W. A. Elwell (Ed.), *Baker encyclopedia of the Bible* (1:767-73). Grand Rapids, MI: Baker.

Pfiffner, L. J., and O'Leary, S. G. (1993). School-based psychological treatments. In J. L. Mattson (Ed.), *Handbook of hyperactivity in children* (pp. 234-45). Boston: Allyn and Bacon.

Quay, H. C. (1986). Classification. In H. C. Quay and J. S. Werry (Eds.), *Psychopathological disorders in childhood* (3rd ed.) (pp. 1-34). New York: Wiley.

Resnick, R. J. (1998). Attention-deficit/hyperactivity disorder through the lifespan. In G. P. Koocher, J. C. Norcross and S. S. Hill (Eds.), *Psychologists' desk reference* (pp. 39-41). New York: Oxford University Press.

Richters, J. E., Arnold, L. E., Jensen, P. S., Abikoff, H. B., Conners, C. K., Greenhill, L. L., Hechtman, L., Hinshaw, S. P., Pelham, W. E., and Swanson, J. M. (1995). NIMH collaborative multisite multimodal treatment study of children with ADHD, part 1: Background and rationale. *Journal of the American Academy of Child and Adolescent Psychiatry, 34,* 987-1000.

Rogers, S. J. (1998). Empirically supported comprehensive treatments for young children with autism. *Journal of Clinical Child Psychology, 27,* 168-79.

Sallee, F. R., and Gill, H. S. (1998). Neuropsychopharmacology III:

Psychostimulants. In C. E. Coffey and R. A. Brumback (Eds.), *Textbook of pediatric neuropsychiatry* (pp. 393-428). Washington, DC: American Psychiatric Association.

Satterfield, J. H., Satterfield, B. T., and Schell, A. M. (1987). Therapeutic interventions to prevent delinquency in hyperactive boys. *Journal of the American Academy of Child and Adolescent Psychiatry, 26,* 56-64.

Scerbo, A., and Kolko, D. J. (1994). Salivary testosterone and cortisol in disruptive children: Relationship to aggressive, hyperactive and internalizing behavior. *Journal of the American Academy of Child and Adolescent Psychiatry, 33,* 1174-84.

Schreibman, L., and Charlop-Christy, M. H. (1998). Autistic disorder. In T. H. Ollendick and M. Hersen (Eds.), *Handbook of child psychopathology* (3rd ed.) (pp. 157-79). New York: Plenum.

Schroder, C. S., and Gordon, B. N. (1991). *Assessment and treatment of childhood problems.* New York: Guilford.

Shadish, W., Montgomery, L., Wilson, P., Wilson, M., Bright, I., and Okwumabua, T. (1993). The effects of family and marital psychotherapies: A meta-analysis. *Journal of Consulting and Clinical Psychology, 61,* 992-1002.

Shaffer, D., Fisher, P., Dulcan, M. K., Davies, M., Piacentini, J., Schwab-Stone, M. E., Lahey, B. C., Bourdon, K., Jensen, P. S., Bird, H. R., Canino, G., and Regier, D. A. (1996). The NIMH diagnostic interview schedule for children version 2.3 (DISC-2.3): Description, acceptability, prevalence rates and performance in the MECA study. *Journal of the American Academy of Child and Adolescent Psychiatry, 35,* 865-77.

Shapiro, E., Shapiro, A. K., Young, J. G., and Feinberg, T. E. (1988). *Gilles de la Tourette syndrome.* New York: Raven.

Silverthorn, P., Frick, P. J., Kuper, K., and Ott, J. (1996). Attention deficit hyperactivity disorder and sex: A test of two etiological models to explain the male predominance. *Journal of Clinical Child Psychology, 25,* 52-59.

Smalley, S. L., Levitt, J., and Bauman, M. (1998). Autism. In C. E. Coffey and R. A. Brumback (Eds.), *Textbook of pediatric neuropsychiatry* (pp. 393-428). Washington, DC: American Psychiatric Association.

Szatmari, P. (1997). Pervasive developmental disorder not otherwise specified. In T. A. Widiger, A. J. Francis, H. A. Pincus, R. Ross, M. B. First and W. Davis (Eds.), *DSM-IV sourcebook* (3:43-55). Washington, DC: American Psychiatric Association.

Torgesen, J. K. (1986). Learning disabilities theory: Its current state and future prospects. *Journal of Learning Disabilities, 19,* 399-407.

Towbin, K. E., and Cohen, D. J. (1996). Tic disorders. In J. M. Weiner (Ed.), *Diagnosis and psychopharmacology of childhood and adolescent disorders* (2nd ed.). New York: Wiley.

Van Leeuwen, M. S. (2002). *My brother's keeper.* Downers Grove, IL: InterVarsity Press.

Verhulst, F. C., Ende, J. V. D., Ferdinand, R. F., and Kasius, M. C. (1997). The prevalence of *DSM-III-R* diagnoses in a national sample of Dutch adolescents. *Archives of General Psychiatry, 54,* 329-36.

Walker, C. E., Milling, L. S., and Bonner, B. L. (1988). Incontinence disorders: Enuresis and encopresis. In D. K. Routh (Ed.), *Handbook of pediatric psychology* (pp. 363-98). New York: Guilford.

Walker, J. L., Lahey, B. B., Russo, M. F., Frick, P. J., Christ, M. A. G., McBurnett, K., Loeber, R., Stouthamer-Loeber, M., and Green, S. M. (1991). Anxiety, inhibition and conduct disorder in children, part 1: Relations to social impairment. *Journal of the American Academy of Child and Adolescent Psychiatry, 30,* 187-91.

Weisz, J. R., and Weiss, B. (1993). *Effects of psychotherapy with children and adolescents.* London: Sage.

Werry, J. S. (1986). Physical illness, symptoms and allied disorders. In H. C. Quay and J. S. Werry (Eds.), *Psychopathological disorders of childhood* (3rd ed.) (pp. 232-93). New York: Wiley.

Wilson, W. J. (1987). *The truly disadvantaged: The inner city, the underclass and public policy.* Chicago: University of Chicago Press.

Zametkin, A. J., and Liotta, W. (1998). The neurobiology of attention-deficit/hyperactivity disorder. *Journal of Clincal Psychiatry, 59*(suppl. 7), 17-23.

RESOURCES

Children and Adults with Attention Deficit Disorder (CHADD)
499 NW 70th Avenue, #109
Plantation, FL 33317
Phone: 305-587-3700
www.chadd.org

Learning Disabilities Association of America
4156 Library Road
Pittsburgh, PA 15234
Phone: 412-341-1515
www.ldanatl.org

American Association on Mental Retardation
Phone: 800-424-3688
www.aamr.org

National Down Syndrome Congress
1605 Chantilly Drive, #250
Atlanta, GA 30324-3269
Phone: 800-232-NDSC
www.ndsccenter.org

13

PROBLEMS IN
OLDER ADULTHOOD

*C*hanging demographics in the United States and throughout the world suggest that older adults will have a significant impact on both the mental health and pastoral care communities. Worldwide demographics are shifting because the "baby boomers," persons born between 1946 and 1964, are entering older adulthood.

Consider that in 1900 the elderly (adults age sixty-five or older) made up 4 percent of the U.S. population, which meant there were approximately 3.1 million older adults (U.S. Bureau of the Census, 1992; U.S. Senate Special Commission on Aging et al., 1991). By 1990, the percentage of elderly in the United States had grown to 12.5 percent of the total population—approximately 31.1 million elderly (U.S. Bureau of the Census, 1992). Among this age group, 18 million were aged sixty-five to seventy-four, 10 million were aged seventy-five to eighty-four, and 3 million were eighty-five or older. It is estimated that by 2030 over 21.8 percent of the U.S. population will be aged sixty-five and older (U.S. Senate Special Committee on Aging et al., 1991).

These demographic shifts are also apparent in the church community; older adults are already overrepresented in many local church bodies. They are recognized as "highly religious" or "most religious" in many polls and on measures of religiosity and religious interest. In fact, religious activities and affiliations are the most common organized participatory experience engaged in by older adults, about half of whom attend religious services weekly (Abeles et al., 1998).

A Christian perspective on problems in older adulthood begins with a Christian perspective on aging. Moberg (1984) discusses several biblical values associated with aging and older adults. The Old Testament speaks of long life as normative and desirable. The shortening of the human lifespan to 120 years is attributed in Genesis 6:3 to human sin rather than either God's intention in creation or what it means to be human. Also, God commands in the Mosaic law—and in the Ten Commandments, at least with reference to one's parents—that the elderly are to be respected. This may become an increasingly important biblical witness for Christians in contemporary culture.

To contrast a biblical view of aging and of older adults with a secular view, we might look at how the mental health community considers older adults and on what basis. Most mental health codes of conduct and ethics identify age as an important dimension of human diversity, and older adults are often seen as an underserved population (e.g., APA, 2002). Yet mental health professionals hold certain beliefs and assumptions about older adults, and these may interfere with proper care. For example, James and Haley reported an age and health bias among psychologists, and they concluded that psychologists tend "to rate older clients as less appropriate for their services and see their prognosis as less positive than for younger clients" (1995, p. 613). This is unfortunate for several reasons. One of them is that research clearly documents the efficacy of interventions for various mental health problems experienced by older adults (for a review of this literature, see Acierno, Hersen and Van Hasselt, 1996; Dick and Gallagher-Thompson, 1996; Schneider, 1995).

Bias, when it is present, may not be expressed as prejudice or discrimination against the elderly, but it may take the form of assumptions about older adults based on an inaccurate understanding of normal adult development, aging and the specific needs of older adults (Hillman et al., 1997). We will return to these issues later in this chapter.

We turn now to a brief discussion of aging and older adults in the pastoral care literature. Although aging and older adults have not received a great deal of attention in this literature, they certainly are mentioned as pastoral insights have drawn on Scripture.

THEMES IN PASTORAL CARE

Scripture is an important resource for understanding how Christians ought to view the aging process and older adulthood. The common Hebrew word for age is *zaqen*, which is an indication of advanced age, as when Scripture speaks of Abraham as being "advanced in years" (Arnold, 1996, p. 13). This word is also related to nobility (e.g., an elderly servant, an officer in a royal court, an elder of Israel), suggesting a biblical theme of respect for the elderly. Other words in the Old Testament include *seba* (gray head), which in Proverbs 16:31 is viewed as a "crown of glory" (ibid.). An elderly person who was seen as defenseless would be referred to by the word *yases*, and the derivative conveys respect for one's age *(yasis)*. The word *kelah* is also used to convey "full vigor" and "ripe old age" (ibid.).

According to Arnold (1996), New Testament terms include *prebytes*, most often applied to leaders, but which means "elder" and can refer to an older adult. In the early church, officers were often called "elders" or "bishops" *(episkopos)*. Another New Testament word is *geras*, which refers to old age.

The biblical witness is that older adults are to be respected and honored for their wisdom (Deut 32:7) and discernment (Job 12:12). Although older adulthood is not a guarantor of wisdom and discernment, lack of respect for older adults is condemned in such passages as Lamentations 5:12 and 1 Timothy 5:1 (Moss, 1995).

As Moss (1995) suggests, aging brings with it a decline in functioning but also a greater appreciation for our dependence on God, both in this lifetime and in the life to come. In this life dependence on God is both direct and indirect, as we rely on others in the body of Christ, whereas in the life to come believers will experience utter dependence on God. Thus aging, when properly experienced from a Christian perspective, points to a transition toward greater dependence on God and ultimately the future hope of the resurrection in Christ (2 Tim 1:10).

THEMES IN PSYCHOPATHOLOGY

The *DSM-IV* does not take a life-span approach to psychopathology per se. Although there are categories for disorders that are first diagnosed in childhood (see chapter twelve), there is no comparable categorization for older adulthood. However, one particular cluster of problems is a concern to older adults more than to younger adults: problems of cognitive impairment.

Problems of cognitive functioning. The problems of cognitive functioning are not addressed elsewhere in this book, but they may be of concern for persons who struggle with any number of clinical problems, such as substance use disorders or acute trauma. They include delirium, dementia and amnestic disorders. We discuss them in this chapter because they are most common among older adults. What the problems of cognitive functioning share in common is impairment of memory, perception, attention and/or thinking.

Delirium is typically a temporary condition characterized by impaired cognition. It has a rapid course (over several hours or days), resulting in a confused or disoriented presentation. The person is typically disoriented first regarding time and then regarding place and people (Maxmen and Ward, 1995). As many as 30 percent of persons in acute care settings (e.g., emergency rooms) may suffer from delirium, but it is most common among older adults.

Dementia is characterized by global deterioration of cognitive functioning, having an impact on memory, language and/or judgment. The two most common types of dementia are dementia of the Alzheimer's type and vascular dementia. Alzheimer's disease accounts for about 50 percent of the cases of dementia, and it is characterized by multiple cognitive deficits that develop gradually over time (Maxmen and Ward, 1995). Vascular dementia leads to very similar cognitive impairments as Alzheimer's disease, but it occurs in more discrete "steps" because it is the result of damage to blood vessels that carry oxygen to the brain. Vascular dementias account for about 10-15 percent of dementias. Dementia can also be caused by other medical conditions (e.g., Parkinson's disease), and together these account for approximately 20-30 percent of dementias (Maxmen and Ward, 1995). Finally, substance-induced persisting dementias (e.g., alcoholic dementia) account for about 7-9 percent of the dementias.

Amnestic disorders are characterized by loss of memory: the person suffering from an amnestic disorder is unable to move information from short-term to long-term memory. There are different types of amnestic disorders due to the various causes of memory impairment. A person can experience memory loss due to a single event such as a stroke located in the hippocampus; toxins such as alcohol can also impair memory over time (Maxmen and Ward, 1995). There are different experiences of memory loss, as one person may have difficulty learning new information, while another may have trouble recalling previously learned material.

Problems of anxiety. For the most part anxiety disorders in older adults mirror anxiety disorders experienced by young and middle-aged adults. The symptom presentation is that of apprehension, tension and dread; those seeking help may struggle with irritability and restlessness and display a range of physical symptoms, including gastrointestinal problems—indigestion, difficulty swallowing and flatulence (Kennedy, 2000).

Among the many problems of anxiety, generalized anxiety disorder and phobic disorders, such as specific phobia, social phobia and agoraphobia, are probably the most common concerns among older adult females and are quite common among older males. Estimates suggest that a little over 6 percent of older women and nearly 3 percent of men meet diagnostic criteria for these disorders (Acierno, Hersen and Van Hasselt, 1996; Abeles et al., 1998). Specific phobias may be of greater concern, followed by agoraphobia and social phobia. Apprehensions and worry are often related to financial strains and health conditions, two concerns faced by most older adults in the United States.

Later-life onset of panic disorder is rare; symptoms of panic disorder in young or middle adulthood often diminish considerably or abate by later life (Abeles et al., 1998). Obsessive-compulsive disorder and posttraumatic stress disorder tend to be less commonly reported as concerns among older adults. Only about 0.1 percent of older adults report panic disorder, while closer to 1 percent meet criteria for obsessive-compulsive disorder (Acierno, Hersen and Van Hasselt, 1996).

Problems of mood. Many people assume that depression is a normal consequence of aging, but this assumption is based on stereotypes and prejudice more than on any specific research finding. A report from the Epidemiological Catchment Area (ECA) studies puts the prevalence rates for depression quite low as defined by the *DSM*. Dysthymic disorder, the experience of a low-grade depression for two years or more, is perhaps the most common depressive disorder among older adults, and its prevalence rate is just 1.8 percent. Major depressive disorder was estimated at 0.4 percent among men and 1.4 percent among women (American Association of Retired Persons, 1990). In fact, in a study of 2,727 persons between twenty-five and seventy-four, Mroczek and Koarz (1998) found that negative emotions were higher among younger adults than older adults, although age and effect appear to be related to other personality and sociodemographic variables, including marriage.

Several subgroups among older adults are, of course, at greater risk for depression. These at-risk groups include the chronically physically ill, the elderly in nursing homes or other institutions, and family caregivers of older adults (Koenig and Blazer, 1992; cf. Fisher, Zeiss and Carstensen, 2001).

In addition, it should be noted that Dick and Gallagher-Thompson (1996) observed that up to 10-30 percent of older adults may report significant symptoms of depression that do not meet diagnostic criteria for a depressive disorder. These researchers think of depression, then, as the "common cold" (p. 182) of mental health concerns for the elderly. Depression might be thought of as common at least in terms of various depressive symptoms, such as loss of sleep, but not common in terms of prevalence rates for specific diagnosed disorders.

The symptoms of depression may also present differently from those seen in younger adults with depression. Older adults are more likely to exhibit anxiety and agitation as well as memory lapses and physical complaints. Hopelessness remains an important indicator of depressed mood among older adults (Abeles et al., 1998). We should note that depression is not a unitary phenomenon and the content and process vary widely across the life span. We need to be careful about imposing our notions on others who may have had vastly different life experiences. Loss is in the eye of the beholder.

Suicide is an important concern among older adults, and it relates to symptoms of depression. The "highest suicide rate of any group is found in older adults, primarily older Caucasian men who live alone, for whom suicide increases dramatically from age 65 to 85 and older" (Abeles et al., 1998, p. 417).

Problems of social impact. It is generally recognized that substance abuse problems, especially alcohol abuse and dependence, are a growing concern among older adults. An estimated 2.5 million older adults have an alcohol-related drinking problem, and as many as one in five hospitalized older adults meet the diagnostic criteria for alcoholism (Dupree and Schonfeld, 1996). These rates are consistent with other research on clinical samples and those referred for outpatient evaluations. Men tend to be at greater risk of alcohol dependence than women, with prevalence estimates of 2-5 percent for men and 1 percent for women.

Illicit drug use and dependence is not as great a concern among

older adults, as the rates of this type of substance abuse decrease for
adults over the age of sixty. Women tend to be at greater risk of pre-
scriptive drug dependence (Dupree and Schonfeld, 1996). Because illicit drug use is not as great a problem among community-dwelling
older adults, most research programs focus on abuse of alcohol and
of prescription and over-the-counter medications.

Problems of body and mind. Somatoform disorders, such as hypochondriasis, conversion disorders, somatization disorder and body
dysmorphic disorders, are present in about 1 percent or less of the
elderly in the community. These rates may jump to as high as 30 percent in clinical samples, however (Kennedy, 2000). Among these, *hypochondriasis* is the most common somatoform disorder diagnosed
among older adults; 10-15 percent of the elderly "exhibit a marked
concern about their health and overestimate their level of physical
impairment" (Abeles et al., 1998, p. 418). Many people believe that
older adults can experience a kind of somatic preoccupation, though
the research in this area is equivocal.

One of the challenges in differential diagnosis is that many older
adults with somatoform disorders will also have any number of physical conditions:

> Older adults with somatoform disorders are at risk for lack of
> appropriate attention from health care professionals, who may
> minimize symptoms of real physical disorders. Those with so-
> matoform disorders are also more likely to take unnecessary
> medications and to undergo unnecessary medical procedures,
> both of which are especially risky for them and may contribute
> to actual morbidity. (Ibid.)

The medications used to treat various physical conditions (and the
side effects of those medications) must also be considered during assessment. A good history can help a clinician rule out hypochondriasis, as onset typically occurs prior to age thirty.

There has been no systematic study of *eating disorders* among older
adults, but case examples suggest that eating disorders do occur,
though in the majority of cases the eating disorder was present in
younger or middle adulthood. It is difficult to say whether the higher
rates of eating disorders in teens and young adults is related more to
their age or to their cohort; if it is the latter, we may find more older
adults who suffer from an eating disorder as these cohorts age.

According to the Abeles et al. (1998), problems in sleeping usually increase with age, with *insomnia* a common concern, especially among women and those who are recently widowed or separated/divorced. The risk of sleep apnea also increases with age; symptoms of sleep apnea are often reported by older adults.

Problems of psychosis and thought disorders. It is commonly assumed that schizophrenia develops in late adolescence/early adulthood and that earlier onset, say before age ten, and later onset, after age forty-five, are rare (Glynn et al., 1996). At least one study, however, reported that almost a third of new cases of schizophrenia occurred after age forty-four and that as many as 12 percent of new cases began after age sixty-four (Glynn et al., 1996). This is referred to as "late-onset" schizophrenia, meaning the person had his or her first schizophrenic episode in middle or later life. This is a condition that is more common among women than men, and it is typically characterized by symptoms such as delusions (typically of paranoia) and hallucinations.

There does not appear to be any significant cognitive decline associated with schizophrenia in later life. In fact, although schizophrenia is considered a chronic condition, people who suffer from it report some improvement over time; about half of those diagnosed with schizophrenia experience a remission of symptoms as they age (Glynn et al., 1996).

Dementia is considered an "age-related disorder" (Kennedy, 2000, p. 45), and dementia of the Alzheimer's type affects about 8-15 percent of older adults. As older adults age, their risk of dementia increases, "doubling every 5 years at least to age 85" (ibid.). A histological examination of actual brain tissue is the only definitive way to diagnose Alzheimer's disease, but accurate diagnoses are typically made based on clinical examination and client and family history (ibid.). Magnetic resonance imaging (MRI) can also be used to confirm diagnosis of vascular dementia, a form of dementia characterized by stepwise progression of symptoms rather than a "smoother" decline in functioning.

Problems of personality. Prevalence estimates of personality disorders among older adults vary considerably. They range from as low as 0.8 percent in community samples to as high as 20 percent of older adults in clinical samples with comorbid major mental illness (Kennedy, 2000). Because personality traits are generally thought to be rather stable across the life span, the rates for older adults in the community are probably closer to what we see in younger and middle-age adults: about 2 percent for paranoid, 3 percent schizotypal, 2 percent antisocial (3 percent of males and 1 percent of females), 2 percent borderline, 2.5 percent histrionic, 1 percent narcissistic, 1 percent avoidant and 1 percent obsessive-compulsive personality disorder (Kennedy, 2000). There is some concern that personality disorder is underdiagnosed in older adulthood (O'Connor and Dyce, 2001).

Problems of sexuality. Older adults are often thought of as having little sexual desire or as being involved in little or no sexual behavior. This perception may reflect our ignorance and biases more than the reality of elder sexuality. There does appear to be a decline in sexual activity as people age (Laumann et al., 1994); however, older adults are more sexually active than the stereotype suggests. The majority of older adults certainly continue to experience sexual desire. For example, in one study 88 percent of men and 71 percent of women fantasized about being intimate with the opposite sex, 72 percent of men and 40 percent of women reported masturbating, and 63 percent of men and 30 percent of women reported engaging in sexual intercourse (Bretshneider and McCoy, 1988; cf. Buono et al., 1998; Marsiglio and Donnelly, 1991; Starr and Weiner, 1981; Steinke, 1994). Marital status predicts sexual activity and interest; this finding is especially true for women (Buono et al., 1998).

There are also important age-related changes that both elderly males and females experience, and some of them can affect sexual behavior. Among women, normal, age-related changes influence their reproductive system, including menopause at about age fifty to fifty-five and the accompanying diminution of estrogen and progesterone production, which can lead to pain during intercourse due to a thinning and drying of the vaginal wall (Whitbourne, 1996).

Although males are still capable of reproducing into old age, they do experience a decrease in the number of viable sperm produced. Normal, age-related changes also include fewer and softer penile erections (Schiavi et al., 1990), a slowing of the sexual response cycle (desire, excitement, orgasm, resolution) and a longer refractory period, which is the time needed to achieve another erection and orgasm (Whitbourne, 1996). Incidence rates of erectile dysfunction increase with age: in one study of 1,709 randomly sampled men the rate was 12.4 cases per 1,000 man-years ages forty to forty-nine, 29.8 cases per 1,000 ages fifty to fifty-nine, and 46.4 cases per 1,000 ages sixty to sixty-nine (Johannes et al., 2000). In addition to age, increased risk of erectile dysfunction was related to lower education and health factors such as diabetes and heart disease.

We turn our attention now to theories regarding causes of the various problems. Rather than reiterate what is discussed in greater detail in earlier chapters, this discussion focuses on antecedents specifically associated with older adulthood.

ANTECEDENTS TO PROBLEMS IN OLDER ADULTHOOD

The range of problems addressed in this chapter makes clear that there is no one antecedent to problems in older adulthood. We consider a number of significant factors, paying special attention to age-related changes and their impact on the problems faced by older adults.

Problems of cognitive functioning. A number of medical conditions, including substance intoxication and withdrawal, infections, and head injury or trauma, may lead to delirium. Older adults are thought to be at greater risk of developing delirium because of mild infections and changes in medications, both of which can be quite common.

There are also a number of potential causes of dementia. These include medical conditions (e.g., stroke, AIDs) as well as substance abuse. But age is perhaps one of the more significant risk factors for dementia, with prevalence rates of about 1 percent for persons ages sixty-five to seventy-four, 4 percent for those ages seventy-five to eighty-four, and 10 percent for those over eighty-five years of age (Patterson, 1996).

Amnestic disorders are most often caused by medical conditions, substance use disorders and head injury. For example, Wernicke-Korsakoff syndrome is caused by damage to the thalamus because of either chronic alcohol use or stroke.

Problems of anxiety. Problems of anxiety often co-occur with various physical illnesses (e.g., Parkinson's disease, hypoglycemia) and with dementia. As Fisher, Zeiss and Carstensen (2001) observe, in the case of anxiety and physical illnesses, it is unclear whether one is the cause of the other. Research to date suggests that either anxiety and physical illnesses develop simultaneously or anxiety follows shortly after the illness.

Age-related changes may also affect anxiety among older adults. For example, it has been speculated that normal, age-related biochemical changes "may result in a decline in cognitive acuity that may in turn reduce the impact of potentially worry-eliciting stimuli," which may explain the lower rates of anxiety disorders reported among older adults than among young and middle-aged adults (ibid., p. 932).

Other explanations for lower rates of anxiety include habituation to stressful events, realistic expectations due to life experience and changes in attitudes associated with normal aging (ibid.).

Problems of mood. Depression is less common among older adults than was once thought. In fact, rates of depression appear to go down in older adulthood as compared to young and middle adulthood. The assumption has also been that medical illnesses cause older adults to be depressed. But what appears to be the case is that loss of function, rather than illness as such, is the key age-related factor associated with depression among older adults (Fisher, Zeiss and Carstensen, 2001). Of particular concern is the psychological toll taken by functional losses. Depression, then, is probably due to this "psychological impact, particularly as functional changes limit valued activities and/or change an older adult's roles and opportunities" (ibid., p. 925).

Changes also occur in older adults' roles and responsibilities. Upon retirement, their role changes can mean diminished reinforcement and add to an experience of loss that may lead to depression.

Bereavement is a common experience among older adults, who may lose their spouse or close friends and other family members. Avoidance of grief, a common problem in the United States, may compound the difficulties of those who experience multiple cumulative losses in older adulthood.

Problems of social impact. Long-term substance abuse that carries into older adulthood has a poor prognosis, and it typically warrants more intensive medical intervention (Fisher, Zeiss and Carstensen, 2001). Onset of alcohol or substance abuse in later life is typically triggered by a specific event. Some of the stressful events associated with aging include retirement, loss of a spouse, family conflicts, health problems, relocation and financial strain (Abeles et al., 1998; Fisher, Zeiss and Carstensen, 2001).

Problems of body and mind. Among the eating disorders, anorexia is more common among older adults. Normal changes associated with aging may affect caloric intake among older adults, including lower metabolic rate; reduced physical activity; changes in vision, taste and smell; and teeth/denture problems (Fisher, Zeiss and Carstensen, 2001).

Normal age-related changes that may affect sleep include a decrease in non-REM sleep (or deep and restorative sleep) and an increase in shallow sleep. This leads to frequent "awakenings (microarousals) throughout the night during shallow sleep and the advancement of the deep-sleep phase into the earlier hours" (Kennedy, 2000, p. 105). Other causes of sleep problems include (1) lack of a set routine in which an established sleep-wake cycle is adhered to and (2) periodic leg movements that may disturb sleep. Finally, physical and mental health concerns, as well as the medications used to treat those concerns, may lead to sleep disruption.[1]

Problems of psychosis and thought disorders. Biological vulnerability is considered a necessary but not sufficient factor in the etiology of schizophrenia. According to the diathesis-stress model, environmental stressors play a role in the symptom onset, and it is understandable that most cases of schizophrenia develop long before older adulthood (though some research has reported surprisingly high rates of middle- and later-life schizophrenia than what might be expected).

Paranoia is a more common presentation in older adulthood, and it is the most common delusional disorder among older adults. It is believed that a number of factors may contribute to paranoia among some older adults, including "never having been married, being childless, being socially isolated, and suffering significant hearing loss" (Fisher, Zeiss and Carstensen, 2001, p. 935). An additional risk factor is any family history of schizophrenia or paranoia.

Problems of personality. Personality disorders are by their very nature chronic, tracing back to childhood and typically crystallizing in young adulthood. As Kennedy observes, the onset of a personality disorder is "no later than early adulthood," though "the disorder may not be apparent until some event makes it impossible to ignore" (2000, p. 114). The intensity of personality distortions is particularly strong during a person's twenties. Some personality disorders soften over time, most notably borderline, narcissistic and antisocial personality disorders (O'Connor and Dyce, 2001).

Problems of sexuality. Medical problems, medications and age-related changes may adversely affect sexual functioning. Age-related changes that may diminish sexual functioning include declining lev-

---

[1]Normally we would address somatoform disorders in the section on problems of body and mind. However, although it is commonly assumed that older adults are preoccupied with their physical health, the research on somatoform disorders in older adulthood does not support this stereotype. Although a number of health-related concerns may arise in later life, there does not appear to be evidence that normal, age-related changes place older adults at greater risk for somatoform disorders. We will instead focus our attention on eating and sleep disorders in the section on problems of body and mind.

els of estrogen in women and testosterone in women and men. Some medications taken by older adults (e.g., hypotensive agents, beta blockers) can lead to diminished sexual desire or ejaculatory problems (Leiblum and Rosen, 2000).

Cultural considerations should not be neglected. Attitudes toward older adults and aging in general can affect the mental health of the elderly. It is generally believed that Western society's many negative messages related to aging can be internalized and leave an older adult doubting her or his own sexual abilities and interest.

THEMES IN TREATMENT

Generally speaking, mental health professionals tend to prefer time-limited, structured interventions to help the elderly (DeVries, 1996). Christian mental health professionals should be aware of treatments that can be especially helpful for older adults who present with a wide range of symptoms (Schneider, 1995).

Problems of cognitive functioning. Behavioral therapy is considered an empirically validated approach for addressing problem behaviors often associated with dementia (Gatz et al., 1998, p. 31). Stimulus control has also been shown to be a well-established treatment approach. Reality orientation and memory and cognitive retraining are considered "probably efficacious" for slowing the progression of "decay of skills" (ibid., p. 34), whereas reminiscence therapy is not believed to be helpful.

Haloperidol is often prescribed for those suffering from acute delirium, but treatment should correspond to the conditions or circumstances that led to the episode. It is common, for example, to prescribe benzodiazepines to the person whose delirium is due to withdrawal from alcohol or some other substance. Support in the form of assurance is often provided to help the person experiencing delirium.

Treatment for dementia is much more difficult due to the nature of the condition and the sheer amount of impairment it can cause. Cutting-edge research is being conducted on substances that may preserve (and in some cases restore) neurons, and there is a controversial line of research that involves transplanting fetal brain tissue into the older adult with dementia.

Problems of anxiety. Most older adults who suffer from an anxiety disorder do not seek mental health services. If they receive help at all, it is typically via their physician, and treatment of problems of anxiety usually takes the form of pharmacotherapy. According to Scogin (1998), benzodiazepines are often used; anxiolytics are used as well, though side effects (e.g., sedation, impaired cognitive functioning) are common. There are currently no treatments that meet the criteria of well-established or probably efficacious treatment for anxiety in older adulthood (Gatz et al., 1998). What appears to be helpful are "both traditional progressive muscle relaxation and imaginal relaxation . . . with the later a useful alternative for those unable to do the tension-release cycles associated with progressive relaxation" (Scogin, 1998, p. 208). Other promising approaches include cognitive-behavioral therapy and supportive therapy for older adults suffering from generalized anxiety disorder.

Problems of mood. As with problems of anxiety, it is rare for depressed older adults to seek treatment for their depression. Kasl-Godley, Gatz and Fiske speculate that this may be because older adults "fail to seek treatment for symptoms of depression," the older adult "does not mention depressive symptoms" when pursuing treatment of physical conditions, or the physician fails to recognize the symptoms of depression in older adulthood (1998, p. 215). Treatment for depression in older adulthood parallels treatment for depression in younger adulthood. Gatz et al. (1998, p. 13) identify cognitive-behavioral therapy as a well-established treatment for adults and "probably efficacious" for older adults (individual behavioral therapy is also considered "probably efficacious"). Interpersonal therapy is also a well-established treatment for adults with depression and thought to be promising for older adults, as is structured life review (Gatz et al., 1998).

Problems of social impact. We noted above that an important distinction should be made between early-onset and late-onset substance abusers. Early-onset substance abusers tend to have a poorer prognosis; later-onset substance abusers generally have turned to alcohol or drugs following a major stressor, such as retirement or the death of a spouse.

No one approach to the treatment of the problems of social impact is considered well established. According to Gatz et al., "reminiscence, age segregation, and a supportive rather than challenging climate may be promising aspects of substance abuse treatment for an older adult population" (1998, p. 27).

At present, interventions for older adults tend to involve a detoxification program, pharmacotherapy and a variety of psychosocial treatment approaches. Gomberg and Zucker (1998) note that there has been some debate about whether older adults need treatment planning that is "elder-specific" and that recent research suggests that older adults who enter elder-specific programs are more likely to complete treatment and to have lower rates of recidivism (the "age segregation" noted in the Gatz et al., 1998, review). It is important to note that withdrawal may take longer for older adults than for younger adults.

Pharmacotherapy is common in substance abuse treatment; however, we know relatively little about the effectiveness of substances such as antabuse with older adults, and the use of such medications places medically ill older adults at risk (Gomberg and Zucker, 1998).

Psychosocial treatment approaches include behavior therapy, group therapy and family therapy. There is empirical support for at least one specific day-treatment program based on behavioral principles that teaches self-management, skill acquisition and the importance of social support (Gomberg and Zucker, 1998). Supportive group therapy has been shown in some studies to be an effective approach with older adults, as has family therapy.

Problems of body and mind. Treatment for eating disorders varies, generally tailored to the idiosyncratic presentation of the particular older adult. Although basic principles for intervention are similar to those used with younger and middle-aged adults, older adults tend to be more vulnerable to weight loss and malnutrition. Nutritional re-education is often an important component of successful treatment, as is reinforcement of appropriate caloric intake.

Gatz et al. (1998) identify cognitive-behavioral therapy and stimulus control as probably efficacious for sleep disorders. In these approaches, mental health professionals generally stress good sleep hygiene, and this is appropriate when working with older adults. Mental health professionals teach stimulus control and essentially tailor behavioral instructions to the specific needs of the older adult who is suffering from sleep disturbance (e.g., avoid caffeine before bedtime, maintain a set daily routine). Older adults can learn sleep restriction, so that they increase "the ratio of time spent sleeping to time spent awake while in bed" (DeVries and Coon, 2002, p. 554). Stimulus control and sleep restriction can be complemented by relaxation training and imagery exercises, which have been used successfully for sleep disturbances (DeVries and Coon, 2002; Nielsen, Nordhus and Kvale, 1998), though by themselves they are not considered probably efficacious (Gatz et al., 1998).

Problems of psychosis and thought disorders. Treatment of schizophrenia in older adulthood is not significantly different from treatment of schizophrenia in younger adulthood, and later-onset schizophrenia has a much better prognosis, an about 50 percent rate of improvement with medication (Karon and VandenBos, 1998). However, there are a few things that set the two apart, including the fact that many antipsychotic medications, at least in high doses, are contraindicated for older adults. Paranoia is more common in persons with late-onset schizophrenia. It is important to recall in such cases that the person has lived successfully for fifty or more years without psychosis or thought disorder, and placing their present circumstances in context may be helpful (ibid.).

Problems of personality. It was noted earlier that the intensity of personality disorders is particularly strong during a person's young adulthood but, at least among some personality disorders, decreases over time. A number of interventions have been used to treat personality disorders, including psychodynamic therapy, cognitive therapy and dialectical behavior therapy. However, there has been very little outcome research on any particular treatment program for older adults with personality disorders (O'Connor and Dyce, 2001). We have seen recent interest in pharmacotherapy for personality disorders, though no medications have been shown to be tremendously effective with younger adults, and the use of pharmacotherapy is increasingly complicated with older adults. Most clinicians today emphasize reducing symptoms "in times of crisis and slow, slight improvements in relationships, living habits, thinking styles, and emotional reactions" (ibid., p. 409).

Problems of sexuality. Treatment for problems of sexuality experienced in older adulthood generally falls into the following categories: psychoeducational programs, pharmacology and over-the-counter aids, and sexual counseling. Psychoeducational approaches are designed to promote healthy sexuality in older adults; such programs may focus on dealing with common sexual dysfunctions, such as erectile dysfunction (e.g., Goldman and Carroll, 1990), or on reducing anxieties about sexual intimacy following treatment for cancer or some other life-threatening illness (e.g., Robinson, Faris and Scott, 1999). Psychoeducational programs have also been developed for "proximal agents," such as family members of older adults or nursing-home staff (e.g., White and Catania, 1982), and these programs typically provide educational material on sexuality and normal aging.

Psychopharmacology is a common approach for specific sexual

dysfunctions. For example, sildenafil (Viagra) has helped to promote sexual functioning, particularly for males (but it is contraindicated for men with some forms of heart disease). Declining levels of estrogen in women and testosterone in women and men can be compensated for with estrogen and testosterone replacement therapies. Some medications (e.g., hypotensive agents, beta blockers) taken by older adults can lead to diminished sexual desire or ejaculatory problems, and when this happens they may be discontinued or replaced with alternative medications (Leiblum and Rosen, 2000). There are many over-the-counter aids to sexual expression for older persons and others. Lubricants can lessen vaginal dryness, and body lotions and oils can enhance sexual performance.

Finally, efforts to promote healthy sexuality do well to recognize the effects on older adults of living in a youth-driven culture. Health professionals can convey positive messages, encouraging older adults to see themselves as having sexual desires that can be expressed in behaviors that are consistent with their personal, cultural and religious beliefs and values.

Sexual counseling of older adults is similar in many ways to sex therapy with younger adults. After a sex history is taken, education is often offered about normal aging. It is important to refer an older adult for a physical examination to rule out chronic diseases and effects of medications to treat chronic diseases. Counseling often includes standard exercises such as sensate focus, directed masturbation and homework assignments tailored to the needs of an individual or couple.

For some of the more common presenting concerns, Heiman and Meston (1997) summarize the research on sex therapy outcomes (not necessarily of older adults) and note the following preferred approaches: directed masturbation in the treatment of primary anorgasmia, with sensate focus enhancing the effects; use of vaginal dilators and relaxation for vaginismus; systematic desensitization and sensate focus for erectile dysfunction; and the "squeeze technique" (applying firm pressure just below the glans of the penis during sexual arousal but before ejaculation) for premature ejaculation. According to Heiman and Meston, insufficient research is available to specify efficacious treatments for desire disorders, dyspareunia and retarded ejaculation.

Emerging trends in treatment. Gerontologists are increasingly aware of the need to train generalists to work competently with older adults, as the changing demographics with "the aging of America" will surely be beyond what only specialists can manage. Emerging trends in training and intervention include an emphasis on adapting treatment to the special needs of older adults, increasing one's awareness of the "aging network" and the intentional use of proximal agents (e.g., family caregivers) as first-line interventionists.

There is increased awareness today of how important it is for mental health professionals to adapt their services to the needs of older adults. DeVries (1996) offers suggestions for such adaptation, including playing a more active role in focusing and structuring therapy sessions. It is recommended that therapists anticipate an overall slower pace in therapy, reflecting normal age-related sensory deficits, such as visual and auditory acuity, that may affect information processing. To compensate for this, DeVries suggests that mental health professionals use multiple sensory modalities when presenting information in session—for example, using handouts or written instructions.

Other specific recommendations include socializing older adults to the nature and structure of therapy. It may be beneficial to reconsider the traditional "fifty-minute hour" that has come to characterize contemporary mental health services (Solomon, Faletti and Yunik, 1982). Older adults may be reluctant to meet for time-limited "sessions" and may question the value of therapy in general. This may be a cohort effect that will change as middle-aged adults grow older. In the meantime, mental health professionals can reduce the stigma of mental health services by developing educational programs formatted in ways that are more attractive to older adults, such as educational workshops or community meetings (Yarhouse and DeVries, 1998).

The "aging network" could be viewed as an extension of a multidisciplinary approach to care. Not only do mental health professionals need to be able to identify and utilize physicians with specialized training and experience in psychopharmacology for older adults, but they should be aware of the importance of identifying and accessing the "aging network"—the "partnership of public and private organizations at the federal, state, and local levels that are involved in providing services to older people" (Waters and Goodman, 1990, p. 78).

According to Tobin and Toseland (1985), it can be helpful for mental health professionals to distinguish between community-based, home-based and residential/institutional-based care. Each of these types of care can be further organized based on level of impairment (minimal, moderate and severe) of the older adult needing services.

For example, community-based care for the minimally impaired might take the form of active involvement in a senior center and adult education through a community college. Home-based needs for a minimally impaired older adult might take the form of home repair and transportation services. Foster family care and home health services are good examples of home-based care for an older adult with more significant impairment (Yarhouse and DeVries, 1998).

Increased emphasis has been placed on identifying and equipping proximal agents to provide early intervention in the lives of older adults. Among these, family caregivers are the most often researched. In fact, mental health professionals who wish to improve the quality of life of older adults must consider the benefits of improving caregiver-recipient relationships. At least one study (Colerick and George, 1986) reports that the caregiver–care recipient relationship is more highly correlated to the recipient's quality of life and likelihood of institutionalization than are other variables, including the patient's condition and stage of illness.

Of particular importance are interventions to help family caregivers (who are more likely to be female) manage negative emotions (e.g., anger, frustration), to reduce the risk of elder abuse. Family caregivers can learn skills for managing feelings of anger and frustration and can challenge assumptions, stereotypes or irrational cognitions that may have kept the caregiver from using resources in the aging network, such as adult daycare centers (Yarhouse and DeVries, 1998).

PREVENTION

There are a number of ways to approach prevention of problems in older adulthood. It may sound simplistic to encourage older adults to follow the adage "Use it or lose it." This may not prevent all problems of older adulthood, but it is true that apart from specific impairments that do not arise from normal aging, how the brain ages will depend on it how it is used. Reading and comprehension actually change little as people age, though it is not uncommon to note some deterioration in verbal and visual memory. Normal aging does lead to some memory loss, thought to occur because of cell loss in the hippocampus, an area of the brain associated with memory. Longer-term memory, however, is less affected, and many older adults are able to recall events from long ago, even from their childhood, particularly if the memory is coded in a way that aids in memory recall, such as if certain smells or a particular song is associated with the event.

Normal age-related changes in memory should be distinguished from the dementias, which always have a specific cause. Dementia involves "cognitive impairments that represent a change from an earlier and higher level of functioning" (Knight, 1996, p. 91). Risk of organic brain diseases does increase with age, and "dementias are presumed to result from diseases of the brain or physical disorders that affect brain functioning" (ibid.).

Rather than focus on preventive efforts for each of the major problem clusters, we will examine the best preventive interventions for older adults. These are organized under the following headings: indicated preventive interventions, selected preventive interventions and universal preventive interventions adapted from Konnert, Gatz and Hertzsprung, 2001.[2]

Universal prevention. Universal prevention programs target all older adults or their families, and they typically emphasize wellness, empowerment and advocacy. These qualities are often found in self-help groups and peer counseling programs, as well as intergenerational services, as when older adults are matched with children to provide advice and encouragement. As Konnert, Gatz and Hertzsprung observe, many universal preventive programs are based on volunteerism. Others emphasize a paraprofessional role that may even include remuneration for services.

When universal programs are broadened to the community, they often take the form of neighborhood networking for mutual assistance, as when older adults actively participate in town hall meetings that provide them with "information about medical care (e.g., insurance, advance directives), health promotion and wellness, and legal, ethical, and financial aspects of aging" (Konnert, Gatz and Hertzsprung, 2001, p. 326).

Selected prevention. In contrast to universal programs, selective preventive programs typically "define their targets in terms of having experienced some particular stressful life event" (ibid., p. 321). As we have mentioned, life events that are predictable and can be planned for include one's changing health and loss of one's partner and close friends. Typically, selective interventions either make changes to the environment or help strengthen coping skills.

---

[2]Adapted from Candace Connert, Margaret Gatz and E. A. Meyen Hertzsprung (1999). Preventive interventions for older adults. In M. Duffy (Ed.), *Handbook of Counseling and Psychotherapy with Older Adults* (pp. 314-34). New York: John Wiley & Sons.

Modifying the environment might involve broadening and strengthening social support networks, as happens in visitor programs, telephone support programs and support groups. Often the most isolated elderly are targeted—for example, institutionalized older adults, older adults in rural communities and recent widows.

The family is also a common focus of education and intervention: "The competency of . . . the entire family system can be enhanced through educational methods for developing new skills, forming new attitudes, gaining new insights, or obtaining new knowledge" (Smith, 1999, p. 383). As Smith observes, these groups often take the form of psychoeducational support groups, but they can also involve family reminiscence and family life enrichment and education.

Interventions intended to strengthen existing coping skills include communication training, assertiveness training, educational and work-related skills training, and a variety of cognitive-behavioral interventions to help older adults manage stress "by anticipating events, altering perceptions of events, and enlarging coping repertoires" (Konnert, Gatz and Hertzsprung, 2001, p. 322).

We mentioned earlier that family caregivers are often the focus of selective preventive programs. Family caregivers can be taught a variety of coping strategies that can be tailored to their circumstances. For example, family caregivers of older adults suffering from Alzheimer's disease can learn to cope with negative emotions such as depression and frustration as well as take advantage of adult daycare programs.

Indicated prevention. The last major category of preventive interventions encompasses indicated prevention programs, which target those who already have a known disorder or condition. Programs typically attempt to prevent institutionalization of those who already have mental and physical health conditions. As Konnert, Gatz and Hertzsprung observe, "many programs have targeted older adults living alone, . . . providing them with services such as transportation, meal programs, homemaker services, personal and nursing aid" (2001, p. 319).

Unfortunately, research on indicated prevention programs suggests that those who are targeted tend not to be at particularly high risk for institutionalization, so there is a need to identify those who are at greatest risk and provide services to them. Like selective prevention programs, indicated prevention programs also tend to provide support to family caregivers.

INTEGRATIVE THEMES

This chapter opened with a discussion of how a Christian understanding of the problems in older adulthood must begin with a biblical perspective on aging. Among several integrative themes, of particular importance are issues in classification, pastoral care and how problems in older adulthood relate to our fallen human condition.

Issues in classification. The major point we want to raise is not whether any particular diagnosis should be added to or removed from contemporary categories but whether mental health professionals' perceptions and stereotypes of older adults may lead to bias in diagnosis, case conceptualization and intervention. Christian mental health professionals may need to advocate for older adults, who are often marginalized in a youth-focused culture that has not retained a place of respect and esteem for the elderly.

To aid in proper assessment and treatment planning, Christian mental health professionals can ask themselves, *Why am I making assumptions about this person's age? What cues am I responding to?*[3] Research from social psychology reminds us to draw on base-rate information when asking ourselves, *What is the probability that such and such characteristic or behavior is true of a group?* Even if a stereotype is true—that is, even if the characteristic or behavior occurs more often among members of the identified group (e.g., the elderly) than in other groups—it can still have a negative effect on how we perceive and treat a particular older adult.

This brings up the issue of prejudice. *Prejudice* refers to a prejudgment of an individual, typically based on a predisposition to discriminate. Prejudices are a form of judgment, and like all judgments, they are based on schemas that influence how people interpret behavior and events (Devine, 1989). Both stereotypes and accurate data reflecting base rates can lead to prejudice. Christian mental health professionals do well to recognize and combat unintentional prejudice against the elderly.

A helpful article on the subject of combating stereotypes and prejudice is offered by Devine (1989), who argues against the inevitability of prejudice. Her research offers evidence that automatic stereotypes can exist independent of an individual's current attitudes and beliefs.

---

[3]These suggestions are adapted from Mark A. Yarhouse (2000), Review of social cognition research on stereotyping: application to psychologists working with older adults (*Journal of Clinical Geropsychology*, 6:121-31).

In her study, both high-prejudice and low-prejudice subjects were aware of various stereotypes; however, low-prejudice subjects evidenced controlled processes that inhibited the effects of automatic processes that would otherwise lead to prejudice.[4]

But how does this change occur? Although change is neither likely nor easy, Devine argues that nonprejudiced responses are a function of "intentional, controlled processes and require a conscious decision to behave in a nonprejudiced fashion" (ibid., p. 15). To combat prejudices, she contends, new responses can and must be learned and practiced. One must "(a) initially decide to stop the old behavior, (b) remember the resolution, and (c) try repeatedly and decide repeatedly to eliminate the habit before the habit can be eliminated" (ibid.).

Devine also observes that stereotypes are not actually eliminated from the awareness of persons who are less prejudiced; rather, they maintain ongoing efforts to bring competing responses to conscious activation. Neglecting this process raises the risk of falling into old habits. To become less prejudiced takes time and effort. But for Christian mental health care providers, such time and effort are important steps toward understanding the needs of and providing effective care to older adults.

Sin and psychopathology. In light of the multitier approach to sin that distinguishes between our sinful state, specific acts of sin and the consequences of sin, the vast majority of concerns that face older adults are the reflection of our sinful state. That is, many of the normal age-related changes associated with older adulthood exist because of the Fall, because to be human is to participate in a fallen world, to realize that our circumstances are not as they should be. So "normal, age-related changes" are best understood as normal within a fallen world in which aging and death are normative. However, there is nothing "normal" about aging and death in terms of God's original plan for his creation. Understanding this puts the Christian mental health professional in a strategic place to help older adults and a broader culture that has not come to terms with aging and death.

A Christian perspective on aging, death and dying is diametrically opposed to our broader culture's view. Our culture does a great deal

---

[4]Devine's (1989) approach can be contrasted with that of Locke, MacLeod and Walker (1994), who argue that it is the relative differences in amount of negative stereotypical information automatically activated that distinguishes high- and low-prejudiced people.

to slow people's aging and to distance people from the elderly and the idea of death. To the secular mind, death is the ultimate loss because it is the end of what a person can experience. Yet because experience is the ultimate authority, quality-of-life experience often guides ethical decision making, so that ending a life is a possibility to the secular mind: "a life can be so broken, disabled, or fading as to be not worthwhile, or of no social value, and hence it may be neglected or even extinguished by voluntary or involuntary euthanasia" (Vere, 1995, p. 284).

Christians see death as a result of sin. Death is not God's intention for human experience, but it is the natural consequence of disobedience (Rom 5:12). We all experience death, but "death is not the ultimate disintegration, though it is in a sense a 'sacrament' or outward sign of universal sinfulness" (Vere, 1995, p. 284). As C. S. Lewis observes, "Human death is the result of sin and the triumph of Satan. But it is also the means of redemption from sin, God's medicine for Man and His weapon against Satan" (1960, p. 128).

Once our lives are separated from any transcendent meaning, then aging is a problem because it points to death, an experience to be avoided at all cost if quality of life can be maintained and if there is no sense of meaning or purpose beyond it.

Furthermore, a secular view of aging and death can find consolation only in achievements and generativity or passing along a part of oneself to future generations. But without a coherent worldview to support these as gains, there is little reason to celebrate the end of one's life. For the Christian, however, because of who God is and because he chose to relate to us in a personal way, he gave our existence transcendent meaning:

> Out of the recognition that life is determined neither by what one did, had, or achieved, nor by one's friends or relatives, nor even by one's own self-understanding, the way might be found to Him whose heart is greater than ours and who says through His own son, the broken servant of Yahweh: "You are accepted." (Nouwen and Gaffney, 1976, p. 131)

Pastoral care and disordered desires. A pastoral perspective on aging and older adulthood builds on the foundation we have laid with respect to death as a consequence of the Fall and the preparation for a life in Christ. To think Christianly about aging and older adulthood is to reflect on what it means to us that we are aging and to come to terms with our mortality. As Nouwen and Gaffney observe, "Care for the elderly means, first of all, to make ourselves available to the experience of becoming old" (1976, p. 102). Elsewhere, the authors state:

> The most important contribution to the elderly is to offer them a chance to bring us into a creative contact with our own aging. Just as the handicapped should remind us of our limitations; the blind, our lack of vision; the anxiety-ridden, our fears; and the poor, our poverty—so the old should remind us of our aging. Thus we can be brought in touch with the fullness of the life experience by an inner solidarity with all human suffering and all human growth. This inner solidarity is the basis of the human community where real care and healing can take place. (p. 154)

The Christian mental health professional and pastoral care provider will have to fight the tendency to keep the elderly in the outgroup while maintaining emotional fidelity to his or her own ingroup (as a young or middle-aged adult). It has been observed that "as long as the old remain strangers, caring can hardly be meaningful" (ibid., p. 104). According to Nouwen and Gaffney:

> No guest will ever feel welcome when his host is not at home in his own house. No old man or woman will ever feel free to reveal his or her hidden anxieties or deepest desires when they only trigger off uneasy feelings in those who are trying to listen. It is no secret that many of our suggestions, advice, admonitions, and good words are often offered in order to keep distance rather than to allow closeness. When we are primarily concerned with giving old people something to do, offering them entertainment and distractions, we might avoid the painful realization that most people do not want to be distracted but heard, not entertained but sustained. (pp. 102-3)

An additional pastoral theme is stewardship of one's life (Ps 90). The fact of our aging and our eventual death is a practical reminder that our lives are not our own. Our lives are fleeting, and what we do with the life we have been entrusted with is of eternal significance. Again, Nouwen and Gaffney issue an important reminder:

> To create space for the elderly means, first of all, that I myself must stop relating to my life as to an inalienable property I am obliged to defend at all cost. How can I ever allow the aged to

enter into my world when I refuse to perceive my life as a fleeting reality I can foster but never cling to? How can I make any old person feel welcome in my presence when I want to hold on to my life as to a possession that nobody can take away from me? How can I create a friendly space for the elderly when I do not want to be reminded of my own historicity and mortality, which make me just as much a "passer-by" as anybody else? (ibid., p. 109)

So there is a necessary relationship between coming to terms with one's mortality and coming to terms with this life as a relatively short and fleeting existence of which one is but a steward.

Similarly, pastoral care for older adults should reorder our very way of living, so that we begin to live as if who we are is more important than what we have or what status we have achieved. As Nouwen and Gaffney observe,

If it is true that people age the way they live, our first task is to help people discover life styles in which "being" is not identified with "having," self-esteem does not depend on success, and goodness is not the same as popularity. Care for the aging means a persistent refusal to attach any kind of ultimate significance to grades, degrees, positions, promotions, or rewards. (ibid., p. 137)

Work, vocation, calling and purpose are important, precisely because God said that these activities are important. But they are not important because of what they accrue for us but for whose purpose they are completed. In this spirit, we are reminded that there is no biblical basis for retirement as we think of today. Arnold suggests that this is a modern concept. Even though the Levites "retired" from service at age fifty, they worked with younger priests.

Without a doubt, in ancient agricultural societies, the nature of physical labor meant cessation from work at a relatively early age. But retirees were then responsible for training their grandchildren and became advisors for the younger generation. The Bible has no concept of ending one's life-work in order to spend the remainder of one's days in leisure. (1996, p. 14)

Of course, for the older adult, connection to family and community is of utmost importance. Connection across generations is a gift to all generations, and delight in these relationships is one aspect of what it means to live a life characterized by shalom (right relationship with God, oneself, others and one's physical surroundings). In an interesting study of one hundred elderly widows, Malatesta et al. found that a variety of activities, such as "conversations with a man" and "going places with a man" were an important part of happiness and quality of life (1988, p. 59). A variety of activities met the "affectional" needs of these women, including "activities [with] children and grandchildren," "wearing attractive clothing" and "expressing . . . spirituality" (ibid.). Are we surprised by these findings? Have we kept older adults at arm's length so long that we do not see them as people with emotional and affectional needs? Is it possible that despite our best intentions we are sometimes guilty of "ageism," disrespect of older adults, ultimately an affront to the experience of aging (Moss, 1995)? As Moss observes, ageism "subtly encourages younger people no longer to identify with their elders as human beings" (1995, p. 149). Older adults are not "other"; they are made in the image of God, and they are living reminders to us of God's future for us in eternity.

An additional consideration is whether it is best to view counseling and pastoral care of older adults as a special kind of care. We commonly think of geriatrics as a specialty, and rightly so, because practicing competently requires bringing together findings from neurology, pharmacology, psychology, biology and so on. However, specialized care is a double-edged sword that can further isolate the elderly:

> It seems important, however, to say that caring for the aging is not a special type of care. As soon as we start thinking about care for the aging as a subject of specialization, we are falling into the trap of societal segregation, which care is precisely trying to overcome. When we allow our world to be divided into young, middle-aged, and old people, each calling for a specialized approach, then we are taking the real care out of caring, since the development and growth of men and women take place, first of all, by creative interaction among the generations. (Nouwen and Gaffney, 1976, p. 117)

So geriatric work *is* a specialty, but we must not allow the recent moves toward specialization to obviate the generalist's responsibility to work with this underserved population and to do so with professional competence. To isolate older adults by having them seen only by specialists is ultimately a disservice both to the older adult and to the broader community. Not only does isolation reinforce gaps in training among generalists, but it is also a disservice to community members who would benefit from interactions across generations.

CONCLUSION

Problems in older adulthood include a wide range of clinical problems. In this chapter we discussed most of the major categories of mental illness. A Christian perspective affirms the integrity of older adults as image bearers of God. Aging can be understood as one consequence of our fallen condition, but also as a marker that indicates God's victory over death and his plan for us in the resurrection.

RECOMMENDED READING:

Martz, S. (Ed.). (1987). *When I am an old woman I shall wear purple.* Watsonville, CA: Papier-Maché Press. Encouraging reflections on aging and older adulthood.

Nouwen, H. J. M., and Gaffney, W. J. (1976). *Aging: The fulfillment of life.* New York: Doubleday. Thoughtful reflections on the aging process.

Waters, E. B., and Goodman, J. (1990). *Empowering older adults.* San Francisco: Jossey-Bass. A helpful resource from a "strengths" or wellness perspective.

Weaver, G. (2004). Embodied spirituality: Experiences of identity and spiritual suffering. In M. Jeeves (Ed.), *From cells to souls* (pp. 77-101). Grand Rapids, MI: Eerdmans. A thoughtful contribution to the literature from a leading Christian scholar.

REFERENCES

Ables, N., Cooley, S., Deithc, I. M., Harper, M. S., Hinrichsen, G., Lopez, M. A., and Molinari, V. A. (1998). What practitioners should know about working with older adults. *Professional Psychology: Research and Practice, 29*(5), 413-27.

Acierno, R., Hersen, M., and Van Hasselt, V. B. (1996). Anxiety-based disorders. In M. Hersen and V. B. Van Hasselt (Eds.), *Psychological treatment of older adults: An introductory textbook* (pp. 149-80). New York: Plenum.

American Association of Retired Persons. (1990). *A profile of older adult Americans.* Washington, DC: Author.

American Psychological Association. (1992). Ethical principles of psychologists and code of conduct. *American Psychologist, 47,* 1597-611.

American Psychological Association. (2002). Ethical principles of psychologist and code of conduct. *American Psychologist, 57*(12), 1060-73.

Arnold, W. T. (1996). Age, old (the aged). In W. A. Elwell (Ed.), *Evangelical dictionary of biblical theology* (pp. 13-14). Grand Rapids, MI: Baker.

Bretschneider, J. G., and McCoy, N. L. (1998). Sexual interest and behavior in healthy 80- to 102-year-olds. *Archives of Sexual Behavior, 17*(2), 109-29.

Buono, M. D., Zaghi, P. C., Padoani, W., Scocco, P., Vrciuoli, O., Pauro, P., and de Leo, D. (1998). Sexual feelings and sexual life in an Italian sample of 335 elderly 65- to 106-year-olds. *Archives of Gerontology and Geriatrics, 6,* 155-62.

Colerick, E., and George, L. (1986). Predictors of institutionalization among caregivers of patients with Alzheimer's disease. *Journal of the American Geriatric Society, 34,* 493-98.

Devine, P. G. (1989). Stereotypes and prejudice: Their automatic and controlled components. *Journal of Personality and Social Psychology, 56,* 5-18.

DeVries, H. M. (1996). Cognitive-behavioral interventions. In J. E. Birren (Ed.), *Encyclopedia of gerontology.* San Diego: Academic.

DeVries, H. M., and Coon, D. W. (2002). Cognitive/behavioral group therapy with older adults. In F. W. Kaslow and T. Patterson (Eds.), *Comprehensive handbook of psychotherapy* (pp. 547-67). New York: John Wiley & Sons.

DeVries, H. M., and Gallagher-Thompson, D. (1994). Older adults. In F. M. Datillio and A. Freeman (Eds.), Cognitive-behavioral strategies in crisis intervention (pp. 200-218). New York: Guilford.

Dick, L. P., and Gallagher-Thompson, D. (1996). Late-life depression. In M. Hersen and V. B. Van Hasselt (Eds.), *Psychological treatment of older adults: An introductory textbook* (pp. 181-208). New York: Plenum.

Dupree, L. W., and Schonfeld, L. (1996). Substance abuse. In M. Hersen and V. B. Van Hasselt (Eds.), *Psychological treatment of older adults: An introductory text* (pp. 281-97). New York: Plenum.

Edelstein, B., Northrop, L., Staats, N., and Packard, N. (1996). Assessment of older adults. In M. Hersen and V. B. Van Hasselt (Eds.), *Psychological treatment of older adults: An introductory textbook* (pp. 35-68). New York: Plenum.

Fisher, J. E., Zeiss, A. M., and Carstensen, L. L. (2001). Psychopathology in the aged. In H. E. Adams and P. B. Sutker (Eds.), *Comprehen-*

sive handbook of psychopathology (3rd ed.) (pp. 921-52). New York: Kluwer Academic.

Gatz, M., Fiske, A., Fox, L. S., Kaskie, B., Kasl-Godley, J. E., McCallum, T. J., and Wetherell, J. L. (1998). Empirically validated psychological treatments for older adults. *Journal of Mental Health and Aging, 4*(1), 9-46.

Glynn, S. M., Muesser, K. T., and Bartels, S. J. (1996). Schizophrenia. In M. Hersen and V. B. Van Hasselt (Eds.), *Psychological treatment of older adults: An introductory text* (pp. 223-44). New York: Plenum.

Goldman, A., and Carroll, J. L. (1990). Educational intervention as adjunct to treatment to erectile dysfunction in older couples. *Journal of Sex and Marital Therapy, 16*(3), 127-41.

Gomberg, E. S. L., and Zucker, R. A. (1998). Substance use and abuse in old age. In I. H. Nordhus, G. R. VandenBos, S. Berg and P. Fromholt (Eds.), *Clinical geropsychology* (pp. 189-204). Washington, DC: American Psychological Association.

Heiman, J. R., and Mestor, C. M. (1997). Empirically validated treatment for sexual dysfunction. *Annual Review of Sex Research, 8,* 148-94.

Hillman, J. L., Stricker, G., and Zweig, R. A. (1997). Clinical psychologists' judgments of older adult patients with character pathology: Implications for practice. *Professional Psychology: Research and Practice, 28,* 179-83.

James, J. W., and Haley, W. E. (1995). Age and health bias in practicing clinical psychologists. *Psychology and Aging, 10*(4), 610-16.

Johannes, C. B., Araujo, A. B., Feldman, H. A., Derby, C. A., Kleinman, K. P., and McKinlay, J. B. (2000). Incidence of erectile dysfunction in men 40 to 69 years old: Longitudinal results for the Massachusetts male aging study. *Journal of Urology, 163*(2), 460-67.

Karon, B. P., and VandenBos, G. R. (1998). Schizophrenia and psychosis in elderly populations. In I. H. Nordhus, G. R. VandenBos, S. Berg and P. Fromholt (Eds.), *Clinical geropsychology* (pp. 219-27). Washington, DC: American Psychological Association.

Kasl-Godley, J. E., Gatz, M., and Fiske, A. (1998). Depression and depressive symptoms in old age. In I. H. Nordhus, G. R. VandenBos, S. Berg and P. Fromholt (Eds.), *Clinical geropsychology* (pp. 211-18). Washington, DC: American Psychological Association.

Kennedy, G. J. (2000). *Geriatric mental health care: A treatment guide for health professionals.* New York: Guilford.

Knight, B. G. (1996). Psychotherapy with older adults (2nd ed.). Thousand Oaks, CA: Sage.

Koenig, H. G., and Blazer, D. G. (1992). Epidemiology of geriatric affective disorders. *Clinics in Geriatric Medicine, 8,* 235, 251.

Konnert, C., Gatz, M., and Hertzsprung, E. A. M. (1999). Preventive interventions for older adults. In M. Duffy (Ed.), *Handbook of counseling and psychotherapy with older adults* (pp. 314-34). New York: John Wiley & Sons.

Laumann, E., Gagnon, J., Michael, R., and Michaels, S. (1994). *The social organization of sexuality.* Chicago: University of Chicago Press.

Leiblum, S. R., and Rosen, R. C. (Eds.). (2000). *Principles and practice of sex therapy* (3rd ed.). New York: Guilford.

Lewis, C. S. (1960). *Miracles.* New York: Macmillan.

Locke, V., MacLeod, C., and Walker, I. (1994). Automatic and controlled activation of stereotypes: Individual differences associated with prejudice. *British Journal of Social Psychology, 33,* 29-46.

Malatesta, V. J., Chambless, D. L., Pollack, M., and Cantor, A. (1988). Widowhood, sexuality and aging: A lifespan analysis. *Journal of Sex and Marital Therapy, 14*(1), 49-62.

Marsiglio, W., and Donnelly, D. (1991). Sexual relations in later life: A national study of married persons. *Journal of Gerontology, 46*(6), 338-44.

Maxmen, J. S., and Ward, N. G. (1995). *Essential psychopathology and its treatment* (2nd ed.). New York: W. W. Norton.

Moberg, D. O. (1984). Aging, Christian view of. In W. A. Elwell (Ed.), *Evangelical dictionary of theology* (pp. 21-24). Grand Rapids, MI: Baker.

Moss, M. J. (1995). Aging. In D. J. Atkinson, D. F. Field, A. Holmes and O. O'Donovan (Eds.), *New dictionary of Christian ethics and pastoral theology* (pp. 148-49). Downers Grove, IL: InterVarsity Press.

Mroczek, D. I., and Kolarz, C. H. (1998). The effect of age in positive and negative affect: A developmental perspective on happiness. *Journal of Personality and Social Psychology, 75*(5), 1333-49.

Nielsen, G. H., Nordhus, I. H., and Kvale, G. (1998). Insomnia in older adults. In I. H. Nordhus, G. R. VandenBos, S. Berg and P. Fromholt (Eds.), *Clinical geropsychology* (pp. 167-75). Washington, DC: American Psychological Association.

Nouwen, H. J. M., and Gaffney, W. J. (1976). *Aging: The fulfillment of life.* New York: Doubleday.

O'Connor, B. P., and Dyce, J. A. (2001). Personality disorders. In M. Hersen and V. B. Van Hasselt (Eds.), *Advanced abnormal psychol-*

ogy (2nd ed.) (pp. 399-418). New York: Kluwer.

Patterson, R. L. (1996). Organic disorders. In M. Hersen and V. B. Van Hasselt (Eds.), *Psychological treatment of older adults: An introductory textbook* (pp. 259-80). New York: Plenum.

Robinson, J. W., Faris, P. D., and Scott, C. B. (1999). Psychoeducational group increases vaginal dilation for younger women and reduces sexual fears for women of all ages with gynecological carcinoma treated with radiotherapy. *International Journal of Oncology, Biology, Physiology, 44*(3), 497-506.

Schiavi, R. C., Schreiner-Engel, P., Mandeli, J., Schanzer, H., and Cohen, E. (1990). Healthy aging and male sexual function. *American Journal of Psychiatry, 147*(6), 766-71.

Schneider, L. S. (1995). Efficacy of clinical treatment for mental disorders among older persons. In M. Gatz (Ed.), *Emerging issues in mental health and aging* (pp. 163-82). Washington, DC: American Psychological Association.

Scogin, F. R. (1998). Anxiety in old age. In I. H. Nordhus, G. R. VandenBos, S. Berg and P. Fromholt (Eds.), *Clinical geropsychology* (pp. 205-10). Washington, DC: American Psychological Association.

Smith, G. C. (1999). Prevention and promotion models of intervention for strengthening families. In M. Duffy (Ed.), *Handbook of counseling and psychotherapy with older adults* (pp. 378-94). New York: John Wiley & Sons.

Solomon, J. R., Faletti, M. V., and Yunik, S. S. (1982). The psychologist as geriatric clinician. In T. Millon, C. Green and R. Meagher (Eds.), *Handbook of clinical health psychology* (pp. 227-49). New York: Plenum.

Starr, B., and Weiner, M. (1981). *The Starr-Weiner report on sex & sexuality in the mature years.* New York: McGraw-Hill.

Steinke, E. E. (1994). Knowledge and attitudes of older adults about sexuality and aging: A comparison of two studies. *Journal of Advanced Nursing, 19*, 477-85.

Tobin, S. S., and Toseland, R. (1985). Models of services for the elderly. In A. Merk (Ed.), *Handbook of gerontological services* (pp. 549-67). New York: Van Nostrom & Reinhold.

U.S. Senate Special Committee on Aging, American Association of Retired Persons, Federal Council on the Aging, and U.S. Administration on Aging. (1991). *Aging America: Trends and projections.* Washington, DC: Department of Health and Human Services.

Vere, D. W. (1995). Death and dying. In D. J. Atkinson, D. F. Field,

A. Holmes and D. O'Donovan (Eds.), *New dictionary of Christian ethics and pastoral theology* (pp. 284-85). Downers Grove, IL: InterVarsity Press.

Waters, E. B., and Goodman, J. (1990). *Empowering older adults.* San Francisco: Jossey-Bass.

Whitbourne, S. K. (1996). Psychological perspectives on the normal aging process. In L. C. Carstensen, B. A. Edelstein and L. Dornbrand (Eds.), *The practical handbook of clinical psychology* (pp. 3-35). Thousand Oaks, CA: Sage.

Yarhouse, M. A. (2000). Review of social cognition research on stereotyping: Application to psychologists working with older adults. *Journal of Clinical Geropsychology, 6*(2), 121-31.

Yarhouse, M. A., and DeVries, H. M. (1998). The general principles of ethical conduct: A framework for psychologists working with older adults. *Journal of Clinical Geropsychology, 4*(2), 141-52.

Part Four

CASTING A VISION

14

THE MODERN
PSYCHOPATHOLOGIES

Challenges and Opportunities

*T*he scientific study of psychopathology arose to meet the challenges faced by those who sought to understand the experience of suffering people. The need was for classification and clarity, for an answer to the question, Can emotional and mental suffering be divided into discrete categories that can be identified, differentiated, researched and communicated? The ongoing revisions of the *DSM* and *ICD* taxonomies evidence these continued efforts and the reality that no absolute and universally accepted classification system has yet been developed. While proponents of these taxonomies continue to refine and revise them, opponents call for complete reform or eradication of taxonomies altogether. Though it is clear that the *DSM* nosology is less than perfect, what is perhaps even clearer is that prior to its development "confusion reigned" (Kendell, 1975, p. 87).

The *DSM* represents arguably the best effort to date to formulate a common nosology that unites researchers and caregivers in their understanding and communication of psychopathology; however, its authors readily admit that its categories are highly debated (Frances et al., 1990; Spitzer, Williams and Skodol, 1980). As Widiger and Clark state, "There might not in fact be one sentence within *DSM-IV* for which well-meaning clinicians, theorists, and researchers could not find some basis for fault" (2000, p. 946). As plans proceed for continued revisions, challenges and opportunities are being identified in hopes to guide future directions for the field of psychopathology. We will highlight a few of those and reflect on the challenges and opportunities that face the church, as Christians are stakeholders in the further development and understanding of psychopathology.

CHALLENGES AND OPPORTUNITIES FOR PSYCHOPATHOLOGY

From the development of the first edition of the *Diagnostic and Statistical Manual of Mental Disorders* (APA, 1952), researchers and clinicians in the field of psychopathology have debated its value and the value of classification systems in general for the work of psychiatry and clinical psychology. The ever-increasing body of research in psychopathology has served as a major impetus for continuing revision of psychopathology classification. This literature has identified numerous challenges and opportunities for the future direction of the field.[1] We will address a few of the many challenges facing the field of psychopathology, including the delimiting nature of research itself, definitions of normality and abnormality, comorbidity, heterogeneity, the organizational structure of the *DSMs*, and the role of clinical testing in diagnosis. We will provide an overview of some criticisms of the existing nosology as well as of suggested new models for classification and diagnosis.

The delimiting nature of research. Although research associated with the development and revisions of the *DSM* nosology has undoubtedly provided a scientific basis for understanding psychopathology, the very existence of this now commonly accepted and utilized system has also served in many cases to limit research to the diagnostic criteria contained within the system. A delineation of scope occurs as specific and discrete symptom clusters are identified and categorized. Perhaps this is an unavoidable reality; nevertheless, it is a challenge to the growth of the field of psychopathology. What we witness as an inductive approach to the study of psychopathology can be subtly trans-

---

[1]In particular, we are indebted to the works of Clark, Watson and Reynolds (1995) and Widiger and Clark (2000) in our discussion of this body of literature.

formed into a deductive approach relying on existing explanatory frameworks for understanding symptom clusters. The risk is that we may foreclose prematurely on other explanatory frameworks for interpreting specific symptoms and conceptualizing various symptom clusters. Rather than science driving our understanding of psychopathology, we may find our present constructs of psychopathology (i.e., the *DSM*) driving the science (Clark, Watson and Reynolds, 1995). Some question whether a scientifically valid nosology of psychopathology is even possible because of the theoretical and interpretive nature of the classification process. Kendler (1990) claims that certain "value judgments" are part of the very fabric of the nosological process, meaning that all of what is studied in psychopathology is viewed through the lenses of a specific explanatory framework.[2] From this perspective, the nosological process can never be truly empirical or objective.

Freedom to explore entirely new ways of conceiving psychopathology needs to be continually embraced and encouraged within the field so that we do not become constrained by our current conceptualizations. Further, researchers need to be freed from pressure to study only existing categories while they continue to contribute to the body of research devoted to further revision of those categories.

Challenges to the current system. Some have argued that the very categorical nature of the current classification system is a misguided direction for the field of psychopathology and the work of clinical diagnosis. Significant attention has been given to a few key aspects of the current categorical system that may point to the need for alternative models of classification to be considered. These include the high rates of comorbidity of psychopathology diagnoses in actual clinical practice, the extent of heterogeneity both within diagnostic classes and across them, and the current organizational structure of the *DSM* nosology. The challenges to the current system actually begin, however, at its foundation with the very definition of psychopathology— the differentiation of abnormal from normal.

The definition of *mental disorder* employed by the *DSM* has under-

---

[2]Recall our discussion in chapter one of how Asperger's syndrome became an explanatory framework that helped mental health professionals organize symptom presentation into a conceptual model they could understand and communicate to others. That specific explanatory model was "unavailable" prior to the mid-1940s. As it gained recognition (closer to the end of the twentieth century), it has become an explanatory framework that helps clinicians "see" the disorder.

gone as many revisions as the classification system itself, and its current form is subject to the same rigorous debate as the entire system
is. Some question the adequacy of the definition, while others ask if it
is even possible to consistently differentiate abnormal behavior from
normal behavior (Widiger and Clark, 2000). An adequate definition of
mental disorder must offer meaningful distinctions and universally
identifiable points of demarcation between normal and abnormal
psychological functioning.

The definition of *mental disorder* in the *DSM-IV-TR* reads as follows:

> In DSM-IV, each of the mental disorders is conceptualized as a
> clinically significant behavioral or psychological syndrome or
> pattern that occurs in an individual and that is associated with
> present distress (e.g., a painful symptom) or disability (i.e., im-
> pairment in one or more important areas of functioning) or
> with a significantly increased risk of suffering death, pain, dis-
> ability, or an important loss of freedom. In addition, this syn-
> drome or pattern must not be merely an expectable and
> culturally sanctioned response to a particular event, for exam-
> ple, the death of a loved one. Whatever its original cause, it
> must currently be considered a manifestation of a behavioral,
> psychological, or biological dysfunction in the individual. Nei-
> ther deviant behavior (e.g., political, religious, or sexual) nor
> conflicts that are primarily between the individual and society
> are mental disorders unless the deviance or conflict is a symp-
> tom of a dysfunction in the individual, as described above.
> (APA, 2000, p. xxxi)

This definition reflects the clinical, academic and political controversy that surrounded the publication of the *DSM-III* (APA, 1980).
Those involved in that *DSM* revision sought to establish unequivocal
criteria for determining whether homosexuality should be considered
a mental disorder (Spitzer and Williams, 1982). The *DSM-IV* revision
includes the stipulation that for a behavior pattern to be considered a
mental disorder, it must "cause clinically significant distress or impairment in social, occupational, or other important areas of functioning"
(p. 7). This made individuals' self-assessment of their experience of
distress or disturbance of their daily functioning the deciding criterion for whether behavior patterns (in this case sexual acts, urges or
fantasies) are pathological. The National Law Center for Children
and Families raised the valid concern that this definition may have

normalized aberrant sexual behaviors, such as pedophilia (Spitzer and Wakefield, 1999). If a person does not experience personal distress because of her or his urges, inclinations or behavior, that person does not meet the criterion for a mental disorder:

> In sum, missing from both the DSM-III-R and the DSM-IV paraphilia criterion sets are the means by which to determine whether the sexually deviant behaviors or fantasies are the result of a dysfunction (or pathology) within the individual. This is not to say that the deviant sexual behaviors are not illegal or that the sexual exploitation of a child is not harmful, but that neither the DSM-III-R nor DSM-IV provides adequate guidance for how to distinguish a willful and voluntary deviant sexual behavior that is engaged in for longer than 6 months from sexual activities that are compelled by the presence of a mental disorder. (Widiger and Clark, 2000, p. 950)

Fortunately, in the text revision of *DSM-IV*, the wording was changed to state that subjective distress in response to sexual attractions, specifically in the case of pedophilia, is not a criterion required to warrant diagnosis. The *DSM-IV-TR* puts it this way:

> Because of the egosyntonic nature of Pedophilia, many individuals do not experience significant distress. It is important to understand that experiencing distress about having the fantasies, urges, or behaviors is not necessary for a diagnosis of Pedophilia. Individuals who have a pedophilic arousal pattern and act on these fantasies or urges with a child qualify for the diagnosis of Pedophilia. (APA, 2000, p. 571)

Greater clarity is still needed in the form of universally recognized and reliably identifiable boundaries between normal and abnormal psychological functioning. Unless we can agree that we heard and saw the same thing, we do not really have much of a science. Whether we are talking about a nosology for classifying mental illness or even basic assertions about religious behavior and experience, we need to have at least some basic shared assumptions about what human suffering "looks" and "sounds" like. The *DSM-IV* may be moving in the right direction with its demand that in order for a diagnosis of mental disorder to be given, a condition "must currently be considered a manifestation of a behavioral, psychological, or biological dysfunction in the individual" (APA, 1994, p. xxxi). However, little mention of such "dysfunctions" is made within the criteria for particular diagnoses, and in many cases the criteria emphasize the person's experience of impairment and distress. In this sense the *DSM* is at least a starting place but certainly not the endpoint for meaningful conversation and collaboration.

The key issue here is the ability of the diagnostic process to determine the presence or absence of pathology within the person. To that end, criterion sets for specific diagnoses need to include explicit criteria to determine the behavioral, psychological or biological pathology or an acknowledgment that the categorical distinction for this diagnosis is imprecise. Where clear criteria are not yet defined, "the concern for defining a precise boundary between normality and psychopathology might become less important than determining the appropriate professional response to different variants and degrees of pathology" (Widiger and Clark, 2000, p. 950; see also Spitzer and Williams, 1982; Widiger and Corbitt, 1994).

Some have expressed concern that continual expansion of the number and range of disorders in the revisions of the *DSM*s is beginning to blur the lines between psychopathology and normal problems in daily living (e.g., the line between depression and normal bereavement). Social and political realities shape concerns that the diagnostic system be stringent enough to keep the prevalence rates of psychopathology low in the general population. On one end of the spectrum, this trend may reflect a genuine hope that psychopathology is a relatively rare phenomenon; on the other end of the spectrum, it may reflect political and economic agendas to decrease the amount of reimbursable treatment for psychopathology. Whatever reason may underlie the pressure to sustain presumptions regarding the prevalence of psychopathology, these hypotheses need to be tested so that the true scope of the phenomena of psychopathology can be determined. As Widiger and Clark state,

> Optimal psychological functioning, as in the case of optimal physical functioning, might represent an ideal that is achieved by only a small minority of the population. The rejection of a high prevalence rate of psychopathology may reflect the best of intensions, such as concerns regarding the stigmatization of mental disorder diagnoses . . . or the potential impact of funding for treatment, . . . but these social and political concerns could also hinder a more dispassionate and accurate recogni-

tion of the true rate of a broad range of psychopathology within the population. (2000, p. 8)

Comorbidity. Another significant challenge to the categorical system utilized by the *DSMs* is the task of differentiating one mental disorder from another, not entirely dissimilar from the aforementioned challenge of differentiating mental disorders from normal functioning. The *DSM-IV-TR* claims to be "a categorical classification that divides mental disorders into types based on criterion sets with defining features" (APA, 2000, p. xxxi). This statement suggests that the divisions are clearly distinguishable one from another based on "criterion sets" and "defining features." The expressed value of such a system lies in its ability to differentiate between normal and pathological functioning and between various categories of pathological functioning. However, the *DSM-IV-TR* also includes a disclaimer that in effect relieves it from this responsibility: "there is no assumption that each category of mental disorder is a completely discrete entity with absolute boundaries dividing it from other mental disorders or from no mental disorder" (ibid.).

If the categories of the *DSM-IV-TR* are in fact not distinct boundaries between mental disorders, then its ability as a system to adequately and reliably classify psychopathology is suspect. Clinicians have typically used the *DSMs* in the practical work of psychiatry and clinical psychology with the assumption that diagnosis is a valid process of differentiating discrete clinical conditions represented by the *DSM* categories. The disclaimer of the *DSM-IV-TR* would suggest that this is an inappropriate use of the category system.

The reality of most clinical diagnoses is that most clusters of symptoms experienced by persons who seek treatment do not fit neatly into any one pure category, and most persons who present with symptoms reflective of one category also meet the criteria for diagnosis of at least one other condition. So most individuals who suffer from psychopathology can be diagnosed with comorbid conditions, and value judgments must be made as to which symptoms belong to which condition and which condition represents the principal area of clinical concern.

According to Clark, Watson and Reynolds, the

data suggest that pure, unmixed cases [of psychopathology] are not likely to be representative of the overall population of individuals with a disorder. Moreover, individuals with comorbid

conditions differ in important ways from pure cases. Most notably, individuals with comorbid conditions generally have a more
chronic and complicated course, poorer prognosis, and lessened response to treatment. (1995, p. 6)

Comorbidity represents a challenge to the *DSM* categorical system.
In future revisions it must define more clearly the criteria by which
categories are distinguished and symptoms are attributed to a given
diagnosis. In clinical practice, the severity of symptoms often is the
most important information for determining course, treatment and
outcome. It may be that "assessing the severity of dysfunction may be
as or more important than specifying the precise nature of the disorder" (Clark, Watson and Reynolds, 1995, p. 7).

Heterogeneity. Persons diagnosed with the same pathological condition may in fact enter a clinician's office with very different presenting symptoms. This heterogeneity evident both within and between
categories reflects another challenge facing the *DSM* diagnostic system. Individuals diagnosed according to the *DSM* categorical system
need meet only a certain percentage of the possible criteria for the diagnosis (e.g., five of the nine criteria for major depression are necessary for the diagnosis). This polythetic approach results in substantial
diversity among individuals with the same diagnosis. An individual diagnosed with major depressive disorder may present with either of
the following symptom patterns (or any of a multiplicity of other combinations of these criterion):

Symptom Pattern A

- depressed mood

- insomnia

- weight loss

- fatigue

- inappropriate guilt

Symptom Pattern B

- anhedonia

- hypersomnia

- weight gain

- concentration problems

- suicidal thoughts

The problem of heterogeneity results when different individuals
experience a broad range of possible symptom combinations that result in the same diagnosis—a problem acknowledged by the authors
of the *DSM* themselves, who note that patients with the same diagnosis "are likely to be heterogeneous even in regard to the defining fea-

tures of the diagnosis" (APA, 2000, p. xxxi). In addition, it opens the door to the second aspect of problematic heterogeneity—boundaries between diagnostic categories.

Clinical diagnosis is based on the ability of a clinician to identify and meaningfully interpret a cluster of symptoms present in a person seeking treatment. The degree to which a clinician is able to reliably do this depends on numerous factors, including the strength of the symptom presentation, the person's ability to articulate his or her symptom experience, and the clarity of the boundaries between diagnoses. If a significant number of symptoms shared among different diagnostic categories, and if the person describes his or her symptom experience with clusters of symptoms that do not exactly match the diagnostic categories of the *DSM* system (as is very often the case), the result is an overriding number of cases that do not clearly fit the categories and fall between them— thus the diagnosis "not otherwise specified" (NOS). According to Clark, Watson and Reynolds, "The so-called atypical case [NOS] often is more properly characterized as the typical diagnosis. Furthermore, additional data document the relative rarity of true prototypical cases" (1995, p. 10).

As Clark, Watson and Reynolds observe, both of these types of heterogeneity suggest problems with the *DSM* nosology: "From a scientific viewpoint, both phenomena suggest an inadequate taxonomy: Excessive within-category heterogeneity challenges the basis for classification, while an overabundance of unclassified boundary cases indicates poor coverage" (1995, p. 7).

***Organization of the* DSM.** Each revision of the *DSM* has sought to offer greater clarity and specificity to the diagnostic process. The addition in *DSM-III* of the five-axis system of diagnosis reflected the desire to differentiate syndromal disorders from deeper characterological problems. It was believed that there is a qualitative distinction between the phenomenological experiences of axis I and axis II disorders. However, in recent research the validity of this distinction between personality disorders and clinical syndromes has been seriously questioned. For example, schizotypal personality disorder (coded on axis II) is viewed by some professionals as a phenotype of what might be thought of as a schizophrenic genotype (coded on axis I), and family, twin and adoptions studies show an increased incidence of schizotypal personality disorder among relatives of those suffering from schizophrenia who are not themselves displaying symptoms of schizophrenia (Barlow and Durand, 2002). Further re-search to either confirm or invalidate this distinction is needed. This is especially salient in light of the growing stigma surrounding axis II diagnoses and the political issues involved where third-party payers decline to pay for the treatment of axis II conditions. The five-axis categorical system opens the door to a misperception that axis II dis-orders represent hopeless cases—people whose experience of pathol-ogy has overtaken their personality in much the same way as when cancer spreads throughout the body. In this analogy, pathology ap-pears beyond the hope of cure.

Another potential challenge arising from the organization of the *DSM* relates to the diagnostic categories themselves. Some question the placement of certain disorders within their diagnostic category, and some are calling for the addition of new categories all together. For example, posttraumatic stress disorder is currently classified as an anxiety disorder; however, the disorder's symptoms have clear disso-ciative features that might warrant its classification as a dissociative disorder. Some have suggested that its etiology in experiences of trauma is similar to that of other disorders and warrants an entirely new classification of "trauma disorders." At the very least, there is jus-tifiable disagreement regarding the boundaries of diagnostic catego-ries and the plethora of categories in the current system. As stated by Clark, Watson and Reynolds,

> These diverse proposals all highlight a taxonomic problem for which no satisfactory solution has been found. That is, al-though the major phenomenologically based diagnostic classes may seem intuitively compelling and relatively straightforward, several specific disorders do not fit comfortably into any one of them. Many disorders are phenomenological hybrids that en-compass dysfunctions characteristic of two or more diagnostic classes. (1995, p. 12)

On some level the concerns noted above are all related. Comor-bidity exists in part because of the heterogeneity of diagnostic classes, which exists in part because of the phenomenological or-ganization of the *DSM* nosology. These challenges to the current categorical system need to be addressed in future revisions of the *DSM*, if the *DSM* system remains the standard for psychopathology. Some are suggesting that categorical taxonomic systems are inade-quate for the work of psychopathology (e.g., Widiger and Shea,

1991), and alternative models are emerging from these discussions for consideration.

Alternative models of classification. The disorders listed in the *DSM* are classified primarily on the basis of the symptoms presented by persons given the diagnosis. They may have little similarity in terms of the etiology of the disorder, and there may be little theoretical justification for the grouping of disorders in a given classification (Widiger and Trull, 1993). Some have argued that symptomatology is an inadequate organizing structure for a system of psychopathology (e.g., Andreasen and Carpenter, 1993); others have focused attention on the need for theoretically unified categories of disorders (e.g., Carson, 1991; cf. Frances et al., 1990; Millon, 1991). What is clear is that the current system is less than perfect, and freedom to explore entirely new ways of conceiving psychopathology needs to be continually encouraged within the field so that we do not become constrained by our current conceptualizations (Clark, Watson and Reynolds, 1995).

One suggestion has been to consider shifting from a categorical model of psychopathology to a *dimensional model*. The challenge, according to proponents of a dimensional model, is that an inordinate number of symptoms are shared by numerous diagnostic categories, making the boundaries of those categories difficult to define. "Eleven of the sixteen major diagnostic classes are based on shared phenomenological features" (Clark, Watson and Reynolds, 1995, p. 3). For example, sleep disturbances can be a symptom of sleep disorder, depression, anxiety and other disorder categories.

The appeal of a dimensional model is the potential for greater specificity in diagnosis. The polythetic categorical model of the *DSM* may not be adequate to offer any greater specificity. A dimensional model would replace phenomenological categories of individual disorders with dimensions of symptom clusters, in which they could be weighted hierarchically based on and reflecting degrees of specificity. These symptom dimensions would serve as the foundation on which a system of diagnoses could then be constructed. The resulting system would consist then of "an ordered matrix of symptom-cluster dimensions, a diagnostic table of the elements that are used in combination to describe the rich variety of human psychopathology" (Widiger and Clark, 2000, p. 13).

A dimensional system would center on specific symptoms that could be assessed on a continuum delineating gradations of severity. Two possible advantages to such a system would be (1) the replacement of the more than three hundred diagnostic categories of the *DSM* with a smaller set of dimensional symptom clusters and (2) a more significant consideration of severity in psychopathology (Clark, Watson and Reynolds, 1995).

A second alternative model under consideration, the *etiological model,* would identify diagnoses not based on the symptoms but rather on the origins of the dysfunction (e.g., Andreasen and Carpenter, 1993). The *DSM* has all but abandoned discussion of the etiology of most mental illnesses. Perhaps the most persuasive arguments for an etiologically based system of classification emerge from studies of neurophysiology and the role that neurotransmitters such as serotonin and dopamine play in the development and maintenance of psychopathological symptoms.

Attempts to develop an etiological model based on experiential criteria are more problematic. For example, some have suggested that trauma or stress serve as an etiological class for PTSD and the adjustment disorders (Davidson and Foa, 1991). Problems associated with such experiential criteria for an etiologically based system have to do with the facts that individual experiences are by nature imprecise and many people who live through similar experiences never develop psychopathological symptoms.

Whether mental health professionals align themselves with those who seek continual revision of the current system or with those who are calling for an entirely new model for psychopathology classification, it is clear that greater clarity, specificity and utility are needed to aid the work of clinical diagnosis. As the field of psychopathology moves forward, an important question will be to what degree this is actually possible. Are the study and practice of diagnosing psychopathology by nature conducive to explicit and incontrovertible classification? If so, will such a classification system emerge from more stringent scientific methodology and ever approach clinical consensus?

The current system, though continually subject to the scrutiny of scientific verification, relies heavily on clinical consensus. Each revision of the *DSM* has resulted from committee deliberation and consensus rather than irrefutable scientific evidence. The inclusion or exclusion of diagnostic categories and disorders ultimately depends on "expert consensus" (Clark, Watson and Reynolds, 1995; Follette and Houts, 1996). This practical reality, as one might expect, has sparked one of the strongest criticisms of the *DSM* taxonomy. Many demand that this process be replaced by a reliance purely on empirical scientific data. However, this position often disregards the fact that scientific data require interpretation by human beings who are subject to faulty presuppositions, biases and agendas (Kendler, 1990; Widiger and Trull, 1993). According to Widiger and Clark,

> No diagnostic manual can be constructed without a group of fallible persons interpreting the results of existing research. These persons ideally would be consensus scholars with no preconceptions and with an adequate understanding of the research and issues, . . . but "participants are [in fact] rarely neutral with respect to the issues they are addressing, and it can be difficult for them to provide a dispassionate, balanced, and objective review and interpretation of the research" (Widiger and Trull, 1993, 73). (2000, p. 4)

Some have argued for the addition of a democratic vote in the decision-making process by which disorders are included in the *DSM* (Sadler, 2002). The idea is that forcing the committee members to deal with the varied perspectives of the broader psychological community would prevent them from developing a minority agenda and protect the process from becoming elitist and theoretically imbalanced. This, however, would open the door to much more political bias in the decision-making process. Decisions based on scientific research are not always comfortable in the political climate of the discipline or in society at large. Clark, Watson and Reynolds (1995) urge that authority be given to those making these decisions and that they base decisions on scientific research, even when specific decisions stand against the majority view of the clinical community. It is this balance between scientific research and clinical wisdom that needs greater clarification as the field of psychopathology moves forward. As it stands now, the authors of the *DSM* have an enormous responsibility and significant power over the future of psychopathology and the work of clinical diagnosis and treatment. And as Widiger and Clark (2000) so appropriately caution, "the selection of those who are to be given this authority might then be as important as the process itself" (2000, p. 948).

One suggestion for strengthening the scientific basis for diagnostic classification has come from those calling for increased emphasis on testing results in the process of diagnosis and in the formation of the criterion sets for the disorders. The *DSM-IV* took a step in this direction with the inclusion of laboratory and physical examination results in the subsection of associated features of each disorder. The field of

medicine relies heavily on laboratory tests for clinical diagnosis
(Frances et al., 1990). Such results provide more objective criteria for
the diagnostic process than the patient's self-description of symptoms.
This is based on the belief that medical diagnosis presumes the presence of a very real and objectively identifiable physiological pathology. A valid question is whether the same is true of psychopathology:

> Anxiety and depression are purportedly the result of neurophys-
> iological mechanisms, and the diagnostic criteria for some men-
> tal disorders include explicit reference to autonomic
> functioning (e.g., palpitations, pounding heart, accelerated
> heart rate, sweating, chest pain, nausea, dizziness, chills or hot
> flushes, and paresthesias in the diagnosis of a panic attack . . .),
> yet no physiological tests are required for their diagnosis. In ad-
> dition, patient self-description within psychiatry can often be
> unreliable and misleading, as respondents will at times be un-
> able or unwilling to describe their symptomatology accurately. . . .
> A hope is that laboratory tests can do the same for psychiatry as
> they have done for other domains of medicine. (Widiger and
> Clark, 2000, p. 956)

Studies of brain structure and function also represent a possible future role for laboratory tests in the diagnostic process (Kennedy, Javanmard and Vaccarino, 1997). But perhaps the most glaringly absent
testing results that might enhance the criterion sets of the diagnostic
categories are psychological tests. These results are included in the
criteria for a diagnosis of mental retardation or learning disorder;
however, they are not included for any other disorder, despite the
vast research base validating their utility for clinical diagnosis.

> The text of DSM-IV refers to specific neurotransmitters that
> might be involved in the pathophysiology of each mental disor-
> der, . . . but no reference is made to cognitive, behavioral, or in-
> terpersonal models of pathology. Instruments that assess
> cognitive, behavioral, affective or other components of psycho-
> logical functioning that comprise explicitly the diagnostic crite-
> rion sets for these disorders and for which substantial research
> already provides specificity and sensitivity rates not obtained by
> the neurophysiological instruments should at least be acknowl-
> edged along with the neurophysiological measures. (Widiger
> and Clark, 2000, p. 958)

From this perspective, the value of standardized psychological instruments needs to be recognized and their results used in the diagnostic process.

Summary. As discussed above, there is clear evidence that the current categorical system of the *DSM* series, which represents the best that the field of psychopathology has yet offered to classify and interpret the wide range of human function and dysfunction, is far from perfect. Comorbidity, heterogeneity, inconsistencies, exclusions and poorly defined boundaries are but a few of the challenges faced by the authors of the *DSM*s. Opportunities exist to refine this system or to consider entirely new ways of conceptualizing psychopathology.

As the field continues to move forward, we believe that perhaps the greatest opportunity is for the addition of a Christian voice to the deliberations. A worldview rooted in the awareness of a divine origin and plan for human functioning—in which an accurate understanding of etiology matters more than symptom reduction—the spiritual as well as material nature of human existence, the moral responsibility and consequences for human attitudes, behaviors and experiences, and the place of transcendental hope in the process of healing must be heard as decisions are made that affect the care of those whose lives are in disarray.

There is a tension, however: the more Christians draw on explicitly religious explanatory frameworks, the less valid such a view will be considered in the broader mental health community. Still, there may come a time when Christians in the field need to speak with greater clarity about the specific issues that face their community, the body of believers, just as mental health professionals from other religious communities will speak to the concerns of those who share their worldview.

CHALLENGES AND OPPORTUNITIES FOR THE CHURCH

The church has, from its inception, been a place of healing, reconciliation and restoration. From the early centuries A.D. until the modern era, the church in Western culture was the predominant instrument in the healing of troubled persons, and its writers demonstrated an increasing knowledge and grasp of the needs of persons with diverse problems. As modern psychology and psychotherapies began to gain acceptance as viable means of caring for those wounded of mind and spirit, the church's once dominant role in this type of care began to wane. A growing distinction began to be accepted between the psychological needs of people and their spiritual needs (Benner, 1998). The church seemed to lose interest, or at least its active role, in the debate over the nature of emotional and mental suffering (Oden, 1987). Faithless worldviews and anthropologies gained preeminence in Western society's deliberations, and the voice of the church fell silent as the field of psychopathology began to emerge.

At its core, psychopathology is the study of wounded souls. Given this, the voice of the church is desperately needed in contemporary deliberations on the nature of human function and dysfunction. The absence of a clear Christian voice in part reflects the discipline's general indifference toward faith-based perspectives on psychopathology. However, some of the responsibility for this must be owned by the church as a whole, and in particular by Christians in the field of psychology who have been reluctant to stand up and be heard within the scientific community. Christians in psychology face many challenges, and these have been thoroughly discussed by others (e.g., Meyers, 1991; Roberts and Talbot, 1997; Van Leeuwen, 1985). Perhaps the most significant challenge in the work of psychopathology is regaining our lost voice.

Christian philosopher Alvin Plantinga (1993) writes about the tensions felt by Christian professionals who are members of multiple communities. Christian psychologists are members of the professional psychological community, the community of Christian psychologists, their local church community, the broader community of faith and many others. Because Christian psychologists are members of multiple communities, they experience tensions that exist for all Christians, regardless of occupation or professional identity. These tensions relate to being residents of both the temporal and the eternal, being "in the world but not of the world" (Jn 17:14-19; see also Hauerwas and Willamon's 1989 discussion of the church as a colony of "resident aliens"). Though we live as the rest of the world in terms of our outward appearance, inwardly we know that we are residents of God's kingdom, heirs with Christ, and we live in anticipation of this future glory. The point Plantinga makes has scriptural foundation: we live with our eyes "fixed" on Jesus (Heb 12:2), no longer "conformed to the pattern of this world" (Rom 12:2), and this reality is meant to shape our decisions and commitments throughout our life. When we profess a faith that is consistent with biblical truth, it must reign as preeminent over all facets of our life (2 Cor 5:1-10), including our professional identity and participation in professional communities.

For the Christian, faith gives meaning to life and, if we are open, undergirds all choices we make. It gives purpose to relationships and provides hope beyond this life. Our faith provides confidence in God's revelation of himself through Scripture and through his creation, and it is only through faith that we can have any measure of confidence in historical or scientific knowledge (Noll, 1990). Christian faith is the lens through which we view all of life, including our professional discipline, and adherence to the standards of participation in the community of faith must be preeminent for every Christian. Potential tension emerges for Christian psychologists in part because faith is informed by an epistemology (or way of knowing) that is different from the epistemology that informs the broader scientific community, and Christian psychologists have explicit faith commitments that shape their priorities and agendas.

Perhaps we now have some words for things we previously did not understand. Perhaps as a result of our study of psychopathology we have a somewhat greater capacity to appreciate the limits on our upward mobility and our continuing dependence on God and on the body of believers. Further, we have the potential to more fully incarnate and "interpersonally mediate" truths that might have previously escaped us. We may even have an enlarged capacity to image God's character, concerns and compassion and put some flesh on what it means to love others as he has loved us.

Psychopathology and the field of psychology in general have firm roots in the disciplines, ideologies and methodologies of science. Christian psychologists attend to the methodologies of science because of their training and professional identification. Yet as *Christian* psychologists we are also firmly rooted in the historic Christian faith with its disciplines, ideologies and methodologies. This has often been experienced and viewed as a conflict of interest. Science and faith both represent the pursuit of Truth; however, they have historically approached this task claiming different but complementary authoritative foundations. Scriptural authority, the life of the church, the indwelling of the Holy Spirit and personal relationship with God have characterized Christian epistemologies, whereas empirical verifiability rooted in logical positivism has dominated the epistemology of science, at least until the postmodern era (Jones, 1994).

These perceived diametrically opposed epistemologies have contributed to the felt tensions of Christians in the scientific disciplines and related scientifically informed disciplines, and have sometimes resulted in a general disregard for faith arguments in professional circles (see Griffiths, 1997; Roberts, 1997). The challenge for Christians in these fields is to live in the tension between these diverse epistemological perspectives. God has chosen to reveal himself through both special revelation (Scripture) and general revelation (creation), and *both* epistemologies are necessary to embrace the breadth of this revelation.

For Christians in the sciences, the two must cease to be competing pathways to truth. The challenge is to appreciate the fact that they complement each other, while we recognize the primacy of our Christian commitments. It is the epistemology of faith that must be the guiding and driving force, because the calling to serve humanity flows from faith in God and scriptural authority. Christian faith, rooted in Scripture, values humanity in a distinctive way and supports an equally distinctive view of health (Evans, 1990). Christians in the mental health fields therefore must root themselves in the epistemologies and core assumptions that flow from Scripture and faith in God and with clarity and integrity integrate their work in the disciplines of science and caregiving.

Faith, and the concerns that flow from it and from the community of faith, ought therefore to shape our priorities and agendas—not to the exclusion of all others, but these should be preeminent. A statement by Plantinga in an address to Christian philosophers can be appropriately adapted to us:

> Christian [psychologists] . . . are the [psychologists] of the Christian community; and it is part of their task as *Christian* [psychologists] to serve the Christian community. But the Christian community has its own questions, its own concerns, its own topics for investigation, its own agenda and its own research programs. (1983, p. 6)

Christian professionals and academicians have a primary obligation, according to Plantinga, to the faith community and to the concerns of the body of Christ in its service to humanity. This, however, is not our only obligation. We are also responsible as professionals to the various professional communities that we represent and to the agendas, priorities and guidelines that shape and govern them.

It is interesting to consider the implications of such a call on our identity as psychologists. If we take this call seriously, it will affect the topics we research, including issues such as prayer, forgiveness, grace and sanctification. It will also affect the populations we serve. To follow a Christian call means to provide services to the underserved and marginalized in a global community in which there are great social injustices that factor into mental health and well-being; this has been referred to as "praxis" integration (see Canning, Pozzi, McNeil and McMinn, 2000). Or consider homosexuality, one of the most divisive topics in the church and the broader society today. Christians in the field of psychology can set a research agenda to address specific questions that the church must wrestle with in this area. The research may delve into questions of etiology and intervention as well as broader questions of sexual identity and what it means to have an identity "in Christ" (Yarhouse and Burkett, 2003).

In any case, Christians struggle with the challenge of being empirically valid, ideologically sound, accepted participants in the professional community and congruent with their Christian faith. They may feel pulled toward competing allegiances: either toward the professional community or toward the community of faith. Movement in either direction creates tension that can silence the distinctly Christian voice that is much needed within the psychological community. These points of tensions may lead some to renounce responsibility to or participation in the professional community at large on one extreme or to segregate their faith from their scientific endeavors on the other. The challenge is not only to be people of faith but also to be intentional in allowing our faith to clarify and give parameters to our work and the very questions we raise with respect to scientific inquiry.

Christian psychologists must be willing to approach their work (including the field of psychopathology) in a way that reflects the priorities and preeminence of the Christian faith. This includes promoting responsible engagement of and participation in the international psychological community and respecting the tensions that exist between it and the church. Plantinga suggests without reservation that the primary allegiance for Christian professionals must be the church and that the research questions in the agenda of the Christian professional must first stem from questions that are preeminent for the church. Such a clear and unmistakable Christian voice is much needed in current deliberations in the field of psychopathology. As we move forward in this direction, opportunities for the church exist as well.

Letting the church influence the study of psychopathology.

Come to me, all you who are weary and burdened, and I will give you rest. Take my yoke upon you and learn from me, for I am gentle and humble in heart; and you will find rest for your souls. (Mt 11:28-30)

My command is this: Love each other as I have loved you. (Jn 15:12)

The teachings of Jesus spoke of a community grounded in love and care for one another's soul. The early church became such a place, and as the gospel began to spread throughout the world, so did the influence of the church. It became a voice of understanding for those who were "weary and burdened" and a place of care. Throughout the centuries, as we discussed in chapter one, the church spoke with confidence and authority to the nature of human pain and struggle. Perspectives rooted in a worldview of faith were heard as societies sought to understand all suffering, including the phenomena we now call psychopathology.

In our time, the scientific study of psychopathology leads the way toward sought-after understandings of the wounds of people's souls but often without the voice of God's people. Thomas Oden reflects on this shift in modern times, as pastoral care was overrun by the modern psychotherapies:

What happened after 1920? It was as if a slow pendulum gradually reversed its direction and began to swing headlong toward modern psychological accommodation. . . . Pastoral care soon acquired a consuming interest in psychoanalysis, psychopathology, clinical methods of treatment, and in the whole string of therapeutic approaches that were to follow Freud. . . . Classical pastoral wisdom fell into a deep sleep. (1988, pp. 22-23)

The Scriptures offer a worldview rooted in the truth of our spiritual nature and the role of sin (on all its levels) in the sufferings of humanity. Throughout history Christians devoted to the care of those wounded of spirit have sought to understand the struggles that we all experience as we strive to live in a world that is not as it was designed to be and as we wage war between our sinful desires and the image of God within us. Much has been written throughout the centuries about the nature of these struggles and their impact on human functioning.

Categories of sin and suffering and pastoral responses of care were once spoken out clearly to a suffering world.

As the influence of modern psychology spread, the voice of the church quickly fell silent: "We have bet all our chips on the assumption that modern consciousness will lead us into vaster freedoms while our specific freedom to be attentive to our own Christian pastoral tradition has been plundered, polemicized, and despoiled" (Oden, 1988, p. 25).

The church must regain a place of influence, particularly when the issues under discussion touch on the lives of believers. The field of psychopathology is moving further away from any moral reasoning at the core of its classifications of human function and dysfunction. Perspectives from faith-based worldviews are afforded little if any credibility in the decision-making process. This is a challenge for Christians who believe that transforming societal structures, including the field of psychopathology, is part of their calling, as well as those who wish to have a more modest impact on how the church deals with these issues.

We recommend that Christians take a two-tier approach in addressing this challenge. First, recognize that a Christian explanatory framework can have an impact on the field by what we choose to dedicate our time and energy to study. Second, recognize that we are both "moral strangers" (insofar as what we believe about right and wrong is different from what other people believe) and "epistemic strangers" (insofar as how we know what we know—through general and special revelation—is different from how others know what they know). Thus some concerns may no longer be relevant to the broader culture but only to those who identify themselves as Christians.

Letting the field of psychopathology influence the church. In many places Christians have turned a deaf ear to the advancements made in understanding human functioning. Theorizing and research have led to discoveries about the complex interconnection between the mind and body, the role of neurophysiology in our feelings and thoughts, patterns of thought and behavior that can overwhelm us or cause us to stagnate, family and interpersonal dynamics that can pass from generation to generation wreaking havoc on people's lives, and so on. Spiritual leaders in the church will benefit greatly from becoming informed about these discoveries and how they can deepen the ministries of the church. The church has benefited from such advancements throughout history, drawing on contemporary understandings of the nature of humanity and the soul (psychologies) and contemporary models of caring (psychotherapies).

> In every historic epoch, pastoring has utilized—and by utilizing has helped to advance and transform—the psychology or psychologies current in that epoch. . . . Nowhere in history has Christianity adumbrated solely from its own lore a distinct psychology, either theoretically or popularly understood. To appreciate traditional pastoring is to stand ready to adopt and adapt current psychological insights and applications without abdicating the distinctly pastoral role. (Clebsch and Jaekle, 1964, pp. 68-69)

A climate of engagement needs to be restored between the church and contemporary deliberations on the nature of human function and dysfunction.

The intellectual and societal leaders of the first century were amazed at the understanding of the apostles as they spoke to them about the gospel. The apostles appeared to be well versed not only in theology but also in contemporary philosophy, literature and politics. In order to bring the truths of God's revelation to a world searching for answers to the problems that confront us, the church must regain a place of respect earned by our ability to dialogue on contemporary issues and to raise questions that arise from a worldview rooted in the Truth.

CONCLUDING THOUGHTS

It has been our intent in this book to offer some perspectives on psychopathology through the eyes of faith. The field of psychopathology is engaged in the very important work of seeking to understand the sufferings of humanity and offer some parameters that will help guide those who seek to bring comfort and healing to hurting people. This has been the work of the church for twenty centuries, and the church needs to resume a prominent role in it. The literature of the church is rich with insights and methods that can offer guidance to this work, if those involved in psychopathology and psychotherapy will heed the voices of those who have gone before and take up their call to seek faith-based understandings of the human condition.

The current system of classification of the *DSM-IV* is a useful yet limited tool. It reflects many diverse agendas and worldviews.

The DSM-IV reflects a compromise of interests. . . . Its primary goal was clinical utility; the interests of lawyers, insurers, parole officers, disability claims personnel, statisticians, educators, and so forth also played a role, however, minor. Although empirical considerations were weighted especially strongly in the latest revision, many decisions were made on the basis of expert consensus in the absence of data. Perhaps the DSM-IV is best viewed as a document with mixed origins and purposes, based in part on scientific principles but also reflecting other influences. (Clark, Watson and Reynolds, 1995, p. 16)

Strikingly absent from its pages and the contemporary debates in the field of psychopathology are voices stemming from a Christian worldview and asking the nosological questions that emerge from it.

Though we live in the world, we do not wage war as the world does. The weapons we fight with are not the weapons of the world. On the contrary, they have divine power to demolish strongholds. We demolish arguments and every pretension that sets itself up against the knowledge of God, and we take captive every thought to make it obedient to Christ. (2 Cor 10:3-5)

We have sought to model for the reader an approach to integration that shows a high regard for both special and general revelation. We want to be responsible citizens of Athens and worthy members of Jerusalem. Toward that end, Christians need to be bicultural and bilingual as we consider what it means to take our faith seriously in the study of psychopathology. Our hope and prayer is that this text represents a first step in that direction.

RECOMMENDED READING

Benner, D. G. (1998). *Care of souls: Revisioning Christian nurture and counsel.* Grand Rapids, MI: Baker. A terrific resource from a leading Christian scholar on the practical dimensions of integrating faith and counseling practice.

Evans, C. S. (1990). *Søren Kierkegaard's Christian psychology: Insight for counseling and pastoral care.* Grand Rapids, MI: Zondervan. A very helpful integration resource from one of the leading Christian philosophers of our day.

Oden, T. C. (1987). *Classical pastoral care* (4 vols.). Grand Rapids, MI: Baker. A wonderful resource for pastors and Christian mental health professionals interested in classic pastoral care.

Roberts, R. C., and Talbot, M. R., (Eds.). (1997). *Limning the psyche: Explorations in Christian psychology.* Grand Rapids, MI: Eerdmans. An excellent edited collection from leading theologians, philosophers and psychologists.

Van Leeuwen, M. S. (1985). *The person in psychology: A contemporary Christian appraisal.* Grand Rapids, MI: Eerdmans. A very helpful resource for Christians interested in the integration of psychology and theology.

REFERENCES

American Psychiatric Association. (1952). *Diagnostic and statistical manual of mental disorders.* Washington, DC: Author.

American Psychiatric Association. (1980). *Diagnostic and statistical manual of mental disorders* (3rd ed.). Washington, DC: Author.

American Psychiatric Association. (1994). *Diagnostic and statistical manual of mental disorders* (4th ed.). Washington, DC: Author.

Andreasen, N. C., and Carpenter, W. T., Jr. (1993). Diagnosis and classification of schizophrenia. *Schizophrenia Bulletin, 19*(2), 199-214.

Barlow, D. H., and Durand, V. M. (2002). *Abnormal psychology* (3rd ed.). Belmont, CA: Wadsworth.

Benner, D. G. (1998). *Care of souls: Revisioning Christian nurture and counsel.* Grand Rapids, MI: Baker.

Canning, S. S., Pozzi, C. F., McNeil, J. D., and McMinn, M. R. (2000). Integration as service: Implications of faith-praxis integration for training. *Journal of Psychology and Theology, 28*(3), 201-11.

Clark, L. A., Watson, D., and Reynolds, S. (1995). Diagnosis and classification of psychopathology: Challenges to the current system and future directions. *Annual Review of Psychology, 46,* 121-53.

Clebsch, W. A., and Jaekle, C. R. (1964). *Pastoral care in historical perspective.* New York: Harper & Row.

Davidson, J. R., and Foa, E. B. (1991). Diagnostic issues in posttraumatic stress disorder: Considerations for the *DSM-IV. Journal of Abnormal Psychology, 100*(3), 346-55.

Evans, C. S. (1990). *Søren Kierkegaard's Christian psychology: Insight for counseling and pastoral care.* Grand Rapids, MI: Zondervan.

Follette, W. C., and Houts, A. C. (1996). Models of scientific programs and the role of theory in taxonomy development: A case study of the *DSM. Journal of Consulting and Clinical Psychology, 64*(16), 1120-32.

Frances, A. J., Pincus, H. A., Widiger, T. A., Davis, W. W., and First,

M. B. (1990). *DSM-IV:* Work in progress. *American Journal of Psychiatry, 147*, 1439-48.

Griffiths, P. J. (1997). Metaphysics and personality theory. In R. C. Roberts and M. R. Talbot (Eds.), *Limning the psyche: Explorations in Christian psychology* (pp. 41-57). Grand Rapids, MI: Eerdmans.

Hauerwas, S., and Willimon, W. H. (1989). *Resident aliens: Life in the Christian colony.* Nashville: Abingdon.

Jones, S. L. (1994). A constructive relationship for religion with the science and profession of psychology: Perhaps the boldest model yet. *American Psychologist, 49*, 184-99.

Kendell, R. E. (1975). *The role of diagnosis in psychiatry.* London: Basil Blackwell.

Kendler, K. S. (1990). Towards a scientific psychiatric nosology: Strengths and limitations. *Archives of General Psychiatry, 47*, 969-73.

Kennedy, S. H., Javanmard, M., and Vaccarino, F. J. (1997). A review of functional neuroimaging in mood disorders: Positron emission tomography and depression. *Canadian Journal of Psychiatry, 42*, 467-75.

Meyers, D. G. (1991). Steering between the extremes: On being a Christian scholar within psychology. *Christian Scholar's Review, 20*(4), 376-83.

Millon, T. (1991). Classification in psychopathology: Rationale, alternatives and standards. *Journal of Abnormal Psychology, 100*(3), 245-61.

Noll, M. (1990). Traditional Christianity and the possibility of historical knowledge. *Christian Scholar's Review, 19*, 388-406.

Oden, T. C. (1987). *Classical pastoral care* (4 vols.). Grand Rapids, MI: Baker.

Oden, T. C. (1988). Recovering pastoral care's lost identity. In L. Aden and J. H. Ellens (Eds.), *The church and pastoral care* (pp. 17-32). Grand Rapids, MI: Baker.

Plantinga, A. (1983). Advice to Christian philosophers. *Faith and Philosophy, 1*, 253-71.

Plantinga, A. (1993). A Christian life partly lived. In K. J. Clark, *Philosophers who believe: The spiritual journeys of eleven leading thinkers* (pp. 45-82). Downers Grove, IL: InterVarsity Press.

Roberts, R. C. (1997). Parameters of a Christian psychology. In R. C. Roberts and M. R. Talbot (Eds.), *Limning the psyche: Explorations in Christian psychology* (pp. 74-101). Grand Rapids, MI: Eerdmans.

Roberts, R. C., and Talbot, M. R. (Eds.). (1997). *Limning the psyche: Explorations in Christian psychology.* Grand Rapids, MI: Eerdmans.

Sadler, J. (2002). Values in developing psychiatric classifications: A proposal for the *DSM-V.* In J. Sadler (Ed.), *Descriptions of prescriptions: Values, mental disorders and the DSMs* (pp. 350-65). Baltimore, MD: Johns Hopkins University Press.

Spitzer, R. L., and Wakefield, J. C. (1999). *DSM-IV* diagnostic criterion for clinical significance: Does it help solve the false positives problem? *American Journal of Psychiatry, 156,* 1856-64.

Spitzer, R. L., and Williams, J. B. W. (1982). The definition and diagnosis of mental disorder. In W. R. Grove (Ed.), *Deviance and mental illness* (pp. 15-32). Beverly Hills, CA: Sage.

Spitzer, R. L., Williams, J. B. W., and Skodol, A. E. (1980). *DSM-III:* The major achievements and an overview. *American Journal of Psychiatry, 137,* 151-64.

Van Leeuwen, M. S. (1985). *The person in psychology: A contemporary Christian appraisal.* Grand Rapids, MI: Eerdmans.

Widiger, T. A., and Clark, L. A. (2000). Toward *DSM-V* and the classification of psychopathology. *Psychological Bulletin, 126*(6), 946-63.

Widiger, T. A., and Corbitt, E. (1994). Normal versus abnormal personality from the perspective of the *DSM.* In Strack and M. Lorr (Eds.), *Differentiating normal and abnormal personality* (pp. 158-75). New York: Springer.

Widiger, T. A., and Shea, T. (1991). Differentiationn of axis I and axis II disorders. *Journal of Abnormal Psychology, 100,* 399-406.

Widiger, T. A., and Trull, T. J. (1993). Borderline and narcissistic personality disorders. In P. B. Sutker and H. E. Adams (Eds.), *Comprehensive handbook of psychotherapy* (2nd ed.) (pp. 371-94). New York: Plenum.

Yarhouse, M. A., and Burkett, L. A. (2003). *Sexual identity: A guide to living in the time between the times.* Lanham, MD: University Press of America.

ABOUT THE AUTHORS

Mark A. Yarhouse is associate professor of psychology at Regent University and a licensed clinical psychologist in the Commonwealth of Virginia. He received his B.A. degree from Calvin College, M.A. in theological studies, M.A. in clinical psychology and Psy.D. in clinical psychology from Wheaton College.

Author of more than forty articles and book chapters, Mark's main interests are in integration of psychology and theology, marriage and family therapy, and human sexuality. He is coauthor of *Homosexuality: The Use of Scientific Research in the Church's Moral Debate* (2000), *Sexual Identity: A Guide to Living in the Time Between the Times* (2003), and *Sexual Identity Synthesis: Attributions, Meaning-Making and the Search for Congruence* (2004).

Richard E. Butman has been a professor of psychology at Wheaton College and a licensed clinical psychologist in Illinois since 1980. He received his B.A. degree from Wheaton College, and an M.A. in theological studies and Ph.D. in clinical psychology from Fuller Theological Seminary in Pasadena, California.

Richard is coauthor of *Modern Psychotherapies: A Comprehensive Christian Appraisal* (1991), and has written many articles and chapters for a wide variety of religious and professional audiences. He is also active as a consultant to several community mental health agencies in the greater Chicagoland area. His interest in faith-based development work has led to extensive travel and work in Latin America, Africa and the Pacific Rim.

Barrett W. McRay is assistant professor of Christian formation and ministry at Wheaton College and codirector of psychological services at Alliance Clinical Associates in Wheaton, Illinois. He is a licensed clinical psychologist in Illinois. He earned M.A. degrees in New Testament studies and clinical psychology and a Psy.D. from Wheaton College.

Barrett served as a youth pastor for two congregations prior to his education in clinical psychology, which contributed to his passion for the pastoral care ministry of the church. His teaching and research center around areas of overlap between the soul care ministries of the church and the resources of the contemporary mental health fields. He has published articles in both psychology and ministry journals.

Subject Index